Uniting against terror

Uniting Against Terror

Uniting Against Terror
Cooperative Nonmilitary Responses to the Global
Terrorist Threat

edited by David Cortright and George A. Lopez

The MIT Press
Cambridge, Massachusetts
London, England

For information about special quantity discounts, please send e-mail to <special_sales@mitpress.mit.edu>.

This book was set in Sabon by SNP Best-set Typesetter Ltd., Hong Kong. Printed on recycled paper and bound in the United States of America.

Library of Congress Cataloging-in-Publication Data

Uniting against terror : cooperative nonmilitary responses to the global terrorist threat / David Cortright and George A. Lopez, editors.
    p. cm.
Includes bibliographical references and index.
ISBN 978-0-262-03368-8 (hardcover : alk. paper)—ISBN 978-0-262-53295-2 (pbk. : alk. paper)
  1. Terrorism—Prevention—International cooperation. I. Cortright, David, 1946– II. Lopez, George A., 1950
HV6431.U56   2007
363.325'17—dc22

                                                          2007000948

10 9 8 7 6 5 4 3 2 1

Contents

Foreword   vii
The Honorable Lee H. Hamilton

Acknowledgments   xi

Acronyms   xix

1 Strategic Counter-Terrorism   1
David Cortright and George A. Lopez

2 Global Cooperation Against Terrorism: Evaluating the United
Nations Counter-Terrorism Committee   23
David Cortright, George A. Lopez, Alistair Millar, and
Linda Gerber-Stellingwerf

3 Strengthening International Law and Global Implementation   51
Eric Rosand and Alistair Millar

4 Unilateral and Multilateral Strategies Against State Sponsors of
Terror: A Case Study of Libya, 1979 to 2003   83
Thomas E. McNamara

5 Cutting the Deadly Nexus: Preventing the Spread of Weapons of
Mass Destruction to Terrorists   123
Alistair Millar and Jason Ipe

6 Terrorism Defanged: The Financial Action Task Force and
International Efforts to Capture Terrorist Finances   157
Kathryn L. Gardner

7 The European Model of Building Regional Cooperation Against
Terrorism   187
Oldrich Bures and Stephanie Ahern

8 Strategies and Policy Challenges for Winning the Fight Against Terrorism 237

David Cortright and George A. Lopez

Bibliography 275

About the Authors 311

Index 315

Foreword

The Honorable Lee H. Hamilton

The United States is engaged in a generational struggle against a catastrophic terrorist threat. There is no quick fix or victory to be won. We need a clear, comprehensive, and sustainable counter-terrorism strategy.

To succeed, we must avoid misunderstanding the nature of the conflict. We are not engaged in a clash of civilizations or in a war against the tactic of terrorism. Both of those definitions are too broad, and those conflicts are unwinnable. Nor are we engaged in a fight against a fixed group of terrorists or a small collection of states that sponsor terrorism. Both of those definitions are too narrow and fail to encompass the expansive nature of the threat.

Our enemies are twofold: Al-Qaida, a stateless network of terrorists that struck us on September 11, 2001 (9/11), and a radical ideological movement in the Islamic world, inspired in part by Al-Qaida, which has spawned terrorist groups and violence across the globe. The first enemy is weakened but continues to pose a grave threat; the second enemy is gathering and will menace American people and interests long after Osama bin Laden and his cohorts are killed or captured. Thus our strategy must match our means to two ends: dismantling the Al-Qaida network and, in the long run, prevailing over the ideology that gives rise to terrorism.

What should this strategy look like? First, it must be balanced. The first phase of our post-9/11 efforts rightly included robust military action to topple the Taliban and pursue Al-Qaida. Although military force can destroy terrorists and their safe havens, it cannot bear burdens as diverse as tracking down funds and changing hearts and minds. Rather, long-term success demands all elements of national power—diplomacy, intelligence, covert action, law enforcement, economic policy, foreign aid, public diplomacy, and homeland defense. If we favor one tool while neglecting others, we leave ourselves vulnerable and miss an opportunity to deploy the United States' full arsenal of power.

Second, these efforts must be integrated. We cannot succeed if the tools of government work in isolation from, or in conflict with, one another. We need focused institutions, White House coordination of our institutions of government, leaders who set clear priorities, and vigorous congressional oversight. Just as we tailored our government to uniformly fight communism through areas as diverse as military strength, Voice of America, the peace corps, and overseas libraries and cultural centers, so, too, must we fashion a government that works as one to counter current threats.

Third, we must also integrate our efforts with friends and allies. We face an enemy that germinates in the cities of Europe, the deserts of Africa, and the islands of Southeast Asia. We cannot possibly root out this enemy alone. We need vigorous bilateral cooperation in everything from law enforcement to aid programs. And we need a multilateral framework that multiplies our strength—through reinvigorated and reformed cold war–era alliances and institutions, a new institution to facilitate dialogue and cooperation between the Islamic world and the West, and new agreements to combat the nexus of terrorism and the proliferation of catastrophic weapons.

Last, and most important, we need to be a force for hope in the Islamic world. Millions of young Muslims grow up lacking political freedom, economic opportunity, and hope. Instead of practical schooling, they often receive unrelenting messages of hatred and fanaticism, along with a tragic distortion of religion. They are taught to blame the United States for the world's ills and their personal suffering and to see Islam as a means for war. Reversing this trend will take time, effort, and resources—reconsideration of some of our alliances; outreach to moderate voices; support for educational reforms; the expansion of trade, jobs, and opportunity; gradual political change; and the resolution of protracted conflicts.

This collection of expert analyses and essays assembled by David Cortright and George Lopez provides a blueprint for moving forward.

Through historical cases and detailed arguments covering the wide array of counter-terrorism strategies and tactics I mention above, the essays demonstrate how a sustainable counter-terrorism strategy can be successfully implemented and integrated. I commend these two scholars and their chapter authors for so capably demonstrating the real victories, best practices, and tasks that lie ahead in the powerful convergence of international law, nonmilitary organization, and diplomatic cooperation in the war on terror.

It is especially important that journalists, policymakers, and other scholars understand the lessons offered by the findings of this book. For instance, that Libya dismantled its dangerous weapon systems as a result of multiyear and multinational diplomatic work, not out of fear of U.S. military power that had been applied in Iraq. Such carrot-and-stick strategies may work with other nuclear or would-be nuclear states, but only if they are vigorously and astutely pursued. Similarly, for all the military victories we have assembled against Al-Qaida, this volume details the equally important policy of locking down terrorist financial assets and stifling their techniques for money transfer and laundering. And the law enforcement networks that have emerged in Europe, as well as the successes and shortcomings in the work of the United Nations and international law, provide valuable lessons.

Sometimes it seems that terrorists are one step ahead of successful policy. Islamist terrorism morphs into an ever-more decentralized series of networks, with new targets and tactics, and the ability to capitalize on new grievances. So it is with weak and failing states and the disturbing number of states with—or actively pursuing—nuclear weapons.

In such a world, no one element of U.S. power can keep us safe; instead, turning the tide on global insecurity depends on our ability to integrate the tools of American power. Military power alone cannot protect America or our allies. The major contribution of this volume is that it clearly shows when diplomatic, economic, and legal tools have worked, and how they can be mobilized to combat the swelling turmoil in the world.

Turmoil is swelling in the world at a moment when American power is preeminent. If we seek to impose our will on the world without acting with others, we will be isolated. If we stress one tool of American power to the exclusion of others, we will be vulnerable. If we integrate America's power and values—both at home and abroad—then we can protect America while making our country stronger. This valuable book outlines a way forward that can do exactly that.

Washington, D.C.
January 2007

Acknowledgments

The research for this volume began soon after the United Nations Security Council passed Resolution 1373 on 28 September 2001. That resolution created the Counter-Terrorism Committee (CTC) and called on all states to engage immediately in specified actions against persons or entities suspected of terrorist activities or affiliations. The resolution urged states to lock down the financial assets of individuals and organizations associated with terrorism and to restrict the international movement of terrorists and those who support them. These measures were essentially the tools of targeted sanctions we had researched in previous years and about which we had written extensively. They were part of the repertoire of smart sanctions techniques we had examined in consultation with Security Council member states and officials in the UN Secretariat. As the CTC began its work, therefore, we were able to carry on our roles of scholars/analysts and practical interlocutors with UN officials, focused now on countering terrorism. Thus began our expanded research agenda and the idea for this volume.

Since that time we have conducted extensive research on specialized techniques and best practices for controlling the movement of assets and persons who would engage in terrorism. We have also scrutinized the effectiveness of the CTC, its related development of the Counter-Terrorism Executive Directorate (CTED), the workings of the Security Council's Al-Qaida/Taliban Sanctions Committee, and other terrorism-related subsidiary committees that have emerged in the past five years. This volume is the product of that examination, the outcome of five years of policy-related research and analysis. In the course of this work we have met with and interviewed literally hundreds of international civil servants, diplomats, technical experts, scholars, bankers, and military officers. We would like to recognize below a few of the numerous individuals who contributed to this book.

We are especially grateful to Jeremy Greenstock, Permanent Representative of the United Kingdom to the UN and the first chair of the CTC, who initially encouraged our counter-terrorism assessment efforts. We received invaluable advice and guidance from Greenstock's senior aide, Anna Clunes, in her former position as First Secretary of the UK Mission to the UN and British representative to the Counter-Terrorism Committee. We also met with and received encouragement from Inocencio Arias, Permanent Representative of Spain to the UN and the second chair of the CTC, and from his senior aide, Gonzalo Quintero Saravia.

We benefited greatly from research support provided by the United States Institute of Peace via a grant made to us in 2004. We had received funding in an earlier time period for our work on smart sanctions, and we were particularly grateful for this second investment in our research at an early stage in the development of our counter-terrorism project. We were uniquely fortunate to receive three distinct research and policy-related grants from three different governments—Denmark, Japan, and the Netherlands—over the past four years to conduct research on the CTC and its processes. The Danish, Japanese, and Dutch foreign ministries worked with us to conduct specific research and develop practical policy recommendations for improving UN counter-terrorism efforts. These contracts offered outstanding opportunities for us to dialogue directly with specialists and diplomats who serve on the front lines of the multilateral challenges presented by transnational extremism and terrorism.

We are grateful to those who provided analysis and comments on our methodology or on initial drafts of research reports related to this volume. We offer special thanks to Hiroshi Tajima of the Permanent Mission of Japan to the United Nations. We owe a singular debt to the members of the Permanent Mission of Denmark to the United Nations in New York, especially Ambassador Ellen Margrethe Løj and Pernille Dahler Kardel, who shared generously of their time and expertise in guiding our research. We thank colleagues in the Foreign Ministry in Copenhagen who participated in and helped organize an April 2004 seminar on counter-terrorism in Copenhagen and who assisted this project in numerous ways, including Peter Tascøe-Jensen, head of the Department of Public and International Law of the Danish Foreign Ministry, Charlotte Laursen, and Anne Ehrenreich. We are grateful to the participants in the Copenhagen seminar who provided analyses of current UN counter-terrorism efforts and offered policy suggestions that helped to inform the findings and recommendations of this report. We specifically thank Eugenio Curia of the Ministry of Foreign Affairs, International Trade, and Worship, Argentina; Lars Erslev Andersen of the Danish Institute for Humanities; E. J. Flynn of the Office of the High Commissioner for Human Rights; Peter Gastrow of the Institute for Security Studies, South Africa; Walter Gehr of the UN Office on Drugs and Crime; Judge Hesham Fathi Ragab, General Department of Legislation, Egypt; Harjit Sandhu of the Action Against Terrorism Unit, Organization for Security and Co-operation in Europe; Karin von Hippel, King's College London; and Joanna Weschler of Human Rights Watch, now of the Security Council Report.

We met with, interviewed, and received encouragement from numerous officials and experts, including Ambassador Javier Rupérez, executive director of the UN Counter-Terrorism Executive Directorate; Richard Barrett of the UN Security Council Analytical Support and Sanctions Monitoring Team; Lars Adam Rehof of the Danish Foreign Ministry; Alexander Konuzin and Sergei Karev of the Russian Mission to the UN; Jean-Luc Florent of the French Mission to the UN; Ambassadors John Dauth and Peter Tesch and Officers Michael Bliss, Bassim Blazey, and Rick Nimmo of the Australian Mission to the UN; Lee Feinstein of the Council on Foreign Relations; Joseph Stephanides, Alec Martinovic, Freda Mackay, and Loraine Rickard-Martin of the UN Department of Political Affairs; Joseph Halligan of the World Bank; Barry Johnson of the International Monetary Fund; Jimmy Gurulé of the University of Notre Dame Law School, formerly Under Secretary for Enforcement, serving several offices at the United States Department of the Treasury; Patricia Holland of the European Commission; Vincent Schmoll of the Financial Action Task Force; Michael Levi of the Crime and Justice Research Group at the University of Cardiff in Wales; Ulrich Kersten of Interpol; and Steven Simon of the RAND Corporation.

We are grateful for the dialogues we have had with two members of the U.S. National Commission on Terrorist Attacks upon the United States (also known as the 9/11 Commission)—Lee Hamilton, vice chair of the commission and current president of the Woodrow Wilson Center for International Affairs, who spent time at the University of Notre Dame as the Hesburgh Lecturer in April 2004 and has been a generous observer of our work; and Timothy J. Roemer, Commission member and former congressional representative from the Second District of Indiana, where the University of Notre Dame is located, who shared with us his insights on effective counter-terrorism. We hope the ideas expressed here further their own important work in getting the remainder of the 9/11 Commission report recommendations approved by the U.S. Congress.

We also acknowledge the important contributions to earlier portions of this research by Ambassador Thomas McNamara of The George Washington University and Douglas Lindores, who is a consultant on international development issues. As the project developed over time, our work with Eric Rosand, formerly of the U.S. Mission to the United Nations and U.S. Department of State, increased when he joined our team as a senior fellow to the point where he exerted a positive influence on this entire work, beyond the chapter he coauthored with Alistair Millar.

We are grateful as well to those who provided analysis and comments on our early reports on the CTC, including Edward Luck of Columbia University; Simon Chesterman of New York University Law School; Tarun Chhabra of the Office of the Secretary-General at the United Nations; John Darby, professor of comparative ethnic studies at the Kroc Institute at the University of Notre Dame; Chantal de Jonge Oudraat, senior fellow and research program coordinator at the Center for Transatlantic Relations, Paul H. Nitze School of Advanced International Studies, Johns Hopkins University; and Helene Seligman, formerly of the Counter-Terrorism Committee staff.

We benefited greatly from the input of participants in the June 2006 Hague meeting on counter-terrorism standards and best practices organized by the Dutch Ministry of Foreign Affairs. We thank the officials in the Dutch Ministry of Foreign Affairs, including Peggy Vissers, Fred Olthof, Andre van Wiggen, Joost van Ettro, Carl Peersman, Pim Dumoré,

Dirk Klaasen, Lex Gerts, Jaap Werner, and Frank Majoor, who participated in and organized the Hague seminar and helped in numerous other
ways. Participants in the seminar included Roberto Maroto of Interpol,
Robert Ireland of the World Customs Organization, Hartmut Hesse
and Chris Trelawny of the International Maritime Organization, Lise
Boisvert and Jalal Haidar of the International Civil Aviation Organiza-
tion, Julio Bravo of Asia-Pacific Economic Cooperation, Jean-François
Thony of the International Monetary Fund, Jakkie Cilliers and Martin
Kimani Mbugua of the Institute of Security Studies in South Africa, Karl
Wycoff and Anton Martynyuk of the Organization for Security and
Co-operation in Europe, Gennady Gatilov of the UN Office of Policy
Coordination and Strategic Planning, and experts on the staff of the UN
Counter-Terrorism Executive Directorate.

While these many specialists and professionals have contributed to our
research, they certainly do not bear responsibility for our own assessments and judgments. That is also true of other colleagues with whom
we have worked most intensely.

As editors and researchers with multiple administrative and teaching
tasks, our work on the chapters here and the wider volume has been sustained throughout the past few years by a team of close colleagues. The
most important contribution has been that of Alistair Millar, vice president of the Fourth Freedom Forum and director of the Center on Global
Counter-Terrorism Cooperation. As his coauthorship of three chapters
in this volume indicates, Millar has contributed significantly to the
success of this work. Millar's work has served the primary focus of our
dialogue with specialists and government officials around the world. His
sound judgment and scholarly expertise combine with extraordinary
organizing abilities.

Jason Ipe of the Fourth Freedom Forum has served as a primary
researcher for many portions of this manuscript and is coauthor of
chapter 5. He has also provided valuable assistance in arranging many
of the conferences and seminars associated with this volume. At various
times he was ably assisted by Lynn Erskine and Matt Martin at the
Fourth Freedom Forum office in Washington, D.C. Additional research
work, as well as organizational management of various dimensions of
our projects, has been provided by Linda Gerber-Stellingwerf, research

director of the Fourth Freedom Forum office in Goshen, Indiana. Gerber-Stellingwerf not only is a coauthor but has been an invaluable assistant in numerous research, writing, and editing tasks associated with the production of this volume. Tomas Valasek made significant contributions to research and editing as staff and consultant to the Fourth Freedom Forum offices in New York and Brussels, Belgium.

Scott Appleby, the Regan Director of the Kroc Institute at the University of Notre Dame, has been extraordinarily supportive in his commitment to our project, providing funding for travel and a continuing atmosphere of encouragement and support. Through the duration of much of the work on this volume, we have been served by the research assistance of three individuals who staffed our project office at the Kroc Institute. These include Benjamin Rooney (2003–2004), who worked especially on international cooperation in the arms embargo area; Oldrich Bures, coauthor of a chapter in this volume, who served as a staff assistant in 2004–2005 and then the following year provided a steady flow of information on European trends from his university base in the Czech Republic. Tona Boyd, sanctions assistant for 2005–2006, also provided significant research support during the writing of contract reports for the Dutch and Japanese governments.

Recognition also goes to members of the Counter-Terrorism Research Seminar convened at the University of Notre Dame during the spring of 2004, who engaged in a series of research topics and papers critical to our research and analysis. Two of the chapters in this volume—chapter 7 by Oldrich Bures and Stephanie Ahern and chapter 6 by Kathryn L. Gardner—result directly from that seminar. We received valuable support from another participant in that seminar, Paul Ahern, a graduate of the Notre Dame Law School and former editor of the *Notre Dame Law Review*. Ahern wrote an important paper that helped to shape chapter 3 in this volume. In the summer of 2006 we relied on former seminar participants and recent Notre Dame graduates Peter Quaranto and Julia Fitzpatrick to provide assistance in last-minute research and updates of earlier work.

The greatest credit for managing the production of this volume goes to Jennifer Glick, publications director of the Fourth Freedom Forum. Glick has surpassed in this volume the level of care and attention to intricate detail from which we benefited in our earlier sanctions volumes. She has labored mightily especially in the final months of the project to ensure a quality publication. We owe a tremendous debt of gratitude to Glick for her meticulous and conscientious work on this volume. We also wish to thank Celeste Kennel-Shank, who was instrumental in assisting Glick in the production of this volume, working diligently to ensure that research was accurately and comprehensively cited in the bibliography. As well, we extend gratitude to the key administrators and financial officers of the Fourth Freedom Forum, Ann Pedler and Kim Minier, for their assistance.

As we bring this sizeable project to fruition, we acknowledge the efficiency and professionalism of Clay Morgan at The MIT Press. Clay expressed interest in the project, secured for us a set of helpful reviews, and pushed us hard to maintain a critical edge to our analysis. We also thank Deborah Cantor-Adams of The MIT Press for her assistance in editing this volume. For their efforts the book is indeed a better volume. We also note the continued support of the board of directors of the Fourth Freedom Forum and especially its chair and founder, Howard S. Brembeck. Since establishing the Fourth Freedom Forum, Brembeck has been challenging us and others to thoroughly scrutinize and produce effective policy recommendations to strengthen international law and improve the use of economic measures and other nonmilitary means to address the great security problems of our time, especially weapons proliferation. As Brembeck enters his ninety-sixth year, we hope he finds this volume a fitting testament to his vision and extraordinary generosity of support. It is in his spirit that we attempt in this volume to assess the successes and shortcomings of international cooperation in freeing the world of the harsh, arbitrary, and criminal violence that is contemporary terrorism.

David Cortright and George A. Lopez
Goshen and Notre Dame, Indiana
May 2007

Acronyms

9/11	September 11, 2001, Al-Qaida terrorist attacks on the United States
AML	anti–money laundering
ANC	African National Congress
ANO	Abu Nidal Organization
APEC	Asia-Pacific Economic Cooperation
APG	Asia/Pacific Group on Money Laundering
ASEAN	Association of Southeast Asian Nations
ASMPs	Air-Sol Moyenne Porté (French missiles)
AU	African Union
AWFs	analysis work files
BCBS	Basel Committee on Banking Supervision
CARICOM	Caribbean Community
CCs	candidate countries
CDD	customer due diligence
CFATF	Caribbean Financial Action Task Force
CFR–CDF	EU Network of Independent Experts in Fundamental Rights
CFSP	Common Foreign and Security Policy
CIA	Central Intelligence Agency
CICTE	Inter-American Committee Against Terrorism
CIS	Commonwealth of Independent States
COTER	Working Party on Terrorism (External Aspects)
CTAG	Counter-Terrorism Action Group
CTC	Counter-Terrorism Committee (UN)
CTED	Counter-Terrorism Executive Directorate (UN)

CTF	counter-terrorism financing
CTG	Counter-Terrorism Group
CTR	Cooperative Threat Reduction
CTTF	Counter Terrorism Task Force of the Asia-Pacific Economic Cooperation
EAs	Europe Agreements
EAG	Eurasian Group on Combating Money Laundering and Financing of Terrorism
EAW	European arrest warrant
EC	European Community
ECJ	European Court of Justice
ECOSOC	Economic and Social Council (UN)
ECST	European Convention on the Suppression of Terrorism
EDU	Europol Drugs Unit
EJN	European Judicial Network
EPC	European Political Cooperation
ESAAMLG	Eastern and Southern Africa Anti-Money Laundering Group
ETA	Euskadi Ta Askatasuna (Basque Fatherland and Liberty)
EU	European Union
Eurojust	European Judicial Cooperation Unit
Europol	European Police
FATF	Financial Action Task Force
FCCs	former candidate countries
FIUs	financial intelligence units
FSRBs	FATF–style regional bodies
G-7	Group of Seven industrial nations: Canada, France, Germany, Italy, Japan, the United Kingdom, and the United States
G-8	Group of Eight major industrial nations: Canada, France, Germany, Italy, Japan, Russia, the United Kingdom, and the United States
GAFISUD	Grupo de Acción Financiera de Sudamerica (against money laundering)
GAO	General Accounting Office (U.S.)

GDP	Gross domestic product
GIABA	Intergovernmental Action Group Against Money Laundering
GPML	Global Programme Against Money Laundering
HEU	highly enriched uranium
IAEA	International Atomic Energy Agency
ICAO	International Civil Aviation Organization
IEEPA	International Emergency Economic Powers Act
IISS	International Institute for Strategic Studies
ILSA	Iran and Libya Sanctions Act of 1996
IMF	International Monetary Fund
IMO	International Maritime Organization
ISA	Iran Sanctions Act
ISPA	Instrument for Structural Policies for Pre-accession
JHA	Justice and Home Affairs
MENA	Middle East and North Africa Region
MENAFATF	Middle East and North Africa Financial Action Task Force
MENAFSRB	Middle East and North Africa FATF–style regional body
MEPs	Members of the European Parliament
MIPT	Memorial Institute for the Prevention of Terrorism
ML/TF	money laundering/terrorist financing
MONEYVAL	Council of Europe's Select Committee of Experts on the Evaluation of Anti–Money Laundering Measures
NAC	New Agenda Coalition
NAM	Non-Aligned Movement
NATO	North Atlantic Treaty Organization
NCCTs	noncooperative countries and territories
NGOs	nongovernmental organizations
NPT	Nuclear Nonproliferation Treaty
NRDC	Natural Resources Defense Council
NSC	National Security Council
NTSB	National Transportation Safety Board
NWFZ	nuclear weapon–free zone
OAS	Organization of American States

OAU	Organisation of African Unity
OECD	Organisation for Economic Co-operation and Development
OECD/DAC	Organisation for Economic Co-operation and Development/Development Co-operation Directorate
OGBS	Offshore Group of Banking Supervisors
OHCHR	Office of the High Commissioner for Human Rights
OIC	Organisation of the Islamic Conference
OLAF	European Anti-Fraud Office (EC)
OPCW	Organisation for the Prohibition of Chemical Weapons
OSCE	Organization for Security and Co-operation in Europe
PAA	Preaccession advisers
PCOTF	Police Chiefs Operational Task Force
PFLP–GC	Popular Front for the Liberation of Palestine–General Command
PLO	Palestine Liberation Organization
PNIs	Presidential Nuclear Initiatives
PSI	Proliferation Security Initiative
PWGT	Police Working Group on Terrorism
SALT II Treaty	Strategic Arms Limitation Talks II Treaty
SAPARD	Special Accession Programme for Agriculture and Rural Development
SEA	Single European Act
STRs	suspicious transaction reports
TEU	Treaty on European Union
TNF	theater nuclear forces
TNWs	tactical nuclear weapons
TPB	Terrorism Prevention Branch (UN)
TREVI Group	Terrorism, Radicalism, Extremism, and Political Violence Group (EC)
TWG	Terrorist Working Group
UK	United Kingdom
UN	United Nations
UNDP	United Nations Development Programme
UNODC/TPB	United Nations Office on Drugs and Crime/Terrorism Prevention Branch

UNSC	United Nations Security Council
USSR	Union of Soviet Socialist Republics
UTA	Union des Transports Aerien (a French airline)
WCO	World Customs Organization
WMD	weapons of mass destruction
WTO	World Trade Organization

Uniting Against Terror

1

Strategic Counter-Terrorism

David Cortright and George A. Lopez

As this book was being written, debates about the effectiveness of the "global war on terrorism" were intensifying. In light of recent major increases in significant terrorist attacks worldwide—including bombings in London and Sharm el-Sheikh in July 2005 and in Amman in November 2005, continuing major attacks in Iraq, and increasing car bombings and suicide attacks in Afghanistan—questions about the appropriateness and effectiveness of current strategies against terrorism have multiplied. The deadly and changing parameters of this age of "new" terrorism are becoming more starkly defined. Various studies note that, despite relative successes in the global campaign against terrorism, more attacks from extremist groups have occurred since September 11, 2001 (9/11) than in the three years prior to that date.[1] Intelligence reports indicate that despite more than five years of intensive efforts to weaken it, the Al-Qaida network remains resilient and may be strengthening.[2] In a number of the world's regions, especially in Europe, the struggle against terrorism has developed primarily within a law enforcement paradigm, with an emphasis on regional cooperation and multilateral crime-fighting measures. The United States has also strengthened law enforcement efforts and transnational cooperation, but it has oscillated between efforts to mobilize United Nations and multilateral cooperation against terrorism and skepticism about the adequacy of such approaches.

Washington has devoted the largest share of resources and political capital to military approaches. In fact, the Bush administration has made the point continually that U.S. efforts prior to 9/11 were relatively ineffective in dealing with Al-Qaida because they relied too heavily on law enforcement approaches, which the administration considered viable only after the fact of a terror attack. Since 9/11, President Bush maintained, the United States has considered the threat and actions of global jihadist terrorists as the major national and global security threat of our time, one that demands a state of war to prevent future attacks. The result has been an expenditure by the U.S. of more than $500 billion for the global war on terror. This has been accompanied by an undervaluation of nonmilitary mechanisms for counter-terrorism and a lack of strategic vision about the role and importance of the UN counter-terrorism program and the efforts of other multilateral institutions. Many have raised doubts about the near-exclusive U.S. reliance on military solutions, particularly the decision to wage war in Iraq. The U.S. has fallen victim to an overemphasis on tactical counter-terrorism (in which the objective is to find, destroy, and defeat operative terrorist groups) and an underemphasis on strategic counter-terrorism (which includes multiple policy responses designed to eliminate the sustaining and underlying conditions of extremist terrorism). Concerns have also been expressed about the tendency in Washington to call for greater international cooperation but then to manifest in its policies a general disdain for international institutions and binding legal arrangements.

Due to the global nature of the terrorist threat, cooperative nonmilitary responses are necessary elements of counter-terrorism strategy. The Al-Qaida movement is spread across more than sixty countries and is increasingly decentralized and self-reliant. Countering this multifaceted and complex threat requires a broadly cooperative effort involving legal, economic, political, and military cooperation from virtually every nation in the world. The United Nations is particularly relevant and important to this fight because of its role as the primary source of international political legitimacy and legal authority for many nations. Although the United Nations frequently lacks resources and operational capacity, it is indispensable in developing political consensus for the international cooperation required to counter the terrorist threat. As several of the chapters in this volume indicate, the United Nations has made important contributions to the global fight against terrorism, although there are also significant shortcomings and problems associated with the UN effort. By offering a critical evaluation of these UN efforts, along with a review of counter-terrorism programs within the European Union, the

Financial Action Task Force (FATF), and other major institutions, we hope to shed light on both successes and failures and to draw lessons on ways to develop more effective strategies against the global terrorist threat.

Despite the burgeoning literature on terrorism, relatively few works have focused on the role of the United Nations and multilateral mechanisms in general.[3] Many works focus exclusively or primarily on U.S. policy and fail to acknowledge the contributions to global counter-terrorism of the United Nations, the European Union (EU), and other international organizations and agencies.[4] The role of diplomacy and the use of economic sanctions against terrorism are often ignored. Only a handful of analysts have attempted to dissect the specific operational components of the UN counter-terrorism program—despite the considerable expansion of these efforts in recent years. Little attention has been given to the work of the Al-Qaida/Taliban Sanctions Committee and its associated Analytical Support and Sanctions Monitoring Team.[5] Very few published works are available on the substantial work of the United Nations Counter-Terrorism Committee (CTC) and the related Counter-Terrorism Executive Directorate (CTED).[6] Even less has been written about the Counter-Proliferation Committee established by Security Council Resolution 1540 (2004).[7] Although international diplomats and law enforcement officials have increasingly focused on these UN counter-terrorism programs, there is little independent evaluation of these efforts among scholars and nongovernmental analysts. We intend this volume as a corrective to this relative neglect. We offer these chapters as documentation and discussion of the strengths and weaknesses of multilateral approaches and as a springboard to future policy research and debate about the contributions that regional and international efforts can make in the global campaign against terrorism.

The Current Debate

Following the September 2001 terrorist attacks, the Bush administration declared that the United States would respond by forging a multilateral coalition to engage in a military campaign in Afghanistan against Al-Qaida and the Taliban regime that protected them there. From the outset the administration stated the global war on terror would be a long-term struggle.[8] It has certainly been that. The administration launched a military invasion and occupation of Iraq that many observers who otherwise might agree with U.S. use of force against regional foes considered a diversion from the central struggle against Al-Qaida. Writing in *Foreign Policy* in January 2003, Stephen M. Walt and John J. Mearsheimer cautioned against invading Iraq and argued that the U.S. national security interest would be best served by finishing the fight in Afghanistan and building the international coalition against terrorism.[9] When, by the fall of 2006, U.S. military engagement in this global war had lasted longer than American fighting in World War II, other analysts called for new thinking about the war, its direction, and its definition.

But is the global struggle against terrorism really a war? The term "war on terror" has value as political metaphor, but as actual policy it can be counterproductive. In the spring and summer of 2005, possibly sensing the declining political power of the phrase, some Bush administration officials acknowledged the one-dimensional nature of the phrase "global war on terror" and started to employ a broader expression, "global struggle against violent extremism." National Security Adviser Steven J. Hadley told the *New York Times* that the campaign against terror is "more than just a military war" and is also a "global struggle against extremism." The change in rhetoric was a partial recognition of the broader dimensions of the campaign against terrorism. But by late autumn, in part because President Bush himself continued to describe the struggle as primarily a war, the phrase "global struggle against extremism" virtually vanished from the policy lexicon.[10]

There is little doubt that the use of force is relevant to the struggle against terrorism and that since 9/11 U.S. action has been effective in countering Al-Qaida and related groups. But the current, relatively singular emphasis on military measures is excessive and is becoming counterproductive. "The Bush administration has seriously overmilitarized the effort to stop jihadist terror," write former National Security Council officials Daniel Benjamin and Steven Simon.[11] Most analysts supported military action in Afghanistan as an appropriate operation that destroyed terrorist training camps and disrupted Al-Qaida capabilities, but growing numbers consider Iraq a major strategic blunder. Military force can be useful for some counter-terrorism missions, but heavily armed troops are rarely able to penetrate terrorist networks.

When military force is used excessively, as the Iraq case illustrates, it is likely to galvanize support for the jihadists and have opposite effects from those intended. A U.S. National Intelligence Estimate, leaked to the press and partially released by the White House in September 2006, acknowledged that the Iraq war "has become the 'cause celebre' for jihadists, breeding a deep resentment of U.S. involvement in the Muslim world and cultivating supporters for the global jihadist movement."[12] According to an intelligence official quoted in the original *New York Times* disclosure, the report showed that "the Iraq war has made the overall terrorism problem worse."[13] An overemphasis on military means is undermining the still ill-defined strategic counter-terrorism effort against Al-Qaida and related jihadist forces.

A growing number of analysts agree that defeating Al-Qaida and related networks will require a multifaceted, strategic counter-terrorism approach encompassing a wide range of policy tools and forms of inter- national cooperation.[14] Although their entry point into the study and policy analysis of terrorism differs, many analysts have emphasized the law enforcement dimensions of the struggle and the need to address the long-term dynamics that give rise to terrorism. Jessica Stern, who inter- viewed dozens of militants to examine their motivations and determine the ways in which extremist groups exploit religion to attract adherents, argues convincingly that jihadism is an idea, not a military target. Thus, she advocates more sophisticated, multifaceted strategies for overcom- ing the terrorist threat.[15] Having served as a CIA case officer with Islamic militants during the Afghan-Soviet war, Marc Sageman writes as both scholar and practitioner to explore the inner dynamics of how terrorist networks form and grow, with particular attention to their transnational tendencies.[16] Karen von Hippel of the Centre for Defence Studies at King's College in London focuses on multilateral mechanisms against ter- rorism and the lessons to be learned from enhanced regional coordina- tion in Europe and cooperative international peace-building efforts during the 1990s.[17] Bruce Hoffman of the RAND Corporation writes extensively on the rise of terrorist networks and the need for multiple approaches that address the core problems of terrorist recruitment and support.[18] Martha Crenshaw argues that states must strike a balance between efforts to reduce terrorism and the preservation of basic civil liberties.[19] Crenshaw also urges greater attention to the motivations of the terrorists themselves to better understand how to mitigate the danger posed by their extremist views and behavior.[20] Andrew Silke points to the need for a deeper understanding of the social and political dynamics that motivate terrorist violence.[21]

The White House *National Strategy for Combating Terrorism*, released in September 2006, acknowledged these scholarly insights in stating that the struggle against the jihadist threat is a "different kind of war." It is a broadly based effort that involves not only military power but diplomatic, financial, intelligence, and law enforcement tools. It is "both a battle of arms and a battle of ideas."[22] The document presented a relatively sophisticated analysis of the nature of the terrorist danger and outlined a range of policies for defeating the jihadist threat through the promotion of freedom and human dignity. Despite these noble intentions, however, U.S. government actions have continued to emphasize the battle of arms. The largest share of counter-terrorism resources has gone into the wars in Afghanistan and Iraq, which the National Strategy document listed as "successes"—notwithstanding a reversal of fortunes in the former and military "fiasco" in the latter.[23] The White House has instituted a militarized system for apprehending, interrogating, and detaining terror suspects that is contrary to international legal standards and that has impeded cooperation with allies in Europe and beyond. Until current policy catches up with available strategy and incorporates the findings of scholarly research on options for international cooperation, U.S. efforts to stem the growing jihadist threat will become increasingly ineffective.

Regional and Institutional Approaches

There is a natural tendency for large and powerful states, when faced with the kind of national security challenge that terrorism poses, to want to "go it alone" in countering the danger. The result is that the multifaceted strategies needed to actually succeed in counter-terrorism are slow to develop. Critical to a multifaceted approach is the effective use of regional and international organizations. Scholars and practitioners of international affairs understand that such institutions are at once a direct extension of member state foreign policies and an organizational space where actions on a particular issue can be more far reaching, comprehensive, and cooperative. To examine the relative effectiveness of regional and international organizations is to scrutinize their work as security organizations, even if this function is not their usual self-definition. Further, it means assessing how these organizations can be more successful than individual nations in facilitating information sharing and policy coordination. In this volume we present and scrutinize the organizational opportunities open to the United States, its European allies, and the United Nations.

In the days following the September 11 attacks and again at the G-8 summits in 2005 and 2006, European and U.S. leaders acknowledged their shared vulnerability and vowed to work together in the global fight against terrorism. Over time, however, the underlying counter-terrorism strategies of the United States and Europe have diverged. As Karen Greenberg and other scholars have noted, while counter-terrorism cooperation remains strong, real differences exist. Most notably, the European community has adopted a more institutionalized, rule-based approach, as opposed to the ad hoc and extralegal efforts employed by the United States. On the continent, information sharing and cooperation among a wide range of agencies are the norm. Europe's open society and removal of border controls make it easier for extremists to operate, but the high degree of law enforcement cooperation among dozens of countries provides important protections. Many terrorist operations have been disrupted and militant suspects arrested through the cooperative efforts of European law enforcement agencies.[24]

The differing institutional and legal approaches of the United States and Europe sometimes impede the successful prosecution of suspected terrorists. A case in point is that of Mounir el-Motassadeq, a Moroccan student in Germany who was prosecuted and convicted for involvement in the September 11 plots. In March 2004 a German appeals court overturned Motassadeq's conviction because U.S. authorities withheld crucial information and refused to allow testimony by terrorist suspect Ramzi Binalshibh, the so-called twentieth hijacker.[25] Europe's emphasis on institutional cooperation and adherence to strict legal guarantees even in the midst of national security challenges stands in juxtaposition to the more secretive, nonjudicial approach in the United States. Complications have also emerged over U.S. detention and interrogation methods in Guantanamo and related facilities, which do not meet European legal standards. Reports that the U.S. used European air bases for refueling and transport of individuals who were "rendered" to third states or secret facilities drew sharp criticism in Europe. Other reports that the U.S. has employed torture in these facilities have compromised evidence and impeded prosecutions. The success of global counter-terrorism efforts depends significantly on these two powerful democratic communities working together effectively and within the same legal framework. This will require a greater emphasis on mutual legal standards and practices and a greater commitment on the part of the U.S. to uphold internationally accepted detention and interrogation standards.

Another major difference between the United States and Europe, indeed between the United States and most of the world, is the degree of importance accorded the United Nations as a principal actor. In Europe and most other regions of the world, the legal authorization and political leadership of the United Nations are indispensable for cooperative international action against terrorism. Security Council Resolution 1373 (2001) and other counter-terrorism measures have provided the essential legal and political authorization permitting nations and regions to act. In the United States, by contrast, there is greater disdain for international legal agreements and a more critical view of the United Nations. The Bush administration has worked through the United Nations to advance global counter-terrorism objectives, but it undermined and humiliated the organization on Iraq. And the U.S. has been highly selective in its adherence to international treaties. The bias against the United Nations among some U.S. policymakers has weakened the underlying legal and political foundations on which multilateral cooperation depends. By focusing instead on ad hoc coalitions and bilateral arrangements of convenience, the United States has given short shrift to international institutions that are vital to the success of global security. One of the central conclusions of this volume is that international mechanisms and legal agreements matter significantly in the fight against terrorism and that more purposeful attention is needed to improve the legitimacy and effectiveness of the UN counter-terrorism program.

The Role of the United Nations: An Overview

The modern era of United Nations involvement against terrorism began in the 1990s when the Security Council adopted Resolution 748 (1992) calling on Libya to cease its support of terrorism and turn over suspects wanted in connection with the bombing of Pan Am flight 103 and French UTA flight 772. Targeted UN sanctions against Libya in combination with more comprehensive measures by the United States were successful in dissuading Libya from further support for terrorism and eventually led to the extradition of the bombing suspects for trial at The Hague in the Netherlands. UN sanctions against Libya were accompanied by extensive diplomatic dialogue and the promise of economic benefit to encourage Libyan reengagement with the world community. This led to Tripoli's agreement in 2003 to dismantle its programs for the development of weapons of mass destruction. Security Council sanctions to counter terrorism were also employed in Sudan (Resolution 1054 in 1996) and Afghanistan (Resolution 1267 in 1999), as the United Nations became more active in applying pressure on regimes that supported or harbored terrorist operations.[26] These Security Council sanctions efforts were closely integrated with intelligence, diplomatic, and occasionally foreign aid efforts by the United States and other countries. They played an important, albeit little noticed, role in mobilizing international pressure against state support of terrorism.[27]

In the wake of the September 2001 attacks, the United Nations launched a second, more expansive phase of its campaign against international terrorism. Targeting the diverse and widely dispersed transnational networks of Al-Qaida and other related nonstate actors, the Security Council adopted Resolution 1373 (2001) mandating a worldwide campaign by all 191 UN member states to deny finances, travel, or assistance of any kind to terrorists and those who support them. Resolution 1373 created the Counter-Terrorism Committee (CTC), and three years later the council adopted Resolution 1535 (2004) to strengthen the CTC through the creation of an unprecedented Counter-Terrorism

Executive Directorate (CTED).[28] The Security Council also adopted Resolutions 1540 (2004) and 1566 (2004) prohibiting the transfer of weapons of mass destruction or related materials to nonstate actors and calling on UN member states to strengthen their cooperation with UN counter-terrorism mandates.[29]

These efforts have produced an unprecedented expansion of UN counter-terrorism activities and a parallel increase in counter-terrorism committees and professional staffing. They stimulated significant international action to build counter-terrorism capacity, particularly in the former Soviet Bloc and in the global South. The UN counter-terrorism program has also sparked greater international cooperation and coordination among regional and subregional organizations, along with specialized international agencies. As the chapters in this volume elucidate, these UN counter-terrorism efforts face numerous challenges, contradictions, and inefficiencies even as they have been partially effective in establishing global legal requirements and building international cooperation in the fight against terrorism.

The third phase of the UN's expanding role in the struggle against terrorism has been marked by proactive involvement of the Secretary-General in analyzing the problems of international cooperation regarding terrorism and in articulating a viable role for the UN as the central collective security regime of the globe. This was particularly evident in Kofi Annan's address at the Madrid Summit in March 2005, delivered on the first anniversary of the terrorist bombing in that city's train station. Although not widely covered by the news media in the United States, the Secretary-General's address was considered by other nations as signaling the need for a more comprehensive strategy against terrorism.

Building from earlier recommendations of his High-Level Panel on Threats, Challenges and Change,[30] and related ideas discussed in various diplomatic-scholarly circles, the Secretary-General proposed a strategy that included five Ds: denying and deterring terrorist activities, dissuading groups from supporting militancy, developing state capacity for the rule of law, and defending human rights. The Secretary-General acknowledged the importance of robust protective and law enforcement measures, but he also called for broader preventive strategies to address the root causes of terrorism. He spoke directly to the growing concern in many parts of the world that counter-terrorism efforts are encroaching on individual freedoms. Undermining human rights in the name of counter-terrorism, the Secretary-General warned, would be counterproductive and would erode the political legitimacy necessary to sustain the struggle against extremism. A more holistic strategy against terrorism must combine preventive and protective measures, he argued, to guard against attacks in the short run and reduce the motivation and social support for political terrorism over the long term.

The ideas in the Madrid speech formed the basis for the March 2005 report, *In Larger Freedom: Towards Development, Security, and Human Rights for All*, which outlined policy recommendations for the world summit held in conjunction with the sixtieth anniversary of the United Nations in September 2005.[31] The Counter-Terrorism Implementation Task Force emerging from that summit helped to produce the Secretary-General's April 2006 report, *Uniting Against Terrorism: Recommendations for a Global Counter-Terrorism Strategy*, which integrated all the previous suggestions into a comprehensive summary of current UN activities and a set of specific proposals for strengthening global efforts to combat terrorism.[32]

Achieving these ambitious objectives will be a difficult and long-term process. Preventive strategies pose enormous challenges for multilateral organizations and especially for the United Nations. A comprehensive approach includes not only coercive measures but also persuasive policies that seek to win hearts and minds of the many young citizens across an array of nations who have yet to decide whether their political participation will take the form of violence or not. Like the other dimensions of successful counter-terrorism strategy, this longer-term preventive effort depends on a greater commitment to cooperation, multilateral action, and the rule of law.

The Chapters in This Volume

The field of counter-terrorism is now so wide-ranging and the volume and scope of published literature so deep that it is difficult to decide where to concentrate an intellectual venture that seeks to be policy relevant. Our choice is to emphasize the role of the United Nations and other major multilateral institutions—particularly the Financial Action Task Force and the European Union. We have also sought to examine the role of international legal mechanisms, sanctions and incentives-based diplomacy, and collaborative efforts to build law enforcement capacity. The result is a set of essays that examine with a critical eye the most important nonmilitary, multilateral strategies for countering terrorism.

In chapter 2 we are joined by our colleagues Alistair Millar and Linda Gerber-Stellingwerf in providing a comprehensive overview of the UN counter-terrorism program. We trace the history of the UN Counter-Terrorism Committee (CTC) from its beginning in September 2001 through the summer of 2006, examining its role as the principal coordinating body for global capacity building and regional coordination efforts. Operating under the mandate of Security Council Resolution 1373 (2001), the CTC has worked with UN member states, regional organizations, and specialized international agencies in support of efforts to deny finances, travel, and other forms of assistance to terrorists. Among the main functions of the committee have been to request and analyze reports from states on their implementation activities and to coordinate the delivery of capacity-building assistance for states needing help to comply with the broad requirements of the resolution. The response of states to CTC reporting requests has been unprecedented, with all 191 (now 192) member states submitting the required reports. As the committee's experts requested additional information, however, states began to bristle at the constant requirement for more paperwork, and a kind of "reporting fatigue" set in. Questions also have emerged about the CTC's role in coordinating the provision of technical assistance. The committee has lacked the staff capacity to monitor and facilitate the expanding international effort to provide assistance for counter-terrorism law enforcement.

Chapter 2 examines this process of UN institutional expansion in detail. We review the accomplishments and the shortcomings of the CTC, noting the gradual loss of institutional and political momentum. The chapter also explores the major challenges facing the UN counter-terrorism program. The relationship between counter-terrorism technical assistance and international developmental aid has stirred debate. Are these programs in competition, or can they be integrated? International coordination remains inadequate, especially in regions of concern such as Northern Africa, the Middle East, and Central Asia. Greater coordination is also needed within the UN system itself. The chapter concludes with a review of the major political and organization obstacles facing the UN as it attempts to play its appropriate role in strategic counter-terrorism. Among these hurdles are the lack of an agreed international definition of terrorism and the absence of universally accepted compliance standards and enforcement policies.

Chapter 3 provides a critical analysis of the UN counter-terrorism program and suggests alternative arrangements for strengthening legal and institutional mechanisms in the future. Eric Rosand, former chief of the Multilateral Affairs Unit in the Office of the Coordinator for Counterterrorism at the U.S. Department of State and deputy legal counsel at the U.S. Mission to the UN, joins with Alistair Millar to explore both present limitations and future options for creating effective international cooperation against terror. Rosand and Millar examine the duplication and overlap that have complicated UN counter-terrorism efforts. The United Nations now has five separate counter-terrorism bodies: the Office on Drugs and Crime/Terrorism Prevention Branch (UNODC/TPB), created by the General Assembly in the late 1990s and expanded after September 2001; the Al-Qaida/Taliban Sanctions Committee and associated Analytical Support and Sanctions Monitoring Team, established by the Security Council in Resolution 1267 (1999) and since reauthorized several times, including in Resolution 1617(2005); the Counter-Terrorism Committee and the Counter-Terrorism Executive Directorate authorized by Resolutions 1373 (2001) and 1535 (2004); the Counter-Proliferation Committee and associated team of experts established by Resolution 1540 (2004); and the working group on additional measures against terrorism established by Resolution 1566 (2004) in the wake of the massacre in Beslan, Russia. The authors argue that this multiplication of underresourced counter-terrorism bodies has led to duplication in analytic and assessment functions at the UN and has imposed excessive reporting obligations on individual UN member states, which can be especially burdensome on smaller, less developed countries. Most important, the existence of separate bodies has impeded the development of more coherent, integrated strategies and programs for combating the terrorist threat.

Rosand and Millar discuss a variety of options for improving program coordination and coherence, ranging from the proposal of Costa Rica and Switzerland for the appointment of a UN high commissioner for terrorism, to the suggestion offered by the prestigious Council on Foreign Relations for the creation of an entirely new international counter-terrorism agency. They present short-term options that might be achieved without extensive political debate or controversy, including integrating the separate Security Council staff bodies, or combining these with the staff of the UNODC/TPB into one consolidated UN counter-terrorism body. Proposals have also been made to consolidate the four separate Security Council counter-terrorism committees into one. These steps could serve as a prelude to the creation of a larger international counter-terrorism body that would be created by the UN and authorized to report to the Security Council but that would operate independently, without the impediments of working within a highly politicized and bureaucratized UN environment. Creating greater institutional capacity for global counter-terrorism is a long-term challenge that will require extensive consultations with stakeholders throughout the world.

In chapter 4 former ambassador and assistant secretary of state Thomas E. McNamara provides an insider's account of one of the most important successes in the global struggle against terrorism and weapons of mass destruction, the case of Libya. McNamara helped to formulate U.S. policy toward Libya during the administration of President George H. W. Bush, and he served as a special assistant for counter-terrorism policy in the State Department in the months after the September 11 attacks. His chapter provides a detailed account of U.S. policy toward Libya and shows how the unique mix of unilateral and multilateral sanctions convinced the Qaddafi regime to end its support of terrorism and dismantle its weapons of mass destruction. The Libya case featured a unique blend of sanctions and diplomatic engagement among an array of actors that included the United States, the UN Security Council, the European community, and Arab and African regional organizations. It illustrated the success of nonmilitary strategies and the effectiveness of sanctions-based diplomacy in achieving counter-terrorism and counter-proliferation objectives.

McNamara's analysis runs counter to the explanation of Libya's behavior posited by the Bush administration and now accepted as conventional wisdom of many media commentators and Washington policymakers. When Libya announced the dismantlement of its weapons programs in October 2003, officials of the Bush administration attributed Libya's dramatic turnaround to what Representative Tom Lantos (D-CA) termed the "pedagogic value" of the war in Iraq. According to this interpretation, Qaddafi had seen what happened to Saddam Hussein and agreed to mend his ways out of fear of American military attack. In fact, as McNamara documents, Libya's policy reversal began many years before in response to sanctions-based diplomacy during the 1990s, and it concluded successfully because of persistent but fair negotiations. Flynt Leverett, senior director for Middle Eastern affairs at the National Security Council in 2003, wrote that the Iraq war "was not the driving force in Libya's move. . . . Libya was willing to deal because of critical diplomatic representations . . . that doing so was critical to achieving their strategic and domestic goals."[33] In a larger and more recent study, Bruce W. Jentleson and Christopher A. Whytock come to a similar conclusion.[34] McNamara's meticulous account of the diplomatic interactions with Libya confirms this analysis and convincingly demonstrates that political and economic pressures, not the threat of war, brought about the historic change in Libyan policy.

As part of post-9/11 security policy, U.S. officials have identified the "deadly nexus" between terrorism and weapons proliferation as the greatest threat to international security. In chapter 5 Alistair Millar and Jason Ipe examine this threat and review the efforts now underway in the international community, especially at the United Nations, to prevent a terrorist-delivered nuclear strike. The authors quote former U.S. secretary of defense William Perry, who said in 2004, "I have never been as worried as I am now that a nuclear bomb will be detonated in an American city. I fear that we are racing towards an unprecedented catastrophe."[35] Chapter 5 reviews the alarming evidence of Al-Qaida's expressed intentions and attempts to acquire nuclear weapons capability. Osama bin Laden has described the acquisition of nuclear weapons as a sacred duty. Senior Al-Qaida officials have met with Pakistani nuclear scientists. Police officials in Europe have arrested suspected members of Al-Qaida for attempting to purchase uranium. Despite these worrisome developments, however, there is no evidence to date that Al-Qaida has succeeded in acquiring nuclear capability. Millar and Ipe examine the problem of unsecured and vulnerable nuclear weapons and materials around the world, particularly in the former Soviet Union. They explore regional approaches to preventing the spread of nuclear materials, especially in the Middle East. The chapter concludes with a critical analysis of UN Security Council Resolution 1540 and the fledging efforts of the UN Counter-Proliferation Committee.

Early in the struggle against Al-Qaida and related networks, international officials recognized the importance of attempting to cut off the financing of terrorist groups. Law enforcement experts and practitioners sought to disable these networks, as they have with criminal syndicates involved in money laundering and drug trafficking, by depriving them of funding. They also attempted to follow the trail of financial transactions as a means of gaining evidence for the indictment and prosecution of terrorist criminals. Since the late 1990s the Financial Action Task Force (FATF) of the Organization for Security and Co-operation in Europe (OSCE) has been at the heart of the struggle to halt the financing of illicit international actions that now include transnational terror. Created in 1989 by the then G-7 nations to combat money laundering, the FATF has been one of the world's most effective organizations for setting standards and monitoring member state progress in implementing anti–money laundering measures. With the increase in terrorist violence in recent years and especially after the attacks of September 2001, the FATF has taken on the additional task of aiding states as they combat the financing of terror.

In chapter 6 Kathryn L. Gardner assesses the Financial Action Task Force's successes and failures in achieving member state compliance with Security Council requirements to freeze the assets of terrorist groups and their supporters. Gardner notes the sharp contrast between financial crime related to money laundering, which involves huge sums of money illegally channeled through banks and conventional financial institutions, and the financing of terrorist networks, where the amounts of money involved are much smaller and where funds are transmitted through informal, nonbanking channels. As a consequence of these differences, the struggle to defund terrorism is extremely daunting and is unlikely to be successful on its own in countering terrorism. Gardner nonetheless points out the ways in which FATF procedures and policies are helpful to the global counter-terrorism struggle and draws lessons for enhancing international cooperation to reduce the funding available for terrorist crime.

In the wake of the September 11 attacks, as Oldrich Bures and Stephanie Ahern document in chapter 7, the European Union acted swiftly to create a counter-terrorism Plan of Action and to increase regional law enforcement cooperation against terrorism. The development of the European program against terrorism was able to grow alongside a historic expansion of the number of states within the Union, which enabled European officials to use the prospect of EU membership as an inducement for new member states of central and eastern Europe to expand counter-terrorism capacity. Bures and Ahern trace the development of European counter-terrorism policy from the 1970s, when members of the emerging European community agreed to a regional approach against politically inspired extremism. In the typical European manner, these programs were grounded in formal legal agreements and were accompanied by the creation of a wide range of organizational structures.

The September 11 attacks provided a jolt to enhance existing protections and add new programs, including the European arrest warrant. As Bures and Ahern note, the idea of a communitywide arrest warrant originated in 1999, but it did not receive serious consideration until after September 11. It took nearly three years for all EU members to approve the new warrant. The program has been a qualified success so far in strengthening law enforcement cooperation and streamlining arrest and extradition procedures. The European Union has also made substantial progress in agreeing to a common definition of terrorism and in designating individuals and entities subject to financial freezes and travel bans. These programs have faced challenges, have stirred controversy, and have a mixture of successes and failures. But on balance, they represent progress in the overall fight against terrorism and can serve as models for other regional organizations.

In chapter 8 we broaden the discussion of counter-terrorism strategy to address the difficult but necessary long-term task of prevention. In the spirit of Secretary-General Kofi Annan's keynote address at the March 2005 Madrid Summit and April 2006 *Uniting Against Terrorism* report, we examine the root causes of terrorism and the challenge of preventing the rise of extremist networks. We address what Shibley Telhami has termed the "demand side" of terrorism, exploring ways to cut off the flow of recruits, financial support, and political sympathy for terrorist groups. By attempting to understand the underlying risk factors associated with terrorist formation, we hope to identify policies that can dissuade groups from supporting militancy and thereby cut off the development of terrorism at its source.

Longer-term preventive strategies require an understanding of the new forms of "superterrorism" that have emerged in the last decade and the ways in which U.S. military policies, particularly the war in Iraq, have inflamed jihadist militancy. Terrorism is ultimately a political act, and it is necessary to understand the political motivations, without justifying the methods of those who resort to such acts. Chapter 8 explores the deeper roots of terrorism in economic deprivation, failed governance and the denial of viable means of political participation, and the exercise of human rights and democratic freedoms. We conclude the chapter with an assessment of protective and preventive strategies that differentiate between hard-core terrorist militants (against whom coercive measures are necessary) and the broader social base of potential sympathizers (where persuasive strategies are likely to be more effective). By addressing legitimate political grievances, improving governance in regions of instability, and expanding economic and social opportunity, the United States and other leading states can alter the underlying conditions that give rise to and sustain terrorist networks. The proposed preventive strategies will require profound changes—including a demilitarization of American policy—and thus will not be welcome in official circles in Washington, but they are in the best interest of the United States and deserve consideration.

The purpose of this volume, then, is to focus attention on the multi-lateral, nonmilitary dimensions of the struggle against terrorism, with a particular focus on the United Nations counter-terrorism program. As we have passed the fifth anniversary of 9/11 in the U.S. and the commemoration of the unprecedented UN foray into counter-terrorist policy and action via Resolution 1373, nothing could be more appropriate than an assessment of the strengths and weaknesses of the UN—and by association U.S.—counter-terrorism efforts. As the chapters in this book suggest, the battle against terrorism is not really a war at all, at least not in any recognizable traditional military sense, but rather a new kind of international campaign encompassing a wide array of policy tools, of which the use of force is but one relatively insignificant element. Our analysis assumes the primacy of cooperative international law enforcement efforts and gives large weight to the role of the United Nations as both legitimizing agency and central hub around which the struggle against terrorism must be organized. We provide a critical look at the strengths and weaknesses of multilateral approaches in general and the UN counter-terrorism program in particular. Our goal is to identify steps that the United States and other states can take to enhance the effectiveness of global counter-terrorism efforts and thereby achieve a shared goal of ending the scourge of terrorism as an expression of political grievance, hatred, or national or religious expression.

Notes

1. Richard A. Clarke et al., *Defeating the Jihadists: A Blueprint for Action* (Washington, DC: Century Foundation Press, 2004).

2. Mark Mazzetti and David Rohde, "Terror Officials See Qaeda Chiefs Regaining Power," *New York Times*, 19 February 2007.

3. There are exceptions to the rule. For an early look at the role of the UN and regional organizations, see *International Terrorism: National, Regional and Global Perspectives*, ed. Yonah Alexander (New York: Praeger, 1976). A more recent examination of these issues is contained in *Terrorism and the UN: Before and After September 11*, ed. Jane Boulden and Thomas G. Weiss (Bloomington: Indiana University Press, 2004). See also Edward C. Luck, "Tackling Terrorism," in *The United Nations Security Council: From the Cold War to the Twenty-first Century*, ed. David M. Malone, 85–100 (Boulder, CO: Lynne Rienner, 2004); and Rob de Wijk, "The Limits of Military Power," *Washington Quarterly* 25, no. 1 (Winter 2002): 75–92.

4. A recent example of this U.S. focus is Daniel Benjamin and Steven Simon, *The Next Attack: The Failure of the War on Terror and a Strategy for Getting It Right* (New York: Times Books, 2005).

5. Eric Rosand, "Current Developments: The Security Council's Efforts to Monitor the Implementation of Al-Qaida/Taliban Sanctions," *American Journal of International Law* 98 (2004): 745–63.

6. David Cortright et al., *An Action Agenda for Enhancing the United Nations Program on Counter-Terrorism* (Goshen, IN: Fourth Freedom Forum, 2004), <http://www.fourthfreedom.org/pdf/Action_Agenda.pdf> (accessed 26 July 2005); see also Eric Rosand, "Security Council Resolution 1373 and the Counter-Terrorism Committee: The Cornerstone of the United Nations Contribution to the Fight Against Terrorism," in *Legal Instruments in the Fight Against International Terrorism*, ed. Cyrille Fijnaut, Jan Wouters, and Frederik Naert, 603, 606 (Boston: Brill Academic, 2004).

7. Alistair Millar and Morten Bremer Maerli, "Nuclear Non-Proliferation and UNSC Resolution 1540," in *Policy Briefs on the Implementation of the Treaty on the Non-Proliferation of Nuclear Weapons* (Oslo: Norwegian Institute of International Affairs, 2005), <http://www.nupi.no/IPS/filestore/PolicyBriefsApril2005.pdf> (accessed 26 July 2005).

8. For contrasting views on what options were open to the U.S. and how and why the Bush administration chose the course it did, see Paul Rogers, *A War on Terror: Afghanistan and After* (London: Pluto Press, 2004), and *America's War on Terror*, ed. Patrick Hayden et al. (London: Ashgate Press, 2003).

9. Stephen M. Walt and John J. Mearsheimer, "An Unnecessary War," *Foreign Policy* 134 (January–February 2003): 50–59.

10. Eric Schmitt and Thom Shanker, "New Name for 'War on Terror' Reflects Wider U.S. Campaign," *New York Times*, 26 July 2005.

11. Benjamin and Simon, *The Next Attack*, 198.

12. "Excerpt from the National Intelligence Estimate," *Washington Post*, 27 September 2006.

13. Mark Mazzetti, "Spy Agencies Say Iraq War Worsens Terror Threat," *New York Times*, 24 September 2006.

14. See, for example, Paul Wilkinson, *Terrorism Versus Democracy: The Liberal State Response* (London: Frank Cass, 2003).

15. Jessica Stern, *Terror in the Name of God: Why Religious Militants Kill* (New York: Harper Collins, 2003).

16. Marc Sageman, *Understanding Terror Networks* (Philadelphia: University of Pennsylvania Press, 2004).

17. See Karen von Hippel, "Improving the International Response to the Transnational Terrorist Threat," in *Terrorism and the UN: Before and After September 11*, ed. Jane Boulden and Thomas G. Weiss, 102–19 (Bloomington: Indiana University Press, 2004); and Karen von Hippel, "Democracy by Force:

A Renewed Commitment to Nation Building," in *The Battle for Hearts and Minds: Using Soft Power to Undermine Terrorist Networks*, ed. Alexander T. J. Lennon, 108–29 (Cambridge, MA: MIT Press, 2003).

18. See Bruce Hoffman, *Inside Terrorism*, revised edition (New York: Columbia University Press, 2006).

19. See, for example, Martha Crenshaw, "The Logic of Terrorism: Terrorist Behavior as a Product of Strategic Choice," in *Origins of Terrorism: Psychologies, Ideologies, Theologies, States of Mind*, ed. Walter Reich, 7–24 (Washington, DC: Woodrow Wilson Center Press, 1998).

20. Martha Crenshaw, "The Psychology of Terrorism: An Agenda for the Twenty-first Century," *Political Psychology* 21, no. 2 (2001): 405–20.

21. See Andrew Silke, "An Introduction to Terrorism Research," in *Research on Terrorism: Trends, Achievements and Failures*, ed. Andrew Silke (London: Frank Cass, 2004).

22. White House, *National Strategy for Combating Terrorism* (Washington, DC: GPO, September 2006), 1.

23. For a critical analysis of the Afghanistan situation, see Barnett R. Rubin, "Still Ours to Lose: Afghanistan on the Brink," prepared testimony for the House Committee on International Relations, 109th Cong., 2d sess., Washington, DC, 20 September 2006, and the Senate Committee on Foreign Relations, 21 September 2006, <http://www.cfr.org/publication/11486/still_ours_to_lose.html> (accessed 9 October 2006). On Iraq, see Thomas Ricks, *Fiasco: The American Military Adventure in Iraq* (New York: Penguin Press, 2006).

24. Karen Greenberg, "From the Editor: European Counterterrorism and Its Implications for the U.S. War on Terror," *New York University Review of Law and Security* (Summer 2005): 2–3.

25. Mark Landler, "German 9/11 Retrial Gets Exculpatory Evidence from U.S.," *New York Times*, 12 August 2004.

26. United Nations Security Council, *Security Council Resolution 1054 (1996)*, S/RES/1054, New York, 26 April 1996; United Nations Security Council, *Security Council Resolution 1267 (1999)*, S/RES/1267, New York, 15 October 1999.

27. The history and details of these cases are chronicled in David Cortright and George A. Lopez, *The Sanctions Decade: Assessing UN Strategies in the 1990s* (Boulder, CO: Lynne Rienner, 2000); and David Cortright and George A. Lopez, *Sanctions and the Search for Security: Challenges to UN Action* (Boulder, CO: Lynne Rienner, 2002).

28. United Nations Security Council, *Security Council Resolution 1373 (2001)*, S/RES/1373, New York, 28 September 2001; United Nations Security Council, *Security Council Resolution 1535 (2004)*, S/RES/1535, New York, 26 March 2004.

29. United Nations Security Council, *Security Council Resolution 1540 (2004)*, S/RES/1540, New York, 28 April 2004; United Nations Security Council, *Security Council Resolution 1566 (2004)*, S/RES/1566, New York, 1 October 2004.

30. United Nations General Assembly, *A More Secure World: Our Shared Responsibility, Report of the Secretary-General's High-Level Panel on Threats, Challenges and Change*, A/59/565, New York, 29 November 2004.

31. United Nations General Assembly, *In Larger Freedom: Towards Development, Security, and Human Rights for All*, A/59/2005, New York, 21 March 2005.

32. United Nations General Assembly, *Uniting Against Terrorism: Recommendations for a Global Counter-Terrorism Strategy*, A/60/825, New York, 27 April 2006.

33. Flynt Leverett, "Why Libya Gave Up the Bomb," *New York Times*, 25 January 2004.

34. Bruce W. Jentleson and Christopher A. Whytock, "Who 'Won' Libya? The Force-Diplomacy Debate and Its Implications for Theory and Policy," *International Security* 30, no. 3 (Winter 2005–2006): 47–86.

35. William J. Perry, Keynote Address at the Conference on Post–Cold War U.S. Nuclear Strategy: A Search for Technical and Policy Common Ground, Committee on International Security and Arms Control, National Academy of Sciences, Washington, DC, 11 August 2004, <http://www7.nationalacademies.org/cisac/Perry_Presentation.pdf>, quoted in Robert S. McNamara, "Apocalypse Soon," *Foreign Policy* 148 (May–June 2005): 28–35.

2

Global Cooperation Against Terrorism
Evaluating the United Nations
Counter-Terrorism Committee

David Cortright, George A. Lopez, Alistair Millar, and
Linda Gerber-Stellingwerf

With the passage of Resolution 1373 on 28 September 2001, the United
Nations Security Council assumed a central role in international efforts
to destroy and disrupt terrorist networks. Faced with the unprecedented
attacks of September 11 (9/11), the Security Council imposed equally
unprecedented obligations on UN member states. The resolution was
adopted under the authority of chapter VII of the United Nations
Charter, which made it legally binding on all member states. Resolution
1373 required every country to freeze the financial assets of terrorists
and their supporters, deny them travel or safe haven, prevent terrorist
recruitment and weapons supply, and cooperate with other countries in
information sharing and criminal prosecution. UN member states were
urged to sign on to twelve existing antiterrorism conventions and to
afford one another "the greatest measure of assistance" in investigating
terrorist acts.[1] They were to intensify and facilitate the exchange of information on matters related to travel, communications, and arms trafficking among terrorists. Simply stated, Resolution 1373 was unparalleled
in establishing legal obligations and mobilizing states for a campaign of
nonmilitary cooperative law enforcement measures to combat global
terrorism.[2]

To monitor state implementation of post-9/11 counter-terrorism mandates and to receive and process the reports of members, Resolution
1373 created the Counter-Terrorism Committee (CTC). The CTC
was fashioned as a committee of the whole, consisting of all fifteen
members of the Security Council.[3] It received priority attention and
resources within the United Nations was described by Secretary-
General Kofi Annan as the "centre of global efforts to fight terrorism."[4]

Subsequently, the Security Council endowed the CTC with a larger, more permanent expert staff in the form of the Counter-Terrorism Executive Directorate (CTED).

The primary function of the CTC and its Executive Directorate is to strengthen the counter-terrorism capacity of UN member states. Its mission, wrote one observer, is to "raise the average level of government performance against terrorism across the globe."[5] The committee serves as a "switchboard," helping to facilitate the provision of technical assistance to countries needing help to implement counter-terrorism mandates. It also attempts to coordinate the counter-terrorism efforts of a wide range of international, regional, and subregional organizations within and beyond the UN system.[6] Contrary to some popularly held notions, the CTC is neither a sanctions committee nor an investigative body.[7]

This chapter assesses the accomplishments and shortcomings of the UN Security Council–led counter-terrorism efforts. The analysis focuses on the CTC and reviews the challenges that lie ahead for the committee and its Executive Directorate. It begins by measuring the overall progress of international counter-terrorism cooperation and capacity-building efforts by the CTC/CTED. It examines the CTC's efforts to facilitate the provision of technical assistance to the many countries that need help in meeting the requirements of Resolution 1373 and its attempts to coordinate the counter-terrorism activities of international, regional, and subregional organizations. It considers the relationship between the CTC and the other counter-terrorism-related Security Council committees (created in 2004 by Resolutions 1540 and 1566), as well as its ongoing relationship to the committee and monitoring team established to enforce sanctions against Al-Qaida and the Taliban. It concludes by examining some of the underlying political challenges that the CTC will have to address, including the lack of an agreed definition of terrorism, as it seeks to enhance global counter-terrorism efforts.

A Mixed Record

Since its establishment, the CTC has had a mixed record in promoting counter-terrorism cooperation. The CTC has played a role in creating and sustaining international momentum to strengthen counter-terrorism efforts. It has helped to establish political and legal authority for the UN counter-terrorism effort and has promoted the creation of specialized systems for coordinating global efforts against terrorism. The cooperative approach embodied in the UN counter-terrorism program has helped to develop and strengthen international norms. The UN program has helped to validate the importance of nonmilitary, cooperative law enforcement efforts as viable means of countering the terrorism threat.

The CTC has sought to focus on the less controversial aspects of counter-terrorism—for example, by working to strengthen states' counter-terrorism infrastructure and enhance counter-terrorism co-operation among states and organizations. It consciously avoids politically charged discussions of definitions and root causes. It has sought to work with all states to help identify their capacity gaps, to serve as a switchboard between donors and interested states, and to minimize duplication and overlap among potential assistance providers. Significantly, the CTC has received and reviewed more than 600 reports from member states and is thus conducting the first worldwide audit of counter-terrorism capacities.[8]

In response to CTC monitoring of these state reports and site visits to a limited amount of countries beginning in 2005, some states have adopted new or improved counter-terrorism legislation, border controls, and executive machinery. The CTC assisted several states to adapt anti–money laundering laws and develop additional legislative restrictions on the financing of terrorism. As a result, countries like the United Arab Emirates and Kuwait have adopted antiterrorist financing legislation. The CTC also assisted countries in placing enhanced controls over informal banking systems such as hawala or hindi that have been exploited by terrorists. Furthermore, partly as a result of the CTC's prodding, the number of countries that are party to all international terrorism treaties has risen from two in September 2001 to more than seventy in 2006. In addition to working with states, the CTC has reached out to some sixty international, regional, and subregional organizations to encourage them to become more involved in the global counter-terrorism campaign—for example, by developing counter-terrorism action plans, best practices, and units within their secretariats, while urging their members to join the international terrorism-related treaties and implement Resolution 1373. The CTC has received high levels of cooperation from UN member states, but it has also faced significant challenges. The Security Council has succeeded in developing a broad counter-terrorism legal framework of resolutions that impose obligations on all 192 UN member states, but it has not developed an effective operational framework. Thus, more than five years after the September 11 attacks, despite pockets of success, the CTC has not yet created a counter-terrorism program capable of implementing its far-reaching legal mandate.

The committee's staff has been engaged in a continuous paper chase with officials in member states, analyzing and responding to hundreds of written reports in a process that created a response backlog in New York and reporting fatigue in state capitals. In its first three years of operation, the committee relied exclusively on the reports from member states and lacked independent means of determining whether countries were actually implementing counter-terrorism mandates in full. In 2005 the CTED initiated a continuing program of site visits that has included missions to Morocco, Albania, Kenya, Thailand, the former Yugoslav republic of Macedonia, and Jordan to evaluate implementation needs.[9] Site visits can substantially increase the committee's capacity to assess counter-terrorism needs, although they require a higher level of preparation and follow-through.

Since its promising beginning under the leadership of its first chair, Jeremy Greenstock, British permanent representative to the United Nations, the CTC has suffered from uneven leadership, administrative and bureaucratic delays, and lack of resources. For the first two and a half years of its existence, the CTC's work was supported by a handful of consultants (many former UN diplomats with little relevant experience) hired by the UN Secretariat on short-term contracts. Given the breadth and long-term nature of the CTC's mandate, it became clear by early 2004 that the Security Council needed to "revitalize" the CTC through the provision of additional resources and authority.[10] These considerations led the Security Council to adopt Resolution 1535 in March 2004. The resolution created the CTED, which significantly expanded the committee's professional staffing and enhanced its capacity to support member state implementation. After lengthy delays due principally to the cumbersome UN budget and personnel processes, the CTED, with its twenty experts, became fully staffed in the fall of 2005, more than eighteen months after it was created. This larger group of experts enabled the CTC to begin site visits and to determine more effectively the areas in which states need the most help. Neither the CTC nor its CTED have the resources to provide technical assistance, however. Thus, even if the CTC can effectively determine the most urgent gaps to be filled, which remains uncertain, it must rely on donors to come forward to deliver the necessary aid.

The committee has served as a useful forum for discussing issues, but it has lacked the political mandate or resources to ensure implementation of counter-terrorism requirements. It has suffered from inattention to fundamental administrative tasks. It has lost momentum as the Security Council shifted its focus to other international emergencies. The result has been mounting discontent among some UN member states with the performance of the CTC. The UN counter-terrorism program has also been caught in various political controversies, including disagreements over how to define terrorism and concerns from civil society that some governments are using counter-terrorism to undermine human rights and political liberties.

To date, the United States, the United Kingdom, and other permanent members of the Security Council have been firmly in charge of shaping the CTC agenda. Developing nations have had little voice in these matters. Partly this reflects the increased counter-terrorism role of the Security Council, where nations from the global South generally have less say. Prior to September 2001 the General Assembly was a major player in shaping the UN agenda on terrorism. The General Assembly created the United Nations Office on Drugs and Crime and its Terrorism Prevention Branch (UNODC/TPB) and authored the thirteen UN counter-terrorism conventions. With the passage of Resolution 1373, the center of antiterrorism activity shifted to the Security Council, a shift that has been further reinforced by a series of subsequent resolutions and the creation of additional Security Council subsidiary bodies. In February 2004 the council adopted Resolution 1540 and created a nonproliferation committee to assist states in keeping weapons of mass destruction out of the hands of terrorists. In October 2004 the Security Council approved Resolution 1566 in response to the school massacre at Beslan in North Ossetia. The new resolution urged greater cooperation in the fight against terrorism and established a working group to consider additional counter-terrorism measures.

The gravitational shift toward the Security Council has meant that nonpermanent members of the Security Council are less able to exert leadership on major policy initiatives. India, South Africa, and other developing countries have actively supported the CTC program and have urged greater efforts to build the capacity of states to crack down on terrorists, but the influence of these countries has not been acknowledged in the Security Council. In Latin America, the Organization of American States (OAS) has developed a vigorous regional counter-terrorism program, in cooperation with the CTC and the United Nations. In Africa and much of West Asia, however, regional and subregional organizations have been less active in counter-terrorism efforts. These areas lack sufficient antiterrorist capacity and have lower ratification rates for counter-terrorism conventions. Some governments in the global South do not share the Western view of terrorism as a priority concern. They consider the current UN emphasis on counter-terrorism a U.S. or Western imposition that diverts attention from other international needs, such as overcoming poverty or resolving conflicts in Africa. This has impeded cooperation with the UN counter-terrorism program.

Some governments have expressed concern that the Security Council exceeded its mandate in Resolution 1373. By imposing sweeping mandates on member states, the council acted as a "global legislator." This was not the intended design of the world body as established in the UN Charter, which gave the authority to draft binding legal agreements to the General Assembly, where all nations are represented. Resolution 1373 included some of the provisions of UN counter-terrorism conventions, which had been crafted previously by the General Assembly. By adopting the resolution under chapter VII, the Security Council made these provisions binding on all member states, even those that had not yet approved the conventions. This continued a trend within UN practice toward greater "legislative" authority for the council, especially since its activation in the post–cold war era, and in response to the perceived urgency of the post-9/11 terrorist threat.[11]

Measuring Progress

It is difficult to measure the success of these nonmilitary counter-terrorism efforts. The core elements of this work—improved information sharing, law enforcement and judicial cooperation, enhanced domestic legal regimes, and strengthened border security—do not make international headlines. One indicator of progress frequently mentioned in the initial work of the CTC was the high rate of response to the committee's requests for information on counter-terrorism capacity and implementation. Member state compliance with CTC reporting requests has been greater than for any previous Security Council mandate. All UN member states submitted first-round reports to the CTC explaining their efforts to implement Resolution 1373.[12] Most states also responded to additional rounds of requests for further information. The more than 600 reports received by the CTC provide a wealth of information about worldwide counter-terrorism capacity. The reports indicate that many states are taking steps to revise their laws and enhance their enforcement capacity for implementation of UN counter-terrorism mandates.

Another measure of progress in UN counter-terrorism implementation is the marked increase in the number of states joining the thirteen UN counter-terrorism conventions. These conventions provide a legal basis for nations to cooperate in preventing the financing of terrorism, suppressing terrorist bombings and hijackings, and carrying out joint law enforcement and intelligence efforts. The increased rate of support for the two main conventions—the *International Convention for the Suppression of Terrorist Bombings* (1997) and the *International Convention for the Suppression of the Financing of Terrorism* (1999)—has been extraordinary. In the first four years after the opening of the convention on terrorist bombings, only twenty-seven states became parties to the agreement. In the years after September 2001, an additional 121 states became parties to the convention. In the case of the convention on terrorist financing, only four states were parties to the agreement in its first two years, but since September 2001, 151 additional nations have become parties.[13] These results show that the United Nations has been successful in creating a stronger legal foundation among states for institutionalizing the battle against terrorism.

While many states have declared their support for UN counter-terrorism mandates, not all states have the full intention or the capacity to make substantive progress in complying with Resolution 1373. Evaluating whether states are actually implementing the requirements of Resolution 1373 and the UN counter-terrorism conventions is a difficult challenge. For example, Sudan has signed and ratified all the conventions relevant to Resolution 1373, but the country clearly has more to do in implementing effective measures against terrorism. Part of the problem is that there are no agreed global criteria for evaluating implementation capacities or for deciding what additional steps a state should take to achieve compliance. The Security Council and the CTC have not established standards for deciding whether and to what extent states are progressing in their implementation of the various requirements of Resolution 1373.[14] Evaluating whether states are actually implementing the requirements of Resolution 1373 and UN counter-terrorism conventions is a more difficult challenge. For example, Kenya and Bangladesh have signed and ratified all the conventions relevant to 1373, but there is little doubt that both countries have much more to do to implement effective measures against terrorism. In a number of countries that have ratified the UN conventions, much more work must be done to create the legal and administrative machinery to extradite terrorist suspects, freeze assets associated with terrorist financing, and deny terrorists safe haven.

The Challenge of Implementation

In its initial operations the CTC developed an approach to assessing state capacity that divided the various implementation requirements into three stages. In stage A states were expected to

• Have legislation in place covering all aspects of Resolution 1373,
• Begin the process of becoming party to the UN counter-terrorism conventions, and
• Establish effective executive machinery for preventing and suppressing terrorist financing.

In stage B states were expected to

• Have executive machinery in place covering all aspects of the resolution,

• Have an effective governmentwide coordinating mechanism for counter-terrorism activity, and

• Cooperate on the bilateral, regional, and international levels, including sharing information.

In stage C states were expected to utilize the legislative and executive machinery to cooperate with other states to bring terrorists and their supporters to justice.[15]

In its communications with member states, the CTC has utilized performance standards that were developed by functional international agencies, including the Financial Action Task Force (FATF) of the Organisation for Economic Co-operation and Development (OECD). The committee has noted, for example, that implementation of paragraph 1 of Resolution 1373 requires states to have a mechanism in place to register, audit, and monitor the collection and use of funds and other financial resources, including by charitable associations, to ensure that such funds are not diverted to terrorist purposes. The committee has urged states to regulate all money and value transfer systems, whether formal or informal, which requires states to license or register all persons involved in such transfers. The CTC has also determined that implementation of paragraph 1 requires financial institutions and other intermediaries to be under legal obligation to identify their clients and report suspicious transactions to a financial intelligence unit or other relevant authorities.[16] These informal assessment criteria indicate that the CTC has already developed initial methodologies for evaluating state capabilities and needs. Much more work is needed, however, to expand on these criteria and develop more formalized performance standards.

The development of a succinct set of standards and best practices related to the obligations imposed by Resolution 1373 would improve the ability of the CTC to

• Monitor and identify gaps in implementation of states' counter-terrorism obligations,

• Provide a basis for improving the coordination of assistance to states lacking the capacity to implement those obligations,

• Strengthen the role of key functional and regional organizations in implementation efforts, and

• Ensure transparency and objectivity of assessments.

As a delegate to the CTC observed, "CTC best practices . . . would go a long way to helping States get a better understanding of what steps should be taken to implement the various provisions of resolution 1373."[17] For the Security Council the existence of uniform standards would permit more objective evaluations of states' implementation of their counter-terrorism-related obligations and could form the basis for decisions that may be necessary to elicit further implementation.

The CTED has developed a "recommended methodology" for the "collection, analysis, development and dissemination of best practices."[18] It has also taken steps to create methodologies that could lead to more formalized evaluation criteria and performance standards. In its December 2005 review of the CTED, the CTC noted that it "attaches importance to the issue of best practices" and called for updated information to be posted on the committee Web site regarding international best practices.[19] The CTC has relied extensively on the best practices and standards developed by international functional agencies. The committee has utilized compliance criteria of the FATF, Interpol, the International Civil Aviation Organization (ICAO), the International Maritime Organization (IMO), the International Monetary Fund (IMF), the Basel Committee on Banking Supervision (BCBS), and the World Customs Organization (WCO). As CTED executive director Javier Rupérez pointed out, international functional organizations have already "invented the wheel."[20] Those agencies and numerous others have devised a vast array of relevant standards and best practices. CTC adaptation of these criteria would greatly advance UN efforts to measure and provide assistance for counter-terrorism implementation.

The creation of evaluation criteria would also benefit member states and regional organizations as they seek to implement counter-terrorism requirements. The creation of formal standards of implementation would end the current situation in which there is a continuous exchange of information between the CTC and state officials but no clear understanding of when or how the process will be completed. Enabling states to see "a light at the end of the tunnel" could serve as an incentive to encourage further implementation efforts. Other inducements will be necessary to encourage nations, especially those facing difficult development challenges, to prioritize implementation of UN counter-terrorism mandates. The most important incentive to date has been the provision of technical assistance and support for capacity-building efforts. These efforts have been partly successful and could be strengthened as part of an enhanced effort to promote development and governance capacity among developing nations.

Related to the issue of compliance is the question of enforcement. If the CTC and the Security Council adopt formal implementation standards, they will then be faced with the challenge of responding to instances where states are unwilling to implement those standards. The United States, the United Kingdom, Russia, and other nations are prepared to consider the imposition of sanctions and other measures against countries that, having received offers of technical assistance to improve capacity, nonetheless fail to meet the implementation standards established by the Security Council. The Secretary-General's High-Level Panel on Threats, Challenges and Change recommended a forceful approach to compliance. "If confronted by States that have the capacity to undertake their obligations but repeatedly fail to do so, the Security Council may need to take additional measures to ensure compliance, and should devise a schedule of predetermined sanctions for State non-compliance."[21] Most states and UN counter-terrorism officials are not prepared to go that far in urging forceful measures to enforce implementation, preferring to emphasize inducements and positive measures to encourage cooperation. Indeed, some have expressed concern that an overly coercive approach to enforcement could jeopardize the high levels of international cooperation that are necessary to fulfill counter-terrorism mandates. These debates will become increasingly important should the Security Council and the CTC take on the issue of enhancing counter-terrorism implementation.

Facilitating Technical Assistance

Meeting at the ministerial level in November 2001, the Security Council adopted Resolution 1377, which encouraged the CTC to work with international, regional, and subregional organizations to explore ways in which states can receive technical, financial, regulatory, legislative, and other assistance to improve implementation of Resolution 1373.[22] Many states face deep deficiencies in their operational and administrative capacity to implement UN Security Council counter-terrorism mandates. Some states lack expertise even to determine their capabilities and deficiencies. Many nations need to make improvements in legislation and legal authority. They also need better administrative machinery and equipment to implement legislative mandates. Their bureaucrats need training and performance guidance in meeting counter-terrorism standards.

The CTC is not an assistance provider, but it has attempted to play a role in facilitating the provision of technical assistance to states that are in need of or request such help. In 2002 the CTC created a "technical assistance team" comprised of just two experts. The meager staff was utterly inadequate to the enormous challenges facing the committee. The technical assistance mandate was to

• Facilitate the sharing of information on standards, best practices, and sources of technical assistance;

• Encourage donors to respond to assistance requests;

• Address regional and sectoral shortcomings; and

• Encourage capacity building by regional organizations.

The goal of the CTC assistance program has been to analyze the needs of states and regional organizations in light of the availability of assistance and to link the two in ways that enhance the ability of states to implement CTC mandates.[23]

Since 2002 the CTC staff has participated in numerous international gatherings and held bilateral meetings with many states needing or requesting technical assistance.[24] From these sessions it has learned that the demand for technical assistance is outpacing supply. One reason for this is that states have realized the extent of their obligations under Resolution 1373 and have recognized the need for assistance in meeting these obligations. Approximately one hundred countries have expressed an interest in technical assistance from the CTC,[25] although the actual number of states needing assistance is greater than this. The CTC assistance team and the more recently established CTED have been unable to keep up with the demand and have failed to perform adequately in facilitating the coordinated delivery of assistance by donor countries and agencies.

Many states have identified legislative drafting assistance as a priority need. Most of the requests in this area have been for general assistance in crafting counter-terrorism legislation, but many states have also requested special assistance in drafting specific legislation to counter the financing of terrorism. Most of the assistance available to states in this area has been provided by the UNODC/TPB, the Commonwealth Secretariat, and the International Monetary Fund (IMF). G-8 member countries have also provided legislative drafting assistance on a bilateral basis. The UNODC/TPB has been the principal provider of general legislative drafting assistance, while the IMF has been the main source of assistance for drafting legislation to counter the financing of terrorism. The Commonwealth Secretariat designed draft model laws for common law countries. The UNODC/TPB has adapted these model laws for use by all UN members, including civil law countries and other legal systems.[26]

The requirements for implementing Resolution 1373 often involve substantial levels of training, the development of new administrative systems, and the purchase and installation of technically sophisticated equipment. Many states need help to improve policing and law enforcement systems and to create financial regulatory mechanisms and financial intelligence units. Assistance is also needed in some instances for the development of computerized links among security-related units, improved systems for identifying fraudulent travel documents, better mechanisms for controlling customs and immigration, and computerized equipment to screen passengers and cargo at border entry points. The CTC has received numerous requests for assistance in these areas, much of it provided by individual donor states. Arrangements have been made bilaterally between donors and countries in need. In some instances the CTC has facilitated these arrangements, but most have developed independently.[27]

The costs of upgrading administrative systems and acquiring and maintaining technical equipment can be substantial.[28] Many states, particularly in the developing world, do not have the necessary financial, technical, and human resources to implement counter-terrorism laws and need help in acquiring these capabilities.[29] This has prompted discussion of a possible multilateral trust fund to assist such efforts. Interest in a trust fund also was expressed by smaller donor countries that provide assistance to some states but lack the broader assessment and facilitation capabilities that a CTC-guided technical assistance fund might provide. These donor nations prefer to coordinate their assistance efforts through the CTC and other multilateral bodies.[30] Early in the CTC process the United Kingdom encouraged the committee and the Al-Qaida/Taliban Sanctions Committee to develop the concept of a specialized technical assistance fund. In 2002 Secretary-General Kofi Annan suggested that the UN Development Programme (UNDP) might play a role in facilitating such a fund, but no action was taken. In 2003 the CTC assistance team held informal discussions on the trust fund idea with representatives of the World Bank, who indicated that the bank might be able to facilitate such a fund. A year later the report of the Secretary-General's High-Level Panel on Threats, Challenges and Change recommended that the UN establish "a capacity-trust fund under the Counter-Terrorism Executive Directorate" to assist in the provision of counter-terrorism technical assistance. The fund has not been established, however.[31]

The United States and other major donor nations have opposed the development of a multilateral-capacity-building trust fund. Washington claims that bilateral assistance programs are sufficient to meet the global need, but critics challenge this assertion. After increasing in the wake of September 11, however, U.S. support for capacity-building assistance has declined in recent years. According to Daniel Benjamin and Steven Simon, U.S. funding for technical assistance globally is only $120 million a year, which is "considerably smaller than is necessary to fulfill" the assistance mandate.[32] These shortcomings in U.S. technical assistance funding have occurred as international legal mandates on countries have grown and the technical needs for counter-terrorism capacity have multiplied.

Linking Technical Assistance and Development Aid

Many of the measures required by Resolution 1373—creating more effective law enforcement capabilities; improving border, immigration, and customs controls; regulating banks and financial institutions; enhancing security at ports and border crossings—parallel the steps needed to strengthen good governance. These steps are increasingly recognized as essential to economic development and the expansion of social and economic opportunity. Trade and investment depend on stable government and the rule of law. Technical assistance programs that build governance capacity also advance the prospects for economic development.

Counter-terrorism activities are traditionally viewed differently by the security and development communities. The former tend to be concerned mainly with enforcement and protection, while the latter have a focus on the structural conditions that give rise to political extremism. The two approaches are interdependent, however, and are connected through a mutual interest in programs of good governance, particularly in the security sector. Development understood as poverty reduction can be obtained and sustained only if there are institutions and mechanisms of governance that ensure the security and safety of citizens.[33] Governance issues have received increased attention in recent years within the development community.[34] In the security community there is growing recognition that short-term operations related to counter-terrorism will not bring sustainable benefit without corresponding attention to underlying development needs. As UN Secretary-General Kofi Annan observed, "The three freedoms which all human beings crave—freedom from want, freedom from war or large-scale violence, and freedom from arbitrary or degrading treatment—are closely interconnected. There is no long-term security without development. There is no development without security."[35]

This linkage between technical assistance and economic development suggests the need for integrated development aid strategies that take account of UN counter-terrorism requirements. Recent policy papers from the Organisation for Economic Co-operation and Development/Development Co-operation Directorate (OECD/DAC) have highlighted the links between development cooperation and terrorism prevention.[36] The DAC has argued that the fundamental goal of poverty reduction shared by all development agencies can help prevent conditions that are hospitable to terrorism. This means that development agencies can continue to do what they are already doing and make an important contribution to counter-terrorism. This enhances the legitimacy of development objectives and indicates that development funders can do much to contribute to the goal of enhancing counter-terrorism capacity. Greater development assistance can help to address the root causes of terrorism. Many of the adverse social conditions in which terrorists thrive fall within the realm of primary concerns for development cooperation.

The DAC has highlighted four specific areas where terrorism prevention could influence and strengthen the development agenda:

- Supporting the structural stability of self-government;
- Dissuading disaffected groups from embracing terrorism;
- Denying groups or individuals the means to carry out acts of terrorism; and
- Sustaining coherent, broadly based international cooperation.

Components of existing development programs that are directly supportive of counter-terrorism capacity building include the following:

- Making political systems more responsive,
- Strengthening the rule of law and improving the professionalism and accountability of the security sector,
- Promoting governance and public-sector reform, and
- Strengthening financial governance systems.

Some officials have encouraged greater dialogue between security and development agencies to identify where counter-terrorism and good-governance agendas overlap and are mutually reinforcing.[37] The challenge is to reinforce development/good governance goals as well as counter-terrorism capacity building in a mutually beneficial manner. Both are interdependent and depend on the same factors for success, including participatory processes, transparency, and other fundamental elements of governance, such as accountability. The prospect of increased development aid and capacity-building assistance could be an inducement for many states to implement more completely relevant UN mandates. A program of providing increased development assistance in combination with security-related capacity-building efforts could be highly attractive to many developing nations. It would help them meet both development and security needs and would facilitate implementation of emerging UN counter-terrorism standards. This type of positive inducement is likely to be more effective in building counter-terrorism cooperation than the threat of sanctions. Honey often works better than vinegar in building the foundations for interstate cooperation.

Enhancing International Cooperation

The UN Counter-Terrorism Committee has facilitated outreach and coordination among a wide array of specialized international agencies and regional and subregional organizations. Attempting to enhance international cooperation is always a formidable challenge, but the mission of the CTC in this regard is truly herculean. The range of regional and international organizations with actual or potential involvement in the UN counter-terrorism mission is vast. Every region of the world is involved, and counter-terrorism programs have emerged in many regional and subregional organizations. The mandates of Resolution 1373 touch on a wide range of public activities—financing, commerce, customs, law enforcement, intelligence sharing, military recruitment and supply—and they affect the mission of dozens of specialized agencies.

Committee experts have worked with several functional international agencies to develop capacity-building programs to improve implementation. As noted, the CTC has cooperated extensively with UNODC/TPB, the Commonwealth Secretariat, and the IMF. Other organizations that have shared information with the CTC include the G-8 and its Counter-Terrorism Action Group (CTAG), the International Civil Aviation Organization (ICAO), the International Maritime Organization (IMO), the International Organization for Migration, the Organization for the Prohibition of Chemical Weapons (OPCW), the World Customs Organization (WCO), and the Financial Action Task Force (FATF).

The CTC has made important strides in encouraging regional organizations to strengthen their counter-terrorism capacity. Many regional organizations have created their own counter-terrorism units, which share information with the CTC and attend semiannual regional coordination meetings. The OAS has played a leading role and has established a counter-terrorism Secretariat within the Inter-American Committee Against Terrorism (CICTE). During 2002 the Secretariat designed and deployed the CICTE online antiterrorism database. The CICTE also participated in the drafting of model regulations for the prevention of terrorist financing and in meetings of the Caribbean Financial Action Task Force (CFATF). The OAS Convention Against Terrorism entered into effect in July 2003 and, as of February 2004, was signed by thirty-three of thirty-four member states. After the Madrid bombings of March 2004, the European Council adopted the *Declaration on Combating Terrorism* and created the position of European counter-terrorism coordinator.[38] The Asia-Pacific Economic Cooperation (APEC) forum had already established a counter-terrorism task force in February 2003. Similar regional bodies exist within the Commonwealth of Independent States (CIS) and the Association of Southeast Asian Nations (ASEAN). The CTC has worked with these and other regional bodies to enhance overall international coordination in the campaign against terrorism.

Some regions continue to lag behind. Much of South Asia and large parts of Africa have not adequately developed the necessary regionally coordinated mechanisms to facilitate local state implementation of counter-terrorism resolutions mandated by the UN Security Council. Progress has been made among fourteen Arab states with the creation of a Middle East and North Africa FATF-style regional body (MENAFSRB), which was formally established in November 2004. The Middle East and North Africa Region (MENA) body held a plenary meeting in April 2005, where it reaffirmed its goal to promote the implementation of the FATF recommendations. Similar efforts are needed in North Africa and other regions to more effectively address other key issue areas covered in Resolution 1373, including border control, law enforcement, and judicial practice. Convening regional and subregional workshops to develop best practices, facilitated by the CTC and coordinated by local bodies, would be an important step toward achieving this task.[39]

Improving coordination among international and regional organizations is a major CTC priority. A call for special meetings among regional, subregional, and international organizations was presented at the ministerial meeting of the Security Council on 20 January 2003. This led to the convening of the first special regional coordination meeting in New York in March 2003, with follow-up meetings in Washington, D.C., in October 2003, Vienna in March 2004, and Almaty, Kazakhstan, in January 2005. Although the CTC convened regular gatherings among regional organizations and international agencies, few concrete results have emerged from these sessions. Coordination among regional organizations has been limited.

For the most part, the CTC has not been able to play an effective coordinating role among states and organizations. Its inability to fulfill that function is largely due to administrative and other limitations imposed by operating within the UN in New York, which, perhaps as a matter of political necessity, gravitates toward bureaucratic procedural approaches to the issues it faces to maintain an element of predictability and avoid potential political disagreements. As primarily a set of political bodies or purely a political body in the case of the UN Security Council, the UN is ill-suited to the task of implementing many of the technical aspects of the resolutions it adopts. The most straightforward uncontroversial matters, such as facilitating technical assistance between consenting donors and recipients, have a tendency to get bound up in red tape and sidetracked by seemingly endless political discussions.

Coordination and Overlap Within the UN System

Coordination and cooperation within the UN system has also been inadequate. Of special concern is the relationship between the CTC and the Security Council committee and monitoring team established to enforce sanctions against Al-Qaida and the Taliban. Through a series of measures—Resolution 1267 (1999), which initially imposed sanctions on the Taliban regime in Afghanistan; Resolution 1390 (2002), which refocused those sanctions on a designated list of Al-Qaida and Taliban leaders; and Resolution 1526 (2004), which established the Analytic Support and Sanctions Monitoring Team to support those measures—the Security Council has applied focused pressure on Osama bin Laden and his supporters.[40] The sanctions require all states to freeze the financial assets and ban the travel and supply of arms to those on the designated list.[41] The Analytic Support and Sanctions Monitoring Team replaced a previous monitoring team, which was criticized for overstepping its mandate and which also stirred controversy because its reports identified specific countries and officials whose implementation efforts it considered unsatisfactory.

Coordination between the CTC staff and the monitoring team of the Al-Qaida/Taliban Sanctions Committee was initially strained but improved with the creation of the CTED. Concerns remain, however, that these efforts need to be linked more closely. Obstacles to coordination stem in part from the concern of Security Council members that the CTC not be seen as a sanctions committee. Resolution 1373 was not designed to impose sanctions but to establish general counter-terrorism requirements and capacity among all states. Chairman Greenstock emphasized at the outset that the CTC was not a sanctions committee. He and other CTC pioneers took this approach to avoid any Iraq-related sanctions backlash and to build the broadest political support and consensus behind the counter-terrorism campaign. This was an effective political approach that helped to win support for the CTC process, but it skirted important issues about how the CTC effort and the Al-Qaida and Taliban sanctions should be coordinated. It also postponed difficult choices that eventually may have to be made about how to ensure enforcement of CTC and Al-Qaida sanctions mandates, as we observe below.

Concerns also have been raised about the need for cooperation between the CTC and the nonproliferation committee established pursuant to Resolution 1540. The staff of the nonproliferation committee reviews reports from states on their efforts to implement prohibitions on the proliferation of deadly weapons to nonstate actors. Some states, especially the least-developed nations in Africa, have indicated that the resolution does not apply to them or that they are incapable of implementing it. This would suggest that the capacity-building efforts that are a primary focus of the CTC are also relevant to the implementation of Resolution 1540. The chair of the CTC has pledged to establish cooperation between the CTED and the staff of the nonproliferation committee, but no specific mechanisms for guaranteeing such cooperation have been established.

Nor have procedures been developed for establishing coordination with the working group established by Resolution 1566. The working group has fewer resources and less political momentum than the other UN counter-terrorism groups, but it is tasked with a potentially significant task, determining whether additional names from other organizations and movements should be added to the list of those subject to targeted financial and other sanctions. This is a potentially explosive issue politically, raising the prospect of Chechen and other militant movements coming under UN sanctions. To date the committee and its working group have been relatively inactive, but when and if it produces results, it will be necessary to coordinate its efforts with those of the CTC and the Al-Qaida/Taliban Sanctions Committee.

There are now four special Security Council bodies working on counter-terrorism issues, each with its own staff of experts: the CTC and the CTED, the Al-Qaida/Taliban Committee and its Analytical Support and Sanctions Monitoring Team, the Resolution 1540 Committee and staff experts, and the Resolution 1566 Committee and working group. These bodies have a combined staff of nearly forty professional experts. While the mandates of the various committees are separate, they have many overlapping purposes and responsibilities. UN member states have obligations with respect to all four committees. As noted in chapter 3, duplication of efforts and bureaucratic inefficiency have created considerable problems and impeded the overall UN counter-terrorism effort.

The problem of inadequate coordination among these various UN counter-terrorism bodies was addressed in the report of the Secretary-General's Counter-Terrorism Implementation Task Force, released in April 2006.[42] The report urged states to focus their efforts on the concrete, practical contributions that the different parts of the UN system can make in the counter-terrorism effort. It called for improving coordination and cooperation among the twenty-three different parts of the system currently engaged in this effort. The General Assembly considered the Secretary-General's report and approved a vaguely worded general strategy against terrorism in September 2006, but it did not act on many of the report's specific policy-related and structural recommendations.[43] Given the General Assembly's track record in dealing with terrorism-related issues, however, it is difficult to imagine that that global body can avoid getting bogged down with the same political issues that have prevented it from reaching agreement on a definition of terrorism.

Defining the Problem

One of the most long-standing and intractable challenges facing the UN is the lack of a universally accepted definition of terrorism. The definitional conundrum has entangled the UN for four decades. Some countries condemn as terrorism all acts that endanger or take innocent life, while others seek to differentiate what they consider legitimate acts of resistance against oppression. Others have emphasized the need to include state-sponsored acts within the definition of terrorism. Middle Eastern states in particular have refused to support counter-terrorism initiatives that might prejudice Palestinian resistance to the Israeli occupation. It is no accident that ratification of counter-terrorism conventions and participation in CTC initiatives are lowest in the Middle East. The CTC has attempted to steer clear of these dilemmas by focusing primarily on procedural issues and generic counter-terrorism capabilities. It has sought to transcend the differences over competing definitions of terrorism by appealing to the consensus among UN member states that greater efforts are needed to counter the global terrorist threat posed by Al-Qaida. How long the CTC will be able to maintain this balance is subject to much debate.

The Secretary-General's High-Level Panel on Threats, Challenges and Change proposed a solution to the definitional problem in the hope that this could gain a consensus within the General Assembly. The panel noted that acts of state terrorism are already prohibited by the Geneva Conventions and other legal agreements. States are required to distinguish between combatants and civilians, to use force proportionately, and to comply with humanitarian law. The use of lethal force against civilians and noncombatants is a war crime or crime against humanity. There is already a "clear normative framework" within international law and United Nations agreements against states intentionally targeting civilians and killing noncombatants.[44] The panel acknowledged the right of resistance to foreign occupation but noted that this right does not justify the targeting and killing of civilians. The panel recommended a definition of terrorism that includes existing prohibitions against the intentional targeting and killing of civilians, and that makes reference to all previous UN conventions and legal agreements against war crimes and terrorism. Within this context it proposed to define terrorism as any action "that is intended to cause death or serious bodily harm to civilians or non-combatants, when the purpose of such an act, by its nature or context, is to intimidate a population, or to compel a Government or an international organization to do or to abstain from doing any act."[45] Whether this proposed definition will attract the political support necessary for approval in the General Assembly remains uncertain. Those concerned about national resistance to foreign occupation are likely to demand a stronger condemnation of governments that continue to violate Security Council or General Assembly resolutions. Those concerned about state-sponsored terrorism will want greater guarantees against government actions that kill innocent civilians.

The Enforcement Dilemma

Perhaps the most difficult political challenge concerns the question of enforcement. What can and will the Security Council do in instances where member states are able but unwilling to implement counterterrorism mandates? The CTC has attempted to avoid this issue by carefully distinguishing itself from the UN sanctions process. Its primary mission has been to build capacity and enhance international coordination, not to impose sanctions. As we have noted, however, the mandate of the CTC overlaps with that of the Al-Qaida/Taliban Sanctions Committee. Its mission is also linked to that of the nonproliferation committee and the 1566 working group. The CTC like the other committees will inevitably face circumstances in which certain member states refuse to implement fully its mandates. This issue will become more pressing as the committee moves toward establishing formal standards. The creation of performance benchmarks will inevitably raise the question of what to do when states willfully fail to implement those standards.

To date the CTC has decided not to sit in judgment of other states or to report to the Security Council on states it has determined to be non-compliant. Over time this may limit the committee's effectiveness, however, if it allows certain countries to avoid responsibility for taking specific action.[46] The CTC could take action short of sanctions to exert pressure. The CTC has within its powers the ability to "name and shame" those that are recalcitrant or obstructionist. Thus far it has not adopted this approach, nor has it gone to the Security Council to gain support for such a tactic. If the CTC is to accomplish its mandate, however, its restrained practice so far may need to be reconsidered.

What additional enforcement measures can be taken beyond naming and shaming? As noted earlier, incentives are a preferable means of encouraging implementation. The Security Council can and should work with donor states and international agencies to develop more substantial assistance and development programs for states needing help implementing counter-terrorism mandates, as part of a general effort to improve governance. In some circumstances, however, it may become necessary to consider other enforcement measures. The current process of requesting reports from countries, coordinating regional cooperation, and providing technical assistance works well with the many states that are supportive of the UN counter-terrorism agenda. How should the Security Council respond, however, to the twenty or more countries that are unwilling to comply fully or that merely pretend to comply with CTC mandates?[47] What can be done to encourage and if necessary pressure states to take stronger measures against Al-Qaida and the Taliban and to prevent the proliferation of deadly weapons to terrorist groups? It is doubtful that the Security Council could find consensus for the kind of automatic sanctions measures recommended by the High-Level Panel, but some consideration of coercive action may be necessary to enforce counter-terrorism mandates. These and other political challenges lie ahead for the UN as it seeks to strengthen the international campaign against terrorism.

Notes

1. United Nations Security Council, *Security Council Resolution 1373 (2001)*, S/RES/1373, New York, 28 September 2001, par. 2f.

2. Nicholas Rostow, "Before and After: The Changed UN Response to Terrorism Since September 11th," *Cornell International Law Journal* 35, no. 3 (Winter 2002): 475, 482; David Cortright and George A. Lopez, *Sanctions and the Search for Security: Challenges to UN Action* (Boulder, CO: Lynne Rienner, 2002), 126–30; Edward C. Luck, "Tackling Terrorism," in *The United Nations Security Council: From the Cold War to the Twenty-first Century*, ed. David Malone (Boulder, CO: Lynne Rienner, 2004), 85–100.

3. United Nations Committee on Counter-Terrorism, "Facilitating the Provision of Technical Assistance," <http://www.un.org/Docs/sc/committees/1373/tat .html> (accessed 8 September 2006).

4. Kofi Annan, "Menace of Terrorism Requires Global Response, Says Secretary-General, Stressing Importance of Increased United Nations Role," United Nations Press Release, SG/SM/8583, SC/7639, New York, 20 January 2003.

5. Eric Rosand, "Security Council Resolution 1373 and the Counter-Terrorism Committee: The Cornerstone of the United Nations Contribution to the Fight Against Terrorism," in *Legal Instruments in the Fight Against International Terrorism*, ed. Cyrille Fijnaut, Jan Wouters, and Frederik Naert (Boston: Brill Academic, 2004), 603–32.

6. Rostow, "Before and After," 475, 485.

7. For an example of the popular mischaracterization of the work and purpose of the CTC, see Anne Bayefsky, "U.N.derwhelming Response: The U.N.'s Approach to Terrorism," *National Review Online*, 24 September 2004, <http://www.nationalreview.com/comment/bayefsky200409240915.asp> (accessed 8 September 2006).

8. According to the CTC's seventeenth work program, as of 30 September 2005, it had received 622 reports from UN member states and others. This includes first reports from all 191 states, 169 second reports, 130 third reports, 101 fourth reports, and 22 fifth reports. See United Nations Security Council, *Work Programme of the Counter-Terrorism Committee*, S/2005/663, New York, 21 October 2005, par. 5.

9. Eric Rosand, "The UN Security Council's Counter-Terrorism Efforts," presentation, American Society of International Law Regional Centennial Meeting, San Francisco, 7 April 2005.

10. United Nations Security Council, *Proposal for the Revitalisation of the Counter-Terrorism Committee*, S/2004/124, New York, 19 February 2004.

11. Rosand, "The UN Security Council's Counter-Terrorism Efforts."

12. Eric Rosand, "Current Developments: Security Council Resolution 1373, the Counter-Terrorism Committee, and the Fight Against Terrorism," *American Journal of International Law* 97, no. 2 (April 2003): 335, 332–41.

13. See United Nations, International Convention for the Suppression of Terrorist Bombings, and United Nations, International Convention for the Suppression of the Financing of Terrorism, *United Nations Treaty Collection*, <http://untreaty.un.org/English/Terrorism.asp> (accessed 7 September 2006).

14. This problem is illustrated by the fact that the analysis outlined in the text was based on an unpublished assessment by a single staff expert. That assessment was not vetted among other UN staff or approved by the CTC. The lack of an approved assessment methodology has become a hindrance to the committee and could become an even greater handicap in the future as it attempts to address problems of lax enforcement in particular states and regions.

15. Analysis of stages drawn from Rosand, "Security Council Resolution 1373 and the Counter-Terrorism Committee," 603, 611–12.

16. See Rosand, "Security Council Resolution 1373 and the Counter-Terrorism Committee," 603, 618–19.

17. United States Mission to the United Nations, "Written Statement of the U.S. Delegation for Inclusion in the Record of the Briefing by the Chairs of the 1267 Al-Qaida/Taliban Sanctions Committee, the 1373 Counter Terrorism Committee, and the 1540 Committee on Non-Proliferation of Weapons of Mass Destruction, in the Security Council, April 25, 2005," USUN Press Release #80[05], New York, 25 April 2005, <http://www.un.int/usa/05_080.htm> (accessed 8 September 2006).

18. United Nations Counter-Terrorism Executive Directorate, "Framework for the Collection, Analysis, Development and Dissemination of Best Practices Relative to United Nations Security Council Resolutions 1373 (2001) and 1624 (2005)," undated and unpublished report.

19. United Nations Security Council, *Report of the Counter-Terrorism Committee to the Security Council for Its Consideration as Part of Its Comprehensive Review of the Counter-Terrorism Committee Executive Directorate*, S/2005/800, New York, 16 December 2005, par. 14.

20. Javier Rupérez, "A Response to the Recommendations for Improving the United Nations Counter-Terrorism Committee's Assessment and Assistance Coordination Function," remarks, International Peace Academy Policy Forum on the Counter-Terrorism Committee/Counter-Terrorism Committee Directorate, New York, 22 November 2005.

21. United Nations General Assembly, *A More Secure World: Our Shared Responsibility: Report of the High-Level Panel on Threats, Challenges and Change*, A/59/565, New York, 2 December 2004, par. 156.

22. United Nations Security Council, *Security Council Resolution 1377 (2001)*, S/RES/1377, New York, 12 November 2001.

23. See United Nations Counter-Terrorism Committee, "Facilitating the Provision of Technical Assistance," <http://www.un.org/Docs/sc/committees/1373/tat.html> (accessed 8 September 2006).

24. The paper of Curtis A. Ward, assistance expert, UN Counter-Terrorism Committee, has provided valuable insights and is one of the few written sources available on CTC assistance facilitation at the United Nations. Curtis A. Ward, "Purposes and Scope: Technical Assistance Activities in the Counter-Terrorism Committee," unpublished paper, 2004, 6. Numerous sources from interviews and written comments have confirmed and corroborated many of the findings articulated by Ward and the authors of this chapter.

25. Curtis A. Ward, e-mail communication with authors, 16 June 2004.

26. Ward, "Purposes and Scope," 16.

27. Ward, "Purposes and Scope," 21.

28. Ward, "Purposes and Scope," 14.

29. Angolan ambassador to the United Nations, quoted in Rosand, "Security Council Resolution 1373 and the Counter-Terrorism Committee."

30. Ward, "Purposes and Scope," 20.

31. UN General Assembly, *A More Secure World*, par. 155.

32. Daniel Benjamin and Steven Simon, *The Next Attack: The Failure of the War on Terror and a Strategy for Getting It Right* (New York: Times Books, 2005), 204.

33. See, for example, Organisation for Economic Co-operation and Development, *Helping Prevent Violent Conflict* (Paris: OECD Publications, 2001), 37, <http://www.oecd.org> (accessed 12 September 2006).

34. A recent example is Organisation for Economic Co-operation and Development, *The Challenge of Capacity Development: Working Towards Good Practice*, DCD/DAC/GOVNET(2005)5/REV/1, DAC Network on Governance [GOVNET], Paris, 1 February 2006, <http://www.oecd.org> (accessed 12 September 2006).

35. Kofi Annan, "Statesmanship, Confidence-Rebuilding Required for UN Capable of Coping with Today's Crises," address to United Nations Association of the United Kingdom, Central Hall, Westminster, United Kingdom, 31 January 2006.

36. Organisation for Economic Co-operation and Development, *A Development Co-operation Lens on Terrorism Prevention: Key Entry Points for Action* (Paris: OECD Publications, 2003), <http://www.oecd.org> (accessed 12 September 2006).

37. Steven Monblatt, "Developing Regional Cooperation," statement of the Executive Secretary, Inter-American Committee Against Terrorism, Organization of American States, at the UN Counter-Terrorism Committee special meeting, Almaty, Kazakhstan, 26–27 January 2005. See United Nations Security Council, *Summaries Provided by Participants in the Counter-Terrorism Committee/Commonwealth of Independent States Special Meeting, 26 to 28 January 2005*, S/2005/87, New York, 14 February 2005, par. 22.

38. For a text of the declaration see European Union, "Declaration on Combating Terrorism," *Council of the European Union Documents*, Brussels, 25 March 2004, <http://www.consilium.europa.eu/ueDocs/cms_Data/docs/pressdata/en/ec/79637.pdf> (accessed 28 September 2006).

39. Reports received by the CTC show deficiencies in regions with less developed regional organizational capacity to assist states in implementing Resolution 1373. For more information on the Eastern and Southern Africa Anti-Money Laundering Group, see *Eastern and Southern Africa Anti-Money Laundering Group,* <http://www.esaamlg.org> (accessed 8 September 2006).

40. United Nations Security Council, *Security Council Resolution 1267 (1999)*, S/RES/1267, New York, 15 October 1999; United Nations Security Council, *Security Council Resolution 1390 (2002)*, S/RES/1390, New York, 28 January 2002; United Nations Security Council, *Security Council Resolution 1526 (2004)*, S/RES/1526, New York, 30 January 2004.

41. Rosand, "The UN Security Council's Counter-Terrorism Efforts."

42. United Nations General Assembly, *Uniting Against Terrorism: Recommendations for a Global Counter-Terrorism Strategy*, A/60/825, New York, 27 April 2006.

43. See United Nations General Assembly, "General Assembly Adopts Global Counter-Terrorism Strategy," press release, unnumbered resolution, and plan of action, New York, 8 September 2006, <http://www.un.org/terrorism/strategy/#resolution> (accessed 28 September 2006.

44. United Nations General Assembly, *A More Secure World*, par. 161.

45. United Nations General Assembly, *A More Secure World*, par. 164.

46. Rosand, "Security Council Resolution 1373 and the Counter-Terrorism Committee," 603, 612–13.

47. Luck, "Tackling Terrorism," 96–97.

3

Strengthening International Law and Global Implementation

Eric Rosand and Alistair Millar

The United Nations has struggled since its inception to formulate an effective response to terrorism due to its continuing inability to agree on a definition that outlaws all indiscriminate attacks against civilians. The adage "One man's terrorist is another man's freedom fighter" continues to permeate the discussion, as the General Assembly's struggle to conclude a comprehensive convention against international terrorism continues into its thirty-fifth year. The General Assembly and UN agencies nonetheless have made important contributions to the development of international norms against discrete terrorist acts, adopting thirteen international conventions and protocols against terrorism between 1963 and 2005.[1] Prior to September 2001 the Security Council was reluctant to address the general threat of international terrorism. This reticence reflected the prevailing attitude that terrorism was largely a localized national problem that in most cases did not constitute a threat to international peace and security, which is the threshold required for Security Council action under the UN Charter. In the period from the end of the cold war in the late 1980s until September 11, 2001, the council responded to specific acts of terrorism—the bombing of Pan Am flight 103 and French UTA flight 772 in the late 1980s and the bombings of the U.S embassies in Kenya and Tanzania in 1998. Since September 11, 2001, with Al-Qaida and like-minded terrorist groups viewed as international threats, the council has placed itself at the center of current global antiterrorism efforts. It has used its authority under chapter VII of the UN Charter to impose binding counter-terrorism-related obligations on all states via a series of ground-breaking resolutions, thus supplementing the existing UN normative counter-terrorism legal framework. It has also established a set of organizational mechanisms to monitor state implementation of the new counter-terrorism mandates and to help those who lack the capacity to do so.

This chapter discusses the legal and institutional framework established by the Security Council and offers an assessment of its performance after five years. It concludes that the framework remains essential and useful but that the monitoring system currently in place to prod and assist countries with counter-terrorism implementation is inadequate. Existing mechanisms have produced lots of paper but few concrete results. The limitations and shortcomings of the present system have overshadowed the council's modest successes to date. This chapter examines options for strengthening and improving current institutional arrangements with the goal of maintaining the credibility of the council and enhancing the effectiveness of global, nonmilitary counter-terrorism efforts.

The Legal Framework

The General Assembly and UN Agencies

During the cold war, support for national liberation movements from a large number of UN member states prevented the General Assembly from formulating a robust response to terrorism. Despite the political obstacles, however, the UN system succeeded in papering over differences on the terrorism issue and made progress in the development of international norms against discrete terrorist acts, generally taking action in response to a specific attack. Following the frequent airplane hijackings of the 1960s, the International Civil Aviation Organization (ICAO) adopted three treaties aimed at securing the safety of civil aviation.[2] The General Assembly also adopted conventions in response to a spate of attacks against diplomats and the taking of U.S. hostages in Iran in 1979.[3] The fact that the General Assembly, in adopting these conventions, often appeared more concerned with the root causes of terrorism than violence against civilians highlighted the difficulty of dealing forthrightly with the issue.[4]

By the end of the cold war, many former colonies had achieved independence, and, in the words of international relations expert Kendall W.

Stiles, a large number of countries had "shifted to a pro-Western orientation and [were thus] inclined to accept the West's interpretation of international law and terrorism."[5] The General Assembly was therefore able to develop a somewhat more vigorous response to the threat. Its nonbinding 1994 *Declaration on Measures to Eliminate International Terrorism* was the first comprehensive, standard-setting instrument at the international level in which states reaffirmed their "unequivocal condemnation of all acts, methods and practices of terrorism, as criminal and unjustifiable, whereby and by whomever committed."[6] The General Assembly's annual terrorism resolutions since 1994 have reiterated this language. In addition, the assembly established an Ad Hoc Committee on Terrorism, which subsequently adopted three additional conventions aimed at addressing specific terrorist acts: the *International Convention for the Suppression of Terrorist Bombings* (1997), the *International Convention for the Suppression of Financing of Terrorism* (1999), and the *International Convention for the Suppression of Acts of Nuclear Terrorism* (2005).

The bombings convention broke new ground by stating clearly that bombings are "not justifiable by consideration of a political, philosophical, ideological, racial, ethnic, religious or other similar nature," reinforcing what the General Assembly had said in the 1994 declaration. Thus, in adopting this convention by consensus, the General Assembly appeared to be taking a clear stand against indiscriminate violence against civilians. This soon proved not to be the case, however. Members of the Organisation of the Islamic Conference (OIC) subsequently adopted their own terrorism convention that explicitly contradicted provisions of both the bombings and financing conventions by distinguishing between acts of terrorism and acts committed in the fight for self-determination or against foreign occupation.[7] The Organisation of African Unity (OAU)—now the African Union (AU)—took a similar approach in adopting its regional counter-terrorism convention in 1999.[8] Furthermore, when deciding to ratify the bombings and financing General Assembly conventions, several countries in the OIC, including Pakistan, Syria, Jordan, and Egypt, reserved the right to continue to distinguish between terrorism and other acts when implementing the conventions. This revealed that the divisions in the General

Assembly that have existed since 1972 remain, despite efforts to hide them in the post–cold war terrorism-related declarations and treaties.

The United Nations Security Council

Like the General Assembly, the UN Security Council has succeeded in developing a broad counter-terrorism legal framework, albeit via a more robust and controversial tool—Security Council resolutions that impose obligations on all 192 (formerly 191) UN member states. Such resolutions have circumvented the traditional international law-making process, which is based on the consent of states. The council's use of this tool has been questioned and criticized by some states, generally those in the global South, as falling outside its mandate. They fear that such action could disrupt the balance of power between the council and the General Assembly as set forth in the UN Charter. Moreover, they assert that having the council, a fifteen-member body not accountable to the other UN organs, impose obligations on all UN members threatens to weaken one of the cornerstones of traditional international law—namely, the principle that international law is based on the consent of states. Defenders of Security Council actions argue that UN practice has evolved to allow the council to act as a global legislator under certain circumstances in the face of an urgent security threat; that the "legislation" in question has already won General Assembly approval and a critical mass of state ratifications; and that the council needs to follow this practice to address effectively, within the state-centered UN Charter system in which it operates, the threats posed by nonstate terrorists and terrorist groups.[9]

The Security Council has established four separate committees to implement its various counter-terrorism mandates. The committees have a combined budget of $13 to $14 million and employ some thirty-six experts. The creation of separate, underresourced mechanisms was part of the council's reaction to particular terrorist attacks. The politics of the moment thus trumped the need to develop a more coherent institutional capability. As a result the overall Security Council counter-terrorism effort has been unable to establish effective programs and mechanisms for implementing its far-reaching legal mandates.

The United Nations Counter-Terrorism Committee

Of the four Security Council counter-terrorism-related bodies, the United Nations Counter-Terrorism Committee (CTC) described in chapter 2 has received priority attention and resources. Established in the aftermath of September 11, 2001, by Security Council Resolution 1373 (2001), the committee has been tasked with monitoring, assessing, and facilitating implementation by states of Security Council Resolution 1373. This groundbreaking resolution required every UN member state to freeze the financial assets of terrorists and their supporters, deny travel or safe haven to terrorists, prevent terrorist recruitment and weapons supply, and cooperate with other countries in information sharing and criminal prosecution. To expedite its adoption, the United States cobbled together a resolution that included provisions from the bombings and financing conventions, which the Security Council made binding on all states overnight.[10]

The committee has received, reviewed, and responded to more than six hundred reports from UN member states.[11] In doing so the committee has encouraged some states to adopt new or improve existing counter-terrorism legislation, border controls, and executive machinery. It has also assisted states in strengthening or establishing laws and mechanisms to prevent the financing of terrorism.

As is discussed below, the CTC has had difficulty transforming itself from a reactive, paper-focused, and process-oriented body to one that is proactive, focused on on-the-ground implementation efforts, results-oriented, and able to respond quickly to try to address the evolving terrorist threat. Rather than addressing concrete country, regional, or thematic issues, the CTC has tended to become unnecessarily consumed in negotiating process-oriented papers and focusing on the political rather than the technical aspects of a particular issue. With its consensus decision-making approach significantly impeding its ability to take decisions in a timely fashion, it took the CTC nearly two years of discussions before it was able to agree on a set of terrorist financing best practices as part of its effort to provide states with a roadmap for effective implementation of Resolution 1373.

The Nonproliferation Committee

As noted in chapter 5, in 2004 the Security Council adopted Resolution 1540, which requires all states to take a series of legislative and regulatory steps to prevent weapons of mass destruction (WMD) and their means of delivery from getting into the hands of terrorists and other non-state actors. It further established a committee with a two-year mandate to monitor states' efforts to implement their 1540 obligations, and a group of eight independent experts to support the committee's work. On 27 April 2006 the Security Council adopted Resolution 1673 to extend the committee's mandate for a second two-year term.[12]

The committee got off to a slow start due to the presence of Pakistan, which, as one of the ten nonpermanent council members, serves a two-year term. Pakistan, which rotated off the Security Council and thus the committee at the end of 2004, viewed itself as a target of Resolution 1540 and only reluctantly voted to adopt it. It then tried to use the negotiations of the committee's rules of procedures and guidelines as a way to dilute both its mandate and the impact of the resolution. Although unsuccessful in the end, Pakistan took advantage of the rule that gives every committee member the ability to block any decision from being taken to prolong the negotiations, thus delaying the start of the committee's substantive work by almost six months.

Although state reporting to the committee has lagged, the committee has made some progress in identifying the different steps states should take to implement fully the provisions of the resolution.[13] Resolution 1673 contained a provision calling on the committee to report by April 2008 to the council on compliance with the council-imposed WMD obligations.[14] Nevertheless, the committee's day-to-day work continues to be impeded somewhat by China's insistence that the committee's experts look only at government, rather than all public, sourced material in analyzing a country's implementation efforts, thus limiting the amount of information the experts can use to analyze each country's performance. As demonstrated in the case of Pakistan, the fact that one state's objections can delay or even paralyze the process for responding to even the most pressing threats to global security is telling of the easy paralysis that is endemic within the political organs of the UN, including all those involved in counter-terrorism related ones. Given the reluctance of UN member states to name specific countries when addressing noncompliance issues, however, it is unlikely that the committee will be able to submit a report on compliance that identifies noncompliant countries by name.

The 1267 Committee (Al-Qaida/Taliban Sanctions Committee)

Although originally established as part of the Security Council's strategy to address the terrorist threat posed by Taliban-controlled Afghanistan, the mandate of the 1267 Committee (which has since become known as the Al-Qaida/Taliban Sanctions Committee) was expanded following September 11, 2001, to deal with the global Al-Qaida threat. It now monitors the implementation of financial, travel, and arms sanctions against Al-Qaida, the Taliban, Osama bin Laden, and their associates. As part of its response to the events of September 11, the council required all states to impose these measures on designated individuals and entities named by the committee, which manages and updates the consolidated sanctions list. To assist the committee with its work, the council established an eight-person Analytical Support and Sanctions Monitoring Team to "collate, assess, monitor, and report on" steps being taken to implement and enforce the sanctions measures against those on the list and to recommend new measures to address the evolving Al-Qaida threat.

Today there are more than 480 names on the committee's list, the vast majority of which were submitted by the United States in the aftermath of September 11 either alone or in conjunction with other UN member states.[15] In the weeks following that day, according to one Security Council diplomat, "there was enormous good will and a willingness to take on trust any name the U.S. submitted."[16] During this period, the creation of the list was based largely on political trust, with the committee having no particular guidelines or standards for states to follow in proposing names. Since then the committee has adopted such guidelines, putting into place minimum evidentiary standards for submitting names and a transparent listing process to help ensure that due process and other human rights standards are respected. Yet concerns about the committee's lack of due process continue to dominate discussions regarding its work, with the procedures for listing and delisting proving to be contentious.[17] European member states generally favor greater transparency and the provision of more rights for those on the list, including possibly allowing them to approach the committee directly.

Maintaining support for the 1267 Committee's work and implementation of the sanctions remain high priorities in the global counterterrorism effort, notwithstanding the mounting controversy surrounding the process (or lack thereof) for adding and removing names from the list. The committee serves as the primary vehicle by which states are empowered to freeze the assets of suspected Al-Qaida and Taliban members. Although countries may be reluctant to freeze the assets of an entity simply because the United States or another powerful country suspects it of having ties to Al-Qaida, they have an obligation under international law to do so if that entity is included on the committee's list.[18]

With respect to state implementation of the sanctions themselves, the record is mixed.[19] As the reports of the monitoring team have revealed, the travel ban and arms embargo have produced few tangible results. The asset freeze requirement has proved valuable in helping internationalize the policy of freezing terrorist assets but has had only limited success.[20] The UN Secretary-General's High-Level Panel on Threats, Challenges and Change, the Secretary-General himself, and world leaders at the 2005 World Summit noted that too often the UN-imposed sanctions are not implemented and that more must be done to ensure that they are. The monitoring team has found a lack of legislative and operational capacity among some states to be the major impediment to implementation.

The Working Group Established Pursuant to Resolution 1566

The Security Council's response to the seizure of approximately 1,200 hostages and the death of hundreds of children at a school in Beslan, Russia, was emblematic of its broader efforts to address the terrorist threat. The desire to satisfy short-term political objectives of one or more council members overcame the need to develop a coherent council-led UN counter-terrorism program.

Using the council's robust response to September 11 as its benchmark, the Russian Federation pushed the council to adopt its strongest condemnation to date of attacks against civilians in Resolution 1566. In fact, only last-minute objections of the two OIC members on the council, Algeria and Pakistan, and Russia's desire to maintain council unity in its response to terrorism stood in the way of the council adopting its own definition of terrorism in this resolution and thus treading on what many UN members view to be within the sole purview of the General Assembly. Many council members, some of which had been victimized by terrorism, wanted to show their solidarity with Russia, and thus were eager to accommodate Moscow's proposals, which had little support on their merits. Most significantly, despite recognizing that the council's three existing terrorism-related committees were having difficulty coordinating their efforts and that the council's counter-terrorism program needed to be rationalized, the council agreed to establish yet another terrorism-related committee, the working group established by Resolution 1566 (2004). The council provided the working group with a mandate, first, to consider practical measures to be imposed on individuals, groups, or entities involved in or associated with terrorist activities, other than those on the Al-Qaida/Taliban consolidated list, and second, to look into the possibilities of creating an international fund for the victims of terrorism. It did this despite the fact that many individual council members objected both to the notion of an expanded UN list of terrorists absent a UN definition of terrorism and to the idea of an international fund for terrorist victims.

Predictably, the differences among council members that were subsumed during the negotiations of Resolution 1566 surfaced during the meetings of the working group, which has rarely met and, not surprisingly, has been unable to reach consensus on any meaningful recommendations. Although one commentator suggested that the working group's 2005 report to the council "would [have] provide[d] a prime vehicle for addressing problems of coherence and overlap" in UN counter-terrorism mandates, its report failed to address this question.[21]

The United Nations Office on Drugs and Crime

While the General Assembly and Security Council have contributed to the development of an international normative and legal framework for combating terrorism, a number of UN agencies have become involved in providing counter-terrorism-related assistance and training to states. The most significant element of this assistance program is carried out by the UN Office on Drugs and Crime (UNODC), which is located in Vienna. Its Terrorism Prevention Branch (TPB) was established a few years prior to September 11, 2001. It was only after September 11, however, as part of a broader push to get states to join and implement the UN counter-terrorism conventions, that the General Assembly shifted the UNODC/TPB's mandate away from producing academic studies on terrorism that seemed to be of little practical value and instead to providing states with assistance in the drafting of the legislation needed to implement these conventions. Since 2001, the TPB, which now consists of some eighteen full-time staff and ten consultants, has delivered country-specific assistance to more than sixty countries and trained more than six hundred lawmakers and other criminal justice officials on ratification and implementation requirements of the international terrorism–related treaties.[22] With staff and consultants stationed in twelve regional offices and nine country offices around the globe, the TPB has a much smaller presence than the UN Development Programme (UNDP), for example, but it has been able to coordinate quite closely with regional organizations, including by cohosting legislative drafting workshops in different regions. In carrying out its activities, the TPB has sought to collaborate with the CTC and CTED to develop a complementary and synergistic relationship.

In addition to the TPB, UNODC has a Global Programme Against Money Laundering (GPML) with a handful of staff that provides technical assistance to states to strengthen their ability to implement measures against money laundering and the financing of terrorism. Although established in the late 1990s to address issues related to organized crime, its focus since 9/11 has expanded to address terrorist financing. Like the TPB, the GPML is funded mostly by voluntary contributions from UN member states (rather than by regular budget allocations) and places mentors in key regions around the globe. There is some overlap between the mandates of the GPML and the TPB. Both offices provide legislative drafting assistance to help states ratify and implement the International Convention on Terrorist Financing and the anti-money laundering and terrorist financing recommendations of the Financial Action Task Force (FATF). Despite this overlap and the fact that they are located in the same Vienna office building, there is little coordination between the two offices.

Duplication

As the above discussion shows, in recent years there has been a proliferation of Security Council subsidiary and other UN bodies tasked to deal with different elements of the threat of terrorism. This has produced overlapping mandates, turf battles, duplication of work, and multiple and sometimes confusing reporting requirements for states. In general, information sharing and other forms of cooperation between and among these groups have been inadequate and often redundant, which has inhibited the overall UN effort.

In addition to the overlap between the UNODC's two main counterterrorism offices mentioned above, there are numerous examples of the ways in which the mandates of the different Security Council initiatives conflict or overlap. The first involves the analysis being done by both the CTED and the monitoring team in the areas of terrorist financing, arms embargoes, and travel bans. The Security Council–imposed Al-Qaida/Taliban sanctions constitute a subset of the measures states are obliged to take under Resolution 1373. Thus, any analysis related to the difficulties of states in implementing the sanctions regime may be relevant to and duplicative of analysis related to the difficulties of states in implementing Resolution 1373. This redundancy is most apparent in the terrorist financing context but also applies to the other two areas. In these, the monitoring team and the CTED have reached many of the same conclusions, not only as to the nature of the gaps in states' capacity to implement the relevant obligations but also what is needed to fill them. This parallel analysis is generally undertaken with little or no coordination between the two analytical teams, despite the fact that their parent committees report to the same fifteen-state Security Council. The problem is exacerbated by the fact that both the CTED and the monitoring team have tended to focus their efforts on the terrorist financing portion of their respective mandates. As a result, there is unnecessary duplication of effort in this field, with few rigorous analyses or assessments being carried out in the other counter-terrorism fields.

There is also duplicative analysis being done by both the CTED and the 1540 Committee's group of experts in the areas of weapons of mass destruction. Among its many different provisions, Resolution 1373 includes language urging states to prevent terrorists from getting their hands on such weapons. Prior to the adoption of Resolution 1540, which is exclusively devoted to this subject, the United States had been pushing the CTC to focus more attention on the WMD-related provisions of Resolution 1373. Despite this overlap in mandates, the CTC and 1540 Committees and their respective staff bodies have yet to agree on a common approach to handling these issues with states.

Another area where there is growing overlap and duplication of effort is in the Security Council's counter-terrorism-related outreach to international, regional, and subregional intergovernmental organizations. Since early 2003, the CTC has sought to deepen its relationships with more than sixty different organizations and has attempted to spur them to do more in the field of counter-terrorism. Today, both the Al-Qaida/Taliban Sanctions Committee and the 1540 Committee are establishing their own separate contacts with the various organizations. Thus, rather than having one Security Council counter-terrorism interlocutor with these bodies, which would help ensure the delivery of a consistent message, with many of them there are three. This redundancy puts an increased burden on the organizations, many of which have only one or two people in their secretariats addressing counter-terrorism issues and thus may lack the capacity to engage substantively with one, let alone three, Security Council counter-terrorism-related committees. Representatives from some organizations may also ask themselves why they need to have three different Security Council counter-terrorism points of contact.[23]

UN Efforts to Strengthen and Streamline Its Counter-terrorism Program

The assessment that the UN's Security Council–led counter-terrorism program has serious shortcomings, including those related to the proliferation of overlapping bodies and mandates, is now widely shared. A March 2006 report of the Secretary-General provides a succinct overview of some of the limitations. The report notes that the council's counter-terrorism bodies "were established in different historical contexts and with different aims, and therefore each is asked to report separately to the Security Council."[24] Despite separate reporting channels, however, there is a certain amount of overlap in their work since the three bodies report on similar issues. The Secretary-General further reports that each body has a somewhat different procedure for dealing with states. In addition to the reporting fatigue that the multiple and somewhat overlapping reporting requirements have produced, the current arrangement has resulted in confusion for noncouncil members and other parts of the UN and other multilateral bodies seeking to cooperate with the different arms of the council's counter-terrorism program.

A number of UN members appear to share the Secretary-General's assessment, believing the current council-led effort to be too diffuse and lacking sufficient coordination to make it effective. This theme was highlighted in the G-8 leaders statement on strengthening the UN counter-terrorism program at the Saint Petersburg meeting in July 2006.[25] The criticisms of the current diffuse approach are not limited to members of the global North, however. In fact, it is the members of the global South that have perhaps been more critical of current arrangements.[26] Many have had difficulty distinguishing among the different mandates of the monitoring team, the CTED, and now the 1540 Committee group of experts; they are inundated with multiple, seemingly duplicative reporting and other requirements.

Although the UN membership has voiced strong support for increased cooperation among the different bodies, in particular among the Security Council staff bodies,[27] there have been few improvements to date. While increased cooperation, if it materializes, might improve the situation somewhat, it will not address the underlying problem of different staff bodies that are unaccountable to each other with separate budgets, different leaders, and overlapping mandates. Thus, absent a formal integration of the multiple staff units into one office under the direction of a single coordinator with day-to-day responsibility for ensuring cooperation, the situation is unlikely to improve significantly. This point has been underscored by Simon Chesterman, executive director of the Institute for International Law and Justice at New York University School of Law, who has written that "if only for reasons of efficiency it appears desirable to rationalise these various supporting offices whose mandates are recognised as overlapping."[28] The shortcomings of the current structure have been at least partially responsible for impeding efforts to move beyond the present paper-driven, process-oriented exercise to one that is results oriented, that is capable of providing both rigorous analyses of states' counter-terrorism capacities and timely assistance to address the identified needs.

The above concerns are not new. As early as 2004 Costa Rica and Switzerland called for the establishment of a UN high commissioner for terrorism to coordinate the growing number of UN counter-terrorism initiatives. The proposal was motivated in part by a desire among non–Security Council members to shift the focus of the UN counter-terrorism effort back to the more inclusive General Assembly by having the General Assembly take control of the currently council-led counter-terrorism program, in particular its staff bodies. In the end, the five permanent members of the council objected to the proposal for just that reason, despite acknowledging that the UN effort could be improved.

Reflecting the broad dissatisfaction with the UN's counter-terrorism program, both the leaders at the UN World Summit and the Sixtieth General Assembly in 2005 requested that the Secretary-General prepare a report with recommendations on how to enhance the UN effort.[29] The Secretary-General's report, *Uniting Against Terrorism*, urged states to focus their efforts on the concrete, practical contributions that the different parts of the UN system can make in the counter-terrorism effort, with a focus on the system's ability to work with states to implement the existing UN legal framework and on improving coordination and cooperation among the twenty-three different parts of the system currently engaged in this effort. The report emphasized the role that the UN can play in helping countries strengthen their counter-terrorism capacities, both by identifying and helping close gaps. The Secretary-General also argued for the development of a more holistic, inclusive UN approach to counter-terrorism, seeking to deepen the coordination between the Security Council's security-focused program and the parts of the UN system that deal with crime, development, human rights, education, and peacekeeping.

The General Assembly started considering the Secretary-General's recommendations in May 2006 with a view to developing its own counter-terrorism strategy. Not surprisingly, given the global body's track record in dealing with terrorism-related issues and the difficulties in getting different parts of the UN system to cooperate and coordinate to address cross-cutting issues effectively, the General Assembly was unable to endorse many of the Secretary-General's recommendations. Instead of trying to put politics aside in the interest of developing a comprehensive and meaningful global strategy with the UN at its center, it got bogged down with the same political issues that have prevented it from reaching agreement on a definition of terrorism and failed to support a number of proposals aimed at improving cooperation and coordination. In September 2006, however, the General Assembly did reach agreement on and adopt an anodyne strategy document. Although largely limited to a repetition of previous general commitments made by one UN body or another, it may provide a framework for enhancing the UN system's counter-terrorism efforts.[30] For the General Assembly to play a meaningful role in implementing the strategy, it will need to be able to put politics aside, at least temporarily. Although the jury is still out as to whether this is possible, the outlook is not promising. Right after the strategy was adopted, a familiar scenario unfolded in the General Assembly, with Israel trading accusations with Iran, Lebanon, and Syria over whom they believe is ultimately responsible for terrorism.[31] While the new strategy indicates the Secretary-General's intention to "institutionalize . . . [his] Counter-Terrorism Task Force within the Secretariat, in order to ensure overall co-ordination and coherence in the United Nations' system's counter-terrorism efforts," the task force will likely serve only an administrative function. It lacks the authority needed to get the different parts of the system to share information, cooperate, and reduce overlapping mandates, all of which are needed to improve the UN effort.

Institutionalizing the Secretary-General's task force may simply add to the problem of duplication if it is not linked organically to the other UN counter-terrorism bodies.

Consolidation Options

With the largest UN counter-terrorism staff's (the CTED) mandate set to expire at the end of 2007, the Security Council has an opportunity to fix the problems within the current UN system. Rather than simply renewing the CTED mandate, as would be the norm in the UN, the Security Council should consolidate its multiple counter-terrorism-related bodies into a single entity to make the council's program more coherent and effective. The Secretary-General has already concluded, in his March 2006 report on streamlining UN mandates, that some form of consolidation would make sense.[32]

Although the Secretary-General's report refers to two possible forms of consolidation, three such options exist. One is to integrate the separate Security Council staff bodies; the second is to consolidate the staff bodies more broadly by integrating the experts in the UNODC/TPB and GPML with those of the Security Council bodies; the third is to combine either of the first two options with a consolidation of the separate Security Council committees into a single member state committee. The Gingrich/Mitchell Task Force on UN Reform, finding the UN counter-terrorism program poorly coordinated, recommended that some of these options be explored.[33] The task force report stated: "Among the solutions that should be explored are mandating closer coordination among the committees (including reducing unnecessary duplication in member states' reports), combining their staffs, and combining the committees themselves."

There would likely be strong support within the UN community for option one, an integration of the Security Council staff bodies while preserving the integrity of the separate council committees. As noted above, a wide range of UN members, including both members and nonmembers of the Security Council, recognizes that cooperation and coordination among these groups remains inadequate and that the resulting duplication of effort and overlapping mandates are hampering its counter-terrorism performance. With reform at the top of most countries' UN agendas in 2006, the idea of consolidating the UN bureaucracy to make it more efficient and effective should resonate both in New York and in world capitals. Ultimately, because this consolidation requires action only by the Security Council and does not affect any existing General Assembly–mandated activity, the council should be able to carry this out with little difficulty, particularly since the mandates of the different council intergovernmental subsidiary bodies would not be affected. The UN Secretariat, which has never fully embraced deepening its involvement in counter-terrorism issues, partly because of divisions among UN members and a resulting lack of understanding of what role the UN Secretariat might play in this field, is unlikely to be an impediment to this effort; consolidation would reduce its already limited role in this area. By design, the Secretariat currently provides more support to the monitoring team and the 1540 Committee group of experts than it provides to the CTED. A consolidation of these two bodies into the larger CTED would reduce Secretariat involvement in the work of those bodies.

Most of the opposition to this type of consolidation would center around three factors. First, the uneven and largely untested performance of the CTED to date might make some states leery about giving it added staff and responsibilities. Second, given the lengthy delays in getting the CTED established and fully operational, council members may be reluctant to embark on yet another restructuring of its counter-terrorism program. Finally, there is a perceived need to maintain the distinction between Security Council counter-terrorism capacity-building and sanctions efforts and its counter-terrorism and WMD efforts.

Yet these differences may not be significant. Many states see the CTC and the Al-Qaida/Taliban Sanctions Committee as having distinct roles and approaches: one is supposed to be a sanctions body with teeth (that is, punitive), and the other a capacity-building body (that is, incentive-based). At the end of the day, however, both committees are charged with monitoring the implementation of similar obligations imposed by the Security Council under chapter VII of the UN Charter. Thus, the same enforcement measures are available for the council to apply against those who fail to comply with the obligations, whether created by Resolution 1373 or Al-Qaida/Taliban sanctions Resolutions 1526 or 1617. The issues become whether each committee will submit to the council a list of states that it has determined are not complying with their obligations and whether the council will decide to take advantage of the available enforcement measures to induce compliance. At this stage neither body appears close to reaching agreement on what standards should measure states' performance, let alone on who should be on a list of the nonperformers and whether to submit such a list to the council.

In addition, although many states view the CTC as a counter-terrorism body and the 1540 Committee as part of the global nonproliferation effort, both are focused on developing the legislative, regulatory, and institutional capacities of states to combat terrorism, with the latter focused on WMD terrorism. Moreover, any consolidation of the committees' expert groups or even the committees themselves need not change the underlying obligations imposed upon states. Rather, it would simply improve the Security Council's efforts to monitor states' implementation efforts and help maximize the synergies between the now separate bodies.

Option two would establish a thoroughgoing staff consolidation by combining the council staff bodies and the UNODC/TPB and GPML into a single unit, thereby formally integrating the technical assistance provision arm of the UN program into the broader capacity-building functions. As both the TPB and GPML have field offices or representatives in a number of countries in Africa, Asia, and Latin America, this consolidation would give the Security Council's counter-terrorism program a more permanent on-the-ground presence that would enhance its global capacity-building efforts.[34]

As with the first option, this fully integrated unit would support the work of and receive policy guidance from the different Security Council counter-terrorism-related bodies. The TPB and GPML, which could be combined as part of this consolidation, could continue to be based in Vienna, with their heads reporting to the head of the CTED in New York rather than the executive director of the UNODC in Vienna. Their mandates, however, would be set by the council rather than by the General Assembly and the UN Economic and Social Council (ECOSOC) as they are currently. Such a consolidation would provide the TPB and GPML with the political clout that comes from being part of a Security Council–mandated staff body. However, while this form of consolidation makes sense on paper it would be difficult to achieve in practice. Consolidation involving the TPB and GPML would require decisions of both the Security Council and the General Assembly. It would involve taking General Assembly–mandated programs—ones that generally receive high marks from a diverse group of UN members—and placing them under the authority of the Security Council. Given the growing tensions between the General Assembly and the Security Council over the latter's ever-increasing counter-terrorism portfolio, there would likely be considerable resistance among noncouncil members to bringing the TPB and GPML under the control of the Security Council.

A third possible form of consolidation would combine the four separate Security Council counter-terrorism-related intergovernmental bodies into a single committee. This could be done in conjunction with either of the first two staff integration options. Such a step would likely meet with resistance, however, due to the emphasis that many UN members tend to place on respecting the different mandates of the Security Council subsidiary bodies. Even the Security Council's calls for greater coordination and cooperation among its subsidiary bodies and staff units are balanced with language recognizing the importance of respecting the distinct mandates. The 2005 UN World Summit Outcome Document makes this point, encouraging the council to consider ways to strengthen its counter-terrorism role, "including by consolidating State reporting requirements, taking into account and respecting the different mandates of its counter-terrorism subsidiary bodies."[35] Although there would likely be support for combining the staff bodies, such support would largely depend on maintaining the mandates of the parent bodies.

Were the council to take the bold step of creating a single counter-terrorism committee, it could maintain the distinct mandates of the separate resolutions by establishing subgroups for each. It could appoint an overall committee chair and a vice chair for sanctions, a vice chair for WMD, and, if the 1566 Committee working group's mandate is extended, a vice chair for issues being considered by that body. Each vice chair could convene meetings whenever a particular issue in his or her purview required urgent attention. This would help assuage the fear that the different elements in the council's counter-terrorism program would not receive the necessary attention should the council consolidate all of its counter-terrorism bodies. A consolidated committee structure could lead to a single council counter-terrorism work plan and mandate. This would reduce, if not eliminate, the problems of duplication of work and overlapping mandates that plague not only the council staff bodies but their parent bodies as well.

With each of these possibilities, the Security Council should consider whether there might be advantages to shifting the locus of its consolidated counter-terrorism program from New York to Vienna, a "technical" UN city, to help depoliticize the effort and enhance the technical focus of the program. In addition, such a move would facilitate greater cooperation not only with UNODC's counter-terrorism assistance offices but with its drugs and crime programs, and the IAEA, the primary international body addressing the threat of WMD terrorism. Relocating the Security Council counter-terrorism program, including its staff functions, to Vienna might facilitate the development of more coherent UN strategies for addressing the connections between terrorism and some of the other major security threats.

In addition, any of these consolidations can and should be carried out in conjunction with two other reforms, which would enhance the council's efforts and build support from noncouncil member states (particularly the smaller ones): the consolidation of the multiple reporting requirements into a single process and consolidated country visits by the various groups of experts. States would submit one report to the council, on a periodic basis, that contains efforts to implement all of the Security Council–imposed counter-terrorism mandates. By addressing the reporting fatigue complaint head on in this way, the council would eliminate a reason (or excuse) many states are giving for not cooperating fully with the various counter-terrorism-related bodies. Also, as recently confirmed by the Japanese permanent representative to the UN, consolidated site visits would enhance the effectiveness of the dialogue between the various council counter-terrorism mechanisms and government officials and improve the information gathering and sharing. The "rationalization of visits would [also] relieve the burden on visited states."[36]

Although not going as far as the Costa Rican and Swiss proposal mentioned above, consolidating some or all of the core elements of the UN counter-terrorism program would make it more coherent and effective. Consolidation would not address the political and institutional limitations of operating within the UN, but it would improve the situation somewhat. Staff integration need not consume significant time and energy. It could be pursued in the short term while states give careful consideration to the questions of (1) whether a consolidated UN program would even be up to the challenge of coordinating global counter-terrorism efforts and (2) if a new counter-terrorism body, either within or external to the UN system, is needed, how to go about creating it.

Limitations of Short-Term Solutions

Even a more unified UN Security Council counter-terrorism program, however, would encounter political, administrative, and budgetary challenges. A combined Security Council and UNODC counter-terrorism staff, for example, would number only some fifty to sixty experts with an annual budget of $17 to $18 million. This would not be sufficient to allow the UN to fulfill its broad mandate of coordinating global capacity-building efforts and the work of dozens of multilateral institutional actors. To highlight this point, the International Atomic Energy Agency (IAEA) has a staff of some 2,200 people (with more than one-half of them technical experts) and an annual budget of some $268 million.[37] Because funding for the UN's counter-terrorism programs comes from the regular UN budget, it is subject to the politics of the Fifth Committee, the main committee of the General Assembly responsible for administration and budgetary matters. It must compete in this committee with other important programs for limited resources.[38] Given the different and at times competing priorities of the global North and South and the Fifth Committee practice of reaching consensus on the budget, it is unlikely that the UN's counter-terrorism program could ever be allocated the resources needed to succeed so long as it is funded outside of the UN regular budget and perceived as a Security Council–led exercise.[39]

The decision-making processes of the Security Council counter-terrorism committees have also presented serious challenges. The practice of taking all decisions by consensus has significantly impeded their ability to act swiftly and at times has diluted their work. To maintain its relevance and effectiveness, the leading multilateral counter-terrorism body needs to be able to act decisively on matters that are often technical in nature and must avoid becoming bogged down in seemingly endless political debates. The same consensus-based practice has made it difficult for any of the Security Council counter-terrorism-related bodies to identify nonperformers ("name and shame") or even to agree on a set of standards against which to measure performance.[40] On a number of occasions, one or two committee members, including the one representing the region in which a targeted country is located, have successfully blocked any efforts to exert meaningful pressure on a particular country.[41] Furthermore, these rules have impeded efforts within the council's counter-terrorism bodies to focus on the more politically sensitive areas of the resolutions. For example, the CTC has been unable to devote meaningful attention to monitoring the implementation of the Resolution 1373 obligation to deny safe haven to terrorists. In practice, the consensus approach has significantly weakened the political and legal power of the different Security Council resolutions on terrorism and impeded the work of the subsidiary bodies created to assist implementation of these mandates.

The political nature of the Security Council means that it is generally focused on responding to specific, time-limited threats to international peace and security. It is less suited to the challenges of managing operations or sustaining institutional commitment to long-term objectives. Thus, it reacts quickly and forcefully to a discrete terrorist incident, meeting at night or on the weekend to adopt the necessary resolution or presidential statement. It has found it difficult, however, to sustain the momentum of its long-term counter-terrorism capacity-building program and the multitude of tasks that are involved.

The UN's comparative advantage in the field of counter-terrorism lies in capacity building and standard setting, both of which have a significant technical component. Yet because the UN's work in this area is overseen by the Security Council and its subsidiary bodies—and because it is based in New York—this effort has been and will continue to be heavily (and perhaps unnecessarily) politicized, with delegations often interjecting tendentious political issues, thus slowing down the legal and technical work. When the Security Council is in the throes of a contentious negotiation outside the purview of its counter-terrorism-related committees, the differences of views and even animosities among certain delegations over these outside issues can spill over into its terrorism-related work. The problem of overpoliticization of technical issues is exacerbated by the fact that the representatives on the CTC and other Security Council counter-terrorism-related bodies are usually political officers (regular diplomats or generalists), often with little or no background in the technical field of counter-terrorism. As a result, rather than focusing on concrete country, regional, or thematic issues, the bodies, in particular the CTC, have tended to become unnecessarily consumed in negotiating process-oriented papers and focusing on the political rather than the technical aspects of a particular issue. This is in contrast to technical organizations such as the International Atomic Energy Agency (IAEA), the Organisation for the Prohibition of Chemical Weapons (OPCW), Interpol, and the International Civil Aviation Organization (ICAO), where member state delegations generally include domestic experts in the relevant field.

Institutional Options for the Future

A long-term consideration for the future of the UN counter-terrorism program is the prospect of creating a new international agency to combat terrorism. Monitoring the implementation of states' counter-terrorism obligations requires a long-term and unwavering commitment—one that will not diminish as the memories of the most recent horrific terrorist attack fade or when the Security Council encounters specific threats to international peace and security that require its urgent attention. It might take some states decades to develop their infrastructure to be able to implement fully the counter-terrorism obligations imposed by the Security Council and international treaties. Given the importance and long-term nature of the task and the above-mentioned political and institutional limitations of working within the UN, serious consideration should be given to studying alternative models to the current approach, including the establishment of a dedicated counter-terrorism organization that reports to the Security Council but operates outside of the UN system.

Creating a new agency would be a means of giving greater priority and more permanence to the global fight against terrorism. Counter-terrorism is one of the few issues for which there is not a dedicated international agency. Human rights, refugees, chemical weapons, children's rights, and many other issues have specialized agencies that usually operate within the UN system and provide a means of focusing international attention and action on the particular concern. The Council on Foreign Relations Task Force on Enhancing U.S. Leadership at the United Nations recommended in a November 2002 report that consideration be given to "the need for an independent body to carry out the CTC's functions over the long term." Both U.S. president Bush and then–UK prime minister Blair highlighted the need to create new multilateral structures to address twenty-first-century security threats such as terrorism.[42] It is conceivable that the CTED might create a precedent for and eventually evolve into a larger counter-terrorism body. Combining the CTED, UNODC, and the staffs of the other Security Council counter-terrorism-related committees as outlined above could pave the way toward the creation of a new entity, which could then be expanded as nations determine. A dedicated counter-terrorism body could be established via a treaty, a political declaration, or a UN General Assembly resolution. Whether directly connected to the United Nations or established as a stand-alone entity, the new organization could focus and build on the work of the existing counter-terrorism-related bodies. Decisions of the Security Council and General Assembly would be needed to transfer the work of their relevant bodies to a new, dedicated counter-terrorism body. It would work to monitor implementation of current and future UN conventions and other instruments against terrorism. Freed from the limitations of the UN political bodies, it could more effectively perform the tasks necessary to build global counter-terrorism capacity. Some states might initially balk at transferring the responsibilities for monitoring the implementation of Security Council counter-terrorism obligations to a new, noncouncil body for fear that such a body would not be as powerful as those under the Security Council, lacking as it would the council's enforcement capacity. The new body could retain a link to the council, however, particularly the authority to refer states to it for remedial action. Thus, no real loss of power or authority need result from such a transfer.

The numerous international bodies that have been created in the past fifty years to address security and other global issues offer a range of models to look to when forming a multilateral counter-terrorism organization. They fit broadly into three categories: a treaty-based body (e.g., the IAEA or OPCW); an informal, political body (e.g., the Wassenaar Arrangement or FATF); or a UN program (e.g., the UNDP or UN High Commissioner for Refugees). Given the *sui generis* nature of a global counter-terrorism organization, a new body would likely draw on elements from many, if not all, of these models. As a first step to establishing a new entity, an international process involving a broad range of stakeholders from both the global North and South should be convened outside the unduly politicized UN setting to discuss the pros and cons of the various possibilities, with a view to recommending the elements of each that should be included in a global counter-terrorism body and what the mandate of such an entity should be. Regardless of which model is chosen, any body needs to attract broad support from a cross-section of countries to obtain the financial and political support necessary for long-term viability and legitimacy. It needs to ensure that an effective and long-lasting mechanism exists both to coordinate the delivery of counter-terrorism capacity-building assistance to the global South and develop a more holistic program of counter-terrorism cooperation across the globe.

Conclusion

As this discussion has indicated, serious problems of organizational duplication and weakness plague the current UN counter-terrorism program. Options for possible consolidation and reform have been discussed, but limited and short-term solutions would not address many of the underlying problems with the UN program. There is need for exploration of more enduring and effective alternatives to achieve the goals of an expanding nonmilitary global campaign against terrorism, including supervising and monitoring the implementation of existing UN counter-terrorism mandates. Increasing state capacity to implement the UN's broad counter-terrorism mandates on a sustainable basis will depend on a level of coordination among states and organizations that the current UN-led institutional arrangements have not reached. A new organizational entity dedicated to combating terrorism and freed from the UN's political and institutional limitations may be needed to help the international community achieve these goals. In the face of a terrorist threat that is constantly transforming and that in the opinion of some analysts continues to grow, slothful, bureaucratic responses are not sufficient. As the record since 9/11 shows, unless serious flaws are addressed, international, nonmilitary counter-terrorism efforts are likely to remain inadequate.

Notes

1. For a list of the first twelve conventions, see United Nations Office on Drugs and Crime, "*Conventions Against Terrorism*," Vienna, n.d., UNODC, <http://www.unodc.org/unodc/terrorism_conventions.html> (accessed 19 September 2006). The thirteenth convention, the *International Convention for the Suppression of Acts of Nuclear Terrorism*, was adopted in 2005. See *International Convention for the Suppression of Acts of Nuclear Terrorism*, New York, 14 September 2005, UN Treaty Collection, <http://untreaty.un.org/English/Terrorism.asp> (accessed 8 October 2006).

2. These include United Nations, *Convention on Offences and Certain Other Acts Committed on Board Aircraft*, signed at Tokyo on 14 September 1963, UN Treaty Collection, <http://untreaty.un.org/English/Terrorism.asp> (accessed 8 October 2006); United Nations *International Convention for the Suppression of Unlawful Seizure of Aircraft*, signed at The Hague 16 December 1970, UN Treaty Collection, <http://www.unodc.org/unodc/en/terrorism_convention _aircraft_seizure.html> (accessed 8 October 2006); and United Nations, *Convention for the Suppression of Unlawful Acts Against the Safety of Civil Aviation*, signed at Montreal on 23 September 1971 (entered into force 26 January 1973), UN Treaty Collection, <http://untreaty.un.org/English/Terrorism.asp> (accessed 8 October 2006).

3. United Nations, *Convention on the Prevention and Punishment of Crimes Against Internationally Protected Persons, Including Diplomatic Agents*, Resolution 3166 (XXVIII), New York, 14 December 1973, <http://www.unodc .org/unodc/en/terrorism_convention_protected_persons.html>   (accessed   8 October 2006); and United Nations, *International Convention Against the Taking of Hostages*, New York, 18 December 1979, UN Treaty Collection, <http://untreaty.un.org/English/Terrorism.asp> (accessed 8 October 2006).

4. See, for example, United Nations General Assembly, *Convention on the Prevention of Punishment of Crimes Against Internationally Protected Persons, Including Diplomatic Agents*, Resolution 3166 (XXVIII), New York, 14 December 1973; and United Nations, *International Convention Against the Taking of Hostages*.

5. Kendall W. Stiles, "The Power of Procedure and the Procedures of the Powerful: Anti-Terror Law in the United Nations," *Journal of Peace Research* 43, no. 1 (January 2006): 42.

6. United Nations General Assembly, *Declaration on Measures to Eliminate International Terrorism*, 9 December 1994, par. 3. The *Declaration on Measures to Eliminate International Terrorism* was approved in the General Assembly resolution on *Measures to Eliminate International Terrorism*. For the text of this resolution and declaration (annex to the resolution), see United Nations General Assembly, *Measures to Eliminate International Terrorism*, A/RES/49/60, New York, 17 February 1995, <http://daccessdds.un.org/doc/UNDOC/GEN/N95/768/19/PDF/N9576819.pdf?OpenElement> (accessed 22 September 2006).

7. Organisation of the Islamic Conference, *Convention on Combating International Terrorism*, annex to Resolution no. 59/26P, completed at the Organisation of the Islamic Conference Convention on Combating International Terrorism, Ouagadougou, 1 July 1999), art. 2(a), <http://www.oic-un.org/26icfm/c.html> (accessed 24 September 2006).

8. Organization of African Unity, *Convention on the Prevention and Combating of Terrorism*, Algiers, 14 July 1999, art. 3.

9. For an in-depth discussion of the Security Council's legislative role, see Stefan Talmon, "The Security Council as World Legislature," *American Journal of International Law* 99 (January 2005): 175–93; Eric Rosand, "The Security Council as 'Global Legislator': Ultra Vires or Ultra Innovative," *Fordham International Law Journal* 28 (May 2005): 542–90.

10. Eric Rosand, "Security Council Resolution 1373 and the Counter-Terrorism Committee: The Cornerstone of the United Nations Contribution to the Fight Against Terrorism," in *Legal Instruments in the Fight Against International Terrorism: A Transatlantic Dialogue*, ed. Cyrille Fijnaut, Jan Wouters, and Frederik Naert (Boston: Brill Academic, 2004), 606.

11. See United Nations Security Council, *Work Programme of the Counter-Terrorism Committee*, S/2005/663, New York, 21 October 2005, par. 5.

12. United Nations Security Council, *Security Council Resolution 1673 (2006)*, S/RES/1673, New York, 27 April 2006.

13. As of October 2005 the committee has received reports from 124 states—that is, about two-thirds of the UN membership. As of April 2006, "The Committee established pursuant to resolution 1540 (2004) and its experts have examined reports from 127 States and one organization (the European Union) on their efforts to meet the requirements of Security Council resolution 1540 (2004)." See Kofi Annan, *Uniting Against Terrorism: Recommendations for a Global Counter-Terrorism Strategy*, report of the Secretary-General to the United Nations General Assembly, A/60/825, 27 April 2006, 26, annex 1, <http://www.un.org/unitingagainstterrorism/sg-terrorism-2may06.pdf> (accessed 24 September 2006).

14. United Nations Security Council, "Security Council Extends for Two Years Mandate of Committee Monitoring Implementation of Resolution 1540 (2004) on Mass Destruction Weapons," press release, SC8708, New York, 27 April 2006, <http://www.un.org/News/Press/docs/2006/sc8708.doc.htm> (accessed 24 September 2006).

15. United Nations Security Council Committee Established Pursuant to Resolution 1267 (1999) Concerning Al-Qaida and the Taliban and Associated Individuals and Entities, *The New Consolidated List of Individuals and Entities Belonging to or Associated with the Taliban and Al-Qaida Organisation as Established and Maintained by the 1267 Committee,* updated 24 August 2006, New York, <http://www.un.org/Docs/sc/committees/1267/1267ListEng.htm> (accessed 11 October 2006).

16. Christopher Cooper, "Shunned in Sweden: How the Drive to Block Funds for Terrorism Entangled Mr. Aden," *Wall Street Journal,* 6 May 2002.

17. See, for example, Thomas Biersteker and Sue E. Eckert, "Strengthening Targeted Sanctions Through Fair and Clear Procedures," report, Watson Institute for International Studies, Brown University, Providence, March 2006; Iain Cameron, "Protecting Legal Rights: On the (In)security of Targeted Sanctions," in *International Sanctions: Between Words and Wars in the Global System,* ed. Peter Wallensteen and Carina Staibano (London: Frank Cass, 2005), 189.

18. Moreover, more than forty have still not reported to the committee on steps they are taking to implement the sanctions, as called for by the Security Council in January 2003.

19. For a critical analysis of the work of the Al-Qaida/Taliban Sanctions Committee, see Eric Rosand, "Current Developments: The Security Council's Efforts to Monitor the Implementation of Al-Qaida/Taliban Sanctions," *American Journal of International Law* 98 (2004): 745–63.

20. As of January 2005, based on informal statements made at the United Nations on 10 January 2005 by Juan Zarate, assistant U.S. treasury secretary, states were reported to have seized or frozen "$147 million in assets belonging to 435 individuals and groups linked to Al-Qaida or the Taliban." Associated Press, "U.S.: Terror Funding Stymied," 11 January 2005, *CBS News,* <http://www.cbsnews.com/stories/2005/01/11/terror/main666168.shtml> (accessed 24 September 2006). In October 2005 the list included 140 individuals associated with the Taliban and 182 people and 117 businesses or groups linked to Al-Qaida. This number is somewhat misleading for a number of reasons. First, between September 11, 2001, and the end of 2001 alone, $112 million in alleged terrorist funds had been frozen. Chantal de Jonge Oudraat, "Combating Terrorism," *Washington Quarterly* 26, no. 4 (Autumn 2003): 163–76. Second, in the two years after that, only about $24 million was frozen. See U.S. Department of Treasury, Office of Public Affairs, "U.S. Designates Individual Tied to Attacks on European Tourists," press release, JS-1043, 5 December 2003. This release indicates that "[w]ith [this] action, the U.S. and our international partners have designated 344 individuals and organizations as terrorists and terrorist supporters and have frozen over $136.8 million [which includes the approximately $112 million in 2001] in terrorist assets," <http://treas.gov/press/releases/js1043.htm> (accessed 24 September 2006); see also unspecified "recently published U.S. Treasury report" cited in United Nations, *Second Report of the Monitoring Group Established Pursuant to*

Security Council Resolution 1363 (2001), S/2003/1070, New York, 2 December 2003, 12. Little if any of the $24 million was linked to individuals or entities listed on the Al-Qaida/Taliban Sanctions Committee's list. Ibid., 36. Finally, according to a 2002 independent U.S. expert panel on terrorist finance, "the frequently cited total amount of terrorist-related assets blocked overstates the amount of money taken from al-Qaida and its supporters specifically, and undoubtedly represents only a small fraction of total funds available to that terrorist organization." See Maurice Greenberg, William F. Wechsler, and Lee S. Wolosky, *Terrorist Financing: Independent Task Force Report* (Washington, DC: Brookings Institution, 2002), 20.

21. Edward C. Luck, "The Uninvited Challenge: Terrorism Targets the United Nations," in *Multilateralism Under Challenge: Power, International Order and Structural Change*, ed. Edward Newman, Ramesh Thakur, and John Tirman, 336–55 (Tokyo: United Nations University and the Social Science Research Council, 2005), 16, available from Center on International Organization, School of International and Public Affairs, Columbia University, <http://www.sipa .columbia.edu/cio/cio/projects/LuckSSRCUNU.pdf> (accessed 7 December 2005).

22. United Nations Office on Drugs and Crime, Terrorism Prevention Branch, *Delivering Counter-Terrorism Assistance*, brochure, New York, April 2005, <http://www.unodc.org/pdf/crime/terrorism/Brochure_GPT_April2005.pdf> (accessed 8 December 2005).

23. For a discussion of the Al-Qaida/Taliban Sanctions Committee and 1540 Committee's nascent outreach efforts, see statements by committee chairmen at the 26 October 2005 and 30 May 2006 Security Council meetings to discuss the work of its counter-terrorism-related committees. For summaries see United Nations Security Council, "Security Council Briefed by Chairmen of Three Anti-Terrorism Committees; Status of Reporting, Technical Assistance, Among Issues Addressed," press release SC/8536, New York, 26 October 2005, <http://www.un.org/News/Press/docs/2005/sc8536.doc.htm> (accessed 24 September 2006), and United Nations Security Council, "Security Council Reviews Work of Committees on Nuclear Non-Proliferation, Counter-Terrorism, Al-Qaida and Taliban," press release SC/8730, 30 May 2006, <http://www.un.org/News/Press/docs/2006/sc8730.doc.htm> (accessed on 30 July 2006).

24. Kofi Annan, *Mandating and Delivering: Analysis and Recommendations to Facilitate the Review of Mandates,* report of the Secretary-General of the United Nations General Assembly, A/60/733, New York, 30 March 2006, paras. 122–23.

25. Group of Eight, "G8 Statement on Strengthening the UN's Counter-Terrorism Program," St. Petersburg, Russia, 16 July 2006, G8/2006 Russia, <http://en.g8russia.ru/docs/18.html> (accessed 24 September 2006).

26. See, for example, the statement by Samoa (Ali'ioaiga Feturi Elisaia) on behalf of the Pacific Island Forum at the 26 October 2005 United Nations Security Council meeting to discuss the council's counter-terrorism program. Samoa commented on the difficulties small states have complying with, implementing, and

even understanding the myriad Security Council counter-terrorism obligations. Concerns were echoed by Fiji. Comments are summarized at United Nations Security Council, "Security Council Briefed by Chairmen of Three Anti-Terrorism Committees." See also statements by Kenya (Wanjuki Muchemi) stating that the cooperation among UN divisions and agencies should be strengthened and by Thailand (Ittiporn Boonpracong) noting that it might be worth exploring the number of UN counter-terrorism offices with perhaps over-lapping mandates and the establishment of a single UN office such as the High Commissioner on Counter-Terrorism. Both statements are available at United Nations General Assembly, "Legal Committee: Reviewing Issues on Completion of Overall Anti-Terrorism Treaty, Notes Outstanding Differences," press release GA/L/3275, New York, 10 June 2005. Also Suriname (Ewald Lomon), speaking on behalf of the fifteen-member Caribbean Community (CARICOM), who stated that "small countries with limited resources . . . were faced with increasingly onerous responsibilities of meeting obligations established by various United Nations mandates on terrorism." Statement available at United Nations General Assembly, "Legal Committee Ends Discussion of Counter-Terrorism Measures; To Receive Group Report on Comprehensive Convention," press release GA/L/3277, New York, 10 October 2005, 2–3. Other statements include Syria, which noted the importance of coordination and cooperation among the Security Council committees and their staff bodies, as they will enhance the committees' work and "lighten the burden on countries, especially with regard to the writing of reports, since there is less duplication of information as a result"; and New Zealand, which spoke on behalf of the Pacific Island Forum and drew attention "to the problems faced by small Member States . . . in meeting the Council's considerable reporting requirements. In the recent Pacific counter-terrorism meeting . . . it was made very clear that the reality of limited resources and the challenge of competing priorities mean that compliance with counter-terrorism remains a significant challenge for many Pacific countries." New Zealand hoped "that the enhanced cooperation among the three committees and expert groups now underway will include some discussion of the consolidation of reporting requirements for small Member States." United Nations Security Council, *5229th Meeting*, S/PV.5229 (Resumption 1), New York, 20 July 2005, 15, <http://daccessdds.un.org/doc/UNDOC/PRO/N05/431/30/PDF/N0543130.pdf ?OpenElement> (accessed 24 September 2006).

27. See United Nations Security Council, *Statement by the President of the Security Council*, S/PRST/2005/16, New York, 25 April 2005; United Nations Security Council, *Statement by the President of the Security Council*, S/PRST/2005/34, New York, 20 July 2005; United Nations Security Council, *Security Council Resolution 1617 (2005)*, S/RES/1617, New York, 29 July 2005; United Nations Security Council, *Security Council Resolution 1624 (2005)*, S/RES/1624, New York, 14 September 2005.

28. Simon Chesterman, "Shared Secrets: Intelligence and Collective Security," paper #10, Lowy Institute for International Policy, Sydney, Australia, 2006, 56.

29. Annan, *Uniting Against Terrorism*, 26, annex 1.

30. Associated Press, "U.N. General Assembly Adopts Counter-Terrorism Strategy," *International Herald Tribune*, 9 September 2006, <http://www.iht.com/articles/ap/2006/09/08/news/UN_GEN_UN_Counter_Terrorism.php> (accessed 28 September 2006).

31. Nick Wadhams, "UN General Assembly Adopts New Counterterrorism Strategy," *San Diego Union-Tribune*, 8 September 2006, available at <http://www.signonsandiego.com/news/nation/terror/20060908-1635-un-counter-terrorism.html> (accessed 9 September 2006).

32. Annan, *Uniting Against Terrorism*, 26, annex 1, par. 123.

33. See *American Interests and UN Reform: Report of the Task Force on the United Nations*, report for Congress of the Task Force on the United Nations, the United States Institute of Peace, 109th Cong., 1st sess., Washington, DC, 2005, 78. The United States Mission to the United Nations has suggested that such a consolidation might be necessary. See Nicolas Rostow, "Statement on the Work of the 1267 Committee, in the Security Council," USUN press release no. 136 [05], 20 July 2005, <http://www.un.int/usa/05_136.htm> (accessed 8 December 2005).

34. The TPB has fourteen experts in the field, four of them on full-time assignments and the others working on a part-time basis as local consultants. Jean-Paul Laborde, TPB director, e-mail communication with authors, 21 September 2005.

35. United Nations General Assembly, *2005 World Summit Outcome*, A/RES/60/1, New York, 24 October 2005, par. 90.

36. See statement by Japan (Kenzo Oshima) at the 30 May 2006 Security Council meeting to discuss the council's counter-terrorism program. United Nations Security Council, "Security Council Reviews Work of Committees."

37. For information about the IAEA's budget and staff, see International Atomic Energy Agency, "Budget and Finance," IAEA, <http://www.iaea.org/About/budget.html> (accessed 24 September 2006), and "IAEA Staff," *International Atomic Energy Agency*, <http://www.iaea.org/About/staff.html> (accessed 24 September 2006).

38. Of those counter-terrorism-related bodies, only the UNODC/TPB accepts voluntary contributions. Voluntary contributions are a major source of funding for most other UN organizations and programs such as the IAEA, the UNDP, and the UN Environmental Program.

39. The total 2005 budget for the Security Council counter-terrorism programs is $12.5 million; for the Al-Qaida/Taliban Monitoring Team, $3,559,300; for the CTED, $6,888,300; and for the 1540 Committee group of experts, $1,794,900. See United Nations General Assembly, *Special Subjects and Questions Relating to the Programme Budget for the Biennium 2004–2005*, A/RES/59/294, New York, 31 August 2005; United Nations General Assembly, *Estimates in Respect of Special Political Missions, Good Offices and Other Political Initiatives Authorized by the General Assembly and/or the Security Council*, A/59/534/Add.1,

New York, 23 November 2004. The TPB's budget for 2005 is $3.5 million, with $1 million coming out of the UN regular budget and the rest coming from voluntary contributions.

40. There are examples of council subsidiary bodies that do not operate by consensus, such as former Yugoslavia and The Hague ad hoc international criminal tribunals. Unlike the council's sanctions and counter-terrorism subsidiary bodies, which are political intergovernmental bodies, these are independent judicial ones where the judges are appointed and act in their individual capacities rather than on behalf of a state.

41. Brazil, for example, opposed putting increased CTC pressure on Paraguay despite the latter's admitted inability to comply with Resolution 1373 due to parliamentary intransigence. It blocked a proposed CTC visit to Peru and generally prevented the CTC from visiting any country in Latin America during its two years on the committee.

42. Prime Minister Tony Blair, "Moment of Reconciliation," foreign policy speech delivered at Georgetown University, Washington, DC, 26 May 2006, Government of the United Kingdom, <http://www.number-10.gov.uk/output/ Page9549.asp>; White House, *National Strategy for Combating Terrorism*, September 2006, <http://www.whitehouse.gov/nsc/nsct/2006/> (accessed 29 September 2006).

4

Unilateral and Multilateral Strategies Against State Sponsors of Terror: A Case Study of Libya, 1979 to 2003

Thomas E. McNamara

The first ten years of U.S. relations with Mohamar Qaddafi's regime in Libya (1969 to 1979) were occasionally contentious. Compared with the last quarter century, however, they were relatively placid and certainly not a major focus of U.S. policy.[1] Beginning with the presidency of Ronald Reagan, intermittent contention turned into constant tension and frequent conflict. This was by no means due solely to Reagan, although he was a central figure in the confrontations and conflicts. Over the final three decades of the century, the driving force in this drama was, above all, Qaddafi, his early embrace of radical Arab nationalism, his progression to sponsorship of Arab terrorism, and until the late 1990s his persistent, unbending determination to confront the United States.

After Reagan left office, President George H. W. Bush adopted a different policy toward Libya, one that has continued *mutatis mutandi* under his two successors. A third period began as a result of Qaddafi's decision to forsake his radicalism and terrorism for a more moderate approach. The last quarter century of U.S. policy toward Libya can be usefully divided into three periods: 1979 to 1989, bilateral confrontation; 1989 to 1998, multilateral containment; and 1998 to 2003, end of isolation.

Note: This study does not deal with the important issue of Libyan weapons of mass destruction (WMD) because WMD and terrorism are most strongly linked to the possibility of nonstate actors gaining access to WMD. This case study examines state-to-state terrorism issues, and it is not yet clear whether Libya's leaders intended to turn WMD over to nonstate actors. Libya's WMD programs and its decision to end them are important matters deserving of close attention, but are beyond the scope of this case study.

Scholars and practitioners increasingly agree on the important lessons to be learned from the Libya case on the value of multilateral co-operation and the appropriate mix of coercive pressure and diplomatic engagement to achieve counter-terrorism and nonproliferation policy objectives.[2] This case study is an attempt to examine the case and draw conclusions.

Setting the Stage: Changes in U.S. Priorities and Middle East Politics

In the years leading up to 1981, five events combined to provide the incoming Reagan administration with diplomatic "breathing space" on many of the major cold war and Middle East issues that had preoccupied the previous administration. First, the Strategic Arms Limitation Talks II (SALT II) Treaty of 1979 put less pressure on Reagan to conclude new cold war arms control agreements, a difficult, time-consuming policy process. Second, the 1979 NATO decision to deploy theater nuclear forces (TNF) in Europe ended an intense period of debate, which left the Reagan diplomatic team with more time for other issues until the implementation phase in 1983. Third, the Camp David Accords of 1980 helped reduce pressure on the incoming Reagan administration to develop immediate new Middle East initiatives. Fourth, the Soviet invasion of Afghanistan in 1980 was met by the Carter administration with a policy of determined opposition that the Reagan team at first adopted and gradually escalated, as both presidents saw an opportunity to further weaken the Soviet Union. Fifth, the Iranian hostage crisis (1979 to 1981), which ended the afternoon of Reagan's inauguration, raised the administration's consciousness of U.S. vulnerability to the growing threat of Islamic terrorism.

The changes in the Middle East raised to a new level the threat to the U.S. of terrorism. Terrorism had not been a priority before 1980 because it was primarily confined to the Middle East and mostly directed at Israel. But that changed dramatically as the Iranian revolution showed Arab radicals that an Islamist "regime change" was possible and that terrorism could be a powerful weapon against the West. Also, the Afghan war became the breeding ground of a new, violent generation of Islamic militants motivated by a new pan-Islamic ideology.

Qaddafi and his military colleagues came to power in 1969 imbued with a secular Arab ideology championed by the leader of the Arab world at that time, Egyptian president Gamal Abdel Nasser. The young and idealistic Qaddafi came to power as a disciple of the older Nasser and initially tended to follow his lead on major Arab issues. By the time Nasser died of a heart attack two years later, the exuberant Qaddafi was already impatient with the more cautious policies of his idol.[3] He expressed his impatience by undisguised support for the anti-Israeli terror of the Palestine Liberation Organization (PLO). At decade's end he was on the first U.S. list of "state sponsors" of terrorism.

By 1979 Qaddafi was more than eager to challenge Egypt's new president, Anwar Sadat. With Nasser gone and Sadat moving toward peace with Israel, Qaddafi made his move to become a leader of the "confrontation" Arabs (later known as the "rejectionist" Arabs), fiercely opposing Sadat's accommodation with Israel. That led, however, to difficulties with a new American government that was no longer preoccupied elsewhere. The Reagan administration was in no mood to ignore a challenge and was willing to use political, economic, and especially military means to respond to Qaddafi.

In December 1979, after a mob burned the U.S. embassy in Tripoli to protest the Camp David Accords, U.S.–Libyan relations declined dramatically. In May 1980 President Carter closed the American mission in Tripoli. Recent terrorist incidents, especially the Iran hostage crisis, had sensitized the president, Congress, media, and public to the threat of terrorism. The stage was set by the confluence of events in the U.S. and the Middle East, so that starting in 1981, contention turned into confrontation, and confrontation into conflict.

1979 to 1989: Bilateral Confrontation

Confrontation between Qaddafi's regime and the Reagan administration persisted throughout the 1980s. Within months after taking office in January 1981, the Reagan administration accused Libya of running training camps for terrorists.[4] In May the United States closed the Libyan diplomatic mission in Washington, giving the reason that Libya was a supporter of international terrorism.[5] These were not the first terrorism charges the U.S. had leveled at Libya. In 1978 the Department of State had banned the sale of military equipment to Libya and cited as the reason Libyan support of unnamed terrorist groups.[6] The following year President Carter put Libya on the original list of state sponsors of terrorism.

Unlike in the 1970s, however, both sides were prepared to confront one another. The two countries had disputed Libyan territorial claims in the Gulf of Sidra since Qaddafi proclaimed it to be Libyan territorial waters in 1973. Qaddafi calculated Libya's waters in the Gulf by drawing a straight line across the 275-mile northern end of the Gulf and maintained this claim over the objections of the U.S., the USSR, and others.

Shortly after taking office, the Reagan administration adopted a worldwide policy of having U.S. armed forces challenge excessive claims of territorial waters and air space. Libyan claims were among the first to be challenged. The U.S. Sixth Fleet conducted "freedom of navigation" maneuvers in the Gulf of Sidra, defying Qaddafi's territorial claims, and in August of 1981 the first military clash occurred in the Gulf as Libyan fighter aircraft challenged U.S. Navy planes. Three Libyan fighter aircraft were downed, and two Libyan patrol vessels were destroyed. Qaddafi vowed to retaliate.[7]

Immediately following the Gulf of Sidra incident, reports of "hit squads" coming to assassinate President Reagan and other senior U.S. officials circulated in the White House and U.S. intelligence community. Reagan himself claimed to have intelligence to this effect.[8] The assassination of the U.S. defense attaché in Paris, France, on 6 December 1981 aroused suspicion that Libya was responsible.[9] In the following six months, the U.S. took additional measures against Libya, including ordering American citizens out of the country, embargoing Libyan oil, and prohibiting high-technology exports to the country.[10] The oil company Exxon took the early cue and closed out its operations in Libya. Other U.S. oil firms replaced Americans with other nationalities and continued operating.[11]

In early 1982 intelligence reports showed that Libya had rebuilt four hundred American trucks to transport tanks and military equipment, after having guaranteed the U.S. that the trucks would be used only for agricultural purposes.[12] The truck rebuild gave the Libyan army added mobility for its 1983 invasion of Chad. Reagan responded by using the powers of the Trade Expansion Act of 1962 to embargo crude oil imports.[13] He also limited the export of modern oil and gas equipment and technology that was not available from non–U.S. sources.[14]

Libya, Chad, and the United States

By mid-1982 Libya was deeply involved in destabilizing neighboring Chad in a dispute over the Aozou Strip. This disputed territory on the border with Chad, thought to have valuable uranium deposits, was claimed and occupied in 1973 by Libya and annexed in 1975. Irregular but frequent clashes resulted between the two countries in the late 1970s as Libyan forces periodically entered Chad and became involved in Chad's internal factional strife. This escalated in 1983 when the Libyan army invaded Chad and drove south against the forces of the Chadian government of Hissen Habre. The U.S. and France strongly supported Habre. In the context of this invasion and Qaddafi's public and covert support of terrorism, and after encouraging Libyan exiles seeking to overthrow Qaddafi, the high-profile head of the CIA, William Casey, made a pointed and not so veiled threat in late 1983 that Libyan activity was serious enough that it might lead to the removal of Qaddafi.[15]

Libya's provocative policy in Chad was part of a long-term Qaddafi effort to project power in Africa. This brought him into serious, direct confrontation not only with the U.S. but with France, whose armed forces were assisting Habre's army. Heretofore, France was solicitous of its economic ties with Libya, above all with its productive and profitable petroleum investments and commerce. However, it regarded its former colonies in Africa as areas of primary French security interest to be protected, if necessary, by the use of French military force. Above all, it was not about to be displaced in Chad by Qaddafi, who, if successful, would be emboldened to redouble his efforts underway to destabilize other Francophone African states on his border, thus undermining French influence in the region and strengthening his own.[16]

Libyan–U.S. relations continued to deteriorate, and by 1985 the confrontation was a regular feature in the American media, and by later that year there were press reports that the U.S. was engaged in covert operations to overthrow Qaddafi on the grounds that only regime change could stop Libyan support of terrorism and other radical policies.[17]

Economic sanctions of the U.S. on Libyan petroleum products were reinforced when all refined petroleum products from Libya were embargoed.[18]

Also, at this juncture the administration was concerned about Libyan "hit squads" seeking to kill American officials in Europe and the Middle East. The credibility of such reports was enhanced by the similar reports early in the Reagan presidency and by the attaché assassination in Paris in 1981. Receptivity in Washington to any such reports was therefore high. Tensions were rising fast, and the perception on both sides that stronger measures were needed to "teach" lessons was growing. It was a dangerous period when careful consideration of overall strategy and of next steps was demanded. The escalation continued, as did the risks of mistake and miscalculation.

Libya and the Abu Nidal Organization

None of these measures by Washington appeared to derail Qaddafi's strong support of Palestinian terrorism. Qaddafi seemed to move forward on this front heedless of Washington's concerns. Indeed, he seemed to revel in his increasing support and involvement as the decade progressed.

One of the most active and deadly of these terrorist organizations in the 1980s was the Abu Nidal Organization (ANO). Qaddafi allowed the ANO to establish a substantial presence in Libya in the early 1980s,[19] a presence that Qaddafi denied.[20] His support went beyond permitting an ANO presence. ANO training camps were opened, banking facilities made available, and movement of personnel and material facilitated. In short, Libya was, along with Syria where ANO was headquartered, its chief state supporter. Syrian fingerprints, figuratively speaking, appeared continually on incidents in and outside the Middle East because ANO's foot soldiers in the terrorist wars remained principally in Syria, the West Bank, and Lebanon. In 1987 Syria expelled the ANO, which then moved its headquarters from Damascus to Tripoli, making Libya the center of the most active, violent Mideast terrorism.[21]

The most spectacular strike by ANO after it established a presence in Libya occurred in December 1985, when ANO terrorists nearly simultaneously attacked passengers at the Rome and Vienna international airports, killing 19 and injuring 110. Most troubling about these and other attacks at this time was the signal that ANO was redirecting its terror from attacks on its Palestinian rivals and on Israel—heretofore its focus—to targets in Egypt, Turkey, and western Europe. Such a change represented a greater threat to Americans and Europeans, who, as in Rome and Vienna, were more likely to become victims of such attacks. The venue of ANO terrorism was expanding.[22]

The Reagan administration was quick to accuse Qadaffi of responsibility in the ANO airport incidents.[23] A month after the attacks Washington pointed to the "considerable amount of assistance" ANO received from Qaddafi and called on other nations to use economic sanctions to stop Libya's state sponsorship of terrorism. Reagan took the lead in January 1986 by using the International Emergency Economic Powers Act (IEEPA) to impose comprehensive trade and financial sanctions on Libya. With the exception of humanitarian cases, most U.S. exports and financial transactions were halted. Among the most important of Reagan's measures were those freezing Libyan government assets in U.S. banks, including hundreds of millions of dollars of deposits held in foreign branches of American banks—a controversial move in Europe.[24]

Reagan appealed to allies and friendly governments not to undermine the U.S. measures, even though they were unwilling to apply similar measures themselves.[25] For the most part the Europeans limited themselves to statements that they would not take advantage of the sanctions to increase trade and economic activity with Libya. The U.S. stepped up the pressure on Qaddafi in March by having the Sixth Fleet again challenge Libya's claims to the Gulf of Sidra. The fleet crossed a Qaddafi-proclaimed "Line of Death" and met the Libyan military response by sinking two Libyan patrol boats and destroying an antiaircraft missile site.[26]

Libya did not delay in responding, as the "tit-for-tat" measures escalated rapidly.[27] On 5 April a bomb destroyed the La Belle Discothèque in West Berlin, killing three and injuring over 150. U.S. servicemen assigned to Berlin heavily patronized the nightclub. In a dramatic television address to the nation on 14 April, Reagan revealed that the U.S. had intercepted communications between Tripoli and its embassy in East Berlin, which produced "evidence [that is] . . . direct, precise, irrefutable" that Libya was responsible for the disco bombing.[28] This bombing reinforced the reports of "hit squads" in western Europe and the belief that Libya was engaged in acts of war against the U.S.

On the morning of 15 April, American aircraft from the Sixth Fleet and from bases in England attacked military and government targets in and around Tripoli and Benghazi. Apart from the British, no other European government agreed to assist in the raid, and most disapproved of it publicly. Nonetheless, the administration went forward without hesitation, flying around rather than over those countries that closed their air space. Qaddafi's headquarters and residence, military airfields, suspected terrorist training camps, and other targets were struck. Reportedly, Qaddafi's adopted daughter was killed in the raid, and other members of his family injured. One casualty was reported on the U.S. side.[29]

American-European Cooperation

It is useful to note that the U.S. actions against Libya were, up to this point, essentially unilateral and for the most part responded to terrorist initiatives that Libya took or supported. The Reagan administration was not getting support from its allies in Europe for its Libyan policy and was reacting to Libya rather than strategically taking decisive actions that could end or greatly diminish the threat.

Administration officials recognized that they did not fully consult with allies before announcing the financial and economic measures in December 1985.[30] Deputy Secretary of State John Whitehead began a round of visits to nine NATO capitals in early 1986 only after the IEEPA sanctions had been imposed in an effort to gain support for U.S. measures already in place.[31] Likewise, on military matters allies complained that they were informed late or perfunctorily, without time to consider the situation. The French and other allies did not cooperate in the April 1986 strikes, at least in part, they said, because they learned of them only a day or so before the operation began.[32]

Certainly, in the mid-1980s Europe, other than the UK, was disinclined to take a proactive stance against Qaddafi, given its heavy dependence on Libyan oil, natural gas, and petroleum products. Some countries in southern Europe imported over half of their petroleum from Libya and had very large, long-term investments there. The U.S., in contrast, imported less that 10 percent of its petroleum from Libya and had substantial but not critical investments there. Much of Europe thought it could deal with Libya without confrontation. Hence, whatever consultations might be held, it was almost certain before the April air raid on Tripoli and Benghazi that, except for Margaret Thatcher's government, Europe would not join or approve.

The resulting disconnects between the U.S. and Europe on responding to Libyan terrorism, particularly after the Rome and Vienna incidents, was a serious U.S. weakness in dealing with Qaddafi. An American policy, such as that undertaken by the Reagan administration, required significant European understanding and cooperation to be successful. Limited military strikes and unilateral economic measures could not succeed on their own. The effort to involve allies was inadequate to the needs of the U.S.[33] Ironically, a different, more aggressive policy—such as invasion and overthrow of the regime in Libya—would not have required as much European support as the policy the administration undertook.

In nonmilitary spheres of counter-terrorism—diplomatic, intelligence, police, and judicial—American cooperation with Europe was extensive and productive throughout the decade, regardless of differences over the use of military force. France, for example, cooperated closely with American agencies on terrorism, even though Paris was at odds with Washington on almost all other important issues. Both nations simply decided they did not want political differences to interfere with their beneficial cooperative work against terrorists. This "CT exceptionalism"[34] continued throughout the 1980s and beyond.

What was not included in this exceptionalism, however, was the use of military force as a counter-terrorism tool against state sponsors of terrorism. Use of military force required high-level political decisions that most European governments were disinclined to take. Any decision in Washington to use force, therefore, was likely to result in little support and substantial criticism in Europe. European attitudes favored police and diplomatic methods for stopping the recognized threat of Arab terrorism. This difference was already apparent in April 1986 and to a large extent continues to this day.

The April 1986 raid, however, did produce a modest change in attitude by European governments. In May 1986 the Europeans, reacting to the U.S. strikes, decided to take nonmilitary measures to rein in Qaddafi. At the Tokyo economic summit that same month, the Group of Seven (G-7, which was the United States, Canada, Japan, France, the United Kingdom, Germany, and Italy) cited Libya as a supporter of international terrorism. The meeting presented a menu of measures recommended for use against countries that supported international terrorism—such as arms embargoes, restrictions on diplomatic missions of states sponsoring terrorism (Libya was not named), stronger cooperation for extradition of terrorists, and closer cooperation by law enforcement agencies. None of these was an economic sanction, however, and they were simply recommendations, which need not be implemented. The administration proclaimed the Tokyo statement a major advance against Libyan terrorism. It was, however, a carefully limited compromise that contained no support for the two most controversial tools Reagan relied on—economic sanctions and military force.

Yet the Europeans could see that the U.S. asset freeze, including investments and real estate, in American banks at home and in branches overseas was one of the more effective measures against Libya. Libya moved quickly after the freeze to try to unblock assets by taking action, for example, in British courts—ultimately successful—to gain access to funds blocked by Bankers Trust in London pursuant to the U.S. freeze. Then, after the G-7 Summit the European Community (EC) applied economic sanctions against Libya, with France taking the lead by reducing its imports of Libyan oil and petroleum products, reportedly by over 90 percent. Others reduced theirs but by much less.[35] Italy, most dependent on Libyan petroleum, took no reductions.

This was the first indication of European policy change, albeit limited, against Libya's strong support and practice of terrorism in Europe and elsewhere.[36] There were two good reasons for Europe to move on this front: first, to delay or make unnecessary further American military action, and second, to warn Qaddafi that his policies were pushing Europe and the U.S. together, not apart.

Qaddafi, the Abu Nidal Organization, and Pan Am Flight 73

The Gulf of Sidra incident in March and the April raid undoubtedly caused Qaddafi to reassess his strategy against the United States. It was clear that the U.S. could exercise its military superiority literally to the shores of Tripoli—and inland. The Libyan leadership's decision to attempt the La Belle disco bombing was probably a calculated strategy to use Libyan terrorist strikes to respond to American military strikes.

The disco bombing was the first time, however, that Libya turned directly and brazenly to terrorism by its own government agents to confront the U.S. Heretofore, Libya employed its own agents primarily to intimidate or murder Libyan exile opponents of the regime. The obvious Libyan "fingerprints" on this major act of international terrorism suggested that Libya did not know how to cover its tracks. It was caught in the act and paid the consequences. In the future it would learn to cover up its clandestine activities more carefully. A powerfully motivated Qaddafi soon escalated the level of terrorism and also his ability to cover his tracks.

Qaddafi turned to the Abu Nidal Organization to help him exact revenge. The ANO had years of experience, strong motivation, and committed cadres to carry out terrorist operations inside and outside the Middle East. Qaddafi had the motivation and the funds, but as the La Belle Disco attack demonstrated, he lacked the experience and the personnel to do the job right. Direct action by his intelligence agents could again lead to severe consequences for Libya if Libyan sponsorship became obvious. The ANO provided Qaddafi what he needed, a non-Libyan capability, and Qaddafi provided the ANO what it lacked, money, training camps, and logistical support. It was a marriage made in hell.

On 5 September 1986, only five months after the April raid, a group of ANO terrorists arrived in Karachi, Pakistan, from Syria and attempted to hijack Pan Am flight 73. The Boeing 747 landed in Karachi from Bombay, India, to take on passengers and fuel before proceeding to Frankfurt, Germany, en route to New York's JFK airport. While it was on the ground, four Palestinians stormed the plane and took it over. They demanded fuel with the intention of forcing the flight crew to fly the plane to an undisclosed destination in the Middle East.[37]

The flight crew unexpectedly managed to escape from the cockpit through an emergency chute, so the plane could not take off. Early in the hijacking the terrorists shot and killed an American to show they meant business. Then they crowded all 378 passengers, including eighty-eight Americans, to the center of the plane and surrounded them.[38]

After sixteen tense hours as the electrical power on board flickered and failed, the hijackers began indiscriminately killing passengers. At that point the Pakistani police and military boarded the plane and captured the hijackers. The toll was twenty-two passengers killed, including three Americans, and 150 wounded. The four ANO hijackers were tried, convicted, and sentenced to long prison terms by a Pakistani court.[39]

Besides the four Palestinians, there was a fifth member of the terrorist group in Karachi, a Libyan, who assisted the four and waited outside the airport during the hijacking. The police arrested him after intercepting his phone call to the Libyan embassy in Islamabad asking for assistance to get out of Pakistan. He was also tried and convicted and is still serving his sentence in Pakistan.

A Lack of Reaction

The U.S. failed to use the Karachi attack, as they did the Rome and Vienna airport attacks, to call attention to Libya's role in international terrorism. Yet circumstances on the ground in Libya were unchanged: ANO was functioning, Libyan support for ANO was strong, and Libyan fingerprints were evident on the Karachi incident as the Reagan administration recognized.[40] Yet the administration did not excoriate Qaddafi.

Several factors explain this silence about the Libyan connection. First, the administration, in explaining the success of the Tripoli and Benghazi strike, had said that it had taught Qaddafi a lesson and that as a result the threat from Libya was greatly reduced.[41] Highlighting Libyan involvement in Karachi would undercut the administration's argument that the air strikes had been effective in reducing the threat. Contradicting the administration's official position were press reports, sourced to unnamed officials, that nothing had changed in Libya and that Qaddafi's commitment to international terrorism was as high as ever.[42] These latter comments were the correct reading of Qaddafi's reaction to the April strike.

Second, the initial information about the four Palestinian terrorists showed that they had traveled to Pakistan from Damascus, strongly suggesting Syrian support for the attempted hijacking. Indeed, ANO was headquartered there, and therefore some Syrian responsibility is clear.[43] The following year, when the ANO headquarters in Syria were closed, Libya quickly agreed to its relocation in Tripoli. The confusion in this case was strikingly similar to that of two years later when the initial suspicion for the Lockerbie bombing fell on Syria and only later fell on Libya.

Third, since the Karachi attack was unsuccessful, and since only three of the twenty-two dead were Americans, the incident did not get the attention it might otherwise have received.

And finally, the Iran-Contra scandal broke several weeks after the Pan Am flight 73 incident. It resulted in a major disruption in American focus on anything but that amateurish, embarrassing, and destructive affair.

In any event, the administration failed to raise a hue and cry against Qaddafi. This now appears to have been a lost occasion to turn the spotlight on undiminished Libyan sponsorship of terrorism, despite the "lesson" of April 1986. It was also a lost chance, possibly, to complicate, interrupt, or stop Qaddafi's next attempt at revenge for the April 1986 air strikes—the Lockerbie tragedy.[44]

Fifteen months after the Pan Am flight 73 incident, on 21 December 1988, Pan Am flight 103 exploded over Lockerbie, Scotland, killing 270 people. This happened a month before Ronald Reagan left office and was Qaddafi's parting shot at his nemesis. This time Libya did not rely on a proxy organization, such as ANO, to do the deed.[45] In the aftermath of the failed ANO Karachi attack, Libya mounted its own operation with its own resources and personnel. It is unnecessary to repeat here the details of the Lockerbie story and Libya's role in it. It has been laid out many times in great detail, in news accounts and academic writings, in the UN Security Council documents, in both U.S. and Scottish indictments, in the Hague trial of the two Libyans, and in the decision of the Hague tribunal. Fifteen years after the event, Libya took responsibility for this abominable, uncivilized crime.

Reagan's Libya Policy: An Evaluation

Ronald Reagan placed terrorism at the center of his foreign policy concerns, with a focus on Lebanon. Libya came in second to the events in Lebanon. The PLO presence in Lebanon after Black September, the Israeli occupation of South Lebanon and Beirut, the series of American hostage takings, and the failed U.S. military peacekeeping operation: all combined to put Lebanon on the map as the major locus of Middle East terror in the 1980s. What was different was that in Lebanon, multiple regional players took leading roles and drove events for their own local reasons. The U.S. was not attempting regime change; it was supporting the Lebanese government and attempting to reduce Syrian and PLO influence.

In Libya, the U.S. was one of two protagonists. France's involvement was chiefly to counter Qaddafi's efforts in Africa and only secondarily to counter his support of terrorism. The U.S. was essentially in a bilateral dispute, especially since the Europeans decided it was not a fight they wished to participate in, and in any event their method of dealing with Libyan terror was, they thought, better than Reagan's approach. Nor was it the case that the Europeans had failed to make clear to the administration their reluctance to support military action. Finally, the Arab states equivocated because they were overwhelmingly focused on the Palestinians and Lebanon and because Qaddafi's pan-Arab nationalism was too appealing to their populations for them to risk open support of the U.S.

An effective regime-change policy in these circumstances required the U.S. to be willing to take decisive measures with minimal expectations of Europe and Middle Eastern support and to be committed to do whatever it took to succeed, including invasion and overthrow of the Libyan regime, if necessary. Given Qaddafi's powerful commitment to oppose the U.S., this required a well-designed strategy that provided a variety of options so that the U.S. would be sure to succeed.

The U.S. was more exposed and more at risk in Libya than in Lebanon in the 1980s. The U.S. actively engaged in Lebanon without suffering disastrous defeat. Indeed, the Marine withdrawal following the barracks bombing was a defeat but not a disaster. A peacekeeping effort failed, but U.S. influence continued strong in the region. In Libya there were no mediating circumstances or players to disguise or reduce the bilateral confrontation.

Policies are judged by results, and hence the final evaluation of Reagan's policy on Libya must therefore be that it was a failure. It openly attempted "regime change," but it could neither change the regime nor change the regime's policies. The failure of U.S. policy resulted from the lack of a strategic concept to guide it. The Reagan approach to Qaddafi's provocations was a series of quick-reaction responses, which were far from decisive.[46] That indecisiveness is fully understandable when one considers the bitter infighting over Libyan policy between Shultz and Weinberger throughout this period.[47] Reagan's two leading advisors were divided, and Reagan appears never to have decided between the two conflicting strategies being proposed by them.

Over the decade the Reagan administration seemed never to step back and consider whether a series of partial and *ad hoc* steps were effectively dealing with a chronic problem. Its calculation was that a tit-for-tat approach would be to America's advantage and to Libya's disadvantage because the U.S. could ratchet up the military pressure on Libya but Libya could not respond militarily. The miscalculation is best exemplified by examining the administration's use of military force in the light of its own "Weinberger Doctrine."

On 28 November 1984—while the confrontation with Libya was a center of administration attention—Secretary of Defense Caspar Weinberger announced at the National Press Club in Washington a policy known as "the Weinberger Doctrine."[48] Entitled "The Uses of Military Power," the speech was prompted by the truck bombing of the U.S. Marine barracks near the Beirut airport on 23 October 1983, in which 241 marines perished and which led to the Marines' withdrawal from Lebanon. Weinberger used the November 1984 speech to announce a policy decision to guide administration military action. It was a way to note the lessons learned from the failed Lebanon experience and also a commentary on the Vietnam War of a decade earlier.

Distilled, the Weinberger speech argued that the U.S. should not put forces into combat unless "vital" national interests were at stake. Such commitments of troops should be with the clear intention of winning and be made with the "assurance" of "sustained" support of Congress and the American people. Furthermore, there must be clearly defined political and military objectives and a capacity to achieve those objectives with the forces committed. Finally, said Weinberger, military action should only be a "last resort."[49]

Weinberger's doctrine was not followed with respect to Libya. At no time did the administration state or act like Libya represented a "vital" threat to U.S. interests, although the growth of terrorism was correctly considered a serious, expanding threat to the U.S. The occasional, limited military strikes were neither "wholehearted" nor "winning" military actions.[50] The military objectives were cloudy at best, as was the likelihood of achieving the political objectives. Congress and public opinion were supportive but only because they assumed, and were told, that military strikes were diminishing Libya's support of terrorism.[51] Finally, the use of force was far from a "last resort"; indeed at times, such as the April 1986 raids, it was a first resort.

Thus, eight years of bilateral confrontation ended in December 1988 with Qaddafi still in power, with the U.S. and its allies at odds on dealing with Libya, and above all with a huge, unsolved tragedy. The aftermath of the Lockerbie horror was a matter to be dealt with by the incoming president, George H. W. Bush.

1989 to 1998: A Multilateral Approach

Intermezzo

For over eighteen months after the December 1988 Lockerbie disaster, the intelligence and evidence were insufficient to determine who was responsible. It was clear that an explosive device, a bomb planted on the aircraft, caused the crash. But it was not clear who planted it or how. By early 1990 intelligence seemed to point inconclusively at Syria and the PFLP-GC (Popular Front for the Liberation of Palestine–General Command). But later in 1990 the forensic evidence collected in the massive effort on the ground in Scotland yielded results. By autumn of 1990 Libya was directly in the crosshairs of the investigators.[52]

During this period of uncertainty, Libya was still active. Since it was not suspect and most important was not identified in the press as a possible suspect, there was no reason for it not to continue its sponsorship and authorship of terrorism. In September 1989 a commercial aircraft of the Union des Transports Aerien (UTA), a French airline, was destroyed in an explosion over the desert of Niger after taking off from N'Djamena, Chad. The 189 deaths in that disaster were fewer than Lockerbie, but the French questions were identical to those of the U.S. about Lockerbie: what caused the explosion, and if it was deliberate, who was responsible?

The results of an intensive and professionally conducted investigation by French authorities led to the conclusion that, like Lockerbie, Libyan agents acting on the authority of the government of Libya conspired to place an explosive device on the plane and bring it down in a remote desert area where it would likely be difficult to find the debris and investigate the cause. (The Lockerbie device was probably intended to explode after the plane was over the Atlantic so that all traces would be lost in the ocean. A delayed departure from London resulted in the explosion over Scotland, where the debris was within reach of investigators.)

Even as Libya carried out these terrorist attacks, Qaddafi was publicly distancing himself from terrorist organizations that he had long supported. This posturing may well have been motivated by a downturn in Libya's economy, domestic tensions, and Qaddafi's need for a respite from the gradually tightening sanctions of the EC and the U.S. He was also looking to accommodate his annoyed and at times hostile Arab and southern neighbors after his embarrassing defeat in Chad and his failed meddling in their (Sudan, Tunisia, Egypt, Niger) internal affairs. His weakened position left him vulnerable to a riposte by these aggrieved states.

As Libya's foreign reserves dipped in 1989, Qaddafi made a public display of "course change." Libya announced that it had stopped the funding to various terrorist and other organizations and requested them to close their offices in Libya. Qaddafi was quoted as saying that "when we discovered that these groups were causing more harm than benefit to the Arab cause, we halted our aid to them completely and withdrew our support."[53] Nonetheless, his animus toward the U.S. was unabated. When the Reagan administration loosened oil sanctions slightly in January 1989, Qaddafi rejected this gesture from his despised foe and maintained his confrontation.[54]

He did, however, make a gesture to France in April 1990 barely six months after the UTA bombing. Again, his agents had covered their tracks well enough that Libyan involvement was still unknown. Qaddafi "intervened" with the Abu Nidal Organization to gain freedom for two French citizens and a Belgian that ANO held as hostages.[55] This intervention took place, it should be noted, eight months after Qaddafi's discovery of the harm ANO and others were doing "to the Arab cause." When the three were released, President François Mitterrand, unaware of the Libyan connection to UTA, offered "personal thanks"—an action that caused his popularity in France to drop. A year later, when leaks to the press suggested that Libya might have been responsible, Libya continued its "withdrawal of support" from known terrorist organizations. In August 1990 as press reports increasingly linked Libya to the Pan Am flight 103 bombing, Libya announced the move of the enfeebled ANO out of Libya and its return to Baghdad, where ANO began its rebellion against the PLO in 1973.[56]

But this intermezzo would soon end as the two criminal investigations reached their conclusions. In early 1991 the Lockerbie attack was traced to Libyan agents, and in succeeding months the UTA explosion was also shown to be a Libyan plot carried out by Libyan government agents and unwitting African operatives.

George H. W. Bush Reexamines American Policy

On taking office the George H. W. Bush administration did not immediately face decisions on the Pan Am/Lockerbie case, although leaks to the press of Syrian and Palestinian roles in the bombing circulated freely and frequently. As a result the families of the victims of Lockerbie were organized and vociferous in wanting strong action taken against those responsible, but they thought mostly in terms of Syria, as did the press and Congress. Pressure built on the administration to move even before the investigations were complete and the perpetrators determined, but President Bush kept his options open. Only in mid-1991, when the investigation was wrapping up and indictments were being prepared, did the administration act.[57]

The U.S. government concluded that Libyan intelligence officers "acted with the approval of the highest levels of the Libyan Government" when they blew up Pan Am flight 103.[58] The State Department's *Patterns of Global Terrorism–1991* report made the case that the pattern of Libyan government actions over a period of years ruled out a less sweeping conclusion. Specifically, it stated that "Libyan Government officials . . . have implemented and directed Libya's use of terrorism over the years as a tool of government policy" and that "[a]n operation of this sophistication and magnitude, involving people so close to the Libyan leadership, could have been undertaken only with the approval of senior Libyan officials."[59] The report also states that Libya continued to be a state supporter of terrorism: "The terrorist case against the [Libyan] government does not begin or end with the destruction of Pan Am flight 103. We have seen a consistent pattern of Libyan-inspired terrorism that continues after the Pan Am flight 103 atrocity to the present."[60]

Virtually simultaneously with the conclusion of the Lockerbie investigation, the French investigation reported equally damning forensic and circumstantial evidence that Libya was responsible for the bombing of UTA flight 772.[61] The position of the U.S. government was that the similarities between the two incidents were numerous and clear. Libya directed its intelligence agents to plan and execute both operations using very similar suitcase bombs with similar sophisticated timing devices to destroy civilian airliners of the U.S. and France in retaliation for the political and military actions taken in opposition to the policies and actions of Libya.

These parallel outcomes presented an opportunity to attempt a different policy with respect to Libya and terrorism. The horrendous attacks on both American and European civil aviation opened the way to trans-Atlantic solidarity. As noted above, Europe was moving slowly toward action against Qaddafi, while the Bush administration, knowing where the investigations were leading, was interested in European support for its Libyan policy. The magnitude of the loss of life (over 450 dead) and the implications of not coordinating and cooperating were such that the first resort of the Bush administration was to work with the French and British and, with their support, with the other European states to develop a strong, common policy against Libya.[62]

The Bush administration put together an initiative to bring the Atlantic community together to quash Libyan terror. The essential new element was that the primary goal was to end Libyan terrorism, not necessarily to end the Qaddafi regime. The U.S. position was made clear to other governments with the caveat that, if nonmilitary means could not stop Libyan terrorism, military action remained a real option. This was a significant change. While keeping the military option on the table, the new administration decided to attempt to achieve its goal, an end to Libya's policies of terrorism, short of military action. The administration adopted a more balanced coercive strategy that was proportional to the limited objective of policy change and that made it easier to mobilize multilateral participation.[63]

From Unilateral to Multilateral in Six Months

The next phase opened even before the French, U.S., or Scottish charges were revealed. Following an American initiative, multiple diplomatic contacts pointed to the possibility of common action once the charges were made public. In November the three injured states—the U.S., Britain, and France—jointly declared Libya responsible for the two attacks and called on it to turn over those charged and cooperate fully with the investigations. In December the EC called on Libya to accede to the demands of the three and threatened economic sanctions if it did not.

This began a period of Libyan backpedaling and concessions in an attempt to stave off the worst of the dangers it faced. The U.S. was seriously considering major military action, and the Europeans were gearing up for serious sanctions. Meanwhile, the American, British, and French governments continued their joint efforts and agreed to move the issue quickly into the UN Security Council.

In response to this mounting pressure, Qaddafi arrested the two men mentioned in the U.S. and Scottish charges[64] but refused to extradite them to either of the two countries. The U.S., UK, and France considered this step inadequate, and the three nations moved the matter quickly to the UN Security Council, asking for council action to condemn Libya and support the turnover of those charged in both cases to the three countries. Qaddafi further prevaricated by announcing he would turn over the two Lockerbie suspects to an acceptable international tribunal. This did little to help him, even within the Arab states, whose moderate leaders were fed up with Qaddafi's disruptive and interfering policies and were repelled by the mass murder represented by the deaths of over 450 innocent international travelers.

There was little resistance in the council to the proposal by the U.S., the UK, and France. United Nations Security Council Resolution 731 received the unanimous support of the fifteen-member Security Council in January 1992.[65] It deplored Libyan stonewalling and gave Libya a sixty-day period to provide "a full and effective" response to the three nations. When the deadline passed without Qaddafi complying, a second resolution, UN Security Council Resolution 748, imposing sanctions, was passed on 31 March without objection—but with abstentions.[66]

Thus, within six months of the U.S. indictment, the decade-long bilateral dispute between Libya and the United States was transformed into a dispute between Libya and the United Nations Security Council. This "multilateralization of sanctions" gave greater coercive credibility to U.S. policy. The joint action of the three veto-wielding members and the revulsion expressed by other council members, as the three detailed their investigations and evidence, put Qaddafi into an international box from which he did not escape for a decade.

For that decade Libyan energies and attention were all but totally consumed by the efforts to break out of the box. For five of those ten years its efforts were to no avail; the box remained firmly closed. Indeed, in November 1993, after Libya refused to cooperate with the council or with any of the three complaining states, a third Security Council resolution, Resolution 883, was approved, tightening the sanctions even further by, *inter alia*, prohibiting the sale of petroleum equipment to Libya and freezing nonpetroleum assets of the Libyan government outside Libya.[67]

Again, this third resolution was passed without a negative vote, although China, Pakistan, Morocco, and Djibouti abstained, and Russia was a reluctant vote in favor. Washington failed to get the complete package of sanctions it argued for, but the sentiment for increasing sanctions in some fashion was strong. The differences among council members revolved around how stringent those increased measures should be.

The three sanctions resolutions against Libya were groundbreaking documents of the UN in its role in countering terrorism. Resolution 731 was the first chapter VII resolution ever passed by the council condemning a terrorist act. Resolution 748 broke new ground by requiring a member state to formally renounce terrorism and "demonstrate" its renunciation. And sanctions imposed by both Resolutions 748 and 883 were the first Security Council sanctions voted against a member state for engaging in terrorism.

This was also the first time the council decided to use so-called smart sanctions, or more accurately "targeted sanctions." The sanctions were "targeted" in the first instance on areas related to the terrorist acts. Hence, Libya's civil aviation was sanctioned, a total arms embargo was instituted, and Libya's diplomatic establishments were reduced because they harbored agents of the country's intelligence services, many of whom participated in and managed the conspiracies that led to the destruction of both airliners. In all of its sanctions the council attempted, insofar as possible, to make the sanctions hurt the government most and the average Libyan least. For example, there was an exception to the aviation ban so all Libyan Muslims could take hajj pilgrimage flights to Mecca for this important religious rite.

These measures, besides being unprecedented, effectively isolated Libya from the world community. No one was allowed to use air travel to enter or leave Libya. Its diplomatic missions were greatly reduced in size worldwide, hampering its ability to use those missions to meddle in the affairs of other nations. There were also parallel efforts regarding Libyan diplomatic personnel in which many nations mutually agreed (in some cases tacitly) that a diplomat expelled or denied a visa to enter one country would not be allowed into other countries. This was a great assist to one of the objectives of that particular sanction, which was to target Libyan intelligence agents and force them back into Libya. This most important and successful element among the sanctions has been among the least noticed by journalists and scholars.

The history of the years following the passage of Security Council Resolution 731 was no longer a story of bilateral confrontation between the U.S. and Libya but one of multilateral insistence that Libya cease supporting terrorism and cooperate or suffer international consequences.

Qaddafi could not bring himself to conform to the demands of the Security Council and thus spent years attempting to get out from under the council's sanctions without complying. The political energy expended on this task effectively took Libya out of the terrorism game for a decade. In fact, since the imposition of the sanctions in 1992, Libya is not known to have been involved in any international acts of terror,[68] according to the records of the U.S. government as published in its annual reports on terrorism, *Patterns of Global Terrorism*. In fact the 1996 *Patterns* report stated, "Terrorism by Libya has been sharply reduced by UN sanctions."[69]

The Four-Year Standoff

From 1992 until 1996 there was no significant movement toward resolving the dispute between Libya and the Security Council. Libya spent the time trying to break the solid support for the sanctions. It went around the council by attempting to convince its neighbors, especially Egypt, to stop enforcing the sanctions along Libya's borders. This would have allowed smuggling of embargoed commercial products and arms. It also attempted to get bordering states and others in Africa to allow flights leaving Libya to land in their countries, thus breaking the aviation restrictions. Qaddafi tried any and all ways of breaking the sanctions, from sympathy appeals to threats, and at times he lashed out in frustration. He was unsuccessful.

Libya claimed in 1993, for example, that the sanctions had caused the deaths of more than 800 Libyan citizens and cost billions of dollars to the Libyan economy. Qaddafi also appealed to his neighbors to assist in brokering an agreement with the UN and suggested he would open Libya's borders to greater investment and tourism if the sanctions were lifted. Then in 1995, taking another tack, Libya expelled foreign workers, claiming that the sanctions had caused domestic unemployment and an economic downturn. To underline its point Libya requested permission for an exception to the civil air sanction so that charter flights could repatriate migrant African workers living in Libya who were unemployed because of the sanctions-caused recession.[70]

Repeated appeals to Arab unity, to African solidarity, and to Non-Aligned Movement (NAM) loyalty and offers of significant financial advantages to many countries made little progress. The sanctions remained in place and were essentially observed by all nations. Although some nations went around sanctions occasionally in minor ways, this unprecedented support for UN sanctions held. It might well have continued for years longer except for disunity among the nations that originally brought the issue to the Security Council. Ironically, it was not the Arab, African, or NAM nations that initiated the collapse of the solidarity but rather the U.S. and the Europeans.

The Collapse of Solidarity
In July 1996 the U.S. Congress passed the Iran and Libya Sanctions Act (ILSA), which required the U.S. government to sanction American and foreign companies that invested more than $40 million in gas and oil projects in Iran or Libya or that exported goods or technology to help Libya acquire weapons or increase its aviation capabilities.[71] The original bill introduced in the Congress targeted only Iran, but before final passage in the Senate a last-minute amendment offered by Senator Edward Kennedy added Libya.[72] The amendment responded to intense lobbying by families of the victims of the Lockerbie bombing. The Clinton administration opposed the bill with the Libya amendment on the grounds that by angering the Europeans it risked undermining the UN sanctions against Libya.[73] This perception was quite accurate. ILSA set in motion a chain of events that did more than undermine them; it ultimately ended them.

The European reaction to the ILSA was immediate, sharp, and negative.[74] The ILSA, the EU said, redefined the restrictions imposed by the Security Council and presumed a U.S. jurisdiction to police and adjudicate the conduct of European companies for activities conducted beyond American territory and not involving American citizens or property. It was done without consultation with or taking account of those allies, who helped create the sanctions. This reaction was hardly a surprise, since earlier and for the same reasons the European Union had expressed outrage and threatened retaliation over the passage of similar legislation—the Helms-Burton Act—that sanctioned foreign companies that purchased or otherwise dealt in expropriated U.S. property in Cuba. The European Commission threatened to make the retaliatory regulations it was formulating against Helms-Burton apply also to the ILSA.[75]

Reflecting their influence in getting the ILSA passed, a delegation of relatives of the victims of the Lockerbie bombing attended the White House bill-signing ceremony. The "Lockerbie families," as they were known informally,[76] were the most important factor in converting the Iran Sanctions Act (ISA) into the ILSA. Earlier in the year they were also instrumental in the passage of the Antiterrorism and Effective Death Penalty Act of 1996, which permitted civil suits in U.S. courts for the compensation of victims and victims' families for terrorist acts committed outside the United States. In May 1996 under the terms of that law, the Lockerbie families opened a civil suit in federal court against the government of Libya for compensation.[77]

The congressional and presidential actions to approve the ILSA were taken under the influence of another significant event. The week before Congress voted on the bill, a TWA airliner, flight 800, exploded shortly after takeoff from JFK airport in New York with the loss of all 230 people aboard. In the immediate aftermath of the tragedy terrorism was strongly suspected. Much later, the final report of the National Transportation Safety Board (NTSB) concluded that the explosion was caused not by terrorism but by an electrical failure that caused a fuel tank to explode.

Two days after Clinton signed the ILSA law, French president Jacques Chirac threatened "immediate retaliation" if any French companies came under ILSA review. His quick reaction to the Clinton administration's backing of the legislation was explained by news that two French petroleum companies, ELF and Total, had expressed interest in increasing investments in Iran and Libya. Later that same month the EU announced that it would appeal to the World Trade Organization (WTO) if the U.S. took action against any European company for doing business with Libya.[78]

The international solidarity on the Libyan issue, which the U.S. had forged in 1991 and which lasted with only minor difficulties for five years, weakened sharply following the enactment of ILSA. Like a well-knit sweater whose last yarn end has been pulled too hard, it started to unravel more rapidly with each succeeding pull on the yarn.

At first there were only a few, hesitant yanks—more to test it than to unravel it—but with time they became more frequent and determined. What Libya had been unable to do in years of concentrated effort, ILSA did in months. In less than a year solidarity was gone, and only high-level attention and strenuous diplomatic efforts could keep the remaining support from dissipating. However, the political will among the Europeans to spend the time and effort against Libya was gone. This gave Libya room to maneuver, and Qaddafi was quick to take advantage. In October 1996 he attributed 21,000 deaths and $19 billion in losses to the sanctions—a "tragic toll," he claimed. Turkey, that same month, signed a new bilateral trade pact during a visit to Libya by Prime Minister Erbakan.[79] In November Italy's state-owned oil company signed an agreement to develop Libyan gas fields and build a pipeline to Italy at a cost of $3 billion—potentially the first significant energy investment in Libya since the sanctions began.[80]

In 1997 the unraveling accelerated. The year's events started incongruously when the Vatican established full diplomatic relations with Libya to "recognize recent positive results in the area of religious freedom."[81] In a bold move in May Qaddafi defied the Security Council, as he had been unable to do for five years. He violated the sanctions by flying from Libya to Niger on an official visit. Niger, with its finger to the political wind, allowed his plane to land.[82] In August the presidents of Chad, Mali, Niger, and Burkina Faso met with Qaddafi and jointly agreed that the five nations would "develop their economic relations and reinforce the mechanisms of cooperation with the goal of reinforcing stability in the region."[83] It was not by accident that, in the aftermath of the public U.S.-French split on ILSA, francophone African states took the lead on that continent in opening the door to Libya. They had likely checked with Paris.

The Arab League joined the march by urging all Arab countries to "take measures to alleviate the sanctions on Libya," including by allowing Qaddafi to travel by plane to member states. The League's resolution also encouraged Arab states to release nonpetroleum funds frozen in their banks.[84]

Other American missteps revealed further weakness. In May 1997, prompted by the Lockerbie families, Senator Kennedy and other senators urged the administration to back a Security Council resolution to impose a complete embargo on Libyan oil. The futility of attempting to move in such a direction, when support for maintaining existing sanctions had been seriously eroded, was so apparent that the initiative went nowhere. Rather, it highlighted the shifting power balance on the issue, thus accelerating, not retarding, the unraveling already underway.

The most dramatic and significant event of 1997 demonstrated that support for sanctions was slipping seriously. The official visit to Libya in October of South African president Nelson Mandela was the first by a global leader since before 1991. It called the sanctions into question with particular force, even though Mandela observed the sanctions by arriving overland in Libya from Egypt. Because Qaddafi had been a strong supporter of the African National Congress (ANC) in its struggle against apartheid, Mandela presented him during the visit with South Africa's highest honor, the Order of Good Hope.[85]

The visit was a turning point. Mandela was a serious world leader who could not easily be dissuaded from his course and whose influence was very strong in Africa. Qaddafi had wooed African governments since sanctions began, thinking that Africa would prove most susceptible to Libyan offers of money and other financial support. He closed out 1997 by playing another card in his struggle to beat the sanctions: letters to the Lockerbie families proposing a financial settlement and urging them to oppose continued sanctions.

As 1998 began, the cracks became fissures, and Qaddafi was hard at work to exploit them. In February 1998 the International Court of Justice in The Hague declared that the court had the right to decide if Libya must surrender its nationals to the U.S. or UK.[86] This represented a partial victory for Libya, since the three nations that were demanding the turnover argued that the court had no authority to act once the UN Security Council had addressed the problem as a threat to international peace and security. Libya quickly went to the Security Council and in March got the debate it wanted on sanctions, at which it presented claims of human and economic losses and injury.[87] The debate served as a useful forum for Libya to accomplish its main goal at that stage: to appeal to the larger international audience. The veto powers of France, the UK, and the U.S. made lifting of sanctions out of the question at that point.

The second major defection came in June 1998. Following the lead of Mandela, his fellow heads of state in the Organisation of African Unity (OAU) called for OAU member states to suspend compliance with the UN's civil air sanctions for all religious, humanitarian, and OAU-related flights. The same communiqué included a statement that, as of September of 1998, the OAU would cease observing UN sanctions on Libya if the American and British governments did not agree to try the Lockerbie suspects in a third country.[88]

Getting to a Compromise

By early 1998 it was clear that a compromise would have to occur if sanctions were not to become completely hollow. Secretary of State Madeleine Albright wrote in her memoirs, "As our prospects for maintaining sanctions dimmed . . . we began to consider other options."[89] As the UN Security Council debate began in early 1998, the U.S. and UK Lockerbie families gathered to discuss their options in light of Libya's offer of compensation. They could not agree on the questions of a financial settlement and accepting a trial of the accused Libyans at the International Court of Justice in The Hague or in a neutral country. While the Lockerbie families were almost never unanimous on strategy or tactics, the disagreement at this time demonstrated that even those most affected by Libyan terrorism did not agree on how to deal with it.

In the face of this string of setbacks, British Foreign Secretary Robin Cook and Secretary of State Albright announced a "take-it-or-leave-it" compromise in August 1998. The trial of the two accused Libyan agents would be held in the Netherlands, but it would be conducted under Scottish law. If convicted, any prison sentence would be served in Britain. Albright added that if Libya did not accept the offer, the U.S. would press for more sanctions, including an oil embargo.[90] The proposal resulted, once again, in a series of moves by various players. Almost immediately Mandela, the Arab League, Egypt, and Sudan endorsed the Anglo-American compromise.[91] With similar speed the Security Council met and voted to suspend sanctions if Libya accepted the offer and, additionally, cooperated with the ongoing French investigation of the UTA bombing. Libyan rejection of this solution would, the council said, open the possibility of additional sanctions.[92]

Qaddafi accepted but insisted on several stipulations and guarantees before the actual surrender of the two Libyans.[93] Libya wanted guarantees that there would be no extradition to the U.S. or the UK and that, if convicted, sentences would be served in a third country or in Libya. By year's end UN Secretary-General Kofi Annan went to Tripoli to attempt to settle the impasse,[94] but it continued into the new year. On 19 March 1999 Nelson Mandela, on another trip to Libya, announced that the Libyan suspects would be surrendered within the month.[95]

On 5 April 1999 the two Libyans were delivered to The Hague for trial, following an agreement that any jail sentences would be served in Britain but under UN supervision.[96] UN sanctions were immediately suspended. The trial began on 3 May 2000 with Abdel Basset al-Meghrahi and Al-Amin Khalifa Fhimah in the dock charged with murder and other crimes. The defense did not present any case to counter the prosecution's case. On 31 January 2001 the three judges unanimously convicted al-Meghrahi of murder and sentenced him to life imprisonment. Khalifa was freed with a verdict of "not proven."[97]

The U.S. held up final settlement until Libya publicly renounced terrorism, fulfilled all requirements of the Security Council resolutions, and agreed to financial compensation for the victims' families.[98] A compensation agreement was reached in August 2003 between Libya and the Lockerbie families (Victims of Pan Am flight 103), including a letter from Libya to the UN accepting responsibility for the Pan Am flight 103 incident.[99] In July 1999 the United Kingdom renewed diplomatic relations with Libya,[100] and the following month Libya paid $31 million to France for the families of those killed aboard UTA flight 772.[101] France stated that Libya's payment constituted acceptance of responsibility by Libya for the UTA flight 772 incident. After the Lockerbie compensation was agreed in 2003, Libya agreed to additional compensation for most of the families of UTA flight 772.[102] Finally, on 12 September 2003 the Security Council lifted the UN sanctions permanently. The United States initially delayed lifting its sanctions and did not remove Libya from the list of states sponsoring terrorism (a severe form of American unilateral sanctions) until May 2006, when it announced that Libya would be removed from the list after a forty-five-day waiting period. This delay in getting off the list caused Libya to delay the final payments to the Lockerbie families.

The Multilateral Policy: An Evaluation

In evaluating the events that led to the suspension of sanctions, one cannot ignore the irony in the role played by ILSA. The U.S. Congress began the unraveling of the sanctions in a futile attempt to strengthen them, and it did so at the behest of the most staunchly anti-Libyan pressure group, the Victims of Pan Am Flight 103.

Without ILSA the sanctions might conceivably have continued indefinitely. Whether, in that event, the matter would have been settled satisfactorily is an open question. Nevertheless, it was settled and by a compromise that left no one fully satisfied but left most with the sense that some small measure of justice had been achieved. The Libyan regime was effectively proven guilty of bombing Pan Am flight 103 and UTA flight 772, and the sanctions were important in getting the regime to admit responsibility, demonstratably renounce terrorism, and pay compensation.

Most important, sanctions took Libya out of terrorism for the decade of the 1990s and, possibly, for good. This is no mean achievement, given the ferocity with which Qaddafi and his government entered that decade, dedicated to using massive indiscriminate terror to advance his Arab nationalist agenda. It showed that sanctions can be a useful tool for the UN, an international institution known for its inability in most cases to agree on tough measures and still less to persevere in implementing them on those rare occasions when they are agreed.

But the outcome also meant that only one low-ranking individual was effectively judged guilty for two of the most horrendous acts of criminal slaughter in the sordid history of modern state-sponsored terror. Such an outcome cannot be considered truly satisfactory. For those who sought to put Qaddafi in the dock or bring his regime down, the results fell far short. To enter the twenty-first century with Qaddafi potentially on the road to rehabilitation and reentry into the normal comity of nations is hard for the victims of his murderous policies, and many others, to accept.

For those who see great value in UN sanctions, it was at most a partial victory in two respects. First, it did demonstrate the force of legitimacy that the UN had: that is, it can promote observance when many nations would wish to avoid the duty (and in this case would desert it as soon as an opportunity came to do so at no cost). But it also showed how essential to the UN's success was the unity, cooperation, and constancy of the major powers. As soon as those powers lost their unity, the sanctions weakened. Legitimacy alone, without that power to back it up, would not have worked.

UN sanctions can encourage and strengthen international norms and promote observance. To do so, however, this case strongly suggests that the UN must have the backing of those nations wielding most of the power. Without that, it will fail. An anecdote underlines this: In an airport meeting with reporters on his return from a negotiating session in Baghdad with Sadaam Hussein in the late 1990s, Secretary-General Kofi Annan replied to a reporter's question about whether diplomacy with Saddam Hussein was of any use. Annan replied that diplomacy can be a powerful tool in preserving the peace but that diplomacy backed by the threat of force can be even more powerful. And so it was in the Libyan sanctions case.

Sanctions were a partial success, but alone they were insufficient to bring Qaddafi to comply with the Security Council resolutions and renounce terrorism. Another powerful factor was at play. Qaddafi's ideology of Nasserite Arab nationalism, which had fueled his terrorism in the 1970s and 1980s, was a spent force by the turn of the century. It had been replaced by a more virulent, pan-Islamic, religious terrorism that aims to destroy both the West and secular Islamic rulers like Qaddafi. Most dangerous of all, the new ideology is very attractive to Libya's youth. Qaddafi was concerned about the rise of Islamic fundamentalism and the influence of jihadists within Libya, and this made him more susceptible to U.S. pressures.

No longer rampaging or defiant, as he was in the 1970s and 1980s, Qaddafi knows that he and other secular Islamic rulers are not the leaders of the new terrorism; they are its primary targets. We should not mistake Qaddafi's change of policy as a change of heart. He is gambling that secular Arab moderates and the Europeans can help him. He calculates that if he forswears terrorism and weapons of mass destruction he will fare better than if he is left isolated to face his implacable, extremist coreligionists alone.

On balance, therefore, the evaluation of the multilateral policy on Libya is that it worked well for over a decade for three presidents—Bush

41, Clinton, and Bush 43. The major credit for this must go to the first of these, George H. W. Bush, who initiated it. It is a wise policy that seriously weakened Qaddafi and advanced American counter-terrorism goals.[103]

Notes

1. A very good, recent one-volume history of modern Libya is Dirk Vandewalle, *A History of Modern Libya* (New York: Cambridge University Press, 2006).

2. One recent example is the excellent essay by Bruce W. Jentleson and Christopher A. Whytock, "Who 'Won' Libya? The Force-Diplomacy Debate and Its Implications for Theory and Policy," *International Security* 30, no. 3 (Winter 2005–2006): 47–86.

3. For detailed examinations of Libya under Qadaffi; see *Qadhafi's Libya, 1969–1994*, ed. Dirk Vandewalle (London: MacMillan, 1995); see also Mansour O. El-Kikhia, *Libya's Qaddafi: The Politics of Contradiction* (Jacksonville, FL: University Press of Florida, 1998), chapters 1, 3, and 5.

4. Bernard Gwertzman, "U.S. Expels Libyans and Closes Mission, Charging Terrorism," *New York Times*, 7 May 1981. See also United Press International, "Qaddafi Is Reported to Prepare Gunmen to Kill the President," *New York Times*, 22 November 1981; Charles Mohr, "Europeans Link Terror to Arabs but Disagree on Soviets," *New York Times*, 23 June 1981. For background information, see *New York Times*, "Exposing the Libyan Link," 21 June 1981.

5. Gwertzman, "U.S. Expels Libyans and Closes Mission."

6. Philip Taubman, "Libya Using U.S. Trucks to Haul Soviet Tanks," *New York Times*, 21 January 1982; see also Thomas W. Lippman, "Trade Ban Irks Libyans; Tripoli Prefers Boeings, but U.S. Won't Sell Them," *Washington Post*, 11 August 1978.

7. Michael Getler, "U.S. Navy Fighters Shot Down Two Libyan Jets," *Washington Post*, 20 August 1981. For details about U.S./Libyan relations surrounding this event, see Haynes Johnson, "The Believe It or Not Show: On Libya, a New Standard of Incredibility," *Washington Post*, 8 December 1981; and Moammar Qaddafi, "We Refuse to Assassinate" (excerpts of interview with Moammar Qaddafi), *Washington Post*, 7 December 1981.

8. Johnson, "The Believe It or Not Show."

9. See Gary Clyde Hufbauer, Jeffrey J. Schott, and Kimberly Ann Elliott, *Economic Sanctions Reconsidered: History and Current Policy*, 2d ed. (Washington, DC: Institute for International Economics, 1990), 140. See also Jeffrey J. Schott, *Trade Sanctions and U.S. Foreign Policy* (Washington, DC: Carnegie Endowment for International Peace, 14 September 1982), 16. See also David A. Flores, "Export Controls and the U.S. Effort to Combat International Terrorism," *Law and Policy in International Business* 13 (1981): 582.

10. Karen Elliott House, "U.S. Will End Libya Oil Buying, Technology Sales," *Wall Street Journal*, 11 March 1982, 2.

11. Walter S. Mossberg, "U.S. Firms Urged to Bring Home Americans Who Have Jobs in Libya," *Wall Street Journal*, 11 December 1981. See also John M. Goshko, "OPEC Turns Down Libya's Request for Retaliation; Oil Companies Bow to Reagan's Wishes; Oil Firms Bow to President on Pullout," *Washington Post*, 12 December 1981.

12. Taubman, "Libya Using U.S. Trucks to Haul Soviet Tanks."

13. *Trade Expansion Act of 1962*, Public Law 87-794, 76 Stat. 872, 87th Cong., 2d sess. (11 October 1962), sec. 232 as amended by 19 U.S.C. 1862, amendment 4907, sec. 1e (10 March 1982).

14. House, "U.S. Will End Libya Oil Buying," 2.

15. Jonathan S. Gration: "William Casey's eagerness to bash Qadhafi was a primary factor in the decision to support Habre. It appears his personal agenda and perception of President Reagan's foreign policy direction pushed the CIA into a more active role in covert operations in Third World countries." See Jonathan S. Gration, "United States Assistance to Chad: Qadhafi-Bashing?," paper written for National Security Policy Process, National War College, Fort McNair, Washington, DC, 18 December 1992, 8–9, National Defense University Special Collections, <http://www.ndu.edu/library/n3/93-E-031.pdf> (accessed 14 July 2005). According to Richard Keeble, "In 1982, away from the glare of the media, Hissene Habre, with the backing of the CIA and French troops, overthrew the Chadian government of Goukouni Wedeye." Human Rights Watch records: "Under President Reagan, the United States gave covert CIA paramilitary support to help install Habre in order, according to secretary of state Alexander Haig, to 'bloody Gadafi's nose.'" Bob Woodward, in his semi-official history of the CIA, reveals that the Chad covert operation was the first undertaken by the new CIA chief William Casey and that throughout the decade Libya ranked almost as high as the Soviet Union as the "'bête noir' of the administration." Richard Keeble, "The Secret War Against Libya," n.d., *Medialens*, <http://www.medialens.org/articles/the_articles/articles_2002/rk_secret_war.html> (accessed 13 July 2005). For more details, see Bob Woodward, *Veil: The Secret Wars of the CIA, 1981–1987* (New York: Simon and Schuster, 1987), 96.

16. Reuters, "Chad Says Rebels Hold a Third of the Country," *New York Times*, 26 June 1983; E. J. Dionne Jr., "France Weighing Troops for Chad," *New York Times*, 12 July 1983.

17. Bob Woodward and Barbara Feinman, "CIA Anti-Qaddafi Plan Backed; Reagan Authorized Covert Operation to Undermine Libyan Regime," *Washington Post*, 3 November 1985.

18. U.S. General Accounting Office (GAO), *Libyan Trade Sanctions*, GAO/NSIAD-87-132BR (Washington, DC: GPO, May 1987), 18. See also David K. Shipler et al., "Trail of Mideast Terror: Seeking a Link to Libya," *New York Times*, 5 January 1986.

19. Elaine Sciolino, "Abu Nidal Backing Is Said to Be Wide," *New York Times*, 19 January 1986; Shipler et al., "Trail of Mideast Terror."

20. Bernard Weintraub, "Terrorists Train at Fifteen Libyan Sites, U.S. Official Says," *New York Times*, 6 January 1986.

21. See below discussion of Pan Am flight 73.

22. U.S. Department of State, *Patterns of Global Terrorism–1985* (Washington, DC: GPO, 1986), 9–12. See also Associated Press, "Abu Nidal Tied to Turkish Attack," *New York Times*, 7 November 1986; "Text of State Department Report in Libya Under Qaddafi," *New York Times*, 9 January 1986. See also Lou Cannon, "U.S. Makes New Bid for Sanctions," *Washington Post*, 16 January 1986.

23. U.S. Department of State, *Patterns of Global Terrorism–1985*, 5; "Transcript of President Reagan's News Conference on Foreign and Domestic Issues," *New York Times*, 8 January 1986.

24. David Hoffman, "President Orders Freeze on Libyans' U.S. Assets; 'Hundreds of Millions' Affected, Official Says," *Washington Post*, 9 January 1986. See also "Transcript of President Reagan's News Conference," *New York Times*, 8 January 1986.

25. Don Oberdorfer, "Reagan Appeals to Allies Not to Thwart Sanctions," *Washington Post*, 10 January 1986.

26. George C. Wilson and David Hoffman, "U.S. Ends Naval Exercises off Libya," *Washington Post*, 28 March 1986. For background information about the exercises, see Global Security, "Operation Attain Document," GlobalSecurity.org, <http://www.globalsecurity.org/military/ops/attain_document.htm> (accessed 14 July 2005).

27. Term attributed to Secretary of Defense Caspar Weinberger. See, by way of comparison, George P. Shultz, *Turmoil and Triumph: My Years as Secretary of State* (Woodbridge, CT: Charles Scribner's Sons, 1993), 680. Shultz's memoir is most revealing of the tensions between him and Weinberger, who favored minimal or no military action against Libya, according to Shultz.

28. Ronald Reagan, "Transcript of Address by Reagan on Libya," *New York Times*, 15 April 1986.

29. George C. Wilson, "Qaddafi Was a Target of U.S. Raid; 'Hoped We'd Get Him,' Official Says; At Least One Jet Aimed at Compound," *Washington Post*, 18 April 1986. See also Edward Schumacher, "Libya a Week After Raid: Qaddafi Seems Firmly in Control," *New York Times*, 24 April 1986; Edward Schumacher, "Wide Damage Seen; Daughter of Qaddafi Is Said to Have Died," *New York Times*, 16 April 1986; "Doctor Describes 'Terror' among Qaddafi Family," *New York Times*, 16 April 1986; Charles Fishman, "For Missing Pilots' Relatives, 'the News Is Nothing Good,'" *Washington Post*, 16 April 1986.

30. Karen DeYoung, "British Dubious About Sanctions; View That Moves Are Counterproductive Is Restated in London," *Washington Post*, 8 January 1986;

John Burgess et al., "Allies Cool to U.S. Call for Sanctions on Libya; Bonn Rejects Plea, Saying Tactics Futile," *Washington Post*, 9 January 1986. For details about the clandestine nature of the discussion about retaliation on Libya, see Bernard Weintraub, "Response to Terrorism: How President Decided," *New York Times*, 12 January 1986.

31. Bernard Gwertzman, "Why Reagan Shuns Attack," *New York Times*, 8 January 1986.

32. R. E. Apple Jr., "U.S. Now Casting Doubt on Allies' Libyan Policy," *New York Times*, 24 April 1986. Initially, France said it refused to allow U.S. fighter bombers based in England to overfly France on their run to Libya in April because they had been "informed a few hours in advance of the decision that was taken." However, in a later interview President François Mitterrand of France indicated that the reasons were largely to protect French interests. See Jim Hoagland, "Mitterand: U.S., France Are United on Essentials; French Leader, Reagan to Meet Wednesday," *Washington Post*, 29 June 1986. See also Emanuel de Margerie, "Why France Said No," *New York Times*, 20 May 1986.

33. See also Jentleson and Whytock, "Who 'Won' Libya?," for a similar conclusion.

34. A phrase used frequently in this period by policymakers to characterize French counter-terrorism cooperation, when other cooperation was at a low point.

35. Robert D. Hershey Jr., "U.S. Effort on Libya Oil Said to Gain," *New York Times*, 1 July 1986.

36. Youssef M. Ibrahim, "France Boycotts Oil from Libya, Joining the U.S." *New York Times*, 6 August 1986; Hershey, "U.S. Effort on Libya Oil Said to Gain."

37. John Kifner, "Hijacking in Karachi; Clues to Attackers Point in Confusing Directions," *New York Times*, 7 September 1986. For background information, see also *Wikipedia*, s.v. "Pan Am Flight 73," <http://en.wikipedia.org/wiki/Pan_Am_Flight_73> (accessed 20 July 2005).

38. James Dunnigan, "Patterns of Islamic Terror," *Strategy*, 28 October 2004, <http://www.strategypage.com/dls/articles/2004102822.asp> (accessed 20 July 2005).

39. Dunnigan, "Patterns of Islamic Terror."

40. U.S. Department of State, *Patterns of Global Terrorism–1986* (Washington, DC: GPO, 1987), 6.

41. This thinking was also shared by Reagan's "hawkish" Secretary of State. See, by way of comparison, Shultz, *Turmoil and Triumph*, 687. See also "Reagan's Response: U.S. Aircraft Attack Libyan Targets in Bid to Preempt Terrorism; Military Airport, Barracks Are Hit; President Vows Further Action If Needed," *Wall Street Journal*, 15 April 1986.

42. Lou Cannon and Bob Woodward, "Reagan's Use of Force Marks Turning Point; More Terror and Retaliation Seen," *Washington Post*, 16 April 1986. See also "Reagan's Response," *Wall Street Journal*.

43. There is reason to believe that Syrian president Hafiz al-Assad was unaware of Syrian military intelligence involvement and that because of the Karachi attack he expelled the ANO from Syria in 1987. See Timothy Naftali, *Blind Spot: The Secret History of American Counterterrorism* (Cambridge, MA: Basic/Perseus Books, 2005), 196–97, for details of meetings between former president Jimmy Carter and Assad that led to that conclusion. As always, Assad hedged his bets, banning Abu Nidal from operating in Syria but allowing ANO terrorist training camps in Lebanon's Syrian-controlled Bekaa Valley. See John Walcott, "Fast End to Mutual Hostility Unlikely as U.S. Reopens Dialogue with Syria," *Washington Insight, Wall Street Journal*, 6 July 1987, 8.

44. See also Stephen M. Walt, *Taming American Power: The Global Response to U.S. Primacy* (New York: W. W. Norton, 2006), 269n.

45. ANO was wracked by internal divisions and violence in 1988 and was never again a force in Arab terrorism. The cause of this turn of events was a clever, successful "psyops" program by U.S. intelligence. See, by way of comparison, U.S. Department of State, *Patterns of Global Terrorism–1989* (Washington, DC: GPO, 1990), 8; and Naftali, *Blind Spot*, 90.

46. For a very similar conclusion, see Jentleson and Whytock, "Who 'Won' Libya?," 60.

47. Compare with Shultz, *Turmoil and Triumph*, especially chapters 32–33; and Caspar Weinberger, *Fighting for Peace: Seven Critical Years in the Pentagon* (New York: Warner Books, 1990).

48. Caspar W. Weinberger, "The Uses of Military Power," speech given at the National Press Club, Washington, DC, 28 November 1984. Airforce Magazine Online <http://www.afa.org/magazine/Jan2004/0104keeperfull.asp> (accessed 24 September 2006).

49. Weinberger, *Fighting for Peace*, 433–45.

50. Colin Powell later modified Weinberger in his own exposition on the subject and used the Libyan example as one where the objective was "short of winning." Colin L. Powell, "U.S. Forces: Challenges Ahead," *Foreign Affairs* 71, no. 5 (Winter 1992–1993): 32–45.

51. See, by way of comparison, Shultz, *Turmoil and Triumph*, 687.

52. See, by way of comparison, U.S. Department of State, *Patterns of Global Terrorism–1990* (Washington, DC: GPO), 35. For an accessible, factual history of Pan Am flight 103, see *Wikipedia*, s.v. "Pan Am Flight 103," <http://en.wikipedia.org/wiki/Pan_Am_flight_103> (accessed 20 July 2004).

53. Associated Press, "Qaddafi Says He Sponsored and Now Forsakes Terrorists," *New York Times*, 26 October 1989.

54. Having just downed an American airliner, this gesture may have perplexed Qaddafi. It is a further indication that the Reagan administration believed the Libyan threat had been contained.

55. Youssef M. Ibrahim, "Arab Militants Release Three After Qaddafi Intervenes," *New York Times*, 11 April 1990.

56. Andrew Gowers, "Crisis in the Gulf; Abu Nidal May Launch Attacks on U.S. Targets," *Financial Times* (London), 11 August 1990; Charles Lane et al., "In Baghdad, a Welcome Mat for Terrorists," *Newsweek*, 3 September 1990, 41.

57. Andrew Rosenthal, "U.S. Accuses Libya as Two Are Charged in Pan Am Bombing," *New York Times*, 15 November 1991.

58. The phrase "highest levels" is a frequently used diplomatic reference to a nation's head of government and most senior advisers. In this case it indicated that, although lacking sufficient evidence to indict, there was no doubt that Qaddafi was involved in the bombing.

59. President George H. W. Bush, "The U.S. and Asia: Building Democracy and Freedom," excerpts from remarks before the Asia Society, New York, 12 November 1991, U.S. Department of State dispatch, vol. 2, no. 46, 18 November 1991, University of Illinois at Chicago Federal Depository Library, <http://dosfan.lib.uic.edu/ERC/briefing/dispatch/1991/html/Dispatchv2no46 .html> (accessed 9 September 2006); see also U.S. Department of State, *Patterns of Global Terrorism–1991* (Washington, DC: GPO), 75–76.

60. Bush, "The U.S. and Asia: Building Democracy and Freedom"; see also U.S. Department of State, *Patterns of Global Terrorism–1991*, 79.

61. Alan Riding, "Four Libyans Charged by France in Air Bombing," *New York Times*, 31 October 1991; see also William Drozdiak and George Lardner Jr., "French Seek Four Libyans in Jet Bombing; One Suspect Also Linked to 1988 Pan Am Blast," *Washington Post*, 31 October 1991; Youssef M. Ibrahim, "Libya Denies Link to Airline Blasts," *New York Times*, 28 June 1991.

62. The author, a member of the National Security Council staff at the time, was deeply involved in the conception, development, and execution of the revised policy.

63. See also Jentleson and Whytock, "Who 'Won' Libya?," 63.

64. Because the aircraft came down in Scotland, Scottish judicial authorities had jurisdiction, and Scottish law and practice were followed.

65. United Nations Security Council, *Security Council Resolution 731 (1992)*, S/RES/731, New York, 21 January 1992.

66. United Nations Security Council, *Security Council Resolution 748 (1992)*, S/RES/748, New York, 31 March 1992.

67. United Nations Security Council, *Security Council Resolution 883 (1993)*, S/RES/883, New York, 11 November 1993.

68. An exception may prove to be an attempt on the life of the crown prince (now king) of Saudi Arabia after a bitter personal and public dispute between the two leaders.

69. United States Department of State, "Overview of State-Sponsored Terrorism," *Patterns of Global Terrorism–1996*, Washington, DC, 30 April 1996, Federation of American Scientists, <http://www.fas.org/irp/threat/terror_96/overview.html> (accessed 12 November 2005).

70. "Sanctions on Libya Seen Behind Repatriation Plan," Journal of Commerce, Trade Briefs. *New York Times*, 20 October 1995; Reuters, "UN Sanctions Prompt Gadaffi to Send Home One Thousand Africans," *Financial Times* (London), 19 October 1995.

71. Jerry Gray, "Foreigners Investing in Libya or in Iran Face U.S. Sanctions," *New York Times*, late edition, 23 July 1996; Nancy Dunne and Robert Corzine, "Politics Sets Tone for Trade Barriers," *Financial Times* (London), 25 July 1996.

72. "Senate Approves Amended Iran Sanctions Bill That Also Targets Libya, *Inside U.S. Trade*, 22 December 1995, 6. For background information, see United States Congress, *The Iran-Libya Sanctions Act (ILSA)*, report for Congress prepared by Kenneth Katzman, 109th Cong., 2d sess., updated 26 April 2006, Committee Print Order Code RS 20871, <http://fpc.state.gov/documents/organization/66441.pdf#search=%22%22edward%20Kennedy%22%20ILSA%22> (accessed 10 June 2006).

73. "Tarnoff Presses House on Changes to Iran, Libya Sanctions Bill," *Inside U.S. Trade*, 10 May 1996, 16.

74. "EU Charges House Iran Sanctions Legislation Violates WTO," *Inside U.S. Trade*, 9 February 1996, 17.

75. Youssef M. Ibrahim, "Planned U.S. Sanctions Anger Europeans," *New York Times*, 25 July 1996; see also Craig R. Whitney, "Europe Gives Cold Shoulder to Clinton on Cuba Law," *New York Times*, 18 July 1996.

76. Formally, their organization was known as Victims of Pan Am Flight 103.

77. Toni Locy, "Families Suing Libya over Pan Am Blast," *Washington Post*, 7 May 1996.

78. "Angered by US Sanctions, EU Threatens to Go to WTO," *New York Times*, 22 August 1996.

79. Associated Press, "U.S. Criticizes Turkish Leader for Libya Trip and Trade Deal," *New York Times*, 8 October 1996.

80. "Italy's ENI Has Deal with Libya," *Wall Street Journal*, 5 November 1996.

81. Reuters, "Vatican Establishes Full Ties with Libya," *New York Times*, 11 March 1997.

82. Reuters, "Qaddafi Flies to Niger, in Defiance of U.N. Ban," *New York Times*, 9 May 1997; see also "Gaddafi Defies UN Sanctions with Trip to Nigeria," *The Independent* (London), 10 May 1997.

83. "Sahel States Call for UN Inquiry into Sanctions on Libya," Agence France-Presse, 17 August 1997.

84. Ian Black, "UN Fury at Sanctions Defiance," *The Guardian* (London), 23 September 1997.

85. "Lockerbie Impasse in Libya," *The Independent* (London), 30 October 1997; see also "South Africa Calls for Lifting of Sanctions on Libya," Agence France-Presse, 22 October 1997.

86. Janet McBride, "Libya Wins a Round in Pan Am 103 Case," *Washington Post*, 28 February 1998; Ian Black, "Lockerbie Families Cheered by Hague Court Ruling; Venue Choice for Trial of Libyans Is Setback for Britain and US," *The Guardian* (London), 28 February 1998; Craig R. Whitney, "World Court Claims Jurisdiction in Pan Am Flight 103 Case," *New York Times*, 28 February 1998; David Buchan, "Libya Claims Victory in Lockerbie Ruling," *Financial Times* (London), 28 February 1998.

87. John M. Goshko, "Libya Sanctions Debated at U.N.: Gadhafi's Backers Call Them Vindictive; Victims' Families Demand They Go On," *Washington Post*, 21 March 1998.

88. General information regarding this decision made in Burkina Faso at the thirty-fourth annual summit of the Organisation of African Unity can be found in Reuters, "OAU Breaks Libya Sanctions," *The Guardian* (London), 10 June 1998; see also United States Department of State, *Communiqué on Libya*, 10 June 1998.

89. Madeleine Albright, *Madame Secretary: A Memoir* (New York: Hyperion, 2003), 329–30.

90. Philip Shenon, "A Decision Is Due Today from Libya," *New York Times*, 26 August 1998; Andrew Parker and Stephen Fidler, "Proposal for Libyans' Trial Unveiled," *Financial Times* (London), 25 August 1998; Thomas W. Lippman, "U.S., Britain Announce Plan for Pan Am Trial; Libya Challenged to Deliver Bomb Suspects," *Washington Post*, 25 August 1998.

91. Severin Carrell and Jenny Booth, "Lockerbie Trial Move Welcomed by Libya's Allies," *New York Times*, 26 August 1998.

92. Steven Erlanger, "U.S. to Ask Wider Libya Ban If Trial Is Refused," *New York Times*, 25 August 1998; United Nations Security Council, *Resolution 1192 (1999)*, S/RES/1192 (1998), New York, 27 August 1998.

93. Stephen Fidler and Mark Suzman, "Gadaffi Warily Backs Trial Plan," *Financial Times* (London), 28 August 1998; Lee Michael Katz, "Gadhafi Demands Negotiations Before Turning in Suspects," *USA Today*, 28 August 1998.

94. Howard Schneider, "U.N. Chief, Gadhafi Meet on Suspects; Annan Praises Libyan's Commitment to Resolving 1988 Lockerbie Bombing Case," *Washington Post*, 6 December 1998, late edition.

95. Mark Huband, "Lockerbie Bomb Suspects Will Face Trial, Says Libya Gadaffi in Pledge to Mandela on Hand-Over," *Financial Times* (London), 20 March 1999.

96. Helene Cooper, "Libya Hands over Pan Am 103 Suspects, as U.N but Not U.S. Suspends Sanctions," *Wall Street Journal*, 6 April 1999.

97. "Judges Find Libyan Guilty of Murder in Pan Am Bombing, Co-Defendant Acquitted in '88 Crash," *New York Times*, 1 February 2001. Scottish law has three verdicts: guilty, not proven, not guilty.

98. Judith Miller, "In Rare Talks with Libyans, U.S. Airs View on Sanctions," *New York Times*, 12 June 1999.

99. Peter Slevin, "Libya Accepts Blame in Lockerbie Bombing, Letter on Flight 103 Is Bid to Ease Sanctions," *Washington Post*, 17 August 2003.

100. Warren Hoge, "New Libyan Cooperation Leads to Renewed Ties with Britain," *New York Times*, 8 July 1999.

101. Craig R. Whitney, "France: Libya Pays for Bombing Plane," *New York Times*, 17 July 1999.

102. For background information, see Colum Lynch, "French Imperil Libyan Deal on Flight 103," *Washington Post*, 19 August 2003; Craig S. Smith, "Libya and France Reach Agreement on Victim Compensation," *New York Times*, 12 September 2003.

103. See the similar evaluations in Jentleson and Whytock, "Who 'Won' Libya?" and in Walt's *Taming American Power*, 228, where he refers to the Libyan case as a "model" for use with the "most recalcitrant regimes."

5

Cutting the Deadly Nexus: Preventing the Spread of Weapons of Mass Destruction to Terrorists

Alistair Millar and Jason Ipe

A guiding principle of U.S. national security since 2001 has been that the most serious threat to global security, in the words of former secretary of defense Donald Rumseld, is the potential "nexus between terrorist networks and terrorist states that have weapons of mass destruction."[1] Concern about the potential effect of these dangers has been expressed by many U.S. policymakers and international experts, including members of the international Weapons of Mass Destruction Commission (WMD Commission) led by Hans Blix. The 2006 report of the WMD Commission noted that terrorist use of weapons of mass destruction (WMD) is an increasing threat; that it could occur "either within or across state borders"; and that it is "important to insist, therefore, on the duty of all states to prevent their territory from being used as a base for such activities."[2] Conventional deterrence will not ensure security against nonstate actors armed with WMD who lack targetable assets and may not value their own lives.[3] The Pentagon has struggled to move beyond traditional deterrence by drafting contingency plans for conventional and preventive strikes against terrorists plotting to use WMD, but in a world of imperfect intelligence the security premise of preemption is questionable.[4] Cutting the deadly nexus requires an understanding of the most potent elements of this multifaceted threat and aggressive preventive measures to keep "the world's most dangerous weapons out of the hands of the world's most dangerous people."[5]

Weapons of mass destruction is a catchall phrase that includes nuclear, chemical, and biological weapons and materials with varying levels of destructive power, all requiring specially tailored strategies.[6] The first known use of the term *weapons of mass destruction* was in a December

1937 Christmas message delivered by Archbishop Cosmo Gordon Lang in reference to bombings in Spain and China, and the term was quoted in a *London Times* newspaper in that year to describe the devastation of a German aerial bomb attack that killed 1,600 civilians in less than three hours in Guernica during the Spanish Civil War.[7] During and immediately following the cold war, the phrase began to be used specifically to refer to nuclear weapons and then also to chemical and biological weapons. In the last decade, radiological and even high explosives and cyberweapons have been included in the definition of WMD.[8] One analyst offers a useful description of the relative destructive power of these weapons on an imaginary line "that begins with nuclear weapons at one extreme, continues through chemical, radiological, and biological and terminates with cyber-weapons (designed to attack computers or critical infrastructure) at the far end."[9]

Of all the weapons of mass destruction available, the immediate and delayed destructive effects of an attack with an intact nuclear weapon would be the most severe.[10] At ground zero, temperatures would reach above ten million degrees Fahrenheit, the surrounding area (a half-mile radius for a Hiroshima-sized bomb) would be destroyed by the blast and direct radiation, charred by thermal radiation, and the population and environment over a larger area would be affected for decades from the fallout.[11] Former Senator Sam Nunn (D-GA) has described the threat as follows:

I am not sure we fully grasp the devastating, world-changing impact of a nuclear attack. If a 10-kiloton nuclear device goes off in mid-town Manhattan on a typical work day, it could kill more than half a million people. Ten kilotons, a plausible yield for a crude terrorist bomb, has the power of 10,000 tons of TNT. To haul that volume of explosives, you would need a cargo train one hundred cars long. But if it were a nuclear bomb, it could fit into the back of a truck. Beyond the immediate deaths and the lives that would be shortened by radioactive fallout, the casualty list would also include civil liberties, privacy and the world economy. . . . Are we doing all we can to prevent a nuclear attack? The simple answer is "no, we are not."[12]

This chapter addresses these issues by focusing on the most significant elements of both sides of the nexus: Al-Qaida and nuclear weapons. It begins by assessing the nature of the threat and examining bilateral, regional, and international efforts to address the danger. It examines the efforts of the United States and countries of the former Soviet Union to secure vulnerable nuclear weapons and materials, focusing on a gaping hole in those efforts—thousands of unmonitored portable nuclear weapons, so-called tactical nuclear weapons (TNWs). It then addresses regional approaches, specifically those in the Middle East, where the twin problems of proliferation and terrorism come into sharp focus. The chapter concludes with an overview of two complementary United Nations resolutions that take direct aim at cutting the deadly nexus.

Al-Qaida's Nuclear Pretensions: Intentions and Capabilities

Vice Admiral Lowell E. Jacoby, the director of the Defense Intelligence Agency, testified before Congress in early 2005 about terrorist attempts to acquire nuclear weapons capability: "Al Qaida's stated intention to conduct an attack exceeding the destruction of 9/11 [September 11] raises the possibility that planned attacks may involve unconventional weapons. There is little doubt it has contemplated using radiological or nuclear material. The question is whether al-Qaida has the capability."[13] The fact that terrorists have not yet used nuclear weapons is due to a "lack of means rather than lack of motivation."[14] Among known terrorist networks, Al-Qaida has demonstrated its ability to meticulously plan and inflict mass-casualty attacks, and indications are that it is trying to acquire WMD. As table 5.1 illustrates, Osama bin Laden has repeatedly voiced his intention to acquire such weapons and even called the quest for them a "religious duty."[15]

As table 5.1 indicates, bin Laden has claimed that his network already possesses nuclear and chemical weapons. The circumstances and timing of the November 2001 interview in which he made this claim during the height of the U.S.-led attack on Taliban forces in Afghanistan suggest that bin Laden was bluffing at the time. However, there is no doubt that Al-Qaida is intent on acquiring a nuclear capability. As table 5.2 indicates, the evidence suggests that it has been actively pursuing nuclear materials, technology, and know-how.

Despite those efforts, the good news is that, based on publicly available information, Al-Qaida does not yet appear to have made significant progress toward obtaining either an intact nuclear weapon or significant

Table 5.1
Al-Qaida's Nuclear Ambitions: Examples of Statements

Approximate Date	Incident
June 1998	"The Nuclear Bomb of Islam," a pamphlet attributed to Osama bin Laden, calls it "the duty of the Muslims to prepare as much force as possible to terrorize the enemies of God."[a]
December 1998	Osama bin Laden: "Acquiring weapons for the defense of Muslims is a religious duty. If I have indeed acquired [nuclear and chemical] weapons, then I thank God for enabling me to do so. And if I seek to acquire these weapons, I am carrying out a duty. It would be a sin for Muslims not to try to possess the weapons that would prevent the infidels from inflicting harm on Muslims."[b]
November 2001	Osama bin Laden: "I wish to declare that if America used chemical or nuclear weapons against us, then we may retort [sic] with chemical and nuclear weapons. We have the weapons as deterrent [sic]."[c]
April 2002	Senior Al-Qaida leader, Abu Zubaydah, tells U.S. interrogators that Al-Qaida has both the intent and know-how to create a radiological weapon.[d]
May 2003	Osama bin Laden obtains a fatwa from the prominent Saudi sheik Hamid bin Fahd justifying the use of a nuclear weapon against Americans.[e]

a. Osama bin Ladin, "The Nuclear Bomb of Islam," statement in *International Islamic Front for Fighting the Jews and the Crusaders*, 29 May 1998, cited in *United States of America v. Usama Bin Laden et al.*, S(9) 98 Cr. 1023 (LBS)(S.D.N.Y. 1998), 7 March 2001, <http://cns.miis.edu/pubs/reports/pdfs/binladen/indict.pdf> (accessed 17 March 2005).
b. Rahimullah Yusufzai, "Wrath of God: Osama bin Laden Lashes Out Against the West," interview, *Time Asia*, 11 January 1999, <http://www.time.com/time/asia/asin/magazine/1999/990111/osama1.html> (accessed 24 August 2006).
c. Hamid Mir, "Osama Claims He Has Nukes: If US Uses N-Arms, It Will Get Same Response," *Dawn*, 9 November 2001, <http://www.dawn.com/2001/11/10/top1.htm> (accessed 17 March 2005).
d. Jamie McIntyre, "Zubaydah: Al Qaeda Had 'Dirty Bomb' Know-How," *CNN*, 22 April 2002, <http://archives.cnn.com/2002/US/04/22/Subaydah.dirty.bomb> (accessed 17 March 2005).
e. Michael Scheuer, "Bin Ladin Expert Steps Forward: Ex-CIA Agent Assesses Terror War in *60 Minutes*," interview by Steve Kroft, *60 Minutes*, CBS, 14 November 2004, <http://www.cbsnews.com/stories/2004/11/12/60minutes/main655407.shtml> (accessed 24 August 2006).

Table 5.2
Examples of Al-Qaida's Efforts to Obtain Nuclear/Radiological Weapons Capabilities[a]

Approximate Date	Incident
Early 1990s	Former Al-Qaida operative, Jamal al-Fadl, claims he witnessed members of Al-Qaida try to buy enriched uranium and that he attempted to procure uranium in Sudan on behalf of Osama bin Laden for use in nuclear weapons.[b]
1998	"Senior deputy" to Osama bin Laden, Mamdouh Mahmud Salim, is arrested in 1998 in Germany for his involvement with Al-Qaida and efforts to purchase enriched uranium in 1993.
Various	Pakistani nuclear scientists, Sultan Bahiruddin Mahmood and Abdul Majid, meet with senior Taliban and Al-Qaida leaders, including Osama bin Laden.[c]
April 2001	Osama bin Laden and a "Pakistani scientist" solicit Bulgarian businessman and former intelligence officer, Ivan Ivanov, to set up a front company to purchase spent nuclear fuel.[d]
Fall/Winter 2001	The invasion of Afghanistan reveals documents that "reinforce assessments that Al Qaeda is highly determined to obtain nuclear weapons and other weapons of mass destruction," including a manual entitled *Superbombs*.[e] Although the documents discovered are alarming, they do not "provide any evidence that Al Qaeda had acquired nuclear weapons . . . [nor] that Al Qaeda had acquired nuclear explosive materials, although this result is less certain."[f]
May 2002	Jose Padilla a.k.a Abdullah al-Muhajir is arrested in the United States for allegedly conspiring with Al-Qaida to carry out a bomb attack on a U.S. city.[g]
January 2005	Police in Germany arrest two suspected members of Al-Qaida and accuse them of, among other offenses, trying to purchase uranium from a dealer in Luxembourg.[h]

a. This table includes only the most credible incidents of Al-Qaida's efforts to obtain nuclear weapons technology, material, and know-how and does not include numerous other incidents that have been reported in the press, such as reports that Al-Qaida has already obtained so-called suitcase nukes from the former Soviet Union.

Table 5.2
(continued)

b. Testimony of Jamal al-Fadl in the trial of Osama bin Laden et al. for the 7 August 1998 bombings of the U.S. embassies in Nairobi, Kenya, and Dar al-Salaam, Tanzania. See *United States of America v. Usama Bin Laden* et al., S(7) 98 Cr. 1023, (S.D.N.Y. 2001), Center for Nonproliferation Studies, <http://cns.miis.edu/pubs/reports/binladen.htm> (accessed 18 March 2005).
c. Peter Baker, "Pakistani Scientist Who Met with Bin Laden Failed Polygraphs, Renewing Suspicions," *Washington Post*, 3 March 2002.
d. Adam Nathan and David Leppard, "Al-Qaeda's Men Held Secret Meetings to Build 'Dirty Bomb,'" Overseas News, *Sunday Times* (London), 14 October 2001.
e. David Albright, "Al Qaeda's Nuclear Program: Through the Window of Seized Documents," Nautilus Institute Policy Forum 47, Berkeley, CA, 6 November 2002, <http://www.nautilus.org/archives/fora/Special-Policy-Forum/47_Albright.html> (accessed 18 March 2005).
f. Albright, "Al Qaeda's Nuclear Program."
g. Susan Schmidt and Walter Pincus, "Al Muhajir Alleged to Be Scouting Terror Sites; U.S. Says Al Qaeda Had Instructed Suspect," *Washington Post*, 12 June 2002.
h. Craig Whitlock, "Germany Arrests Two Al-Qaeda Suspects; Men Accused of Planning Attacks in Iraq," *Washington Post*, 24 January 2005.

amounts of fissile material. Such is the best estimate of the U.S. intelligence community. The assistant secretary of state for intelligence and research, Thomas Fingar, provided the following written testimony to the Senate Select Committee on Intelligence in 2005: "We have seen no persuasive evidence that al-Qaida has obtained fissile material or ever has had a serious and sustained program to do so. At worst, the group possesses small amounts of radiological material that could be used to fabricate a radiological dispersion device (dirty bomb)."[16] Before the war in Afghanistan, the best guess of U.S. intelligence was that "fabrication of at least a 'crude' nuclear device was within al-Qa'ida's capabilities, if it could obtain fissile material."[17] As a formal hierarchical network, today Al-Qaida is a shell of the organization it once was. Years of offensive military operations against it and its leadership and other efforts to disrupt its operations have degraded Al-Qaida's capacity to centrally orchestrate large-scale attacks. The result is a wider, more disparate and dispersed movement. In many ways it is just as dangerous but is perhaps less capable of mustering the necessary resources for a nuclear weapon.

Examining the obstacles to acquiring a nuclear weapons capability can provide a useful analytical framework for diagnosing the threat. Al-Qaida has only three avenues by which it could acquire a nuclear weapons capability:

• Processing uranium or plutonium into weapons-grade material and then designing and constructing a bomb,

• Acquiring rather than processing weapons-grade fissile material and then designing and constructing a weapon, or

• Obtaining an intact nuclear weapon.[18]

The first option would be feasible only with state sponsorship to acquire the assets necessary to reprocess enough plutonium or enrich a sufficient amount of uranium for a weapon. Both processes require immense resources, including well-equipped laboratories with sophisticated, precisely machined equipment in fixed locations staffed with highly trained, experienced scientists. While Iran and North Korea are testing the limits of existing nonproliferation regimes, such as the Nuclear Nonproliferation Treaty (NPT), International Atomic Energy Agency (IAEA) safeguards and myriad export controls make it difficult for even the most dedicated states to develop nuclear weapons undetected. These international restrictions combined with the immense financial, scientific, and technical hurdles involved make it highly unlikely that even the most sophisticated terrorist group could process the necessary fissile material on its own. The fact that Al-Qaida has been deprived of territorial bases and facilities in Afghanistan makes such a path all the more improbable.

It would be more plausible for Al-Qaida to pursue option two: building a crude device with illegally acquired fissile material either purchased on the black market or stolen from vulnerable locations—in the former Soviet Union, for example. If Al-Qaida was able to obtain sufficient fissile material, actually assembling a nuclear weapon would present its own obstacles. Although basic designs and information on the physics of nuclear weapons are openly available, significant technical and practical hurdles remain. Given sufficient time, however, these obstacles could certainly be overcome. Enlisting the expertise of trained nuclear scientists would obviously greatly facilitate such a process. Most states would be deterred from assigning experts or passing materials to terrorists or would want deniability at a minimum, but there are no guarantees against potential rogue actors. Discoveries of illegal supply networks emanating from Pakistan (on whom the U.S. relies as a key ally in the war on terror) have not led to significant reprisals.[19]

Given the obstacles inherent to procuring enough fissile material and to constructing a nuclear weapon itself, option three—stealing an intact weapon—would also be an attractive and potentially feasible method for Al-Qaida.[20] This and option two present the most likely route by which Al-Qaida could obtain a nuclear capability. This means that securing existing nuclear weapons and stocks of fissile material should be the most pressing concern for policymakers. As one group of senior nuclear physicists explained, "The main concern with respect to terrorists should be focused on those in a position to build, and bring with them, their own devices, as well as on those able to steal an operable weapon."[21] It then follows that the most efficient use of resources devoted to this task should be the protection of areas with the highest concentration of inadequately secured nuclear materials and weapons.

Vulnerable Locations

Russia is probably the most vulnerable location. Russia's nuclear complex is not adequately protected or maintained and contains hundreds of tons of plutonium and highly enriched uranium as well as thousands of intact nuclear weapons. As Graham Allison describes,

> Russia is the most likely source, not because the Russian government would intentionally sell or lose weapons or materials, but simply as an instance of the Willie Sutton principle. When asked why he robbed banks, Sutton answered: "Because that's where the money is." Russia's eleven-time-zone expanse contains more nuclear weapons and materials than any other country in the world, much of it vulnerable to theft.[22]

In January 2001, a bipartisan commission chaired by Howard Baker, former Senate Republican majority leader, and Lloyd Cutler, senior counsel to President Reagan during the Strategic Arms Limitation Talks

II (SALT II), concluded that "[t]he most urgent unmet national security threat to the United States today is the danger that weapons of mass destruction or weapons-usable material in Russia could be stolen and sold to terrorists or hostile nation states and used against American troops abroad and citizens at home."[23]

The consensus within the U.S. intelligence community is that significant amounts of nuclear material have already been stolen from the former Soviet Union. According to the National Intelligence Council's 2004 annual report to Congress on the safety and security of Russian nuclear facilities and military forces, "we assess that undetected smuggling has occurred, and we are concerned about the total amount of material that could have been diverted or stolen in the last 13 years."[24] Table 5.3 highlights a few of the most worrisome, confirmed incidents of nuclear smuggling from the former Soviet Union.

As table 5.3 indicates, in each of the examples Russian authorities claim to have recovered all of the missing nuclear material. Those claims are judged to be suspect by some intelligence analysts.[25] The additional question is, what about undetected diversions?

In addition to the known incidents, Russian agents have uncovered and prevented two "attempts by known terrorists to scout out nuclear weapons storage sites." According to a press report, "two sabotage and reconnaissance groups associated with Chechen separatists were spotted at several major railway stations in the Moscow region, in apparent attempts to gather intelligence about a special train used to transport nuclear weapons."[26] The Russian media has reported several other incidents where terrorists have plotted to steal large amounts of weapons-grade materials.[27]

Although Russia is the most obvious vulnerable location, the nuclear weapons of other countries—and even more so the stocks of fissile material widely distributed throughout the world—may also be vulnerable to diversion by terrorist groups. First on that list might be Pakistan because of its nuclear weapons, materials, and expertise; Al-Qaida's large presence in the country; President Musharraf's less than firm grip on power; and the sympathy of some within Pakistan's nuclear program for Al-Qaida's Islamist ideology. Revelations in February 2004 of the nuclear black market run by Pakistani nuclear scientist A. Q. Khan highlight

Table 5.3

Examples of Significant Incidents of Nuclear Smuggling from the Former Soviet Union[a]

Approximate Date	Incident	Status
1992	An employee of the Luch Production Facility in Podolsk, Russia, steals 1.5 kilograms of highly enriched uranium (HEU) (90 percent enriched) from the facility over a five-month period.	Recovered
March 1994	Three individuals are arrested in St. Petersburg, Russia, for attempting to sell 3 kilograms of HEU (90 percent enriched) stolen from the Elektrostal nuclear facility outside Moscow.	Recovered
1998	Russian authorities in the Chelyabinsk region reportedly thwart an attempt to steal 18.5 kilograms of HEU (unspecified level of enrichment), allegedly enough to construct a nuclear weapon.	Recovered
1999	Four grams of HEU (90 percent enriched) originating from Russia are seized by Bulgarian authorities at a border crossing.	Recovered

a. This table was adapted from United States General Accounting Office, *Nuclear Nonproliferation: U.S. Efforts to Help Other Countries Combat Nuclear Smuggling Need Strengthened Coordination and Planning*, GAO-02-426 (Washington, DC: GAO, 2002); and National Intelligence Council, *Annual Report to Congress on the Safety and Security of Russian Nuclear Facilities and Military Forces*, 108th Cong., 2d sess., Washington, DC, December 2004, <http://www.cia.gov/nic/special_russiannuke04.html> (accessed 18 March 2005). For a more comprehensive list of incidents involving the smuggling of nuclear materials, see the IAEA's "List of Confirmed Incidents Involving HEU or Pu," International Atomic Energy Agency, <http://www.iaea.org/NewsCenter/Features/RadSources/table1.html> (accessed 18 March 2005).

those concerns. Khan, the founder of Pakistan's bomb program, was discovered to have provided enrichment technology and possibly weapons designs to states such as Iran and Libya.[28] Although Pakistan's nuclear weapons complex and stockpile is relatively small, the confluence of these various factors makes it particularly vulnerable.

Controlling the Former Soviet Nuclear Arsenal

Since the end of the cold war, the United States and Russia have embarked on a number of innovative bilateral initiatives, collectively referred to as Cooperative Threat Reduction (CTR), which have helped Russia and other countries of the former Soviet Union deal safely with their cold war legacies of nuclear, biological, and chemical weapons–related expertise and materials.[29] Despite limited resources and bureaucratic logjams, CTR and similar innovative bilateral and ad hoc multilateral efforts have been relatively successful in improving control of and overseeing destruction of numerous strategic systems—although funding for CTR programs remains insufficient in the opinion of many U.S. experts. CTR and similar efforts have not sufficiently addressed what are perhaps the most attractive types of nuclear weapons to terrorists, TNWs. Thousands of TNWs—many with a yield capacity greater than the atomic bombs dropped on Japan in 1945—were deployed for battlefield use during the cold war and still exist today.[30] Also referred to as "battlefield" nuclear weapons, "mini-nukes," "sub-strategic," or "nonstrategic" nuclear weapons, TNWs are regularly overlooked in arms control negotiations and have never been the subject of a formal international treaty. As such they represent one of the most significant unaddressed challenges in the deadly nexus.

An increase in terrorist dangers has made the existence of TNWs a particularly grave concern. Large numbers of these weapons, such as artillery shells, land mines, and rockets, were designed for war-fighting missions. Many are small and portable and can be used in the field without the authority of centralized command and control oversight mechanisms. In some cases, field commanders can be given predelegated launch authority or preapproved authority to respond with nuclear weapons when confronted with certain battlefield conditions. Some older versions of these weapons have no permissive action links—control mechanisms that prohibit uncontrolled or accidental nuclear launches— and can be used by whomever possesses them.

TNWs are arguably more susceptible to unauthorized or accidental use than strategic nuclear weapons. They are often deployed near the front line, they are far more sensitive to communications problems under crisis conditions, and they can be fired by an individual combatant on the battlefield without employing stringent safety precautions that govern the launch of strategic nuclear weapons. Estimates indicate that there could be three to four thousand and as many as ten thousand relatively portable nuclear weapons in the former Soviet Union.[31]

Lack of information confirming the location and safety of these weapons is perceived, particularly among Western experts and officials, to be a serious security problem. Without reliable data on the vast number of Soviet-era tactical weapons, no one can be sure if they have fallen, or could still fall, into the wrong hands. It is difficult to determine whether the security threats posed by Russian TNWs have become more acute in recent years, but the confluence of corruption and the increased sophistication of organized crime have made the theft of entire weapons more likely (table 5.4).[32]

In 1991 and 1992 Presidents Bush, Gorbachev, and Yeltsin announced diplomatic efforts toward the reduction and control of tactical nuclear weapons in what came to be known as the Presidential Nuclear Initiatives (PNIs). In September 1991, after an aborted coup in Moscow, it became evident that the nuclear arsenal of a disintegrating Soviet Union posed an urgent risk to global security. To prevent these weapons from falling into the wrong hands, President Bush announced the unilateral reduction of U.S. TNWs, estimated to have been 7,165 weapons,[33] and proposed that the Russians respond in kind with their own reductions. The Soviet Union under Mikhail Gorbachev and then Russia under Boris Yeltsin reciprocated President Bush's initiative by agreeing to reduce the Soviet/Russian TNW arsenal. The total reductions were significant. Reductions in the Russian TNW arsenal were estimated at more than 11,000 warheads.[34] However, except for the occasional vague announcement stating that progress is being made on reaching targeted

Table 5.4
Estimates of World Tactical Nuclear Weapons (TNWs) Forces

Country	Estimates of Deployed TNWs
Russia	2,330–3,400[a]
United States	500[b] (an estimated 480 of which are deployed in Europe)[c]
China	0–150[d]
Israel	75–300[e]
France	60[f]
India	40–50[g]
Pakistan	24–48[h]
United Kingdom	0–200[i]

a. According to Alexei Arbatov, member of the Russian Duma, "Whereas in 1991 the USSR had about 22,000 tactical nuclear weapons, at present Russia retains around 3,800." Alexei Arbatov, "Deep Cuts and De-alerting: A Russian Perspective," in *The Nuclear Turning Point: A Blueprint for Deep Cuts and De-Alerting of Nuclear Weapons*, ed. Harold Feiveson (Washington, DC: Brookings Institution, 1999), 320. Other analysts put the number somewhat lower. Nikolai Sokov, for example, estimates that, based on Arbatov's calculations and sub-tracting eliminations supplied as percentage-of-force reductions by the Russian government, the number of Russian tactical nuclear weapons perhaps would be around 3,000 deployed. Nikolai Sokov, e-mail message to the author, 25 October 2005. The NRDC Nuclear Notebook states, "Russia maintains approximately 2,330 operational nonstrategic warheads and some 4,170 nonstrategic warheads in reserve." See Robert S. Norris and Hans M. Kristensen, "Russian Nuclear Forces, 2006," NRDC: Nuclear Notebook, *Bulletin of the Atomic Scientists* 62, no. 2 (March–April 2006): 64–67, <http://www.thebulletin.org/article_nn.php?art_ofn=ma06norris> (accessed 25 August 2006).
b. Norris and Kristensen, "Russian Nuclear Forces, 2006," 64–67.
c. Robert S. Norris and Hans M. Kristensen, "U.S. Nuclear Forces, 2005," NRDC: Nuclear Notebook, *Bulletin of the Atomic Scientists* 61, no. 1 (January–February 2005): 73–75, <http://www.thebulletin.org/article_nn.php?art_ofn=jf05norris> (accessed 25 August 2006). It was previously estimated that the U.S. had approximately 150 nuclear weapons deployed in Europe; however, that estimate has since been revised to nearly triple that number. For a discussion of the revised estimate, see Robert S. Norris and Hans M. Kristensen, "U.S. Nuclear Weapons in Europe: 1954–2004," NRDC: Nuclear Notebook, *Bulletin of the Atomic Scientists* 60, no. 6 (November–December 2004): 76–77, <http://www.thebulletin.org/article_nn.php?art_ofn=nd04norris>.

Table 5.4
(continued)

d. According to the definition proposed in this chapter, all of China's nuclear weapons would be classified as "nonstrategic"; however, given the absence of reliable data, it is impossible to determine how many or even whether China has deployed nuclear weapons that, based on their range or yield, may be described as tactical. Although China likely possesses some tactical nuclear capabilities, it is much less clear whether it has stockpiled or deployed such weapons. See, for example, Charles D. Ferguson, Evan S. Medeiros, and Phillip C. Saunders, "Chinese Tactical Nuclear Weapons," in *Tactical Nuclear Weapons: Emerging Threats in an Evolving Security Environment*, ed. Brian Alexander and Alistair Millar (Washington, DC: Brassey's, 2003), 110–26. Jeffrey Lewis similarly notes that although China may have a tactical nuclear weapons capability, intelligence assessments indicate that these weapons are not deployed. Moreover, Lewis estimates that China may only have "about 100" deployed nuclear weapons total. See Jeffrey Lewis, "Nuclear Numerology Chinese Style," Letter to the editor, *Arms Control Today* 35, no. 2 (March 2005).

e. Because of the limited range and regional nature of Israel's nuclear arsenal, all of its nuclear forces may be described as tactical. Specific estimates of the size and composition of its nuclear arsenal are inherently difficult to make and vary widely due to Israel's policy of "strategic ambiguity" and attendant secrecy. According to the 2002 NRDC Nuclear Notebook, estimates of Israel's nuclear forces range from 75 to 200, but other estimates put the total number as high as 300. Robert S. Norris, William M. Arkin, Hans M. Kristensen, and Joshua Handler, "Israeli Nuclear Forces, 2002," NRDC Nuclear Notebook, *Bulletin of the Atomic Scientists* 58, no. 5 (September–October 2002): 73–75, <http://www.thebulletin.org/article_nn.php?art_ofn=so02norris> (accessed 25 August 2006). See also William Burrows and Robert Windrem, *Critical Mass: The Dangerous Race for Superweapons in a Fragmenting World* (New York: Simon and Schuster, 1994). Israel also may have developed tactical nuclear weapons specifically for battlefield use such as nuclear artillery shells and landmines. See, for example, Robert S. Norris, William M. Arkin, Hans M. Kristensen, and Joshua Handler, "Israeli Nuclear Forces, 2002," NRDC: Nuclear Notebook, *Bulletin of the Atomic Scientists* 58, no. 5 (September–October 2002): 73–75, <http://www.thebulletin.org/article_nn.php?art_ofn=so02norris>.

f. According to the definition proposed in this chapter, all of France's approximately 350 nuclear weapons are "nonstrategic," but more practically, based on range, only about 60 so-called Air-Sol Moyenne Porté (ASMPs) may be described as tactical. The ASMP is a medium-range air-to-surface missile deployed on carrier and land-based aircraft. See, for example, Robert S. Norris, William M. Arkin, Hans M. Kristensen, and Joshua Handler, "French Nuclear Forces, 2001," NRDC: Nuclear Notebook, *Bulletin of the Atomic Scientists* 57, no. 4 (July–August 2001): 70–71, <http://www.thebulletin.org/article_nn.php?art_ofn=ja01norris>.

Table 5.4
(continued)

g. Robert S. Norris and Hans M. Kristensen, "India's Nuclear Forces, 2005," NRDC: Nuclear Notebook, *Bulletin of the Atomic Scientists* 61, no. 5 (September–October 2005): 73–75, <http://www.thebulletin.org/article_nn.php?art _ofn=so05norris>. According to Timothy Hoyt, "Both India and Pakistan claim to have tested subkiloton nuclear weapons in their May [1998] tests. If correct, these weapons are relatively optimized for tactical nuclear use in the subcontinent. . . . Even if subkiloton devices do not exist, the consensus of most analysts is that Indian and Pakistani weapons have yields in the low-kiloton range, roughly equivalent to the fission weapons used in Hiroshima and Nagasaki. In appropriate terrain, like the desert regions in Rajasthan, these weapons could still be used as battlefield weapons." Timothy D. Hoyt, "The Buddha Frowns? Tactical Nuclear Weapons in South Asia," in *Tactical Nuclear Weapons: Emerging Threats in an Evolving Security Environment*, ed. Brian Alexander and Alistair Millar (Washington, DC: Brassey's, 2003), 95.

h. Robert S. Norris, Hans M. Kristensen, and Joshua Handler, "Pakistan's Nuclear Forces, 2001," NRDC: Nuclear Notebook, *Bulletin of the Atomic Scientists* 58, no. 1 (January–February 2002): 70–71, <http://www.thebulletin.org/ article_nn.php?art_ofn=jf02norris>.

i. Although the UK no longer deploys its WE177 gravity bombs, its remaining submarine-launched Trident missiles are capable of performing a substrategic or tactical role. According to the Natural Resources Defense Council, "Some Trident II SLBMs already have a single warhead and are assigned targets once covered by WE177 gravity bombs. This means that when Vigilant is on patrol, 10, 12, or 14 of its missiles may carry as many as three warheads, while the other two, four, or six may be armed with only one warhead. There is some flexibility in the choice of yield of the Trident warhead. (For instance, choosing to detonate only the unboosted primary could produce a yield of 1 kiloton or less. Or choosing to detonate the boosted primary could produce a yield of a few kilotons.) With dual missions, an SSBN would have approximately 36–44 warheads on board during patrol." See Robert S. Norris, William M. Arkin, Hans M. Kristensen, and Joshua Handler, "British Nuclear Forces, 2001," NRDC: Nuclear Notebook, *Bulletin of the Atomic Scientists* 57, no. 6 (November–December 2001): 78–79.

reductions,[35] a comparative lack of transparency from Moscow has fueled doubts and concerns about the extent to which Russia has actually fulfilled its pledges.[36]

Uncertainties surrounding implementation of the PNIs, and qualities of the agreements themselves leave this entire class of nuclear weapons still largely unmonitored and uncontrolled.[37] Despite numerous efforts at the United Nations to strengthen the PNIs, these agreements, as with unilateral arms control initiatives in general, are not legally binding, allowing either side to modify or withdraw from the arrangement.[38] They do not provide any consistent means for data sharing and verification, thereby increasing uncertainty regarding stockpile levels, implementation, and the manner in which and timing when information is shared. They do not limit research and development into other similar, newer, or related weapons systems. They provide no way of assuring the public that any reduction is actually taking place. They are vulnerable to changes in other international agreements and shifts in strategic relations or international attitudes that may undercut a long-term commitment to nuclear reduction.[39]

Former senator Sam Nunn (D-GA), former Clinton administration defense secretary William J. Perry, and former commander of U.S. strategic nuclear forces retired Air Force General Eugene E. Habiger argue that an accurate accounting of both U.S. and Russian tactical nuclear arsenals should be a priority in the effort to prevent terrorists from obtaining and using weapons of mass destruction, noting that "[t]hese are the nuclear weapons most attractive to terrorists—even more attractive to them than radioactive bomb-making material, and much more portable than strategic warheads."[40]

In the early 1990s the limited time that Moscow had to move its TNWs from various Soviet republics into Russia led to a substandard accounting of the number and exact location of those weapons. "Dozens of small nuclear weapons, ideal for terrorist use, may have fallen into the wrong hands, or perhaps not," said Congressman Curt Weldon, chair of the U.S. House of Representatives Military Research and Development Subcommittee.[41] "The important point is that crime, corruption, incompetence, and institutional disintegration are so advanced in Russia that the theft of nuclear weapons, unthinkable in the Soviet era of the cold war, seems entirely plausible in the Russia of today." To date there is no publicly available evidence to corroborate claims that terrorists have procured intact TNWs,[42] although there have been smuggling incidents reported by the International Atomic Energy Agency (IAEA) and at least one case where two Lithuanian arms brokers were accused of offering to sell Russian TNWs to U.S. undercover agents.[43] Said Weldon, "The mere possibility that terrorists or rogue states may have acquired some Russian nuclear weapons should be a matter of the gravest concern to the governments and the people of the West."[44]

The work of controlling TNWs has been greatly hampered by the growing impression in Russia, particularly in more nationalist circles, that cooperative threat-reduction efforts are aimed at disarming Russia. In February 2005 at a summit in Bratislava, President Bush and Russian leader Vladimir Putin announced a series of initiatives to improve cooperative efforts to secure nuclear weapons and materials, including the establishment of a senior interagency group to oversee implementation and the sharing of best practices for improving security at nuclear facilities. However, widespread reports in even some of the mainstream Russian press in advance of the summit hinted that Russia was preparing to allow U.S. or international control of its nuclear weapons, sparking nationalist protests in Russia.[45] Although such suspicions are by no means new, they are increasingly widespread and have served to make the Russian leadership far more reluctant than in the past to discuss TNW control.

In the summer of 2006, Russia released its first white paper on the subject of nonproliferation in over ten years. It stated that "the greatest threat faced by Russia and other states in the area of nonproliferation will emanate from the possible use by terrorists of some type of WMD."[46] Nikolai Sokov, an analyst at the Center for Nonproliferation Studies, noted however that it "estimates the risk of terrorists acquiring or building a nuclear weapon as extremely low" and instead concludes that "the greatest risk is the possibility that terrorists might acquire radioactive materials to build a radiological device." This assumption "has direct implications for policy with regard to security of nuclear weapons and fissile materials as opposed to radiation sources and probably proceeds from Moscow's premise that the security of nuclear weapons and weapons grade materials in nuclear states (including Russia, of course) is adequate."[47]

Regional Approaches

The 9/11 terrorist attacks have made nonproliferation norms more important than ever and the issue of controlling existing TNWs and preventing the development of new ones even more urgent. The vast majority of TNWs are deployed as remnants of the cold war in Russia and to a lesser extent in Europe, where confidence-building measures and data exchanges are needed between two former enemies in regional security fora, such as the NATO-Russia Council. Involving NATO not only as an alliance but as a regional player makes sense. Canada and twenty-four European nations in NATO have concerns about the threat of Russian and U.S. tactical weapons in locations either within or proximate to their own territory and can help to encourage continued dialogue to increase transparency and improve security measures taken by the U.S. and Russia.

A regional approach to the problem of terrorism and nuclear weapons is also necessary in other parts of the world. Nuclear weapon–free zones (NWFZs) have been common means of achieving regional nonproliferation goals. The Nuclear Nonproliferation Treaty (NPT) gives all states the right to create them. Regional nuclear weapon–free zones have been adopted with considerable success over the last forty years and may offer long-term means of controlling nuclear weapons and materials. In 1967 the Treaty of Tlatelolco established the first NWFZ in Latin America with all parties agreeing not to manufacture or acquire control of atomic weapons. A group of states in the Pacific joined an NWFZ under the 1985 Treaty of Rarotonga. Eleven years later the Pelindaba Treaty was signed by several African nations but has yet to be entered into force. A Southeast Asia Nuclear Weapons Free Zone treaty was signed in Bangkok in 1995. Despite opposition from the UK, France, and the U.S., a Central Asian Nuclear Weapons Free Zone was established with the signatures of Kazakhstan, Kyrgyzstan, Tajikistan, Turkmenistan, and Uzbekistan on 8 September 2006. An initiative to create a free zone in Central and Eastern Europe has not come to fruition.[48]

The greatest need for a nuclear free zone is in the Middle East, where proliferation exacerbates already dangerous threats to local and global security. The region that stretches from North Africa to the Persian Gulf contains a high concentration of biological and chemical weapons in the hands of states with hostile relations toward their neighbors. It includes Israel, an undeclared nuclear weapon state; Iraq, which was forced to disarm; and Iran, which is suspected of seeking to acquire nuclear weapons capability. Several of the states in the region face hostile relations within and along their own borders. Inter-Arab and regional rivalries continue to have a profound effect on the security policies of every nation in the vicinity, particularly those nations that have sought, developed, and in some cases proliferated nuclear weapons and materials. There is no region in greater need of coordinated proliferation control. Calls for a nuclear weapon-free zone in the Middle East have been persistent. Iran and Egypt formally suggested a regional NWFZ nearly thirty years ago. Since then, there have been dozens of resolutions passed in the UN General Assembly affirming that the creation of such a weapons-free zone in the Middle East would lead to increased regional and international peace and security. UN Security Council Resolution 687, which ended the Gulf War in 1991, described the mandated measures for Iraqi disarmament as "steps toward establishing in the Middle East a zone free from weapons of mass destruction."[49] The demand for a denuclearized Middle East was repeated in the declarations of the NPT Review and Extension Conference in 1995.

There are several reasons why these proposals for a regional NWFZ have been ignored. The principal factor has been the Israeli-Palestinian conflict. It will not be possible to advance regional nonproliferation objectives without a concerted effort to address broader issues of Middle East peace and regional demilitarization based on the uniform acceptance of international law and compliance with UN resolutions. There is an abiding connection between nuclear nonproliferation measures and efforts to resolve the conflict between Israelis and Palestinians. Forward progress in the peace process would greatly increase regional enthusiasm for the implementation of IAEA safeguards and regional nonproliferation objectives.[50]

Israel's status as a de facto nuclear power and its refusal to join the NPT are also obstacles to regional agreement. Despite UN Security Council Resolution 487 (1981) specifically calling on Israel to place its nuclear facilities under IAEA safeguards, the country's program is not subject to any international monitoring.[51] This has been a source of concern among neighboring governments. Arab states have led other nations in accusing the United States of applying double standards by trying to crack down on Iraq, Syria, North Korea, and Iran while ignoring Israel's advanced nuclear, chemical, and biological weapons capabilities. The director general of the International Atomic Energy Agency, Mohamed ElBaradei, has used the following analogy to describe the dilemma: "as long as you have countries dangling a cigarette from their mouth, you cannot tell everyone not to smoke with a high degree of credibility."[52] Without a greater commitment to transparency and consistency, progress toward nonproliferation objectives will be difficult.

Global Approaches

Multilateral approaches to nonproliferation, ad hoc and general, have made significant contributions to increasing awareness and pooling resources to prevent nuclear materials from getting into the hands of terrorists. A recent U.S.-sponsored program is the Proliferation Security Initiative (PSI). This is an ad hoc series of international agreements designed to enable the United States and cooperating nations to interdict shipments of WMD materials on the high seas. A state department fact sheet on PSI describes it as "partnerships of states working in concert, employing their national capabilities to develop a broad range of legal, diplomatic, economic, military and other tools to interdict shipments of such items." The primary legal basis for such interdictions is through bilateral boarding agreements among PSI partners such as Panama and Liberia.[53] The initiative is not covered by a UN resolution, although the former under secretary of state for arms control and U.S. ambassador to the UN, John Bolton, made carefully worded statements that inappropriately attempt to answer questions about the legality of the PSI by mentioning international support for UN Security Council Resolution 1540:

When PSI first emerged, it was criticized inaccurately as an initiative with a shaky legal underpinning. There is in national legal systems and relevant international authorities ample authority to support interdiction actions at sea, in the air, and on land. States around the world have concurred with this fact and made political commitments to the PSI Statement of Interdiction Principles. Importantly, the unanimous passage of U.N. Security Council [UNSC] Resolution 1540 establishes clear international acknowledgement that active cooperation among states, such as PSI, is both useful and necessary. Paragraph 10 of the resolution . . . calls upon all states to "take cooperative action to prevent illicit trafficking in nuclear, chemical, and biological weapons, their means of delivery and related materials."[54]

Despite a number of widely publicized interdiction exercises coordinated between PSI participants, it remains unclear what PSI has accomplished since it was established in May 2003. Advocates point to Libya as a success story. In October 2003 American and British officials, acting on intelligence tips, diverted a German ship heading for Libya. On inspection of the vessel, they discovered equipment for processing nuclear weapons-grade material. Two months later Libya made its announcement to abandon all unconventional weapons programs. Some claim that the seizure speeded up Libya's decision to dismantle its WMD programs. The interdiction was a factor, but it should not be overstated. It did not create the necessary diplomatic conditions for reaching a successful agreement with Libyan president Mohamar Qaddafi. As described in chapter 4, the roots of the Libya agreement preceded the shipping incident and the war in Iraq. The favorable outcome in Libya flowed from years of negotiation and dialogue with the U.S. and multilateral organizations.

The Group of Eight (G-8) Global Partnership against the Spread of Weapons and Materials of Mass Destruction is another ad hoc multilateral effort to prevent nuclear materials from getting into the hands of terrorists. The G-8 member nations have pledged $20 billion over a ten-year period to this effort, including $10 billion from the United States (10 + 10 over 10).[55] The focus of the partnership has been to encourage cooperative projects to address nonproliferation, disarmament, counterterrorism, and nuclear safety issues. The G-8 started its work in Russia, where it adopted a set of guidelines for the negotiation of specific nuclear safety projects. The G-8 countries have invited other nations to participate in the initiative. Australia, Belgium, the Czech Republic, Denmark,

Ireland, the Republic of Korea, and New Zealand have joined as donors, and the Ukraine and other former Soviet republics are being encouraged to participate as recipients.

The most comprehensive multilateral effort is the UN counter-terrorism program, which has shown that addressing security issues in a cooperative framework is a successful model for encouraging states to comply with international mandates. United Nations Security Council Resolution 1373 (2001) created an innovative campaign of cooperative law enforcement measures to combat global terrorist threats. In 2004, motivated by a heightened sensitivity to nuclear security after the 9/11 attacks and the revelations of A. Q. Khan, the Security Council adopted Resolution 1540, extending UN counter-terrorism mandates to address the problem of proliferation. The resolution requires all UN member states to undertake a series of measures to prevent the proliferation and transfer to terrorists and other nonstate actors of biological, chemical, and nuclear weapons; their delivery systems; and related materials. It specifically prohibits countries from providing any kind of support to nonstate actors for the development of WMD and mandates that states adopt laws to prevent the diversion of WMD and related materials. It calls on all states "to promote the universal adoption and full implementation, and, where necessary, strengthening of multilateral treaties to which they are parties, whose aim is to prevent the proliferation of nuclear, biological or chemical weapons." The resolution also requires states to adhere to the 1980 Convention on the Physical Protection of Nuclear Materials. Resolution 1540 was an effort by the United States and other governments to enhance institutional multilateral cooperation against proliferation. The resolution came at a time when the international security climate was increasingly characterized by unilateralism and ad hoc coalition building, as practiced by the Bush administration. Resolution 1540 reverted to the common diplomatic language of nonproliferation, multilateralism, and cooperation, without any reference to counterproliferation or military preemption and/or prevention.[56]

Resolution 1540 calls on all states to take cooperative action to stop, impede, intercept, and otherwise prevent the illicit trafficking in WMD, their means of delivery, and related materials. As Mohamed ElBaradei noted:

The operative paragraphs of the Resolution cover legal measures, accountancy and control measures, physical protection measures, border controls, measures to detect, deter, prevent and combat illicit trafficking, and export and import measures. They closely mirror the structure and activities of the Agency's existing nuclear security Plan of Activities.[57]

Accordingly, the resolution could bolster relevant IAEA activities, and if requested, the agency will be able to offer technical advice in support of implementation efforts.

International controls over the export of sensitive nuclear material and technology could also be tightened by the resolution. Again, according to ElBaradei,

[T]he nuclear export control system should be binding rather than voluntary, and should be made more widely applicable, to include all countries with the capability of manufacturing sensitive nuclear related items. . . . As prescribed in . . . Security Council Resolution 1540, it [the international export control system] should ensure effective national control over sensitive items, and criminalize the actions of individuals and companies involved in efforts to acquire nuclear weapons.[58]

Moreover, Resolution 1540 could provide a unique opportunity to engage NPT holdouts in concerted and formalized nonproliferation activities. Now, for the first time, such states have similar obligations as the rest of the world. Pakistan, for example, like India and Israel, is not a member of the NPT. Yet its government used Resolution 1540 to justify more stringent export controls.[59]

Resolution 1540 created a nonproliferation committee to monitor and oversee implementation. The committee hired a group of experts to examine documentation provided by states. The resolution requires every state to report to the committee on efforts to comply with the mandated measures. As of 20 September 2006, 132 out of 192 UN member states had submitted reports to the committee and a further seventy-nine submitted second-round reports in response to requests for additional information.

State compliance with Resolution 1540 would be aided by the establishment of clear criteria for compliance. The creation of a transparent, fair, and clearly defined evaluation process would enable the Nonproliferation Committee to better assess states' compliance needs and potential problems. It would also have the practical effect of establishing a higher minimum standard for control list requirements of treaty-related materials. Currently, Resolution 1540 has two different standards on control lists: one for states party to multilateral treaties and arrangements and the other pertaining only to national control lists. This allows states that are not party to multilateral agreements to apply lower standards established by often inadequate national control lists. Terrorists could take advantage of this to acquire prohibited items in countries with looser standards.

Long-standing efforts to raise awareness and encourage collective action on the issue of nuclear terrorism in the UN General Assembly received a boost on 13 April 2005 when the assembly adopted the *International Convention for the Suppression of Acts of Nuclear Terrorism*. Once the convention enters in force, after twenty-two nations ratify it, UN member governments will be required to amend national laws and take other appropriate actions to prosecute or extradite any persons who possess radioactive material or a radioactive device with the intent to cause, or threaten to cause, death or injury or to damage property or the environment. Along with UN Security Council Resolution 1373 and the other twelve UN conventions on terrorism, the nuclear terrorism convention requires enhanced cooperation among states on information sharing and legal assistance.[60]

Conclusion

Al-Qaida's attempts to acquire a nuclear weapons capability pose unique challenges in an international system currently confronting an upsurge in threats to international security from nonstate actors. Russian tactical nuclear weapons and the proliferation of weapons-related materials in South Asia and the Middle East raise particular vulnerabilities that require urgent attention. Dealing with nonstate actors is an important part of the work that is now being done at the UN, in the G-8, and in other international fora to prevent terrorists from acquiring WMD and to improve control of potentially dangerous materials. Existing norms—particularly export control regimes, which prohibit transfer of proscribed items to nonstate entities—go a long way to address evolving nonconventional threats from nonstate actors. These are best met by rigorous national systems of protection, control and accounting, and strong international nonproliferation norms. Nonproliferation treaties and agreements will continue to play important roles and must be strengthened by the careful implementation of Resolution 1540 and by state parties affirming, through actions and not just words, their commitment to reduce and eliminate nuclear weapons. Efforts to control weapons and keep all relevant components and materials (particularly fissile material) out of terrorists' hands require a multilevel response that focuses on prevention at the source as the only realistic option to sever the deadly nexus and prevent its unthinkable destructive consequences.

Notes

1. Donald Rumsfeld, U.S. secretary of defense, quoted by the Associated Press's military writer, Robert Burns, "Defense Secretary Says Potentially Deadly Link Between Terrorist Networks and 'Terrorist States' Must Be Stopped," Associated Press, 31 January 2002. This appraisal was one of the few issues George W. Bush and his presidential campaign opponent Senator John Kerry agreed on during a heated election campaign in 2004.

2. Weapons of Mass Destruction Commission, "Reviving Disarmament," in *Weapons of Terror: Freeing the World of Nuclear, Biological and Chemical Arms* (Stockholm: Weapons of Mass Destruction Commission, June 2006), 28, <http://www.wmdcommission.org/files/Weapons_of_Terror.pdf> (accessed 23 August 2006).

3. Charles D. Ferguson, *Preventing Catastrophic Nuclear Terrorism*, Council on Foreign Relations Special Report No. 11 (New York: Council on Foreign Relations Press, March 2006), 1.

4. Walter Pincus, "Pentagon Revises Nuclear Strike Plan Strategy; Includes Preemptive Use Against Banned Weapons," *Washington Post*, 11 September 2005; see also William M. Arkin, "A New Trident II Is an Illusion of Defense," *Washington Post*, 22 May 2006, <http://blog.washingtonpost.com/earlywarning/2006/05/a_new_trident_ii_is_an_illusio.html> (accessed 8 August 2006).

5. White House, *The National Security Strategy of the United States of America* (Washington, DC: GPO, March 2006), 19, <http://www.whitehouse.gov/nsc/nss/2006/nss2006.pdf#search=%22The%20National%20Security%20Strategy%20of%20the%20United%20States%20of%20America%202006%22> (accessed 23 August 2006).

6. For a discussion of this issue, see Christopher F. Chyba, "Toward Biological Security," in *Terrorism and Counterterrorism: Understanding the New Security Environment—Readings and Interpretations*, rev. and updated by Russell D. Howard and Reid Sawyer (Guilford, CT: McGraw-Hill/Dushkin, 2003), 198–99.

7. In a Christmas message delivered on 28 December 1937, Cosmo Gordon Lang, archbishop of Canterbury, posed the question, "Who can think without horror of what another widespread war would mean, waged as it would be with all the new weapons of mass destruction?" See Cosmo Gordon Lang, archbishop of Canterbury, "Archbishop's Appeal: Individual Will and Action," *London Times*, 28 December 1937, quoted in Dave Wilton, *Etymologies and Word Origins*, s.v. "weapons of mass destruction," <http://www.wordorigins.org/index.php/site/comments/weapon_of_mass_destruction/> (accessed 15 June 2005).

8. In 1998 U.S. Secretary of Defense William Cohen added radiological weapons to the definition of WMD, and in an interview with CNN's Wolf Blitzer, then chairman of the Joint Chiefs of Staff General Richard Myers explained that the president should have "all the options that a president would want to have in case this country or our friends and allies were attacked with weapons of mass destruction, be they nuclear, biological, chemical or, for that matter, high explosives." Chyba and others include cyberweapons. See "Officials: Nuclear Strategy a Deterrent," *CBS News*, 10 March 2002, <http://www.cbsnews.com/stories/2002/03/13/national/main503608.shtml> (accessed 17 March 2005).

9. Chyba, "Toward Biological Security."

10. Chyba, "Toward Biological Security."

11. According to the Federation of American Scientists, "Nuclear detonations are the most devastating of the weapons of mass destruction. To make this point one need only recall the pictures from Hiroshima or the international furor over the accidental but enormous radiation release from the Chernobyl power plant. The contamination from Chernobyl was significantly larger than would have been expected from a nuclear detonation of about 20 kT at ground level, but was comparable in extent to what might result from a small nuclear war in which a dozen or so weapons of nominal yield were exploded at altitudes intended to maximize blast damage." See John Pike, "Nuclear Weapon Effects," *Special Weapons Primer*, Federation of American Scientists, <http://www.fas.org/nuke/intro/nuke/effects.htm> (accessed 17 March 2005).

12. Sam Nunn, cochair, Nuclear Threat Initiative, "The Race Between Cooperation and Catastrophe: Reducing the Global Nuclear Threat," speech before the National Press Club, Washington, DC, 9 March 2005, Nuclear Threat Initiative, <http://www.ntinitiative.org/c_press/speech_nunnpressclub_030905.pdf> (accessed 17 March 2005).

13. Vice Admiral Lowell E. Jacoby, director, Defense Intelligence Agency, "Current and Projected National Security Threats to the United States," statement before the Senate Select Committee on Intelligence, 109th Cong., 1st sess., Washington, DC, 16 February 2005.

14. Matthew Bunn, John P. Holdren, and Anthony Wier, *Securing Nuclear Weapons and Materials: Seven Steps for Immediate Action*, report, Project on Managing the Atom and Nuclear Threat Initiative, Belfer Center for Science and

International Affairs, John F. Kennedy School of Government, Harvard University, Cambridge, MA, 20 May 2002, <http://bcsia.ksg.harvard.edu/publication.cfm?ctype=book&item_id=90> (accessed 17 March 2005).

15. Rahimullah Yusufzai, "Wrath of God: Osama bin Laden Lashes Out Against the West" (interview with Osama Bin Laden), *Time Asia*, 11 January 1999, <http://www.time.com/time/asia/asia/magazine/1999/990111/osama1.html> (accessed 24 August 2006).

16. Thomas Fingar, assistant secretary of state for intelligence and research, "Current and Projected National Security Threats to the United States," statement before the Senate Select Committee on Intelligence, 109th Cong., 1st sess., Washington, DC, 16 February 2005), quoted in Dana Priest and Josh White, "War Helps Recruit Terrorists, Hill Told; Intelligence Officials Talk of Growing Insurgency," *Washington Post*, 17 February 2005.

17. National Intelligence Council (NIC), Title Classified, ICA 2001-07HC, 22 October 2001, 4; see also Commission on the Intelligence Capabilities of the United States Regarding Weapons of Mass Destruction, *Report to the President of the United States* (Washington, DC: GPO 31 March 2005), <http://www.wmd.gov/report/index.html> (accessed 24 August 2006).

18. Cyberterrorism could possibly be used to manipulate command and control nuclear weapons delivery systems, and an attack on a nuclear power plant could produce mass destruction from radiation. These options would not require a terrorist to possess a nuclear weapon.

19. Gary Ackerman and Laura Snyder argue that states of this sort would "want to be able to maintain 'deniability.'" If a target state or the international community should discover (or perhaps only suspect) that a country may have handed over a nuclear bomb or a bioweapon to a terrorist group, retribution would be almost certain. While they are happy to supply terrorists with conventional arms, finances, and training, most state sponsors of terrorism would ordinarily have little incentive to supply terrorists with weapons of mass destruction. See Gary Ackerman and Laura Snyder, "Would They If They Could?," *Bulletin of the Atomic Scientists* 58, no. 3 (May–June 2002): 40–47. For background on the A. Q. Kahn network and Pakistan, see Global Security, "Weapons of Mass Destruction (WMD): A. Q. Khan," <http://www.globalsecurity.org/wmd/world/pakistan/khan.htm> (accessed 18 March 2005).

20. Thomas Fingar, assistant secretary of state for intelligence and research, judges that the "so far theoretical possibility of nuclear weapons falling into the hands of terrorists constitutes a very different type of threat": "We have seen no persuasive evidence that al-Qaida has obtained fissile material or ever has had a serious and sustained program to do so. At worst, the group possesses small amounts of radiological material that could be used to fabricate a radiological dispersion device ('dirty bomb'). The only practical way for non-state actors to obtain sufficient fissile material for a nuclear weapon (as opposed to material for a so-called dirty bomb) would be to acquire it on the black market or to steal it from one of the current, want-to-be, or used-to-be nuclear weapons states." Fingar, "Current and Projected National Security Threats to the United States."

21. J. Mark Carson et al., "Can Terrorists Build Nuclear Weapons?," paper prepared for the International Task Force on the Prevention of Nuclear Terrorism, Nuclear Control Institute, Washington, DC, 1987, <http://www.nci.org/k-m/makeab.htm> (accessed 18 March 2005).

22. Graham Allison, *Nuclear Terrorism: The Ultimate Preventable Catastrophe* (New York: Times Books, 2004), 68.

23. Howard Baker and Lloyd Cutler, *A Report Card on the Department of Energy's Nonproliferation Programs with Russia*, draft paper of the Secretary of Energy Advisory Board, United States Department of Energy, 10 January 2000 (released 10 January 2001), <http://www.seab.energy.gov/publications/rpt.pdf> (accessed 24 August 2006).

24. National Intelligence Council, *Annual Report to Congress on the Safety and Security of Russian Nuclear Facilities and Military Forces*, 108th Cong., 2d sess., Washington, DC, December 2004, <http://www.cia.gov/nic/special_russiannuke04.html> (accessed 18 March 2005).

25. National Intelligence Council, *Annual Report to Congress on the Safety and Security of Russian Nuclear Facilities and Military Forces*.

26. Agence France-Presse, "U.S. Intelligence Concludes Theft of Russian Nuclear Material 'Has Occurred,'" 23 February 2005.

27. According to Matthew Bunn, "The Russian state newspaper reports that the 41 heavily armed terrorists who seized a theater in Moscow in October 2002 considered seizing the Kurchatov Institute, a Moscow site with enough HEU for dozens of bombs." See Matthew Bunn, "Preventing a Nuclear 9/11," *Issues in Science and Technology* (Winter 2005): 55–62.

28. Raymond Bonner and Craig S. Smith, "Pakistani Said to Have Given Libya Uranium," *New York Times*, 21 February 2004; Farhan Bokhari, et al., "Pakistan's 'Rogue Nuclear Scientist': What Did Khan's Government Know about his Deals?" *Financial Times* (London), 6 April 2004; David E. Sanger, "In Face of Report, Iran Acknowledges Buying Nuclear Components," *New York Times*, 23 February 2004.

29. Led by Senators Sam Nunn (D-GA) and Richard Lugar (R-IN), the U.S. Congress laid the foundations for handling the threats posed by unsecured stockpiles of WMD. Since 1991, this cooperative initiative has evolved into a broad set of programs across different agencies, primarily the departments of defense, energy, and state. Together these programs have helped to protect, secure, and begin destroying nuclear warheads, delivery vehicles (such as bombers, missiles, and submarines), and hundreds of metric tons of weapons-usable material. Additional programs have helped to redirect weapons scientists and engineers from defense work to civilian employment. These scientists, many of whom live under severe economic distress due to Russia's economic climate, may be tempted to sell their skills to terrorist groups or states. Helping to redirect the skills of the weapons scientists to productive civilian industries reduces the likelihood that a terrorist group or nonnuclear state could construct a nuclear weapon.

30. Estimates by the Natural Resources Defense Council (NRDC) indicate that there are nearly 2,000 U.S. tactical gravity bombs and Tomahawk cruise missiles suitable for submarine launchers. See Robert S. Norris and Hans M. Kristensen, "U.S. Nuclear Forces, 2005," *Bulletin of the Atomic Scientists* 61, no. 1 (January–February 2005): 73–75, <http://www.thebulletin.org/article_nn.php ?art_ofn=jf05norris> (accessed 25 August 2006). Estimates for Russia are much less certain. Norris and Kristensen believe there are around 3,400; other estimates are as high as 8,000 and are summarized in Andrea Gabbitas, "Non-Strategic Nuclear Weapons: Problems of Definition," in *Controlling Non-Strategic Nuclear Weapons: Obstacles and Opportunities*, ed. Jeffrey Larsen and Kurt Klingenberger (Colorado Springs, CO: United States Air Force Academy Institute for National Security Studies, 2001), 25.

31. See table 3.1 in Charles D. Ferguson and William C. Potter et al., *The Four Faces of Nuclear Terrorism* (Monterey, CA: Monterey Institute of International Affairs, 2005), 49.

32. "[A] few high-profile episodes point to a spreading ethos of corruption in the Russian nuclear establishment that could presage major covert exports of fissile material, weapons components, and even intact nuclear weapons." Rensselaer Lee, "Nuclear Smuggling from the Former Soviet Union: Threats and Responses," *Global Beat*, 27 April 2001, <http://www.bu.edu/globalbeat/ nuclear/FPRI042701.html> (accessed 25 August 2006).

33. Harold Müller and Annette Schaper, "Part II: Definitions, Types, Missions, Risks and Options for Control: A European Perspective," in *Tactical Nuclear Weapons: Options for Control*, ed. William Potter et al. (Geneva: United Nations, 2001), 19–78.

34. Joshua Handler, "The September 1991 PNIs and the Elimination, Storing and Security Aspects of TNWs," presentation at the Time to Control Tactical Nuclear Weapons seminar hosted by the United Nations Institute for Disarmament Research et al., New York, 24 September 2001, <http://www.princeton.edu/ ~globsec/publications/pdf/untalk.pdf> (accessed 18 March 2005), 22 n.6, quoting United States Department of Defense, *Proliferation: Threat and Response*, 3d ed. (Washington, DC: GPO, 10 January 2001).

35. For example, Russian Foreign Minister Igor Ivanov stated at the Review Conference on the Treaty on the Non-Proliferation of Nuclear Weapons on 25 April 2000 that "Russia also continues to consistently implement its unilateral initiatives related [to] tactical nuclear weapons. Such weapons have been completely removed from surface ships and multipurpose submarines, as well as from the land-based naval aircraft, and are stored at centralized storage facilities. One third of all nuclear munitions for the sea-based tactical missiles and naval aircraft has been eliminated. We are about to complete the destruction of nuclear warheads from tactical missiles, artillery shells and nuclear mines. We have destroyed half of the nuclear warheads for anti-aircraft missiles and for nuclear gravity bombs." See H. E. Igor S. Ivanov, *Statement to the Non-Proliferation Treaty 2000 Review Conference*, New York, 25 April 2000, Federation of

American Scientists, <http://www.fas.org/nuke/control/npt/news/00_04_25.htm> (accessed 18 March 2005). Information from Russia on the extent to which it has fulfilled its Pressidential Nuclear Initiative commitments has been very sparse. At the 2000 NPT Review Conference, the Russian foreign minister said publicly that his country had nearly completed implementation of the PNIs, but two years later contradictory Russian statements indicated that the process would not be completed until some future date and that only provided funding was available. In May 2004 Russia announced that half of its total arsenal of sea-based and naval aviation tactical nuclear warheads had been "liquidated." In October 2004 the U.S. assistant secretary of state, Stephen Rademaker, asserted, "The Russian side has not fully met its commitments to reduce TNWs in Europe." The Russian response illustrates how precarious unilateral initiatives are in comparison to codified arms control treaties. The spokesman for the Russian ministry of foreign affairs noted that it was "incorrect" to refer to the PNIs as commitments and that they should be seen rather as "a goodwill gesture on the part of Russia." Russia also points out that the United States still deploys TNWs in Europe for NATO and is therefore in violation of its PNI commitments.

36. For an appraisal of the extent to which Russia has implemented the 1991–1992 commitments, see David Yost, "Russia and Arms Control for Non Strategic Forces," in *Controlling Non-Strategic Nuclear Weapons: Obstacles and Opportunities*, ed. Jeffrey Larsen and Kurt Klingenberger (Colorado Springs, CO: United States Air Force Academy and Institute for National Security Studies, 2001), 133–37.

37. Tactical nuclear weapons do receive periodic mention in international non-proliferation discourse. For example, the 2000 Nonproliferation Treaty Review Conference calls for "the further reduction of non-strategic nuclear weapons, based on unilateral initiatives and as an integral part of the arms-control process." For more information on this, see Tariq Rauf, *Towards NPT 2005: An Action Plan for the 'Thirteen Steps' Towards Nuclear Disarmament Agreed at NPT 2000* (Monterey, CA: Monterey Institute for International Studies, 2001), Center for Nonproliferation Studies, <http://www.cns.miis.edu/pubs/reports/pdfs/npt2005.pdf> (accessed 18 March 2005). However, concrete steps or actual implementations of measures to reduce or control TNWs have not occurred, other than the 1991–1992 presidential initiatives.

38. The New Agenda Coalition (NAC) of Brazil, Egypt, Ireland, Mexico, New Zealand, South Africa, and Sweden has had significant impact at the United Nations on the issue of verification and control of nonstrategic nuclear weapons within the Nonproliferation Treaty (NPT) agenda. The Final Document from the Sixth NPT Review Conference in 2000 reflected agreement among all NPT states parties on the need to reduce tactical nuclear weapons, calling for "further reduction of non-strategic nuclear weapons, based on unilateral initiatives and as an integral part of the nuclear arms reduction and disarmament process." The NAC has continued to apply pressure on this point in the UN First Committee and the UN General Assembly. In 2002 the General Assembly adopted Resolution 57/58, titled the *Reduction of Non-Strategic Nuclear Weapons*, submitted by

Ireland on behalf of the NAC. From 2002 to 2004 several working papers by individual states and groups of states set forth proposals for moving these issues forward within the NPT. Austria, Sweden, and Ukraine, for example, produced a working paper at the 2004 Preparatory Committee for the 2005 Review Conference of the NPT on "Reductions of Non-Strategic Nuclear Weapons," which suggested nine succinct recommendations for reducing and enhancing the security of TNWs to the 2005 Review Conference. One major point addressed in the working paper and in the NAC resolutions underscores "the importance of preserving, reaffirming and implementing the 1991 and 1992 Presidential Nuclear Initiatives." See Preparatory Committee of Austria, Sweden, and Ukraine, "Reductions of Non-Strategic Nuclear Weapons," working paper prepared for the Conference of the Parties to the Treaty on the Non-Proliferation of Nuclear Weapons, Third Session, New York, NPT/CONF.2005/PC.III/WP.13, 29 April 2004, Reaching Critical Will, <http://www.reachingcriticalwill.org/legal/npt/prepcom04/WPX.pdf> (accessed 7 July 2005).

39. See William Potter and Nikolai Sokov, *Tactical Nuclear Weapons: The Nature of the Problem* (Monterey, CA: Monterey Institute of International Studies, 4 January 2001): 6, 11, Center for Nonproliferation Studies, <http://cns.miis.edu/pubs/reports/tnw_nat.htm> (accessed 18 March 2005).

40. Paul Richter, "Tactical Devices Still Present Major Threat," *Los Angeles Times*, 25 May 2002.

41. See Rep. Curt Weldon of Pennsylvania, "Opening Statement of the Chairman, Military Research and Development Subcommittee, at the Hearing on Nuclear Terrorism and Countermeasures," remarks before the House Committee on National Security, Military Research, and Development Subcommittee, 105th Cong., 1st sess., 1 October 1997, Terrorism Research Center, <http://www.terrorism.org/modules.php?op=modload&name=News&file=article&sid=5695> (accessed 20 May 2005).

42. According to the IAEA, since 1993 there have been 175 cases of trafficking in nuclear material and 201 cases of trafficking in other radioactive sources (medical, industrial, etc.). However, only eighteen of these cases have actually involved small amounts of highly enriched uranium or plutonium, the material needed to produce a nuclear bomb. IAEA experts judge the quantities involved to be insufficient to construct a nuclear explosive device. "However, any such materials being in illicit commerce and conceivably accessible to terrorist groups is deeply troubling," says Mohamed ElBaradei. See International Atomic Energy Agency, "Calculating the New Global Nuclear Terrorism Threat," press release, New York, 1 November 2001, <http://www.iaea.org/NewsCenter/PressReleases/2001/nt_pressrelease.shtml> (accessed 21 March 2005). On the case of the two Lithuanian arms dealers, see Aleksey Agureyev, "Two Lithuanians Sentenced in Missile Plot in USA," *ITAR-TASS*, 20 August 1998.

43. See Gary Milhollin, "Can Terrorists Get the Bomb?," *Commentary* 113, no. 2 (February 2002): 45–49.

44. Weldon, "Opening Statement."

45. See, for example, Interfax, "Moscow Rally Calls to Prevent US Control Over Russian Nuclear Facilities," 20 February 2005.

46. Center for Nonproliferation Studies, trans., "The Russian Federation and Nonproliferation of Weapons of Mass Destruction and Delivery Systems: Threats, Assessments, Problems and Solutions," a Russian government white paper translated by Monterey Institute for International Affairs, Center for Nonproliferation Studies, Monterey, CA, June 2006, <http://cns.miis.edu/pubs/other/rusfed.htm> (accessed 8 August 2006).

47. Nikolai Sokov, "CNS Analysis of the Russian Government's White Paper on WMD Nonproliferation" Monterey Institute for International Affairs, Center for Nonproliferation Studies, Monterey, CA, 25 July 2006, <http://cns.miis.edu/pubs/week/060726.htm> (accessed 8 August 2006).

48. Scott Parrish and William Potter, "Central Asian States Establish Nuclear-Weapons-Free-Zone Despite U.S. Opposition," research story, Monterey Institute for International Studies, Center for Nonproliferation Studies, Monterey, CA, 8 September 2006, <http://cns.miis.edu/pubs/week/060905.htm> (accessed 20 September 2006).

49. United Nations Security Council, *Security Council Resolution 687 (1991)*, S/RES/687, New York, 3 April 1991.

50. On 22 November 1967, after the Six-Day War, the United Nations Security Council passed Resolution 242 with the aim of providing a solution for the conflict in the Middle East. Resolution 338 passed on 22 October 1973 during the Yom Kippur War. It called on the Arab states and Israel to engage in direct peace talks and to establish an effective framework for future peace negotiations.

51. United Nations Security Council, *Security Council Resolution 487 (1981)*, S/RES/487, New York, 19 June 1981.

52. "Iran and Israel: Chain Reaction," *Christian Science Monitor*, 9 July 2004.

53. United States Department of State, Bureau of Nonproliferation, "Proliferation Security Initiative Frequently Asked Questions (FAQ)" Fact Sheet, 11 January 2005, <http://www.state.gov/t/np/rls/fs/32725.htm> (accessed 21 March 2005).

54. John Bolton, then undersecretary of state for arms control and international security, "Bolton Outlines Bush Administration's Nonproliferation Efforts," US Info, U.S. Department of State, 19 October 2004, <http://usinfo.state.gov/eap/Archive/2004/Oct/20-535618.html> (accessed 30 August 2006).

55. Claire Applegarth, "G-8 Global Partnership Selects Ukraine for Nonproliferation Funds," *Arms Control Today* 34, no. 1 (December 2004): 41.

56. William Walker, "Weapons of Mass Destruction and International Order," Adelphi Paper 370, International Institute for Strategic Studies, London, November 2004, 75.

57. Mohamed ElBaradei, "Nuclear Security: Measures to Protect Against Nuclear Terrorism," report by the director general to the International Atomic

Energy Agency, Board of Governors General Conference, GOV/2004/50-GC(48)/6, Washington, DC, 11 August 2004, Global Security, <http://www.globalsecurity.org/security/library/report/2004/gc48-6.pdf> (accessed 21 March 2005).

58. Mohamed ElBaradei, "Nuclear Non-Proliferation: Global Security in a Rapidly Changing World," statement, Carnegie International Non-Proliferation Conference, Washington, DC, 21 June 2004, International Atomic Energy Agency, <http://www.iaea.org/NewsCenter/Statements/2004/ebsp2004n004.html> (accessed 21 March 2005).

59. "Counter-Proliferation in Asia: No Place to Hide, Maybe," *Economist*, 30 October–5 November 2004, 47.

60. Colum Lynch, "U.N. Votes to Outlaw Nuclear Terrorism, No New Restrictions Put on Atomic Arms," *Washington Post*, 14 April 2005.

6

Terrorism Defanged: The Financial Action Task Force and International Efforts to Capture Terrorist Finances

Kathryn L. Gardner

For terrorists, money laundering and forms of financial crime provide potent weapons.[1] Terrorism experts recognize money laundering as the "Achilles heel of criminal activity" and as a crucial pressure point in terrorist organizations.[2] Disrupting terrorist financing has become a major task for the United States government and for the international community in the prevention of future terrorist attacks. If the money flow can be shut down, so can the terrorist activities that it was meant to finance. The challenge presented to lead organizations in the fight against terrorism is that they are working within a context of a morphing transnational threat that requires an equally dynamic counter-terrorist strategy. The central tension in this fight is how to structure a response that adapts to the shifting threat, both transnational and local, while simultaneously increasing levels of compliance with existing standards.

Since 2001 the Financial Action Task Force (FATF) has become the lead institution of the world community's fight to detect and counter-terrorist financing. Created in 1989 by the Group of Seven (G-7) nations to combat money laundering activities associated with the international drug trade and other transnational crimes, the FATF is one of the most effective mechanisms in the contemporary international system for capturing the financial resources of would-be terrorists. Composed of thirty-three member jurisdictions, the FATF sets and promotes the adoption of global standards to combat money laundering and terrorist financing and monitors members' progress in implementing anti–money laundering and counter-terrorist financing trends and techniques. Where necessary it imposes countermeasures on noncompliant members and non-members. As an instrument of international cooperation the FATF has achieved marked success. By U.S. government calculations, 130 juris-dictions representing more than 85 percent of the world's population and 90 to 95 percent of economic output have made political commitments to implement FATF recommendations.[3]

This chapter assesses the FATF model in each of the areas in which the organization has become relevant to defunding terrorism. The chapter examines the mandate, structure, and accomplishments of the FATF. It analyzes those factors that have contributed to the FATF model's achievements, including the body's three main processes of developing, adapting, and securing compliance with anti–money laundering and counter-terrorist financing standards from both FATF members as well as nonmember states. The chapter shows the significance of the peer-review process in addressing the central tensions inherent in the inter-national fight to "defund" terrorism. It reviews the practices of other organizations that have attempted to replicate the FATF model and the accomplishments of this model both on regional and global levels. It concludes with an evaluation of the viability of a global-style FATF and addresses whether FATF or its imitators can adequately adjust their measures to the flexible, dynamic enemy of contemporary terrorism.

Capturing Terrorist Monies

An effective counter-terrorist strategy must be proactive, assess threats, and understand the financial goals and structures in which terrorists operate, including their adaptive capabilities. This creates an important tension in the cooperative enterprise: institutions seek to ensure com-pliance with existing standards, while simultaneously seeking new and updated solutions sensitive to the evolving threat. Compliance with FATF and related standards comprises the key issue for the fight against ter-rorism; noncompliance means ineffectiveness. As more states and inter-national organizations join the fight, it is vital to have a unified purpose and approach. This section briefly highlights the nature of the terrorist financing threat, emphasizing its ability to adapt to the international community's counter-terrorism efforts.

Until September 11, 2001 (9/11), tracking terrorist financing was not viewed as a priority either nationally or internationally. Money

laundering—the process by which money with criminal origins or destinations is concealed through multiple, layered transactions in the financial system—has for many years been practiced by organized crime, drug
traffickers, blue-collar criminals, and white-collar embezzlers.[4] It is estimated that between 2 to 5 percent of the world's annual gross domestic
product is derived from money laundering activities—some $600 billion
to $1.5 trillion.[5]

Money laundering is conceptually and empirically tied to contemporary terrorist activity, but the latter differs from global crime in critical
ways: the direction of the related financial transactions, the tolerance for
failure, the motivations of the participants, and the scale of the activity
to be suppressed.[6] In the period after 9/11 analysts highlighted several
important differences in terrorist financing trends. First, terrorist financing generally involves financial flows that originated in legitimate activities to support illegitimate activities rather than the reverse. This makes
one of the key questions for experts not "Who benefits?" but "Who
gives?"[7] As leading terrorist expert Monica Serrano has noted, the "deep
financial logic of terrorism, then, is to be found in the symbolic structures of philanthropy."[8] The legitimate origins of terrorist financing
introduced a significant complication for authorities as they "follow the
money." Second, the stakes are higher in combating terrorist financing.
Therefore, the goal is not to contain or reduce but to eliminate the flow
of funds and to capture the assets. Moreover, traditional money laundering involves a profit motive, while in terrorist financing the profit
motive is replaced by noneconomic motives. While money laundering for
criminals and drug traffickers is mostly for financial gain, for terrorists
the ultimate goal is not money but the end product of committing a
violent act.[9] A final distinction between the two activities is operational:
traditional money launderers deal with large cash deposits, while terrorists deal with substantially lesser amounts of money. This small scale
of the activity makes terrorist financing more evasive. To move the
money into the financial system, the terrorists use mechanisms that
enable them to conceal assets through nontransparent trade or financial
transactions such as the use of charities,[10] informal banking systems,[11]
bulk cash,[12] and commodities, including precious stones and metals,[13]
that serve functionally as forms of currency.

As the international community has responded to the terrorist financing threat through different international and national efforts, there is significant evidence that Al-Qaida and other terrorist organizations have adapted their structure and methods significantly. This makes detecting terrorist financing a more difficult task. Experts have called the evasive strategies used by money launderers and terrorists varied and "highly evolved."[14] The U.S. 9/11 Commission report underscored the obstacles by noting that it is difficult to distinguish the terrorist funds of Al-Qaida from legitimate vast sums moving in the financial system.[15] In particular, global networks such as Al-Qaida, operating autonomously in sixty to one hundred locations worldwide, can "exploit their geographically diffuse structure to move the location of their operations if they are notified that authorities are pursuing their financing activities in a particular location."[16]

As noted, the amount of money required to launch a terrorist attack is small in comparison to the amounts of money laundered by other criminals. The costs are especially low for homegrown terrorist attacks, such as the bombings in Madrid and London. In the first report of the Analytical Support and Sanctions Monitoring Team appointed under UN Security Council Resolution 1526 (2004), the authors argue that "Only the sophisticated attacks of 11 September 2001 required significant funding of over six figures. Other Al-Qaeda terrorist operations have been far less expensive."[17] The report details that the bombings of the U.S. embassies in Kenya and Tanzania in 1998 cost less than $50,000, the 2000 attack on the USS *Cole* cost less than $10,000, the Bali bombings in 2002 cost less than $50,000, the Madrid bombings in 2004 cost about $10,000, and the London bombings in 2005 cost about $2,000.[18] Attacks such as the London bombings involve very small operational budgets and little to no cross-border communication, indicating that attention must be paid not only to the transnational nature of the terrorist actions but to their local manifestations as well.

Another important adaptation by terrorist cells involves their diffusion and autonomous operation. In adapting to the international regulatory and enforcement environment, Al-Qaida and related groups have evolved into self-perpetuating cells with only a distant attachment to the centralized structure of the larger group. As a result, self-sufficient cells must raise their own funds, leading to a rise in illegal activity, similar to traditional patterns of financial crime and money laundering.[19] Thus, although previous efforts to disrupt terrorist financing have looked to more legitimate activities such as charities, recent trends indicate the increasing use of illegitimate activities, from narcotic trafficking to the sale of counterfeit compact disks, credit card fraud, robbery, and the production of false identity documents.[20]

With the evolving nature of terrorist financing, traditional anti–money laundering (AML) and counter-terrorism financing (CTF) efforts share parallel organizational response challenges. The similarities allow countries to utilize the same techniques and institutions in countering both. First, regime tools such as customer due diligence (CDD) and suspicious transaction reports (STRs) can be used as investigative devices to learn about both the origins of funds and their destinations.[21] Customer due diligence can help determine not only who the suspicious customers are but also how they manage their money, its origin, and where they are transferring money. Second, the regime can be used as a prosecutorial device. In both the money laundering and terrorist financing fields, evidence from financial transactions is a key tool in obtaining criminal prosecutions. Close international cooperation is crucial to the success of any AML/CTF regime, especially in exchanging information, blocking funds, and closing down channels used to transfer funds. For all of these challenges, the FATF model and experience are vital.

The Financial Action Task Force Model

Originally composed of sixteen industrialized states, the FATF's initial task was to examine money laundering techniques and trends, review national and international actions that had already been taken, and identify what still needed to be done. In April 1990 the FATF introduced its set of *Forty Recommendations on Money Laundering* now recognized as the international standard in combating money laundering. To keep pace with the changing tactics of illicit money changers, these recommendations were subsequently revised in 1996 and 2003. After the events of 9/11 the FATF's mandate expanded to include capturing terrorist finances and locking down their financial networks. This new mandate was encapsulated in the Nine Special Recommendations Against Terrorist Financing. The FATF model involves these AML/CTF standards as well as processes to ensure compliance by member states and nonmember states. Since 1990 the FATF has expanded to include seventeen new member jurisdictions that have been identified as strategically important (fifteen countries and two regional organizations). Currently, the full FATF membership includes thirty-one nations and two international bodies, representing a high percentage of the world's financial activity.[22]

Similar to other international organizations with successful member state compliance rates, the FATF has highly developed processes. As Edith Brown Weiss emphasizes, "Research suggests that while it is essential to use compliance strategies that are tailored to the intent and capacity of the individual states and other relevant actors to comply with particular instruments, it is also essential to develop and maintain the processes joining the participants to elaborate mechanisms of accountability among states and other relevant actors."[23] There are three main FATF processes: (1) developing recommendations and making them more precise and adaptive, (2) assessing compliance with accepted standards (the *Forty* plus *Nine Recommendations*), and (3) extending the standards to other entities.

Process 1 (The Standards Process): The *Forty Recommendations* and the Expanded Mandate

The FATF first issued its *Forty Recommendations on Money Laundering* in 1990. These recommendations were designed to prevent proceeds of crime from being utilized in future criminal activities. They have been widely acknowledged as *the* international standards in this area.[24] The *Forty Recommendations* are designed to set out a comprehensive anti–money laundering framework and universal application. Even though these recommendations are not manifested in a binding commitment by the international community, a majority of the countries in the world have made a political commitment to implement them. This process includes periodic revisions to the base recommendations as deemed necessary. Revisions made in 1996 and 2003 address a number of deficiencies in earlier versions, such as the need to prohibit shell banks and to cover "gatekeepers" like lawyers, accountants, and notaries who work outside the financial sector but can nevertheless help with arranging and structuring accounts.

The *Forty Recommendations* are the prevention and enforcement pillars of the international AML regime. The cornerstone of the prevention pillar is the "Know Your Customer" approach embodied in Recommendation 21. Financial institutions are urged to secure the identification of customers whose financial transactions originate or pass through the FATF system. This pillar aims to limit criminal access to the financial system, alert authorities of suspicious activity, and ensure compliance.[25] As a part of the "Know Your Customer" approach, financial institutions are required to eliminate anonymous accounts, maintain records of transaction for at least five years, make all records available to legal authorities on request, and notify appropriate authorities if unusual or suspicious transactions have transpired.[26]

The enforcement pillar calls for states to criminalize money laundering and other illicit financial transactions and to include negligence and willful blindness as punishable offenses.[27] To increase interstate cooperation, the FATF recommends that nations monitor and keep records of cross-border flows and make such information available to central banks and multilateral financial institutions.[28] This recommendation has led to the creation of financial intelligence units (FIUs) in over 150 states. FIUs are tasked with analyzing suspicious transaction reports and coordinating with other FIUs.

With the events of 9/11 the FATF expanded its mandate to include specific measures against terrorist financing in its initial *Eight Special Recommendations on Terrorist Financing*. In October 2001 the FATF responded to governments' calls to establish a coordinated effort to detect and prevent the misuse of the international financial system by terrorists. Since then the FATF has worked to identify weaknesses in worldwide efforts to combat the financing of terrorism. It has also worked to identify those countries with priority technical assistance needs in implementing measures to combat the financing of terrorism. It has established guidelines for fighting terrorist financing with its *Special Recommendations* and *Interpretative Notes*.

The FATF's *Nine Special Recommendations on Terrorist Financing* are intended for universal application and, accordingly, the FATF has called on all states to adopt and implement the measures. The original eight

Table 6.1
The FATF's Nine Special Recommendations on Terrorist Financing

Recommendation Number	Description
I	Ratify the 1999 UN International Convention for the Suppression of the Financing of Terrorism and implement relevant UN resolutions against terrorist financing.
II	Criminalize the financing of terrorism, terrorist acts, and terrorist organizations.
III	Freeze and confiscate terrorist assets.
IV	Require financial institutions to report suspicious transactions linked to terrorism.
V	Provide the widest possible assistance to other countries' law enforcement and regulatory authorities for terrorist financing investigations.
VI	Extend anti–money laundering requirements to alternative remittance systems.
VII	Require financial institutions to include accurate and meaningful originator information in money transfers.
VIII	Ensure that nonprofit organizations cannot be misused to finance terrorism.
IX	Ensure measures are in place to detect physical cross-border transportation of currency and that authorities have the legal authority to stop or restrain such movements.

recommendations include designating the act of money laundering a crime; providing investigative agencies with the authority to trace, seize, and confiscate criminally derived assets; and building a framework for sharing relevant information cross-nationally. FATF introduced a ninth recommendation, a call to interdict cross-border cash movements, in October 2004 to reflect changes in terrorist financing. The FATF's *Nine Special Recommendations on Terrorist Financing* are specified in table 6.1. As was done for the *Forty Recommendations*, the FATF has established a methodology for assessing compliance with the special recommendations. It has focused on developing best practices for several of the recommendations, such as the freezing of terrorist assets, the establishing of alternative remittance systems, and the monitoring of nonprofit organizations.

Not only the thirty-three FATF members but a majority of states and regional organizations in the world have accepted the *Forty Recommendations* and the *Nine Special Recommendations on Terrorist Financing*. Many of the FATF recommendations are similar to measures required by United Nations Security Council Resolution 1373 (2001). In July 2005 the Security Council adopted Resolution 1617 calling on states to implement the FATF special recommendations.[29]

The standards process has two specific subprocesses that are important to adapting the organization's principles to a dynamic environment: (1) *Interpretative Notes* and *International Best Practices* and (2) typology exercises. The *Interpretative Notes* and the *International Best Practices* provide a mechanism to increase precision and ensure more uniform interpretation of the *Forty Recommendations* plus *Nine Special Recommendations*. In its initial years, the FATF's recommendations were purposefully imprecise to allow for wide interpretation to accommodate different legal systems and institutional environments. As the organization has learned more about the nature and practice of money laundering and terrorist financing—and how to counter them—the nonbinding norms have become increasingly more precise, enhancing both the legitimacy of the norm and the organization. *Interpretative Notes* are issued as needed to clarify certain provisions, facilitate greater compliance, and explain the obligations set forth in the original recommendations. *International Best Practices* papers give additional details and guidance for states and the relevant national institutions on how to properly implement the standards. This increased precision narrows the scope of contested interpretation by detailing conditions of application and elaborating required or proscribed behavior.[30]

The organization also conducts typology exercises that identify emerging trends in money laundering and terrorist financing to assess the effectiveness of the recommendations and suggest preemptive actions to be taken. As terrorist organizations adapt to emerging regulatory and security environments, a counter-terrorist strategy must adapt as well.[31] Success often depends on an ability to anticipate how terrorist groups will evolve over time. These typology exercises reflect the organization's persistent effort to combat terrorism by "[changing] the environment of the terrorist group, making its current knowledge and capabilities obsolete."[32] Typology exercises involve a "series of money laundering or terrorist financing schemes that are constructed" to describe current and emerging money laundering and terrorist financing trends.[33] A significant focus is on the weaknesses of anti–money laundering and counterterrorist financing regimes with a critical eye to the elements that should be changed. Through the process of studying typologies, experts can detect weaknesses. Ultimately, the goal is to develop indicators that can be used by private institutions and investigative authorities. This detection of weakness process allows for countermeasures to be taken by international, national, and local officials. With a fuller understanding of money laundering and terrorist financing (as well as their linkages), the organization aims to identify and alert relevant actors to potential areas of vulnerability.[34] The FATF utilizes typology exercises to go beyond a "how-to" knowledge to a more accurate and systematic understanding of the larger context in which money laundering and terrorist financing (ML/TF) takes place, identifying "credible and relevant ML/TF trends."[35] With these goals in mind, typology exercises prioritize measures at the international and national level to effect a wider change.

If there is a critique to be leveled against the FATF, it lies in this area. The organization has only recently focused attention on terrorist financing in its typology exercises, resulting in a significant lead time for terrorist organizations to adapt to these countermeasures. It is not yet clear whether the FATF can increase the pace of national proactive measures in the international community in a manner that closes the gap between terrorist adaptation and state action.

Process 2 (Assessing and Ensuring Compliance): Self-Reporting and Mutual Review

Establishing international standards is only the first step toward denying terrorists and criminals access to the international financial system. Consistent implementation of these standards throughout the international community is equally important to prevent terrorists from taking advantage of the weakest seams in the international financial network. Monitoring and assessment are key to the success of the Financial Action Task

Force. In this second process, the FATF has developed specific mechanisms to assess the adherence of countries with the *Forty Recommendations* plus *Nine Special Recommendations*, including the self-assessment and mutual evaluation processes. As a condition of membership, FATF members participate in annual self-reporting exercises and mutual evaluations that are designed to scrutinize progress by (1) objectively assessing all countries against the recommendations, (2) providing capacity-building assistance for key countries in need, and (3) ensuring appropriate consequences for countries and institutions that fail to take reasonable steps to implement standards to prevent terrorist financing and money laundering. For nonmember states, the FATF has employed a "naming and shaming" initiative that makes public a list of noncooperative countries and territories (NCCTs), as described below.

Self-Assessment Mechanism   Self-assessment reports and the peer-review processes aim to increase transparency and compel member states to comply. Each state must submit a report detailing its actions to implement FATF recommendations, which is followed by an evaluation process by a peer government to assess this report and the state's overall progress. In the self-assessment exercise, member countries are required to provide information on the status of their implementation of the *Forty Recommendations* and *Nine Special Recommendations* through a standard questionnaire. The organization then compiles and analyzes the information which is subsequently detailed in the annual report.

Peer-Review Mechanism   The FATF also assesses compliance levels through mutual evaluations. During this process, each member country is assessed by a team of three or four selected experts of other FATF members during an on-site visit. A report for the eyes of the member country only is the product of the visit, thus providing a "comprehensive and objective assessment of the extent to which the country in question has moved forward in implementing effective AML/CTF measures and to highlight those areas in which further progress may still be required."[36] At present, the FATF is conducting the third round of mutual evaluations of member countries, utilizing the FATF's new joint

AML/CTF methodology with the International Monetary Fund (IMF) and World Bank to assess compliance with the *Forty Recommendations* and *Nine Special Recommendations.*

A central component of the self-reporting and mutual evaluation system is graduated peer pressure on noncomplying members. When a member country is judged to be out of compliance, the FATF initiates a four-step countermeasure program. The first step involves a requirement of the noncompliant country to deliver a report to the FATF plenary meeting. If further measures are required, the FATF president will send a letter and/or a high-level mission to the country. Third, the FATF can issue a statement requiring financial institutions to pay special attention to business transactions from the particular country, its citizens, and its businesses. The final countermeasure is revoking membership status in the FATF. The last two measures are sanctions. In particular, the third measure, enjoining financial institutions of member states to pay special attention to business transactions, has the potential to constitute a heavy sanction. Although nominally requiring increased "scrutiny" of financial transactions, essentially this third measure restricts the access of the state, its financial institutions, and its citizens to international financial markets (at least the large percentage controlled by FATF member states) through higher barriers to entry. However, it is important to highlight the noninstitutionalized nature of this process; it does not entail binding obligations on member states.

Process 3: Exporting the Model Through Regional FATFs
One of the key features of the contemporary terrorist threat is its diffused, global character. Many major terrorist attacks have been carried out by militant cells based in the Middle East, Africa, Asia, and the Caucuses.[37] A thirty-three-member body comprised primarily of the OECD countries (countries that are members of the Organisation for Economic Co-operation and Development) is not sufficiently global in reach. The fight against terrorism entails both global cooperation and a response that is sensitive to regional differences. To address this need the FATF has sought to replicate its model and expand its reach beyond the core membership. It has done so through the creation of FATF-style regional bodies (FSRBs) in regions of concern. FSRBs are regional bodies

with structures and processes based on the FATF model. Over 130 countries throughout the world are now members of FATF-style regional bodies. Currently, there are seven FSRBs covering the Asia/Pacific, the Caribbean, South America, eastern and southern Africa, Europe, Eurasia, and the Middle East and the North Africa and West Africa regions.[38] FSRBs are tasked specifically to act as standard-setting bodies in the regional context, ensuring the adoption, implementation, and enforcement of the *Forty Recommendations* and the *Nine Special Recommendations on Terrorist Financing*. FSRBs strengthen the work of the FATF by participating as observers in all FATF meetings, assessing their members against the FATF standards, creating regionally specific standards, and in many cases, participating in the IMF/World Bank assessment program.

FSRBs play an important role in the reach of the anti–money laundering/counter-terrorism financing standards in two ways. First, FSRBs expand the FATF's geographic scope beyond OECD countries. This is crucial for the global fight against money laundering and terrorist financing. Second, regional bodies allow the organization to focus on specific regional needs and capacities. Many developing regions face problems of weak regulatory oversight and substantial use of alternative remittance systems such as hawala. One cannot simply graft a U.S. or European regulatory structure onto these financial markets. As one leading scholar argued, "U.S.-based terrorist financing initiatives will not apply effectively when enforced in other countries."[39] Regional bodies are able to address regional characteristics through additional standards and targeted financial assistance. The need for assistance is more salient in these regions due to the informality of banking structures.

The establishment of a Middle East and North Africa FATF-style regional body (MENAFATF)[40] in November 2004 was particularly important in enhancing the geographic reach of the FATF. Member states of the new FSRB have agreed "[t]o work together to identify money laundering and terrorist financing issues of a regional nature, to share experiences of these problems and to develop regional solutions for dealing with them" and "[t]o build effective arrangements throughout the region to combat effectively money laundering and terrorist financing in accordance with the particular cultural values, constitutional framework and legal systems in the member countries."[41] The region's structural problems include the weak financial regulations of the Islamic banking system and the widespread use of the hawala system.[42] One of MENAFATF's first tasks has been setting a regional standard for regulating Islamic charities, acknowledged as the heart of Al-Qaida's financial structure.[43] Reports have stressed the problem of Islamic charities in Saudi Arabia, a member of MENAFATF.[44]

The FATF has undertaken several actions to forge closer alliances with its FATF-style regional bodies. One initiative affords members of FSRBs much greater participation in the processes within the FATF as associate members. This new arrangement allows those FSRBs that meet requirements to have full access to FATF work and discussions. Associate members also have greater influence within the organization, although what this means operationally is unclear. Of the five FSRBs that have applied, three have been granted immediate approval.[45] In addition, the FATF has conducted joint plenary sessions, such as the one completed with Eastern and Southern Africa Anti–Money Laundering Group and typology exercises with FSRBs.

The Noncooperative Countries and Territories Initiative

In 2000 the Financial Action Task Force initiated a process of identifying specific jurisdictions that posed significant risks to the financial sector and FATF member states. These jurisdictions were labeled noncooperative countries and territories (NCCTs) under the Noncooperative Countries and Territories Initiative. The FATF started to release a biannual list of noncooperative countries and territories with "serious systemic problems." This "naming and shaming" process was intended to identify serious flaws in a country's AML system and to subject nonperforming countries to countermeasures.[46] Financial institutions were advised to give greater scrutiny to transactions with persons, businesses, or banks in listed countries or territories that the FATF deemed to have "inadequate anti–money laundering and counter-terrorist financing infrastructure."[47] Placement on the NCCT list was an effective sanction that prompted many of the listed countries to take immediate action to improve compliance. In many cases this involved the enactment of legislation and regulatory measures to address financial oversight deficiencies.[48] Overall, more than 85 percent of the countries with initial deficiencies responded by bringing their regimes into better alignment.[49] Countries on the list that have enacted necessary legislation and have moved to implement the FATF recommendations have been subsequently delisted.[50] Since the introduction of the list in June 2000, only one out of twenty-three NCCTs remains on the list.[51] Table 6.2 traces the list's lifespan. At present Myanmar is the sole country to maintain NCCT status. Additionally, increased international scrutiny of Saudi Arabia, targeted in many U.S. reports as the epicenter of Al-Qaida financing, led that kingdom to submit its financial system to FATF inspection.

It is widely recognized that the NCCT initiative was successful in eliciting a positive response from most named countries. Yet the future effectiveness of the program is questionable. Despite the present era of increased attention to combating the financing of terrorism, it appears that the program's energy has decreased. Since September 2001 the FATF has named only two countries to the NCCT list. In comparison, the U.S. Department of State listed fifty-four jurisdictions as "Jurisdictions of Primary Concern" in its 2004 annual report on major money launder-ing countries. The difference between the lists reflects decreased will at the FATF to utilize this substantial tool for enforcement. This is a promi-nent example of failure by the international community to use every financial and economic tool at its disposal. A significant indicator that the NCCT Initiative will be less effective in the future is the shift in the program toward a greater role and purview for the IMF and World Bank. IMF and World Bank officials have expressed their desire to focus on capacity building rather than "naming and shaming." Analysts worry that the movement of the assessment and evaluation functions to other international institutions and away from the FATF's exclusive sphere will dampen and diffuse this process and reduce the organization's capacity to apply "meaningful leverage."[52]

The Peer-Review Process

This section offers an analysis of the Financial Action Task Force model and its processes in light of declared goals and ongoing challenges. The

Table 6.2
Financial Action Task Force Noncooperative Countries and Territories Initiative

Date	Added to List	Removed from List
June 2000	Bahamas Dominica Cayman Islands Cook Islands Israel Lebanon Liechtenstein Marshall Islands Nauru Niue Panama Philippines Russia St. Kitts and Nevis St. Vincent and the Grenadines	
June 2001	Burma Egypt Guatemala Hungary Indonesia Nigeria	Bahamas Cayman Islands Liechtenstein Panama
September 2001	Grenada Ukraine	
June 2002		Hungary Israel Lebanon St. Kitts and Nevis
October 2002		Dominica Marshall Islands Niue Russia
February 2003		Grenada
June 2003		St. Vincent and the Grenadines
February 2004		Egypt Ukraine
July 2004		Guatemala
February 2005		Cook Islands Indonesia Philippines
October 2005		Nauru
June 2006		Nigeria
September 2006		Myanmar

relevance of international regimes such as the FATF derives from their ability to establish recognizable standards, put in place effective enforcement measures, and adapt organizational processes to a changing environment. In each of these areas FATF has had some successes but also has faced limitations. Peer reviews and mutual evaluations are the cornerstone of the FATF assessment process. International relations scholars who have examined compliance issues have focused almost exclusively on static treaties and regimes. However, what if the goal or end point is continually reassessed and changing? Compliance, it would seem, is trying to catch a moving target. Problems in the real world are not static; to be effective, international agreements and institutions that deal with these problems cannot remain static. As is the case with the *Forty Recommendations* plus *Nine Special Recommendations*, standards must adapt through frequent reassessment and revision. Managing the tension of improving compliance levels with existing standards while adapting these standards to a changing environment is a major challenge. The progress of deeper cooperation depends on a high degree of willingness to ensure permanent cooperation, which necessitates "zones of acceptance in which parties may consider compromise solutions."[53] International relations scholars are virtually silent on this tension of maintaining existing levels of compliance and cooperation while simultaneously seeking to deepen the commitment of states.

The peer review and mutual evaluation process is utilized by FATF and other international organizations to increase transparency and encourage state compliance. At its core, peer review is a process of external monitoring and assessment. In a self-reporting process like the one described in the previous section, the actor provides information on its own behavior. Each state is usually expected to submit a report detailing its actions to implement principles set forth by the regime. As Ronald Mitchell stresses, the incentives to provide information in self-reporting systems depend on the actors' normative commitment to the regime and its principles.[54] In peer reporting, information is provided by a peer on another actor's behavior. Peer reporting is normally used in conjunction with a self-reporting system, as is the case with the FATF process. An evaluation by a peer government assesses the self-report and the state's overall progress toward regime goals.

Peer review is a potent method when the process has clearly defined standards as well as reasonable consequences. The process scrutinizes progress by objectively assessing all countries against clearly defined standards, identifying deficiencies in compliance responses, and ensuring appropriate consequences for countries and institutions that fail to take reasonable steps to implement standards. Regular and detailed feedback identifies gaps between reality and the standards. Mitchell argues that peer reporting is used when the probability of honest self-reporting is questioned. The incentives to report on noncompliance by others depend on the "degree of perceived harm from others' regime-inconsistent behaviors."[55] In many cases external actors have greater incentives to assess the behaviors of other actors, either because they have a normative commitment to regime rules or merely because they are making an instrumental calculation based on short-term interests. It seems plausible that peer reporting may serve additional functions that the analysts do not highlight. In particular, external reporting creates a process that builds relationships among the actors in the regime, which can facilitate the process of persuasion. Persuasion is more likely to be effective when the persuader-persuadee interaction occurs in less politicized settings. A peer-review process can be structured to provide such a setting. In the case of the FATF, mutual evaluation reports are not publicized. However, the peer-review mechanism can also serve to politicize the process. If the peer relationship is decidedly unbalanced (for example, in terms of structural power), the nature of the interaction may result in a less effective compliance process.

Depending on the particular structure of the process, an additional function of peer review is mutual support. Peer review provides a means to move beyond the highlighting of particular deficiencies or merits in a compliance situation. It may also assist in building capacity through passing along valuable techniques, lessons learned, and experience. One unique and critical aspect of the European Union's successful preaccession process is its twinning program, which pairs member states and candidate countries to help smoothly implement needed changes. The FATF utilizes mutual evaluations as a mechanism to highlight deficiencies in member states and also to identify those areas in which technical assistance and aid should be targeted. The FATF utilizes international carrots in the form of positive inducements, partnering with international bodies such as the IMF, World Bank, and Counter-Terrorism Action Group (CTAG) to assess the needs of countries for technical assistance in complying with the *Forty Recommendations* plus *Nine Special Recommendations* and match these needs with the donor community.[56] The peer review process is most effective when the method moves beyond identifying particular deficiencies or merits of a state's compliance situation to serve as a system to build capacity through the identification of areas in need of technical assistance. States are more willing to subject their internal processes to evaluation when assistance, not approbation, is the end product. When the peer-review method is oriented toward the sanctioning process, the method has proven controversial among states.

Judging the FATF Model

Two potential drawbacks of the peer-review process are the time and the resources required for efficient functioning. These demands limit the number of countries that can be reviewed in a given period. In the third round of mutual evaluations that commenced in 2005, only ten countries have been assessed. While it is certainly true that the FSRBs are also conducting mutual evaluation processes similar to the FATF, and thus the number of states assessed is higher than ten, the overall number of evaluations remains relatively limited. If the success of the FATF rests on a timely process of highlighting deficiencies and targeting technical assistance, this is a critical limitation.

The level of compliance within the organization's *Special Recommendations* and standards serves as the crucial litmus test in the assessment of the success of the FATF model. The organization's annual reports show that compliance within the organization is not universal. It is not merely a matter of countries being entirely compliant or noncompliant. In most cases, a country is only partially compliant.[57] FATF compliance benchmarks include the nature of the deficiency (whether it is discrete or systematic), the presence of a response, and the quality of this response (whether it addresses it in a reasonable time period).[58] Based on the above, a country is deemed compliant, largely compliant, materially noncompliant, or noncompliant. While member states have a higher level of compliance than nonmember states, the organization still encounters noncompliance with specific recommendations. Progress in compliance with the *Forty Recommendations* has been exemplary, but the level of compliance with the *Nine Special Recommendations* is more uncertain. Implementation of several provisions of the *Nine Special Recommendations* has been slow. For instance, a year after accepting the new recommendations, almost half of FATF member states had not yet complied fully with Special Resolution I, which calls on members to ratify the appropriate UN instruments against terrorist financing,[59] and with Special Resolution VII, which calls on members to monitor wire transfers. Only two jurisdictions, France and Italy, were approved by the organization as being in full compliance with all provisions.[60]

Assessing the FATF's overall success is difficult for several reasons. The organization does not prioritize principles or establish relative weight to its recommendations. Nor does it have a clear definition of overall "compliance." Because of this ambiguity and open-endedness, member states may be unsure of required action or unwilling to move beyond the minimum. A related difficulty appears in how the organization measures compliance. As is clear through its evaluation process, the measure of compliance is the extent to which national rules reflect FATF recommendations. However, this measure does not address the prosecutorial or punitive rates within the country. These are tougher and more relevant criteria.[61] However, implementation is not a sufficient condition. A law on the books does not amount to an enforced law. This is especially the case in money laundering and terrorist financing regimes, where it is vital to enlist the cooperation of the financial and private sector in following the accepted standards.

Another weakness in the FATF model lies in the disconnect with the private sector in the form of banking and financial institutions. The FATF is an intergovernmental body in which states play the dominant role, but bank officials, financial advisers, and auditors are the first line of contact with money launderers and terrorist financiers and are crucial actors in this effort. In an effort to coordinate a more effective regime, the FATF has initiated a dialogue with the private sector. In December 2005 the

FATF held several consultations with private-sector representatives to discuss issues and challenges associated with implementing FATF standards on the ground. These consultations showed a significant gap between recommendations and concrete guidelines for the field. Many of the financial institutions asked for increased guidance on what to look for as possible identifiers to be used in detecting money laundering and terrorist financing. Financial institutions have flooded authorities with suspicious transaction reports, as many as 13 million a day in the U.S. Without more reliable indicators, reports generated by these institutions are of little value to financial intelligence units and the intelligence community. *Interpretative Notes* and *Best Practice* papers are intended to give the additional guidance, but a continual consultation process with the private sector is needed. Although the FATF and the private sector have established a dialogue, a significant increase in contact and standard formulation will be needed to ensure consistent implementation and coordination by the myriad of actors who deal with the anti–money laundering and counter-terrorism financing standards daily.

A fundamental problem for the FATF and for nearly all international standard-setting bodies is that compliance is voluntary in nature. A senior FATF official noted, "The FATF standards are not mandatory in terms of international law. They are not backed by a specific international convention or treaty, although some measures have become international obligations through certain international instruments in recent years, and yet others have been taken up through other international or regional instruments as well."[62] For example FATF Recommendation 21 requires financial institutions to establish "Know Your Customer" procedures, but there are no guarantees of implementation. The FATF cannot force members to implement Recommendation 21, and individual member states are given the discretion to determine how to apply this recommendation. Moreover, by its very nature, this measure does not prevent the transfer of illicit funds through other means such as alternative remittance systems. FATF's focus on the formal financial sphere decreases the effectiveness of its program. As stricter regulations have been applied to the formal financial sector, such as the "Know Your Customer" requirements, money laundering activity has increased in alternative nonbank and nonfinancial sectors.[63] With the evolution toward home-grown terrorism, with its lower costs and more informal modes of operation, the importance of greater monitoring of nonbank transfers has grown. This will pose continuing challenges to an intergovernmental body like FATF.

FATF as a Global Solution

As more states and international organizations join the fight against terrorism, it is vital to have unified purpose, approach, and methods in counter-terrorist financing.[64] Some have called for the international community to establish a "global FATF." Former U.S. under secretary of treasury Jimmy Gurulé has proposed a worldwide organization to fight terrorist financing because "[t]errorist financing networks are global, and consequently, efforts to identify and deny terrorist access to funds must also be global. Moreover, because the overwhelming bulk of terrorist assets, cash flows, and evidence lie outside the United States, international alliances against terrorism are crucial."[65] While the FATF's reach is broader than its member states, it is still unable to regulate 5 to 10 percent[66] of international financial transactions, including those in the world's most troubled spots. Moreover, the challenge is to have not just a transnational response but one that is robust in local circumstances as the terrorism threat has morphed into a home-grown enemy. The rise of self-radicalized terrorism and the link to criminal endeavors have linked counter-terrorism with anti–money laundering efforts.

This chapter demonstrates that the FATF has been partially effective in facilitating transnational efforts to address terrorist financing and to enhance compliance with globally recognized standards. The organization has adjusted its structure and program to meet the demands on the financial system of the transnational terrorist threat. It has provided leadership in the international community to establish standards against terrorist financing in the *Nine Special Recommendations* and *Best Practices* for these recommendations. This has led analysts and international bodies to promote the organization as an international leader and to push for its replication in developing regions. A report issued by an independent task force of the Council on Foreign Relations recommended that the FATF be empowered to "lead international efforts not only to articulate international standards relating to anti–money laundering and counter-terrorist financing (AML/CTF), but also to monitor and assess implementation and compliance with those stands."[67] The United Nations Security Council has also called on the international community to comply with FATF standards as the model in counter-terrorist financing. The fight against terrorism will necessitate a broader global effort and new organizational forms to address continuing inadequacies in financial regulation and enforcement that impede further progress.[68] The FATF processes will remain at the center of that effort.

Notes

1. Sean D. Murphy, "Contemporary Practice of the United States Relating to International Law: Multilateral Listing of States as Money-Laundering Havens," *American Journal of International Law* 94, no. 4 (2000): 695, 695–96.

2. United States Department of State, Bureau for International Narcotics and Law Enforcement Affairs, *International Narcotics Control Strategy Report 2003*, Vol. 2, *Money Laundering and Financial Crimes*, Washington, DC, 1 March 2004.

3. United States Department of State, Bureau for International Narcotics and Law Enforcement Affairs, *Money Laundering and Financial Crimes*.

4. See Peter Reuter and Edwin M. Truman, *Chasing Dirty Money: The Fight Against Money Laundering* (Washington, DC: Institute for International Economics, 2004), for a more detailed discussion.

5. The volume from the informal banking sector was estimated by the United Nations to be $200 billion while the World Bank and International Monetary Fund estimate tens of billions of dollars flow through informal transactions. See United States General Accounting Office (GAO), *Terrorist Financing: U.S. Agencies Should Systematically Assess Terrorists' Use of Alternative Financing Mechanisms*, GAO-04-163, no. 24, report to congressional requesters, 108th Cong., 1st sess. (Washington, DC, November 2003); and United States Department of State, Bureau for International Narcotics and Law Enforcement Affairs, *Money Laundering and Financial Crimes*.

6. United States Department of State, Bureau for International Narcotics and Law Enforcement Affairs, *Money Laundering and Financial Crimes*.

7. Monica Serrano, "The Political Economy of Terrorism," in *Terrorism and the UN: Before and After September 11*, ed. Jane Boulden and Thomas Weiss (Bloomington: Indiana University Press, 2004), 204.

8. Serrano, "The Political Economy of Terrorism," 204.

9. See Reuter and Truman, *Chasing Dirty Money*, for a more detailed discussion of these implications.

10. Charities can serve the dual purpose of raising money for the organization and also covering the moving of funds. The GAO report recounts that an Illinois-based charity, Global Relief Foundation, diverted more than 90 percent of its donations abroad. The Department of Justice charged the organization with connections to and providing assistance to individuals associated with Osama bin Laden, Al-Qaida, and other terrorist groups. See United States General Accounting Office, *Terrorist Financing*, 15.

11. The hawala system has been cited in many government and independent reports as an important tool used by terrorist groups because of its informal, nontransparent nature.

12. Bulk cash transfers are particularly attractive to terrorists because of the ease of transfer: between 1 October 2001 and 8 August 2003 the Department of Homeland Security's Operation Oasis seized more than $28 million in bulk cash according to the 2003 GAO report. United States General Accounting Office, *Terrorist Financing*, 20.

13. United States General Accounting Office, *Terrorist Financing*, 10.

14. David Cortright and George A. Lopez, *Sanctions and the Search for Security: Challenges to UN Action* (Boulder, CO: Lynne Rienner, 2002), 102.

15. United States National Commission on Terrorist Attacks upon the United States, *Monograph on Terrorist Financing*, staff report to the Commission prepared by John Roth, Douglas Greenburg, and Serena Wille, 108th Cong., 2d sess., 2004, Committee Print, 186.

16. When accentuating the intricacies of tracking, seizing, and ultimately ceasing terrorist financing, the GAO report highlights the adaptability of terrorist groups to thwart such efforts. United States General Accounting Office, *Terrorist Financing*, 30.

17. United Nations Analytical Support and Sanctions Monitoring Team, *First Report of the Analytical Support and Sanctions Monitoring Team Appointed Pursuant to Resolution 1526 (2004) Concerning Al-Qaida and the Taliban and Associated Individuals and Entities*, S/2004/679 (New York: United Nations, 25 August 2004), 12.

18. For details about the Kenyan and Tanzanian bombings, see United States National Commission on Terrorist Attacks upon the United States, *The 9/11 Commission Report, Final Report of the National Commission on Terrorist Attacks upon the United States* (New York: Norton, 2004), 498 n.127. For information about other costs, see Eben Kaplan, "Tracking Down Terrorist Financing," background paper, Council on Foreign Relations, New York, 4 April 2006, <http://www.cfr.org/publication/10356/tracking_down_terrorist_financing.html> (accessed 10 October 2006); see also Eben Kaplan, "The Rise of Al-Qaedism," background paper, Council on Foreign Relations, New York, 30 June 2006, <http://www.cfr.org/publication/11033/rise_of_alqaedism.html> (accessed 8 September 2006).

19. Kaplan, "The Rise of Al-Qaedism."

20. United Nations Analytical Support and Sanctions Monitoring Team, *Third Report of the Analytical Support and Sanctions Monitoring Team Appointed Pursuant to Resolution 1526 (2004) Concerning Al-Qaida and the Taliban and Associated Individuals and Entities*, S/2005/572, New York, United Nations, 9 September 2005.

21. These methods include targeted legislation and regulations, suspicious trans-action reporting systems (SARs), financial intelligence units (FIUs), on-site super-vision of the financial sector, internal controls, trained financial investigations, modern asset forfeiture and administrative blocking capacity, and the ability to cooperate and share internationally information for the purpose of detecting, investigating, and prosecuting money laundering. United States Department of State, Bureau for International Narcotics and Law Enforcement Affairs, *Money Laundering and Financial Crimes*, xiii–8.

22. Membership status is contingent on the adoption of its anti–money laun-dering legislation and a successful mutual evaluation. The thirty-one member countries are Argentina, Australia, Austria, Belgium, Brazil, Canada, Denmark, Finland, France, Germany, Greece, Hong Kong, Iceland, Ireland, Italy, Japan, Luxembourg, Mexico, the Netherlands, New Zealand, Norway, Portugal, Russia, Singapore, South Africa, Spain, Sweden, Switzerland, Turkey, the United Kingdom, and the United States. Additionally, the European Commission and the Gulf Cooperation Council are members of the FATF. The FATF continues to discuss membership with India, while China has been granted observer status.

23. Edith Brown Weiss and Harold K. Jacobson, eds., *Engaging Countries: Strengthening Compliance with International Environmental Accords* (Cam-bridge, MA: MIT Press, 2000), 553.

24. United States Department of State, Bureau for International Narcotics and Law Enforcement Affairs, *Money Laundering and Financial Crimes*.

25. Reuter and Truman, *Chasing Dirty Money*, 46.

26. Financial Action Task Force, *Methodology for Assessing Compliance with the FATF Forty Recommendations and the FATF Nine Special Recommendations* (Paris: OECD, 27 February 2004).

27. Financial Action Task Force, *Methodology for Assessing Compliance with the FATF Forty Recommendations and the FATF Nine Special Recommendations*.

28. Financial Action Task Force, *Methodology for Assessing Compliance with the FATF Forty Recommendations and the FATF Nine Special Recommendations*.

29. See United Nations Security Council, *Security Council Resolution 1617 (2005)*, S/RES/1617, New York, 29 July 2005.

30. Precision is a variable of legalization. See Kenneth W. Abbott et al., "The Concept of Legalization," *International Organization* 54, no. 3 (2000): 401–19. The authors identify three components of legalization: obligation, precision, and

delegation. *Precision* means that rules define the conduct they require, authorize, or proscribe in an unambiguous way.

31. Brian A. Jackson et al., *Aptitude for Destruction*, Vol. 1, *Organizational Learning in Terrorist Groups and Its Implications for Combating Terrorism*, monograph prepared for the National Institute of Justice (Santa Monica, CA: RAND Corporation Monograph Series, 2005), 9.

32. Jackson et al., *Aptitude for Destruction*, 23.

33. Financial Action Task Force, *Money Laundering and Terrorist Financing Typologies 2004–2005* (Paris: OECD, 10 June 2005), 90.

34. Financial Action Task Force, *Money Laundering and Terrorist Financing Typologies 2004–2005*.

35. Financial Action Task Force, *Money Laundering and Terrorist Financing Typologies 2004–2005*, 90.

36. Financial Action Task Force, *Annual Report 2003–2004* (Paris: OECD, 2 July 2004), 8, art. 34.

37. See Audrey Kurth Cronin, "Rethinking Sovereignty: American Strategy in the Age of Terrorism," *Survival* 44, no. 2 (2002): 119–39; Rohan Gunaratna, ed., *The Changing Face of Terrorism* (London: Easter Universities Press, 2004).

38. These FSRBs are the Asia/Pacific Group on Money Laundering (APG), Caribbean Financial Action Task Force (CFATF), Eastern and Southern Africa Anti–Money Laundering Group (ESAAMLG), the Eurasian Group on Combating Money Laundering and Financing of Terrorism (EAG), the Grupo de Acción Financiera de Sudamerica (GAFISUD), Intergovernmental Action Group Against Money Laundering (GIABA), the Council of Europe's Select Committee of Experts on the Evaluation of Anti–Money Laundering Measures (MONEYVAL), the Middle East and North Africa Financial Action Task Force (MENAFATF), and the Offshore Group of Banking Supervisors (OGBS).

39. Mark Basile, "Going to the Source: Why Al Qaeda's Financial Network Is Likely to Withstand the Current War on Terrorist Financing," *Studies in Conflict and Terrorism* 27, no. 3 (May–June 2004): 178.

40. The membership of the Middle East and North Africa Financial Action Task Force (MENAFATF), based in the regional standard-setter Bahrain, includes Algeria, Bahrain, Egypt, Jordan, Kuwait, Lebanon, Morocco, Oman, Qatar, Saudia Arabia, the Syrian Arab Republic, Tunisia, the United Arab Emirates, and Yemen.

41. See "Inaugural Ministerial Meeting of the Middle East and North Africa Financial Action Task Force (MENAFATF) Against Money Laundering and Terrorist Financing," press release, MENAFATF, Kingdom of Bahrain, 30 November 2004, <http://www.menafatf.org/ArticleDetail.asp?rid=548> (accessed 18 September 2006).

42. See Basile, "Going to the Source"; United States National Commission on Terrorist Attacks upon the United States, *Monograph on Terrorist Financing*;

United States General Accounting Office, *Terrorist Financing*; Council on Foreign Relations, *Update on the Global Campaign Against Terrorist Financing: Second Report of an Independent Task Force on Terrorist Financing* (New York: Council on Foreign Relations, 2004).

43. Basile, "Going to the Source," 169–88.

44. Basile, "Going to the Source"; United States Department of State, Bureau for International Narcotics and Law Enforcement Affairs, *Money Laundering and Financial Crimes*; Council on Foreign Relations, *Update on the Global Campaign Against Terrorist Financing*.

45. Financial Action Task Force, *Annual and Overall Review of Non-Cooperative Countries or Territories, 2005–2006* (Paris: OECD, 23 June 2006), 5, art. 21.

46. Financial Action Task Force, *Report on Non-Cooperative Countries or Territories* (Paris: OECD, 14 February 2000), 9, art. 50.

47. Financial Action Task Force, "FATF Tackles Terrorism Financing, Delists Guatemala," press release, OECD, Paris, 2 July 2004, <http://www.fatf-gafi .org/dataoecd/29/36/33616642.pdf> (accessed 10 September 2006).

48. Financial Action Task Force, *Annual Review of Non-Cooperative Countries or Territories 2003* (Paris: OECD, February 2004), 4.

49. For example, the United States State Department helped provide technical assistance or training to thirteen countries on the FATF noncooperative countries and territories list. Six of the jurisdictions to whom the U.S. provided this technical assistance and training were removed from the list.

50. Financial Action Task Force, *Annual Review of Non-Cooperative Countries and Territories 2003*.

51. In June 2000 the initial FATF noncooperative countries and territories list included fifteen jurisdictions. One year later four countries—the Bahamas, the Cayman Islands, Liechtenstein, and Panama—were removed. At that time six more countries were assessed and added to the list: Burma, Egypt, Guatemala, Hungary, Indonesia, and Nigeria. See Financial Action Task Force, *Review to Identify Non-Cooperative Countries or Territories: Increasing the Worldwide Effectiveness of Anti–Money Laundering Measures 2001* (Paris: OECD, 22 June 2001), 3. In September 2001 FATF identified two new jurisdictions—Grenada and Ukraine—as noncooperative. See Financial Action Task Force, "Developments in Non-Cooperative Countries and Territories," press release, OECD, 7 September 2001, <http://www.oecd.org/document/57/0,2340,en_2649_201185 _1890937_1_1_1_1,00.html> (accessed 10 September 2006). In June 2002 four countries were removed from the list after having implemented reforms: Hungary, Israel, Lebanon, and St. Kitts and Nevis. See Financial Action Task Force, *Review to Identify Non-Cooperative Countries or Territories: Increasing the World-Wide Effectiveness of Anti–Money Laundering Measures* (Paris: OECD, 21 June 2002). That same year, in October 2002, four additional countries were removed: Dominica, Marshall Islands, Niue, and Russia. See

Financial Action Task Force, "Russia, Dominica, Niue, and Marshall Islands Removed from FATF's List of Non-Cooperative Countries and Territories," press release, OECD, Paris, 11 October 2002, <http://www.fatf-gafi.org/dataoecd/45/31/33693981.pdf> (accessed 18 September 2006). In February of 2003 Grenada was removed from the list, and in June 2003 the FATF removed St. Vincent and the Grenadines from the NCCT list. See Financial Action Task Force, "FATF Withdraws Counter-Measures with Respect to Ukraine and Decides on Date for Counter-Measures to Philippines," press release, OECD, Paris, 14 February 2003; Financial Action Task Force, *Annual Report 2003* (Paris: OECD, 20 June 2003). Due to their "substantial implementation of anti–money laundering reforms," the FATF removed Egypt and Ukraine from the NCCT list in February 2004. See Financial Action Task Force, *Annual Review of Non-Cooperative Countries and Territories, 27 February 2004* (Paris: OECD, 27 February 2004). In July 2004 the FATF delisted Guatemala. See Financial Action Task Force, "FATF Tackles Terrorism Financing, Delists Guatemala," press release, OECD, Paris, 2 July 2004. As of February 2005 the FATF delisted Cook Islands, Philippines, and Indonesia. See Financial Action Task Force, *Annual Report 2004–2005* (Paris, OECD, 10 June 2005), 12, art. 35.

52. Reuter and Truman, *Chasing Dirty Money*, 185.

53. Christer Jönsson and Jonas Tallberg, "Compliance and Post-Agreement Bargaining," *European Journal of International Relations* 4, no. 4 (1998): 371–408.

54. Ronald B. Mitchell, "Sources of Transparency: Information Systems in International Regimes," *International Studies Quarterly* 42, no. 1 (March 1998): 109–30.

55. Mitchell, "Sources of Transparency."

56. Financial Action Task Force, "FATF Intensifies Anti-Terrorist Financing Campaign," press release, OECD, Paris, 3 October 2003, <http://www.fatf-gafi .org/dataoecd/43/32/33690944.pdf> (accessed 10 September 2006).

57. This brings up the question of whether there is a magic number when defining *compliance*. Currently, the FATF has not identified certain measures as carrying more weight over others.

58. A requirement is considered *compliant* whenever it is fully observed. A requirement is considered *largely compliant* whenever only discrete and nonsystemic shortcomings are observed that do not raise major concerns and when corrective actions to achieve full observance with the requirement are readily identified and have been scheduled within a reasonable period of time. A requirement is considered *materially noncompliant* whenever discrete or nonsystemic shortcomings are observed that are not addressed or whenever numerous or systemic shortcomings are observed and corrective actions are identified and have been scheduled within a reasonable period of time. A requirement is considered *noncompliant* whenever the jurisdiction has not addressed the issue or has addressed it in a manner that cannot reasonably lead to substantial observance.

A requirement is considered *not applicable* whenever, in the view of the assessor, the requirement does not apply given the structural, legal, and institutional features of a jurisdiction. Financial Action Task Force, *Methodology for Assessing Compliance with Anti–Money Laundering and Combating the Financing of Terrorism Standards* (Paris: OECD, 11 October 2002), 7.

59. Special Recommendation I calls for the ratification and implementation of UN instruments (including both the 1999 United Nations International Convention for the Suppression of Financing of Terrorism and Security Council Resolution 1373). See Financial Action Task Force, *Methodology for Assessing Compliance with the FATF Forty Recommendations and the FATF Nine Special Recommendations*, 59.

60. Special Recommendation VI had the third highest noncompliant incident rate. This recommendation deals with alternative remittance systems. Three countries are noncompliant with the third recommendation, freezing and confiscating of terrorist assets. Recommendations IV (reporting suspicious transactions relating to terrorism) and V (international cooperation) have the fewest member states noncompliant. Two member states are noncompliant for both recommendations. See Financial Action Task Force, *Annual Review of Non-Cooperative Countries or Territories, 2002–2003* (Paris: OECD, 10 June 2003). For background information on the Nine Special Recommendations, see Financial Action Task Force, *Methodology for Assessing Compliance with the FATF Forty Recommendations and the FATF Nine Special Recommendations*, 64–66.

61. Beth Simmons, "International Efforts Against Money Laundering," in *Commitment and Compliance: The Role of Non-Binding Norms in the International Legal Systems*, ed. Dinah Shelton (Oxford: Oxford University Press, 2000), 244–63.

62. Vincent Schmoll, "Liechtenstein Dialogue on the Future of Financial Markets," summary of remarks for focus group 2, n.d., 2, <http://www .dialogue.li/0/Downloads/2005_referenten_summary_schmoll.pdf> (accessed 10 October 2006).

63. See Financial Action Task Force, "Combating the Abuse of Alternative Remittance Systems: International Best Practices," In *FATF Annual Report 2002–2003*, annex B (Paris: OECD, 20 June 2003).

64. Chantal de Jonge Oudraat, "Combating Terrorism," *Washington Quarterly* 26, no. 4 (Autumn 2003): 163–76; Chantal de Jonge Oudraat, "The Role of the UN Security Council," in *Terrorism and the UN: Before and After September 11*, ed. Jane Boulden and Thomas G. Weiss (Bloomington: Indiana University Press, 2004).

65. Jimmy Gurulé, "The Global Effort to Stop Terrorist Financing," *U.S. Foreign Policy Agenda* 8, no. 1 (2003): 21–24, <http://www.ciaonet.org .lib-proxy.nd.edu/olj/fpa/fpa_aug03_gurule.pdf> (accessed 20 September 2006).

66. "By the U.S. government's calculations, around 130 jurisdictions—representing 85 percent of the world's population and 90 to 95 percent of global

economic output—have made political commitments to implementing [FATF] recommendations." See Joseph Myers, "International Standards and Cooperation in the Fight against Money Laundering," *Economic Perspectives* (U.S. Department of State) 6, no. 2 (May 2001), <http://usinfo.state.gov/journals/ites/0501/ijee/treasury.htm> (accessed 20 September 2006).

67. Council on Foreign Relations, *Update on the Global Campaign Against Terrorist Financing*, 30.

68. Serrano, "The Political Economy of Terrorism," 209.

7

The European Model of Building Regional Cooperation Against Terrorism

Oldrich Bures and Stephanie Ahern

On 11 March 2004, exactly two and a half years after the September 2001 (9/11) attacks on the United States, a series of blasts killed more than 200 train passengers in Madrid. As the implications sank in of an Al-Qaida–linked terror attack on their own home soil, the European countries began a much needed appraisal of all the measures they had taken thus far to combat terrorism. This chapter contributes to this important process by offering a critical analysis of the counter-terrorism policy of the European Union (EU), based on the analyses of official EU documents, internal reports, and a handful of existing scholarly studies. We contend that, notwithstanding the wide array of innovative legal measures that have strengthened cooperation among the EU member states after 9/11, the EU's counter-terrorism policy still appears to be more of a paper tiger than an effective counter-terrorism device.

This chapter begins with an analysis of the origins of the EU's counter-terrorism policy, followed by an overview of the key developments in this area prior to 9/11. The EU's Plan of Action that was adopted immediately after 9/11 and has functioned as a road map for all subsequent developments and changes of EU counter-terrorism policy is introduced in the third part of the chapter. The following five sections offer in-depth analyses of the major measures and instruments that have been adopted in the area of Justice and Home Affairs (JHA) according to the Plan of Action. These include the introduction of a European arrest warrant (EAW), enhancement of enforcement cooperation and intelligence sharing via the European Police (Europol), enhancement of judicial cooperation via the European Judicial Cooperation Unit (Eurojust), adoption of a binding definition of terrorism, and identification of presumed terrorists and terrorist groups and the freezing of their assets. In the next section, we present a succinct overview of the most recent EU enlargement process with a special focus on a series of preaccession planning, monitoring, mentoring, and funding programs and mechanisms devised by Brussels to assist the candidate countries (CCs) in their efforts to conform to the JHA standards of the European Union. Finally, the concluding part of this chapter offers an assessment of the impact that the EU counter-terrorism policy has made thus far.

European Community/European Union Counter-Terrorism Policy Prior to 9/11

The European Union's counter-terrorism policy predates the 9/11 terrorist attacks on the United States. Its roots can be traced to the early 1970s when the European Political Cooperation (EPC)[1] came into being. An early impetus for greater intergovernmental security cooperation among member states was the growth of terrorist incidents perpetrated by indigenous western European and Middle Eastern groups in the late 1960s and early 1970s.[2] Furthermore, by the mid-1970s the then nine European Community (EC) member states were becoming increasingly dissatisfied with the failure of international measures against terrorism[3] and felt that a regionally inspired program might stand a better chance of implementation.[4] Consequentially, in addition to the diplomatic efforts taken to combat state-sponsored terrorism within the EPC framework,[5] the EC member states began to develop what could be termed an EC counter-terrorism policy at two key levels: the legal and the operational.

At the legal level the EC member states adopted a strategy designed to ensure that the existing international counter-terrorist provisions would be fully applied within the EC. Moreover, since the respective national criminal codes and definitions of terrorism diverged so greatly, "the aim was to inject a degree of predictability into the EC's public position vis-à-vis terrorism."[6] To this end, in 1979 the EC member states negotiated the so-called Dublin Agreement to ensure that the Council of Europe's 1977 European Convention on the Suppression of Terrorism (ECST) would be applied uniformly among them.[7] The implementation of both the Dublin Agreement and ECST has, however, been beset by difficulties as a number of EC member states refused to ratify the treaty and convention, primarily because these states feared that their autonomy to deal with terrorism on an independent, intergovernmental basis would be thwarted.[8] Consequentially, it was not until the mid-1980s that the idea of a European judicial area was seriously considered under the banner of the completion of the European Common Market.[9]

At the operational level special mention must be made of the TREVI (Terrorism, Radicalism, Extremism, and Political Violence) Group, which the EC established in 1976 as a forum for discussion and cooperation on police and intelligence matters. It was within the TREVI framework that the justice and interior ministers of EC member states initiated regular systematic work concerning terrorist threats. This included the exchange of intelligence information, compilation of a blacklist of terrorists, analysis of external terrorist threats, studies on specific terrorist groups, and facilitation of apprehension and subsequent prosecution of terrorists in the EC.[10] Following a series of terrorist attacks in the mid-1980s, the TREVI Group increased cooperation in combating terrorism even further, assembling a working party to study problems of improving checks at the community's external frontiers, the coordination of national visa policies, and cooperation in combating passport fraud.[11]

Overall, TREVI's work was considered by both the EC and the contiguous European states to be useful, despite the fact that both its legal basis and its relationship to other EC institutions remained unclear. As Juliet Lodge has noted, by the late 1980s many EC member states seemed to feel that "TREVI is a more effective forum than Interpol in matters relating to the security of databank and information exchanges on international terrorism."[12] Perhaps most important, it was also becoming clear that "[security in] the internal market cannot be completed unless the issues currently being addressed by TREVI are discussed within the EC."[13] Consequentially, when the Treaty on European Union (Maastricht treaty) was signed in February 1992, the previously informal European Political Cooperation and TREVI frameworks were brought under the new legal and structural framework of the EU and formed the basis of the Justice and Home Affairs pillar.

The Maastricht treaty specifically referred to terrorism as a serious form of crime to be prevented and combated by developing common action in three areas:

• Closer cooperation between police forces, customs authorities, and other competent authorities, including Europol;

• Closer cooperation among judicial and other competent authorities of EU member states; and

• Approximation, where necessary, of rules on criminal matters.[14]

Prior to 9/11 some progress had been made in developing common actions in all three areas, but their practical implementation was often painfully slow.

In the area of police cooperation the Maastricht treaty made a provision for the establishment of Europol, the EU police coordination unit. Europol started limited operations on 3 January 1994 in the form of the Europol Drugs Unit (EDU). Subsequently, other areas of criminal oversight were added to Europol's mandate, including "dealing with crimes committed or likely to be committed in the course of terrorist activities against life, limb, personal freedom or property."[15] Nevertheless, Europol was unable to commence full activities until July 1999, when the Europol Convention was finally ratified by all EU member states.

In the area of judicial cooperation, two important legal instruments were adopted in the 1990s: the Convention on Simplified Extradition Procedures Between Member States of the European Union (March 1995) and the Convention Relating to Extradition Between Member States of the European Union (September 1996). The main purpose of both conventions was to supplement and improve the application of both the 1957 European Convention on Extradition and the 1977 European Convention on the Suppression of Terrorism by imposing a lower threshold for extraditable offenses and by specifying those offenses for which extradition may not be refused.[16] As such, the two conventions represented yet another attempt to ensure uniform application of existing crucial antiterrorist provisions within the EU.

Regarding the rules on criminal matters in the member states, article 31(e) of the 1992 Maastricht treaty already called for the establishment of minimum rules relating to the constituent elements of terrorist acts and penalties. This call was repeated in paragraph 46 of the December 1998 Action Plan of the European Council and in the commission on how best to implement the freedom, security, and justice provisions of the 1997 Treaty of Amsterdam, which entered into force in May 1999.[17]

In the Treaty of Amsterdam, the EU member states committed themselves to constructing this "area of freedom, security and justice." It was acknowledged that the member states needed to better coordinate their justice and home affairs policies and, in some areas, grant the EU new powers.[18] In subsequent years, however, the EU has made only slow progress in working on these commitments. To inject new life into the JHA pillar, the October 1999 Tampere European Council supplied a number of targets and deadlines for the implementation of policies on immigration, border control, police cooperation, and asylum. Few of these targets, however, were met before 9/11, and as discussed below, some are still to be met as of 2006.

In conclusion, it is apparent that a number of key pillars of the EU counter-terrorism policy were adopted well before the 9/11 events. As Monica den Boer and Jörg Monar put it:

[O]ne could argue that several strata of counter-terrorism activities were already in place within the EU before 11 September: institutionally, a European police office competent to deal with terrorism-related offences; legally, conventions and additional legal instruments to facilitate extradition; and operationally, direct and regular contact between the heads of the European security services, an anti-terrorism repertory, and a regular update of the security situation.[19]

However, the delays in the ratification of the Europol convention and other key counter-terrorism measures by several EU member states suggest that the impact of 9/11 on EU counter-terrorism policy should not be underestimated. As Anastassia Tsoukala noted, prior to 9/11, "The position of the European Union toward terrorism has been limited to a strictly political level."[20] While all EU institutions had constantly condemned terrorism,[21] the definition of a common counter-terrorism policy and the articulation of their role in combating terrorism was fully integrated into their agenda only after the 9/11 terrorist attacks on the United States.

EU Counter-terrorism Policy After 9/11

The counter-terrorism dynamics prevalent in the aftermath of 9/11 were seized by the EU as both opportunity and proof of the necessity to reinforce its internal coherence. The representatives of the EU member states immediately engaged in a long series of meetings, which ultimately led to the Extraordinary European Council meeting on 21 September 2001. Building on the conclusions adopted by the Justice and Home Affairs Council the day before, the Extraordinary Council approved a comprehensive "European policy to combat terrorism," titled the Plan of Action.[22] In this document the European Council called for the adoption of instruments and measures in five areas:

• Enhancing police and judicial cooperation,
• Developing international legal instruments,
• Putting an end to the funding of terrorism,
• Strengthening air security, and
• Coordinating the European Union's global action.[23]

One important implication of this Plan of Action is that it binds the EU member states to a single long-term counter-terrorism strategy, implying that the rotating presidencies will no longer be able to set the EU counter-terrorist agenda solely on the basis of their own national priorities. As Dorine Dubois points out, "The events of 11 September have indirectly allowed the EU to become a consistent actor in the fight against terrorism."[24] Once the Plan of Action was accepted, the EU turned its attention to implementing the plan through a series of steps, one of which was the establishment of the European arrest warrant.

Introduction of a European Arrest Warrant

The idea of a European arrest warrant (EAW) originated from the Tampere European Council of 1999, in which leaders of all member states expressed their desire to improve judicial cooperation in the EU by abolishing the formal extradition procedures for persons "who are fleeing from justice after having been finally sentenced."[25] The European Commission, one of the most outspoken proponents of the EAW, "regarded the arrest warrant as one of the first genuine steps towards the harmonization of (criminal) procedure laws and, ultimately, towards the realization of a European judicial area."[26] Nevertheless, prior to 9/11, the idea of a European arrest warrant proved to be highly controversial in a number of EU member states,[27] rendering impossible the necessary unanimous agreement on a framework decision. It was only because of the momentum generated by 9/11—which forced European leaders to finally recognize that the EU's open borders and different legal systems allowed terrorists and other criminals to move around easily and evade arrest and prosecution—that the council was able to reach a political agreement in December 2001 on the Framework Decision on the European arrest warrant.[28] The binding council Framework Decision was duly approved in June 2002,[29] and in January 2004 the EAW began to replace the formal extradition procedures among the member states. In April 2005 Italy became the last EU member state to transpose the EAW into national law.

The EAW allows for a significant expediting of the entire extradition process. First of all, the state in which the person is arrested must return the suspect to the state issuing the warrant within ninety days of the arrest. Moreover, if the detained person gives consent to the surrender, the extradition shall occur within ten days. This acceleration is achieved by requiring only one judicial decision for both arrest and surrender.[30] As a result of this innovation, which excludes any political involvement of the ministers of justice or foreign affairs, it is possible to argue that the entire EAW procedure is completely "judicialized."

The EAW also considerably simplifies the entire extradition procedure by abolishing the principle of double criminal liability for thirty-two serious criminal offenses, including participation in a criminal organization and terrorism. In practical terms, this means that in these thirty-two cases, the crime for which the convicted person is requested no longer needs to be recognized in both the requesting and the requested states. The EAW also abolishes the classification of political offense and nationality as legitimate criteria for refusal for extradition, further ensuring a smooth extradition process. The EAW Framework Decision does, nonetheless, specify a certain number of exceptions. For example, the implementation of extradition can be postponed for humanitarian reasons. Specific provisions were also made in the Framework Decision to ensure adequate protection of human rights.

Despite offering a smoother and simpler extradition process to the EU, some experts see the EAW as a threat to national sovereignty. Jonathan Stevenson, for example, suggests that the EAW, "although proposed on the pretext of counterterrorism, appears to be part of a larger agenda, one that aims . . . to expand the EU's supranational legal jurisdiction," and warned that this could lead to significant backlash from member states that "are becoming more worried about hemorrhaging national authority."[31] In contrast, while admitting that the new model "implies the transfer of another element of intergovernmental cooperation to the supranational level," Filip Jasinski argues that the EAW "would not be a breach of national sovereignty in respect of extradition decisions, since surrender of a suspect within the Union would not be regarded as classic extradition."[32] In either case, the EAW represents the first realization of the principle of mutual recognition of judicial decisions that was established by the Tampere European Council as the cornerstone of judicial cooperation. By reinforcing the internal EU procedures to act coherently and cooperatively, the EAW should significantly increase the credibility of the EU as a major player in the global fight against international terrorism and improve EU abilities to investigate and prosecute other transnational crimes.[33]

While it is still too early to provide an authoritative assessment of the practical impact of the EAW on the judicial cooperation of EU member states, some preliminary observations can already be made. First, there has been a significant delay in implementing the EAW in a number of member states. Even though the Framework Decision set 1 January 2004 as the final deadline for implementation, only eight member states incorporated all of the required provisions of the EAW in their national legislation by this date.[34] In several countries the enactment of the necessary constitutional provision took longer than expected, but in other countries the delay was at least partly due to the objections of conservative opposition parties that feared that "their fellow citizens will be exposed to the whims of other judicial systems that they consider less than trustworthy."[35] Some European legal scholars have also argued that the introduction of EAW was a "step too far too soon," warning that a number of practical problems are already beginning to emerge, in particular in relation to the protection of individual rights and legal certainty in the European judicial space.[36]

Despite the initial implementation delays, the EAW is now operational in most of the cases planned in all twenty-five EU member states. According to the first assessments by the European Commission, EAW's impact has been positive in terms of depoliticization, efficiency, and speed in the procedure for surrendering people who are sought:

The effectiveness of the EAW can be gauged provisionally from the 2,603 warrants issued, the 653 persons arrested and the 104 persons surrendered up to September 2004.... Since the Framework Decision came into operation, the average time taken to execute a warrant is provisionally estimated to have fallen from more than nine months to 43 days. This does not include these frequent cases where the person consents to surrender, for which the average time taken is 13 days.[37]

The EC, also warned that this overall success should not make people lose sight of the effort that is still required by some member states to comply fully with the EAW Framework Decision. Its recent report highlights the difficulties that remain in that respect. A few member states considered that, with regard to their nationals, they should reintroduce a systematic check on double criminality. Noticeable in some member states is the introduction of supplementary grounds for refusal, which are contrary to the Framework Decision, such as political reasons, reasons of national security, or those involving examination of the merits of a case. Moreover, there are cases in certain member states where the decision-making powers conferred on executive bodies are not in line with the Framework Decision. Lastly, by ruling out the warrant's application to acts that occurred before a given date, a few member states did not comply with the Framework Decision. The extradition requests that they continue to present therefore risk being rejected by the other member states.[38]

Although the EAW applies only within the territory of the EU and relations with third countries are still governed by extradition rules, EAW's introduction has also raised some concerns outside of the EU. The U.S. government, in particular, has been concerned that with the EAW in place, the EU member states would give extradition and assistance requests from other EU member states a higher priority than requests from the United States and other third parties. As before 9/11, the death penalty has been a particularly controversial issue that has hindered the negotiation of a workable transatlantic standard for extradition and legal assistance.[39] Bilateral treaties with individual EU members have generally contained assurances that suspects extradited to the United States will not face the death penalty, but U.S. officials have been reluctant to agree to such a blanket guarantee in a treaty negotiated with the EU as a whole.[40] According to Kristin Archick, the Bush administration's main objective for an eventual extradition accord is to secure a provision permitting any EU national to be handed over to U.S. judicial authorities.[41] The EU officials, however, remain largely circumspect on whether they would be prepared to meet such a requirement given the national sensitivities involved and the likely objections of some EU member states.[42]

Enhancing Law Enforcement Cooperation and Intelligence Sharing: Europol

The importance of Europol in the fight against terrorism was stressed once again in the conclusions of the Extraordinary European Council of 21 September 2001. The European Council issued instructions aimed to elevate Europol to an effective information and intelligence exchange medium. Although Europol did not gain supranational authority to conduct its own investigations, undertake searches, or arrest suspects, its mandate was somewhat expanded in the aftermath of 9/11. Most important, Europol gained the authority to ask police forces of EU member states to launch investigations and to share information with the U.S. and other third parties.[43] It was also assigned to open and expand the so-called terrorist analysis work files (AWFs) created from information and intelligence provided by the police forces and intelligence services of the EU member states.[44] This task was further discussed in the November 2002 JHA Council, which issued a recommendation on developing "terrorist profiles" that focused on the identification of terrorist targets and organizations. Finally, the December 2002 Council Decision 2003/48/JHA specifically stipulated that "each Member State shall take necessary measures to ensure that at least the following information collected by the specialized service is communicated to Europol":

- Data that identify the person, group, or entity;
- Acts under investigation and their specific circumstances;
- Links with other relevant cases of terrorist offenses;
- The use of communications technologies; and
- The threat posed by the possession of weapons of mass destruction.[45]

The Framework Decision also provided for the appointment of specialized services or magistrates (articles 2 and 3) within the police services and judicial authorities (Eurojust or other); an optimal exchange of information with Europol; an immediate priority to be given to requests for mutual assistance concerning persons, groups, and entities listed (article 6); and maximum access by the authorities of other member states to information on those targeted (article 7).

Building on the proposals from the JHA Council meeting on 20 September,[46] the Extraordinary Council of 21 September also launched several institutional innovations, including the installation of a twenty-four-hour alert counter-terrorism unit within Europol.[47] Later known as the Counter Terrorist Task Force (CTTF), the unit was comprised of national liaison officers from police and intelligence services. It was supposed to collect all relevant information and intelligence concerning current terrorist threats in a timely manner, analyze the collected information and undertake the necessary operational and strategic analysis, and draft a threat assessment document based on information received. In practice, however, the CTTF was criticized for serious shortcomings in handling real-time data.[48] Consequentially, when its original mandate expired in the spring of 2003, all counter-terrorism work had been taken over by the Serious Crime Unit.[49] A "new" CTTF was put in place in the aftermath of the Madrid terrorist attacks but as of October 2004, it had performed only limited operations with limited staff.[50]

According to some observers, Europol has begun to play an increasingly important role in the fight against terrorism after the 9/11 events. Jonathan Stevenson, for example, suggested that

Europol has already proven useful as a vehicle for distributing general information and assessments among national law-enforcement authorities. It has also served the useful political function of enshrining pre-existing bilateral law-enforcement relationships that had arisen in connection with transnational threats such as narcotics trafficking and the "old" pre–al Qaeda terrorism. Europol also has some potential . . . to help harmonize the national policies of EU member states on territorial security.[51]

Other observers, however, pointed out that "most Europol-related measures are still in the stage of planning,"[52] and the skeptics have warned that even after the recent budgetary and staff increases,[53] Europol remains too small and minimally funded.[54] For its part, the European press noted that when it came to real action, Europol looked rather marginal in a number of recent events. Perhaps most notably, it was not even given a role in the investigation when a spate of letter bombs was sent to several top EU officials at the end of 2003, despite the fact that its own chief was among those targeted.[55] Examples like this confirm that even after 9/11, Europol continues to be more of a coordination office than an operational headquarters.

In the area of counter-terrorism, however, even coordination has proven to be a difficult task. In part this is because the political, administrative, and judicial framework varies from one member state to another, which adds further impediments to effective information sharing and coordination.[56] Moreover, according to a report by the European Commission, free circulation of information is hindered by two additional obstacles:

The first is that the information tends to be compartmentalized at both organizational and legal levels. For example, it is divided between different ministries and services and is intended for use in different procedures, thereby affecting the nature and sensitivity of the information that can be handled by the services. The second obstacle is the lack of a clear policy on information channels, resulting in disagreement on the choice of channel and on how to handle sensitive and confidential information.[57]

More important, it seems that some do not necessarily welcome coordination from Brussels. A recent study by the EU counter-terrorism coordinator, for example, found that while all member states "deplore the failure to set up a Europol information system, which prevents rapid and effective cooperation between them . . . they do not all seem to have the same level of involvement in this project."[58] As of 2004, for example, only seven member states seconded the necessary intelligence analysts to the EU's Situation Centre, and the special working groups on counter-terrorism that report to the council were still based in the capitals instead of feeding directly to EU security experts in Brussels.[59]

Another important area of the counter-terrorism campaign where, according to a recent report by the RAND Corporation, "the EU has not made a significant contribution" is intelligence sharing.[60] The report explicitly pointed out that the reluctance of some member states to share information about terrorism with Europol has repeatedly led to situations where Europol lacked "a complete understanding of current threat levels, international connections among suspected terrorists, and the counterterrorism efforts of its own members."[61] The fact that intelligence sharing between the EU member states and Europol has so far been extremely slow was also acknowledged in the March 2004 "European Commission action paper in response to the terrorist attacks on Madrid." The commission urged the member states to use Europol "more and better" and stressed that they "should consider it their duty to give the Europol Terrorism Task Force . . . all operational information, not just limited and filtered strategic and technical intelligence."[62]

Overall, however, it is still questionable whether all EU member states are truly committed to giving Europol a serious counter-terrorism role. It was primarily for political reasons that terrorism was originally not included on Europol's agenda, and, as of this writing, full consensus has not yet emerged on the role and future of Europol. While some member states, including Germany, would like to see Europol evolve into an organization with an independent investigative role like the U.S. Federal Bureau of Investigation, others, including the United Kingdom, oppose such evolution, preferring instead to keep investigative authority at the national level with Europol as a coordinating body.[63] Disputes like this indicate that at least for some member states, it may still be too early to allow the EU to have an influential role in traditionally state-specific areas such as policing, criminal justice, and intelligence gathering. In the early 1990s the desire of EU member states to keep control over the two most sensitive policy areas (Foreign and Security Policy and Justice and Home Affairs) was one of the primary reasons that the EU was established with three discrete "pillars."[64] As of early 2006 it appeared that regarding JHA, most member states continue to prefer the intergovernmental principle of decision making, which means that any common policy must emerge through consensus and cannot be dictated by supranational EU institutions.

Some observers have also noted that the apparent lack of agreement on the role of Europol is due to the fact that a number of member states consider bilateral cooperation as "the most workable instrument" from an intelligence perspective.[65] Consequently, while formally supporting political initiatives at the EU level, many member states simultaneously participate in informal, practitioner-led networks such as the Police Working Group on Terrorism (PWGT) and the Club of Berne, often at the expense of supporting Europol.[66] The police forces and intelligence services of EU member states also "generally view Europol with a great deal of suspicion, believing that it infringes on their authority and autonomy."[67] As Europol director Jürgen Storbeck explained: "For a policeman, information about his own case is like property. He is even reluctant to give it to his chief or to another department, let alone giving it to the regional or national services. For an international body like Europol, it is very difficult."[68]

Regardless of the fact that the enlargement of Europol's operational counter-terrorist capacities has been mostly theoretical, the need to address issues of judicial control and the inclusion of binding human rights provisions has already been raised and is likely to become even more pressing in the years to come. A recent report by the EU Network of Independent Experts in Fundamental Rights (CFR-CDF), for example, stated that at the present stage, the procedures devised by the JHA Council session of 28 and 29 November 2002 for the development of terrorist profiles "appear insufficient in terms of the accuracy and reliability of information, which is taken into account, notwithstanding its confidentiality, which cannot justify a total absence of control."[69] The report also criticized the lack of adequate human rights safeguards in a number of other data-sharing measures, including several agreements between Europol and non-EU states, as well as the council's proposals to intensify the monitoring of personal communications.[70]

Enhancing Judicial Cooperation: Eurojust

Although the establishment of Eurojust was not specifically mentioned in the Plan of Action adopted by the Extraordinary European Council on 21 September 2001, the conclusions of the Justice and Home Affairs

Council meeting on the preceding day underlined the urgent need for a European Judicial Cooperation Unit (Eurojust).[71] The original decision to establish Eurojust was made already by the Tampere JHA Council in October 1999, and the 2001 Treaty of Nice provided an explicit basis for this new organization. In accordance with the original timetable, the new unit became fully operational in February 2002.[72]

The council's underlying idea behind the decision to establish Eurojust was that "the efficient prosecution of criminal acts makes . . . cooperation between member states at the judicial level necessary."[73] In practical terms Eurojust is essentially a high-level team of senior magistrates, prosecutors, judges, and other legal experts who are seconded from every EU member state. Although they work in one building as a team, they continue to function as members of their respective national organizations. The main advantage of this arrangement is that the individual team members know the legal systems and practical arrangements of their home countries inside out. In addition, they can consult other team members at any time. This accessibility and consolidation of information and expertise enables Eurojust to put "any cases referred to them into an EU context and more easily spot any patterns or trends in EU crime than colleagues in their home countries."[74] Eurojust also enables direct contact between judges so that, for example, a judge in Greece can ask a judge in France to issue an order against a suspect living in France.[75]

The primary task of Eurojust is to provide "immediate legal advice and assistance in cross-border cases to the investigators, prosecutors and judges in different EU member states."[76] It can also handle letters rogatory, which ask for information, or enquiries to be carried out by the authorities in another country and direct them to the appropriate authorities for action. Eurojust also assists and cooperates with OLAF, the EU's Anti-fraud Office, in cases affecting the EU's financial interests. Eurojust can recommend certain steps to national authorities, "such as to initiate and/or coordinate investigations or to set up investigation teams."[77] On its own, however, Eurojust has no legal authority to launch or execute investigations. Like Europol, it instead relies on a system of lateral links among its members, which are based on the idea that "cross-border issues such as terrorism and organized crime require increased cooperation among judicial authorities."[78]

In addition to its primary intra–EU coordination tasks, article 1 of the 28 February 2002 Council Decision setting up Eurojust entitled the organization to "have legal personality," thus allowing it to directly engage in formal relations with third partners. The U.S., for example, has already provided a specific liaison magistrate to take part in Eurojust activities.[79] However, this cooperation with non–EU counter-terrorist magistrates has been criticized by the European Parliament because "it entails an exchange of personal data, while there are no data protection provisions in force for Eurojust."[80] Indeed, as Nicola Venne-mann pointed out, "Eurojust as an entity with legal personality is not itself bound by the human rights obligations contained in Article 6 TEU [Treaty on European Union] and is not accountable to the ECJ [European Court of Justice] either."[81] In response to these critiques, a decision was recently made to establish a Joint Supervisory Body to Eurojust, which will be composed of "judges or comparably independent professionals from the Member States." This new body will monitor data processing at Eurojust to "ensure that it is carried out in accordance with the relevant data protection rules."[82]

In the wake of the Madrid bombings and following the conclusions of the European Council of 25 and 26 March 2004, the European Commission adopted a "Communication on the Fight Against Terrorism." This initiative proposes a number of new measures to improve the exchange of information in the EU, enabling counter-terrorist services to do their jobs more effectively. It also paves the way for a future "European criminal record" that would ensure that information is exchanged on all offenses, convictions, and disqualifications linked to terrorism, including any form of financing of terrorist activities. Furthermore, the commission proposed that the member states be equipped with systems for registering bank accounts to facilitate the gathering of evidence—especially where financing of terrorism is suspected.[83] In the long run, the European Commission hopes that Eurojust will become the functional equivalent of Europol, thus representing "the next major step in ensuring that there are no safe havens for criminals and terrorists in the European Union."[84]

As of 2005 Eurojust was still a very young organization trying to establish its own procedures and mechanisms for cooperation. Nevertheless, two high-profile reports have already criticized the slow progress of implementation of the relevant EU decisions and the persistent lack of tangible results in the area of judicial cooperation at the EU level. The first report, drawn up by the EU Council's security experts following the March 2004 terrorist attacks in Madrid, claimed that EU member states adopted "a minimalist approach to Eurojust" and criticized several of them for paying lip service to this important EU organization.[85] The second report, the "European Commission Action Paper in response to the Terrorist Attacks on Madrid," suggested the following regarding the future role of Eurojust:

> Eurojust should be given a stronger role in the fight against terrorism. The Council should give it a clear mandate to coordinate the activities of national prosecuting authorities across the Union in relation to terrorism. We should open an urgent debate about giving Eurojust an initiating role in this regard too. Presently, Member States may, provided they come forward with a justification, refuse to pursue an investigation requested by Eurojust. This should be abrogated, at least when Eurojust's request would relate to investigations on terrorism.[86]

As in the case of Europol, it is questionable whether all EU member states fully support the strengthening of Eurojust's role in the fight against terrorism. As Jasinski noted, the negative attitude of some EU member states toward Eurojust "testifies to still inadequate harmonization of 'pro-integration thinking' in the justice and home affairs sphere."[87] Alternatively, the adoption of a minimalist approach to Eurojust may reflect the preference of national agencies and officials to work through the existing state-to-state contacts rather than through a new, untested EU organization. One may also suspect that along with their law enforcement counterparts, national judiciaries may view Eurojust as a threat to their own authority and autonomy. The experiences so far with Europol and Eurojust indeed seem to suggest that it is one thing for Europe's political elites to make public promises on the international exchange of counter-terrorism intelligence and EU-wide judicial cooperation and quite another thing for them to persuade the relevant national agencies, over which politicians usually exercise less than perfect control, to comply.[88]

Adoption of a Common Definition of Terrorism

A binding EU definition of terrorism was elaborated in December 2001 when the council reached political agreement on a Framework Decision on Combating Terrorism.[89] The decision was subsequently duly approved in June 2002.[90] It specifically delineates acts of terrorism and acts of terrorist groups. Article 1 sets out a three-part definition of *terrorism*, consisting of the *context* of an action, the *aim* of the action, and the *specific acts* being committed.[91] First, it stipulates there must be "intentional acts . . . which, given their nature or context, may seriously damage a country or an international organization." Second, the acts must be committed with the aim of either "seriously intimidating a population" or "unduly compelling a Government or international organization" to act or fail to act or "seriously destabilizing or destroying the fundamental political, constitutional, economic or social structures of a country or an international organization." Third, there is a list of eight types of specific acts that can be identified as terrorist:

• Attacks on a person's life that may cause death;

• Attacks on the physical integrity of a person;

• Kidnapping or hostage taking;

• The causing of extensive destruction to a government or public facility, a transport system, an infrastructure facility, including an information system, a fixed platform located on the continental shelf, a public place or private property likely to endanger human life or result in major economic loss;

• Seizure of aircraft, ships, or other means of public or goods transport;

• Manufacture, possession, acquisition, transport, supply or use of weapons, explosives, or of nuclear, biological, or chemical weapons, as well as research into, and development of, biological and chemical weapons;

• Release of dangerous substances, or causing fires, explosions, or floods, the effect of which is to endanger human life; and

• Interference with or disruption of the supply of water, power, or any other fundamental natural resource, the effect of which is to endanger human life.

Threatening to commit any of the above acts is also included. According to article 2.2, the EU member states must also punish the following intentional acts:

• Directing a terrorist group; and

• Participating in the activities of a terrorist group, including by supplying information or material resources or by funding its activities in any way, with knowledge of the fact that such participation will contribute to the criminal activities of the (terrorist) group.

The Framework Decision on Combating Terrorism ensures that these offenses are punished by heavier sentences than common criminal offenses in all the EU member states. It does not, however, spell out specific penalties and standardized sanctions from terrorist activities as originally recommended by the European Commission because member states "could not agree on such exact penalties and found the proposed system too complicated."[92] As a result, the Framework Decision spelled out specific penalties for only two offenses—a fifteen-year minimum custodial sentence for leading a terrorist group and an eight-year minimum custodial sentence for other offenses relating to involvement with a terrorist group. Sanctions for other offenses—such as murder, kidnapping, or hijacking—are largely left to the discretion of each member state, although the Framework Decision allows for the imposition of a heavier sentence if the acts were committed with a terrorist intent.

It is important to note that the preamble to the Framework Decision specifically excludes from its scope "[a]ctions by armed forces during periods of armed conflict, which are governed by international humanitarian law . . . and, inasmuch as they are governed by other rules of international law." Both Protocol 1 and Protocol 2 Additional to the Geneva Conventions recognize peoples "fighting against colonial domination and alien occupation and against racist regimes in the exercise of their right of self-determination." These protocols also recognize "dissident armed forces or other organized armed groups, which under responsible command, exercise such control over a part of its territory as to enable them to carry out sustained and concerted military action operations" as legitimate armed forces in the sense of international humanitarian law. These provisions imply that parties to an internal conflict or a civil war are excluded from the range of persons capable of committing terrorist offenses as defined by the Framework Decision. The same exclusion applies also for regular armed forces, including police, as far as they exercise official duties.

The Framework Decision's definition of *terrorism* has nonetheless been criticized by some human rights advocate groups as being "too extensive and as not reflecting particular dangers inherent in terrorist acts."[93] The 2003 report by the CFR–CDF, for example, asserted that "this definition as such is not adequate to meet the requirement of lawfulness."[94] The only available scholarly legal analysis of the Framework Decision definition of *terrorism* concluded that it contains "adequate protection of human rights *if* its preamble and statements attached to it are fully applied" but warned that "the ambiguity of the Framework Decision taken by the EU Council makes it necessary to keep a close eye on the Union's and its member states' implementation of the policy because of possible abuses of human rights in certain cases."[95]

Given that prior to the 9/11 events, terrorism was recognized as a special offense only in six EU member states,[96] there is little doubt that even with the aforementioned shortcomings, the council's definition of terrorist offenses represents a crucial prerequisite for enhanced police and judicial cooperation at the EU level. A number of subsequent common positions and decisions, including those on the freezing of terrorists' assets, were adopted on the basis of this definition. Furthermore, as Dorine Dubois pointed out, the Framework Decision is favorable to EU-U.S. cooperation in the fight against terrorism because the two partners can now deal with a crime legally recognized as a special offense on both sides of the Atlantic. In fact, the EU Council definition of terrorism is similar to that of the U.S.[97]

As has been the case with a number of other post-9/11 counterterrorism measures, the impact of the Framework Decision on the fight against terrorism has been negatively influenced by the lengthy transposition of its provisions into the national legislation of some of the EU member states. This was confirmed in the recent "European Commission Action Paper in Response to the Terrorist Attacks on Madrid," which points out that "[t]hree Member States have not fully reported on the implementation of this legislation, and for the others it is not yet clear that national measures fully implement the requirements of the Framework Decision." In the same report, the commission promised "to report the failings in no uncertain terms to the Council" and to "do all it can to ensure that the Member States take the necessary measures" in the coming weeks.[98] It remains to be seen how persistent the commission will be in this delicate endeavor and what impact it will ultimately make.

Notwithstanding the similarity of EU and U.S. definitions of *terrorism*, there remain many important difficulties resulting from the differences between the EU counter-terrorism model, based on strict law enforcement, and the U.S. model, based on the use of force. The recent request by an independent Italian judge for arrest and extradition of a number of CIA agents that allegedly mounted a secret operation inside Italy (kidnapping an Egyptian Islamic cleric as he walked on the streets of Milan and deporting him to Egypt) without even letting the Italians know, clearly exposed a wider clash of cultures between the U.S. and Europe when it comes to fighting terrorism. As Jörg Friedrichs, an expert in international police cooperation at the University of Bremen, put it: "Americans think they are fighting evil and that you can't play by the rules when you fight an enemy that does not. But in general, Europe, with its history of dealing with domestic terrorism, is convinced that the problem must be tackled using the law, not flouting it."[99] In practical terms, this means that the European judicial inquiries, which are independent from state intelligence operations, must work painstakingly to build cases against suspected terrorists and arrest them only when there is sufficient evidence for a court case. The U.S. approach since 9/11, however, has been to eliminate the threat first and ask questions later. Consequentially, according to Ian Cuthbertson, a counter-terrorism expert at the World Policy Institute, "Americans will never think Europe is doing enough. For every hundred terror-related arrests, only a handful are ever convicted. And even then, sentences in Europe for any crime are trivial compared to those in the United States. Suspected terrorists are often allowed to walk free."[100] In the case of the Milan abduction, Cuthbertson states: "[T]he Americans felt the information this man had was too valuable; if they entered into the European justice system, that information would never come out."[101] In short, the key difference is that while the U.S. treats the fight against terrorism as a war, the majority of EU member states still see it primarily as a criminal justice matter.

Identification of Presumed Terrorists and Freezing of their Assets

In reaction to UN Security Council Resolution 1373 (2001), which requires all UN member states to freeze funds and other financial assets of persons and groups engaged in terrorist activities, in December 2001 the council adopted Common Position 2001/931/CFSP on the application of specific measures to combat terrorism.[102] Referring to the 2002 Council Framework definition of terrorist offenses, the common position draws a comprehensive list of persons, groups, and entities considered terrorist. Most interesting, another list of "certain persons and entities" considered terrorist was adopted by the council in its December 2001 Regulation (EC) No. 2580/2001, which specifically tasked the first pillar of the EU—the European Communities—with the actual execution of freezing of terrorist assets.[103] This cross-pillar approach clearly "shows to what extent internal and external security aspects have merged with the internationalization of terrorism."[104] Moreover, as Dubois suggested, "This strange mix of legal bases originating in all three pillars of the EU emphasizes the EU's willingness to take action, even though its competence to implement the UN SC Resolution may not clearly appear."[105]

The list of individuals and entities established by the Common Position 2001/931/CFSP distinguishes between two different statuses. For the first group of persons or organizations, the council calls for the EU member states to enhance their third pillar of cooperation to prevent terrorist acts. As for the second group of persons or organizations concerned, the EC is actually to freeze their financial or economic assets. The list contains names and personal identification data that is regularly updated twice a year. Originally, only twenty-nine individuals (twenty-one of whom were members of the Euskadi Ta Askatasuna, or Basque Fatherland and Liberty, ETA) and thirteen organizations were placed on the list. After the revision in May 2004 there were forty-five individuals and forty-six organizations, including the Kurdistan Workers' Party and the Revolutionary Armed Forces of Colombia.[106] The inclusion of the latter organization, which currently controls an area of Colombian territory the size of Switzerland, demonstrates that the restrictive approach to terrorism of the Framework Decision—that excludes from its scope actions by armed forces during periods of armed conflict governed by international humanitarian law—is not adopted by the present common position.

The council updates the list unanimously, and it must meet the criteria spelled out in article 1(4) of the Common Position 2001/931/CFSP:

The list in the Annex shall be drawn up on the basis of precise information or material in the relevant file which indicates that a decision has been taken by a competent authority in respect of the persons, groups and entities concerned, irrespective of whether it concerns the instigation of investigations or prosecution for a terrorist act, an attempt to perpetrate, participate in or facilitate such an act based on serious and credible evidence or clues, or condemnation for such deeds.[107]

Proposals for listing or maintaining persons, groups, and entities on the lists are examined by the relevant national authorities of the member states before the council endorses them. This procedure grants these authorities a minimum period of two weeks for vetting and consideration. The council's discussions about the list are secret.[108]

The procedure, as well as the criteria for placing individuals on the list, has been criticized by nongovernmental organizations (NGOs) and human rights experts. A recent report by the CFR–CDF raised the following objections:

Aside from questions of the confidentiality of the collection of information, which must not result in a complete absence of control, an important question remains, that of the veracity and reliability of information which results in inclusion in the list, the danger of abuse of asset freezing increasing with a lack of a definition of a terrorist offence. Undeniably, the means of drawing up this list do not appear to be satisfactory in their present form, since the choice of an administrative procedure (inclusion in a list by a governmental body) concerns a field which should fall strictly within the authority of the judiciary.[109]

Another serious matter of concern is that the list established within the December 2001 Common Position 2001/931/CFSP differs in both number of persons and groups from the list established and updated by the council for the purposes of its December 2001 Regulation (EC) No. 2580/2001.[110] In absence of any explanation by the EU authorities, this discrepancy clearly demonstrates the lack of transparency in the establishment of these lists. This assertion is further justified by the existence of a number of other terrorist lists established by several EU member states that do not correspond to either of those mentioned above. For example, as of March 2005 the Consolidated List of Financial Sanctions Targets in the UK (managed by the Bank of England) contained the names of sixty individuals and fifty-five entities that are considered terrorist.[111]

In addition to all the previously discussed measures that are aimed at implementing Resolution 1373, the EU has also taken a number of measures to comply with the October 1999 UN Security Council Resolution 1267, which calls for the freezing of funds and financial assets of the Taliban and Al-Qaida. Although there is still some debate among legal scholars as to the extent to which the EU is bound by Security Council Resolutions,[112] there is no longer any doubt that the implementation of embargo orders by the UN Security Council falls under the competence of the EU. Article 301, also known as the "embargo Article," was incorporated into the Maastricht treaty precisely with the aim of putting an end to such discussions on whether and to what extent Community law provides the basis for an exclusive EC competence in implementing trade embargoes.[113]

In the case of Al-Qaida, however, the council had to rely on a number of other treaty articles because the embargo article referred only to embargoes directed against state actors. Over time this innovative approach allowed the council to agree on three common positions that in turn opened the path for the adoption of corresponding council regulations aimed at implementing Security Council Resolution 1267.[114] Similarly to the Common Position 2001/931/CFSP, there is a list of persons and entities whose assets should be frozen by relevant EU authorities. However, unlike the two lists established by designated EU authorities in 2001, in the case of Al-Qaida the EU simply adopted the list that was established by the UN 1267 Committee, which oversees the implementation of Resolution 1267. This has been heavily criticized by a number of human rights NGOs because the Resolution 1267 Committee proceedings for drafting the list are secret and Resolution 1267 does not contain any substantive criteria for determining who should be on the list. Some experts have also expressed concern that the list is not based on an act by an entity bound by EU law, which raises concerns about the adequacy of protection of fundamental rights and freedoms of the individuals who are added to this list.[115]

The suspicious lack of official, publicly available data concerning the actual amounts and types of terrorist assets frozen by the relevant EU authorities makes the evaluation of the real impact of the EU's counter-terrorism policies to eliminate terrorist finances a difficult endeavor. The figures that were published by various journalists and experts in the field are quite diverse. In April 2002 a special inquiry by the *Financial Times* revealed that "European countries have frozen nearly $35 million in terrorist assets since the September 11 attacks in the U.S., a figure equal to the assets blocked by the U.S."[116] Between 2002 and March 2004, according to a news report by the Associated Press, banks across the EU allegedly froze close to $2 million dollars in assets belonging to terrorist groups.[117] A January 2004 press release by the U.S. Department of the Treasury stated that "[a]t least $139 million in assets has been kept out of the control of terrorists as a result of efforts by the United States and its allies."[118] According to Jimmy Gurulé, the former U.S. under secretary of treasury in the current Bush administration, 75 percent of this amount has been frozen by U.S. authorities.[119] Provided that these figures are roughly correct, it appears that since 2002 EU efforts to cut off terrorists from their financial sources have delivered only modest results, at least in comparison to the actions taken by the U.S.[120] Moreover, according to the European Strategic Intelligence and Security Center, the real impact of the freezing of millions of terrorist assets has often been overestimated because the preparation of a terrorist attack can be financed by microfinancing involving more complex tracing.[121]

The importance of strengthening the fight against the financing of terrorism was nonetheless reiterated in the "European Commission Action Paper in Response to the Terrorist Attacks on Madrid." In this report, the European Commission proposed a number of innovative measures to curb terrorist financing, which could be interpreted as an indirect acknowledgement of the weaknesses of the current EU financial control mechanism. The list of proposals includes the following:

• Introduction of custom controls on cash movements at the external frontier;

• Broadening of the exchanges of information on convictions for terrorist offenses and cooperation between member states, Europol, and Eurojust;

• Establishment of a European register on convictions and disqualifications for individuals and corporate bodies, with direct access "given to the competent";

• Establishment of a database of persons, groups, and entities covered by restrictive measures for the fight against terrorism or under criminal proceedings for terrorist offenses;

• Establishment by member states of systems allowing holders of bank accounts to be identified and facilitating investigations into bank accounts and movements of funds;

• Streamlining of the lists of terrorist organizations/assets to make them "operational and reactive on a 'real time' basis."[122]

It remains to be seen how many of these innovations will ultimately be accepted and implemented.

The Enlargement Process

Along with championing the cause of transnational counter-terrorism cooperation among its original fifteen member states, the EU has simultaneously attempted to bolster the counter-terrorism capabilities in Europe en masse. These efforts have been especially apparent in the successful enlargement process that was completed on 1 May 2004, when ten new member states joined the EU: Cyprus, the Czech Republic, Estonia, Hungary, Latvia, Lithuania, Malta, Poland, the Slovak Republic, and Slovenia (further referred to as the former candidate countries, or FCCs).[123] These FCCs were willing to change—but were not necessarily independently capable of changing, at least within the relatively short accession time frame—their administrative, legal, economic, social, and policy frameworks to conform to the EU's standards. It was only through intense planning, monitoring, mentoring, and generous funding assistance that the EU was able to facilitate these countries' successful transitions.

The European Union's accession process is a complex, resource-intensive system that has evolved along with the integration of the EU itself. Over time it has been refined into an identifiable series of six distinct steps.[124] First, the EU clearly defined its standards for accession by adopting the *acquis communautaire* and creating a written agreement with each state desiring membership. Second, the EU identified and prioritized the gaps between each state's current situation and the EU standard. Third, the EU required each state to devise its own (but EU-approved) plan to meet the standard. Fourth, the EU identified the funding and technical assistance available for each state to reach the standard. Fifth, the EU provided regular and detailed feedback on each state's successes and failures, relative to the standards identified in its accession agreement. Sixth, the EU actively communicated to all involved, from heads of state to individual citizens, the benefits of undertaking this dramatic—and at times painful—process.

Already in the preaccession stage, the FCCs gained a number of privileges in the area of Justice and Home Affairs, such as access to European early warning systems, institutional support, and subject matter experts for technical assistance and advice, including all terrorism-related measures. Perhaps most important, the FCCs received significant financial assistance to implement the structural and institutional changes required by the *acquis*.[125] The EU judiciously planned its accession program with parallel funding measures, which ultimately enabled the ten FCCs to enter in 2004. The combined preaccession assistance for the FCCs was €3 billion per year (1997 figures) during the 2000 to 2006 period.[126]

In May 1998 the EU launched its twinning program as a new way of delivering assistance for institution building programs within the Phare Programme,[127] using the same logic but different processes as its popular town twinning program between cities of separate European countries.[128] Although not generally considered to be a central component of the EU's accession process, twinning has served as a valuable tool to expedite and facilitate the accession states' implementation of their Europe

Box 7.1
The Twinning Program: A Success Story

In one of the EU's "great success stories," Hungary twinned with the United Kingdom and Germany to counter organized crime activities, harmonize its legislation, and examine systems and structures at its Interior Ministry to implement the Justice and Home Affairs chapter of the *acquis*. This program drastically increased in importance after Romania's accession plans were delayed, since this border was then the "Schengen frontier" or would become the EU's external border after accession. Within the project, the checkpoints were renovated; over 300 border guards, customs officials, and police officers were trained for their new tasks; and a completely new information network system was established. They completed this training within a "Training to Combat Organized Crime Activities" project that covered seven areas, including cross-border criminality, criminal intelligence activities, criminal terrorism, corruption, witness protection, and financial investigation. The Hungarians also created a new unit to fight cross-border crime and have included a series of enhanced and sophisticated skills into their police academy as a follow-up to the Phare Training Programme. In the area of criminal terrorism, they used improved bomb-scene management, trained officers in specialized analytical skills in the field of detecting organized crime, practiced techniques of undercover work, and introduced improved methods of fingerprinting and photographic evaluation. The drastic changes occurred in only eighteen months (1 February 2000 to 31 August 2001) and cost only €1.4 million.*

* European Commission, "On Time, on Target: Training to Combat Organized Crime in Hungary," *Phare National Programmes Highlights* 4 (February 2000): 40.

Agreements (EAs), allowing them to come into compliance with the EU's standards. By pairing the "old" EU member states with FCCs to share their counter-terrorism expertise, the FCCs could more quickly create or adapt their administrative and democratic institutions to comply with membership requirements in the area of JHA.[129]

Most interesting, countries using the twinning program have been the most successful in instituting changes related to legislation, the judiciary, and administrative procedures. This is in part because the general population does not always have to support these changes for them to be effective, unlike other EU twinning projects with goals such as integrating minorities or changing educational curricula. In addition, twinning incorporated an agreed-upon standard that the "old" EU member states were already successfully employing.[130] There were also many indirect benefits from twinning for both the FCCs and member states. For example, one external evaluation of the EU's Phare Programme found that the EU twinning partners introduced good management practices outside of the specific twinning project. Although the twinning projects do not guarantee lasting relationships, "twinning partners tend to keep in touch through e-mails and phone calls, which is not the case with technical assistance."[131] The evaluators found this was a common occurrence with far-reaching possibilities for sustainability and community building. As one manager in an agricultural agency participating in the twinning program told an evaluator, "When I am encountered with a problem or have some doubts, I simply ring my new friends from Germany and Austria for their second opinion."[132]

Since 1998 the EU has also continued to annually complete regular reports on the progress and shortcomings of each former candidate country with respect to its accession partnership and *acquis* implementation progress. Together with the accession partnership, the regular reports define the priorities within each FCC for specific institution building, which is generally defined as "the process of helping the FCCs to develop the structures, strategies, human resources and management skills needed to strengthen their economic, social, regulatory and administrative capacity."[133] Within each regular report's section covering the JHA, the EU recapitulated what was the FCC's original status as per its July 1997 report and then described the FCC's current status in meeting the EU standards specifically pertaining to the areas of immigration/border controls, asylum, police, drugs, and judicial cooperation. The report clearly identified progress toward and away from the FCC's Action Plan, and prioritized the short- and medium-term objectives that the FCC needed to address to remain in good standing in the accession process.

These reports and the financial assistance the EU provided to help make the required preaccession changes have had a significant effect on the compliance of the former candidate countries' administrative, legal, economic, social, and policy frameworks with the EU *acquis*. Despite the significant hardships that each FCC and its people incurred due to the (at times drastic) changes demanded by Brussels, these efforts yielded some impressive results. For example, before accepting the EAs, which formalized their plans toward accession in the 1990s, the ten FCCs collectively had a 35 percent acceptance rate of the twelve international terrorism-related treaties. After signing the EAs but before Resolution 1373 went into effect in 2001, an additional 32 percent of the treaties were accepted, while 27 percent more have been accepted since Resolution 1373 and before the FCCs were granted EU membership. Combined, the FCCs have accepted 93 percent of all treaties relating to combating international terrorism, and almost 98 percent of the treaties have at least been signed.[134]

The Impact of Madrid

The brazen terrorist attack on the Madrid train system in March 2004 stood as a grim reminder to EU member states of the costs of moving too slowly to implement counter-terrorism measures. At the EU level a number of internal reports revealed that implementation of the measures agreed on years prior had been "slow, poor and inadequate,"[135] and top-level EU officials suddenly became unusually outspoken in their sharp criticisms of the tendency of the EU member states to produce "networks and institutions and then refuse to provide them with necessary tools to perform their jobs or simply not [use] them."[136] Austrian chancellor Wolfgang Schuessel suggested that the measures previously taken by the EU had been "absolutely not sufficient as a protection against terrorism."[137]

Seizing the momentum created by the Madrid attacks, the European Commission has been particularly outspoken in its sharp criticism of the lack of intelligence data sharing and has proposed a number of ways to enhance operational coordination and cooperation in the area of counter-terrorism at the EU level, including the following:

• The development of a new coordination mechanism for the exchange of information;

• The implementation of a European information policy for law enforcement purposes;

• The enhancement of controls to prevent goods linked to terrorist actions from entering the Community;

• The outlining of an EU approach to the use of travelers' data for border and aviation security and other law enforcement purposes;

• The development of comprehensive and interoperable European information systems;

• The execution of an "urgent review" to determine if EU member states have adequate measures in place to monitor and trace bomb-making materials;

• The strengthening of the identification, control, and interception of illegal trafficking in weapons of mass destruction (WMD) materials;

• The early ratification of the Protocol to the United Nations Transnational Organised Crime Convention on trafficking of illegal firearms;

• The consideration of making fingerprints mandatory for EU identity cards and EU passports;

• The enforcement of a stronger role to the Task Force of EU Police Chiefs in operational activities concerning the prevention and fight against terrorism; and

• The fostering of internal coordination within the commission and within the council of various policies that are linked to EU counter-terrorism efforts.[138]

A number of individual member states have also capitalized on this same momentum to enhance the EU counter-terrorism policy in the area of intelligence sharing. Austria and Belgium, for example, put forward a proposal suggesting that the EU should create a "CIA-style intelligence agency to pool information on the extremist threat."[139] The proposal failed, however, to generate enough support from either the other member states or the European Commission. In a comment that was subsequently echoed by his French and German counterparts, British home secretary David Blunkett suggested the priority should be implementing those counter-terrorism measures already agreed on after the 9/11 terrorist attacks: "We don't want new institutions. What I'm interested in is hard, practical action. Let's cut out the waffle and let's make sure that whatever we do, we're practicing what we preach at home."[140]

The member states did, nevertheless, agree on the need to appoint an EU security coordinator, an idea that was first circulated by the Irish EU presidency immediately after the Madrid terrorist attacks.[141] Quickly nicknamed the EU's "Mr. Terrorism" and the "European terrorism czar" by the media, the EU security coordinator was tasked with addressing some of the shortcomings in the coordination of EU counter-terrorism policy. The very acknowledgment of a need to create such a position reflects the fact that despite the frequent calls by European governments to step up cooperation in intelligence sharing, the Council of Ministers, the Commission, and even the member states on a bilateral level often cannot agree how to coordinate.

The 25 and 26 March 2004 European Council took notice of many of the aforementioned critiques and confirmed the need to review what has been done to combat terrorism in Europe. It also issued a Declaration on Combating Terrorism, which outlines seven of the EU's strategic objectives to combat terrorism in a Revised Plan of Action:

• To deepen the international consensus and enhance international efforts to combat terrorism;

• To reduce the access of terrorists to financial and other economic resources;

• To maximize capacity within EU bodies and member states to detect, investigate, and prosecute terrorists and prevent terrorist attacks;

• To protect the security of international transport and ensure effective systems of border control;

• To enhance the capability of the European Union and of member states to deal with the consequences of a terrorist attack;

• To address the factors that contribute to support for, and recruitment into, terrorism;

• To target actions under EU external relations toward priority third countries where counter-terrorist capacity or commitment to combating terrorism needs to be enhanced.[142]

While it is clear that the primary aim of the Revised Plan of Action is to eliminate the previous EU counter-terrorism policy's tactical shortcomings, the wording of objectives six and seven seems to suggest that some changes may also be necessary at the strategic level. In particular, as British home secretary Blunkett suggested, "Moves must be made to address the wider context of terrorism by tackling its roots, whether this be the crisis in the Middle East or chronic unemployment [in the Arab states]."[143] This seems to confirm the conclusion of a scholarly study, which suggests that the EU counter-terrorism campaign has been developed primarily as a matter of judicial and police authority and described the current EU efforts to address the underlying roots of terrorism as "woefully inadequate."[144]

In many respects the Revised Plan of Action represents the first call to address terrorism in a comprehensive fashion. In November 2004 this call was reinforced at another European Council meeting in The Hague, where the so-called Hague Program was adopted. In this document, the heads of state and government of twenty-five EU member states declared that

The European Union can contribute decisively to the defeat of terrorism, by working together towards a global strategy to be established on the basis of its founding values: democracy, fundamental rights and the rule of law. The Union's attention must focus on different aspects of prevention, preparedness and response to further enhance, and where necessary complement, Member States' capabilities to fight terrorism.[145]

The Hague Programme is effectively the EU's current agenda for further development of the Justice and Home Affairs pillar, and counter-terrorism is clearly one of the key areas where the council would like to see a number of policy decisions within the next five years.

The overall priorities set out in The Hague Programme were further elaborated by the European Commission in May 2005 when a five-year Action Plan for Freedom, Justice, and Security was launched. This policy initiative sought to turn The Hague Programme's agenda into concrete actions, including a timetable for their adoption and implementation. It contains detailed proposals for EU action on terrorism, migration management, visa policies, asylum, privacy and security, the fight against organized crime, and criminal justice, while recognizing that none of these issues can be effectively addressed in isolation. Among the measures being introduced by the commission in the area of counter-terrorism are proposals aiming at greater cooperation between the law enforcement services of member states, particularly by means of improved exchange of information; a European framework for the protection of related data; a communication on the radicalization and recruitment of terrorists; proposals on the protection of vulnerable infrastructures; a proposal aimed at preventing charitable organizations from being used to fund terrorism; and a monitoring of the pilot project in place for the victims of terrorism.[146]

Similarly to all previous EU plans of action, the Revised Plan of Action, the Hague Programme, and the Action Plan for Freedom, Justice, and Security must be implemented to make a difference. A key prerequisite for meeting political objectives is adequate funding. In this regard the Hague Programme stands a good chance of being implemented since it was adopted at a time when the Commission was preparing its proposals for the financial perspective 2007 to 2013. This made it possible to ensure that the objectives of the program were in phase with the financial means available for them. As of 2006 only 0.5 percent of the total EU budget is dispensed in the area of Freedom, Security, and Justice, but the percentage should gradually increase to 1.3 percent in 2013. This amounts to almost a trebling of the total expenditure. Moreover, if the amounts proposed for 2007 to 2013 are compared to the current levels of funding, it is clear that the most significant progression is in the field of security. In 2013 amounts allocated to this policy will have increased by almost twelve times when compared to funding in 2006.[147] This demonstrates the political importance that the European Commission attaches to EU action in the field of prevention of and the fight against crime and terrorism.

The political commitment of the EU member states' representatives to the fight against terrorism also appears to be somewhat stronger after March 2004. When they resolutely rejected a "truce offer" from Osama Bin Laden, their message was a lucid one: "The threat of terrorism is a threat to our security, our democracies, and our way of life in the European Union. We will do everything in our power to protect our people from this threat."[148] A series of similar proclamations followed in July 2005 after the terrorist attacks in London. One can only hope that this time the EU politicians will be more successful in matching the rhetoric with action. Their past track record in implementing the EU counter-terrorism policy is unfortunately not particularly encouraging.

Conclusion

Following the tragic events of 9/11 the European Union acted on several fronts to reinforce its existing nascent capabilities to combat terrorism. By 21 September 2001 the Extraordinary European Council had already approved a comprehensive "European policy to combat terrorism" in the form of a Plan of Action, which was subsequently supplemented by a number of other important legal initiatives, including the following:

• Framework Decision on the European arrest warrant,

• Decision on the implementation of specific measures for police and judicial cooperation to combat terrorism,

• Framework Decision on Joint Investigation Teams,

• Decision establishing Eurojust,

• Framework Decision on Combating Terrorism,

• Common Position on the application of specific measures to combat terrorism, and

• Framework Decision on money laundering, the identification, tracing, freezing, and confiscation of instrumentalities and the proceeds of crime.

In light of this wide array of innovative legal measures, some observers suggested that "it certainly must be acknowledged that European Union law contributed to a great extent to the fight against terrorism in Europe, especially through the strengthening of cooperation between Member States."[149] Others noted that the 9/11 events generated tremendous political impetus, which not only enabled the EU to rapidly adopt a number of significant JHA instruments that attested to the EU's credibility as a partner in JHA but also augmented the EU's capacity to act as a single unit on the international stage.[150]

The findings of this analysis, however, reveal that while the unprecedented post-9/11 ability of the council to rapidly reach a political agreement on a number of highly sensitive issues may perhaps represent "a precedent for future developments in the field of JHA, as Third Pillar decision making has proven not to be inherently slow and cumbersome,"[151] serious doubts remain about the extent to which these agreements have been translated into effect thus far. Often, decisions adopted at the EU level have not been fully implemented by the member states. There have been cases of different interpretations of the agreed measures. EU enforcement capabilities remain quite weak, and there is a lack of effective coordination between EU institutions and EU member states in a number of important areas. The national intelligence and law enforcement agencies do not always cooperate with Europol as they should and occasionally prefer to act bilaterally rather than collectively. Cooperation of national judiciaries with Eurojust is also far from ideal due to ongoing national sovereignty concerns and various domestic preoccupations. These shortcomings represent an important reminder that the EU is ultimately its member states, without whose wholehearted support even the most elaborate and innovative counter-terrorism structures and mechanisms remain useless. Most important, however, they testify to the prevailing lack of genuine pro-integration thinking in the Justice and Home Affairs pillar.

The findings of this analysis also indicate that human-rights pressure groups and the European Parliament have consistently opposed the adoption of counter-terrorism measures that neglect the protection, or limit the provisions, of human rights and civil liberties. This opposition reflects the deeply rooted conviction of many members of the European Parliament (MEPs) who believe in the words of their Dutch liberal colleague Johanna Boogerd-Quaak that "[i]f we give away our freedoms in the fight against terrorism, the terrorists will have won."[152] In the past the involvement of the European Parliament and the ongoing monitoring by independent human-rights pressure groups like Statewatch and Amnesty International have led to several major changes in the EU's counter-terrorism policy, with the result that "in general, the human rights protection can be considered to be satisfactory."[153] It is therefore clear that all future efforts to combat terrorism at the EU level need to have adequate built-in safeguards for protection of human rights and liberties to avoid criticisms from members of the European Parliament, NGOs, and human-rights pressure groups.

On a more positive note, the findings of our analysis show that the EU's efforts to bolster the meager counter-terrorism capabilities of the candidate countries have produced some impressive results. Along with the billions of euros and extensive technical assistance, the refining of the EU's accession process into an identifiable and replicable series of six specific steps helped the ten former candidate countries to bring their administrative, legal, economic, social, and policy frameworks closer to the much higher EU standards. It is our contention that the EU's accession process offers a number of valuable lessons regarding the provision of counter-terrorism assistance to those developing countries that are willing to change—but not necessarily independently capable of changing—their administrative, legal, economic, social, and policy frameworks to combat international terrorism more effectively. These lessons could be emulated by other regional organizations and by the UN Counter-Terrorism Committee.

The analysis of recent developments suggests that both the EU institutions and the EU member states responded to the 11 March 2004 and the 7 July 2005 terrorist attacks with a much needed critique of the measures they have taken to combat terrorism thus far. The EU Council adopted a Revised Plan of Action, the commission launched a five-year Action Plan for Freedom, Justice, and Security, and a new EU security coordinator post was created to remedy the current shortcomings in intelligence sharing and coordination. These are all laudable developments that correspond to changed citizens' expectations about what should be priority issues at the European Union level. According to a recent Eurobarometer survey, 91 percent of EU citizens expect the EU to take action to fight terrorism and to maintain peace and security.[154]

Past experience, however, suggests that translating recent EU political agreements into effective counter-terrorism tools will not be easy. Most observers acknowledge that a multitude of political, legal, and cultural challenges lie ahead, and some have also criticized the EU's failure to adequately address the root causes of terrorism, which in turn suggests that the EU counter-terrorism policy needs to be adjusted both at the tactical and strategic levels. A year after the London terrorist attacks, the political commitment of EU leaders to make these adjustments appears to be stronger than ever before. Whether it will be strong enough to make the EU's counter-terrorism policy less of a paper tiger and more of an effective counter-terrorism device remains to be seen.

Notes

1. The main feature of the European Political Cooperation (EPC) was consultation among the member states on foreign policy issues. Launched in 1970, EPC was formally enshrined in the Single European Act (SEA) in 1987.

2. Malcolm Anderson, "Counterterrorism as an Objective of European Police Cooperation," in *European Democracies Against Terrorism: Governmental Policies and Intergovernmental Cooperation*, ed. Fernando Reinares (Burlington, VT: Ashgate, 2000), 229.

3. Paul Wilkinson, *Terrorism and the Liberal State* (London: Macmillan, 1986), 292.

4. Juliet Lodge, "Terrorism and the European Community: Towards 1992," *Terrorism and Political Violence* 1, no. 1 (January 1989): 30.

5. For further information, see Meliton Cardona, "The European Response to Terrorism," *Terrorism and Political Violence* 4, no. 4 (Winter 1992): 252–53; Lodge, "Terrorism and the European Community: Towards 1992," 36–40.

6. Lodge, "Terrorism and the European Community: Towards 1992," 30.

7. Cardona, "The European Response to Terrorism," 251.

8. M. P. M. Zagari, "Combating Terrorism: Report to the Committee of Legal Affairs and Citizens' Rights of the European Parliament," *Terrorism and Political Violence* 4, no. 4 (Winter 1992): 292.

9. Lodge, "Terrorism and the European Community: Towards 1992," 32.

10. Cardona, "The European Response to Terrorism," 252.

11. Zagari, "Combating Terrorism: Report to the Committee of Legal Affairs and Citizens' Rights of the European Parliament," 293.

12. Lodge, "Terrorism and the European Community: Towards 1992," 42.

13. Lodge, "Terrorism and the European Community: Towards 1992," 42.

14. Council of the European Union, *Treaty on European Union,* Maastricht, 7 February 1992, art. K.1, <http://www.eurotreaties.com/maastrichteu.pdf>. After subsequent Treaty of Amsterdam revisions, art. 29.

15. Council of the European Union, *Council Decision of 3 December 1998 Instructing Europol to Deal with Crimes Committed or Likely to Be Committed in the Course of Terrorist Activities Against Life, Limb, Personal Freedom or Property,* EN 30/01/1999 0022 (1999), Brussels, 3 December 1998.

16. Monica den Boer and Jörg Monar, "Keynote Article: 11 September and the Challenge of Global Terrorism to the EU as a Security Actor," in *The European Union: Annual Review of the EU 2001/2002,* ed. Geoffrey Edwards and Georg Wiessala (Oxford, UK: Blackwell, 2002), 21.

17. European Commission, *Proposal for a Council Framework Decision on Combating Terrorism,* 2001/0217 (CNS), Brussels, 19 September 2001, 2.

18. These include powers to make national criminal laws more similar, make national police forces and prosecutors work together more effectively, build a common border guard, develop common asylum and visa policies, make the EU courts more efficient, and guarantee the rights of individuals. Adam Townsend, "Can the EU Achieve an Area of Freedom, Security and Justice?," opinion, Center for European Reform, October 2003, <http://www.cer.org.uk/pdf/opinion _at_jhaoct.pdf> (accessed 6 October 2003).

19. Den Boer and Monar, "Keynote Article: 11 September and the Challenge of Global Terrorism to the EU as a Security Actor," 21.

20. Anastassia Tsoukala, "Democracy Against Security: The Debates About Counterterrorism in the European Parliament, September 2001–June 2003," *Alternatives: Global, Local, Political* 29, no. 4 (August–October 2004): 429.

21. In October 1995, for example, the council adopted the *La Gomera Declaration*, which "affirmed that terrorism constitutes a threat to democracy, to the free exercise of human rights and to economic and social development." Council of the European Union, *Council Framework Decision of 13 June 2002 on Combating Terrorism*, EN 2002/475/JHA 0003, Brussels, 13 June 2002, art. 2. The representatives of EU member states also repeatedly publicly condemned terrorist acts as contradictory to the basic universal values of human dignity, liberty, equality, and solidarity on which the European Union is founded.

22. Council of the European Union, *Conclusions and Plan of Action of the Extraordinary European Council Meeting on 21 September 2001*, Brussels, 21 September 2001, <http://europa.eu.int/comm/external_relations/110901/ actplan01.pdf> (accessed 6 September 2006).

23. In addition to the comprehensive European policy to combat terrorism, there were two other areas where the Council specifically reaffirmed "its firm determination to act in concert in all circumstances": "Solidarity and cooperation with the United States" and "The Union's involvement in the world." Council of the European Union, *Conclusions and Plan of Action of the Extraordinary European Council Meeting on 21 September 2001*. For the purposes of this chapter, we discuss only those aspects of the EU's cooperation with the U.S. that fall primarily in the area of Justice and Home Affairs. For a comprehensive analysis of other aspects of EU–U.S. cooperation in the area of counter-terrorism, see Deniz A. Akgül, "The European Union Response to September 11: Relations with the US and the Failure to Maintain a CFSP," *Review of International Affairs* 1, no. 4 (Summer 2002): 1–24; Den Boer and Monar, "Keynote Article: 11 September and the Challenge of Global Terrorism to the EU as a Security Actor"; Dorine Dubois, "The Attacks of 11 September: EU-US Cooperation Against Terrorism in the Field of Justice and Home Affairs," *European Foreign Affairs Review* 7 (2002): 317–35. For an official overview of the EU's external actions in the area of counter-terrorism, see European Union, *Supplementary Report by the European Union to the Committee Established Under Paragraph 6 of Security Council Resolution 1373 (2001)*, technical report. no. S/2002/928 (New York: United Nations, 2002), 4–9; Commission of the European Communities,

Commission Staff Working Paper, EC External Assistance Facilitating the Implementation of UN Security Council Resolution 1373: An Overview, SEC(2002) 231, Brussels, 25 February 2002, 1.

24. Dubois, "The Attacks of 11 September: EU-US Cooperation Against Terrorism in the Field of Justice and Home Affairs," 324.

25. European Commission, "Extradition and Surrender Procedures Across the EU," Brussels, updated May 2005, <http://europa.eu.int/comm/justice_home/fsj/criminal/extradition/fsj_criminal_extradition_en.htm> (accessed 6 September 2006).

26. Den Boer and Monar, "Keynote Article: 11 September and the Challenge of Global Terrorism to the EU as a Security Actor," 21.

27. Italy was the most reluctant of all EU member states to give its assent to the European arrest warrant. It claimed that the thirty-two offenses were too many and wanted the warrant's thirty-two offenses reduced to six, including terrorism but excluding financial crimes. Press reports speculated that this position was due to allegations of corruption and tax evasion pending against Prime Minister Berlusconi in Italy and elsewhere in Europe. United States Congress, *Europe and Counterterrorism: Strengthening Police and Judicial Cooperation,* report for Congress prepared by Kristin Archick, 108th Cong., 2d sess., updated 23 August 2004, Committee Print Order Code RL31509.

28. Council of the European Union, *Proposal for a Framework Decision on the European Arrest Warrant and the Surrender Procedures Between the Member States, Outcome of Proceedings of the Council,* EN 14867/1/01 REV1, Brussels, 12 December 2001.

29. Council of the European Union. *Council Framework Decision of 13 June 2002 on the European Arrest Warrant and the Surrender Procedures Between Member States: Statements Made by Certain Member States on the Adoption of the Framework Decision,* EN 2002/584/JHA 0001, Brussels, 26 June 2002.

30. In contrast, the traditional international extradition procedure requires a separate procedure for arrest and surrender.

31. Jonathan Stevenson, "How Europe and America Defend Themselves," *Foreign Affairs* 82, no. 2 (March–April 2003): 83.

32. Filip Jasinski, "The European Union and Terrorism," *Polish Quarterly of International Affairs* 11, no. 2 (2002): 44.

33. United States Congress, *Europe and Counterterrorism: Strengthening Police,* 2.

34. European Commission, "Extradition and Surrender Procedures Across the EU."

35. United States Congress, *Europe and Counterterrorism: Strengthening Police,* 7, 12.

36. Susie Alegre and Marisa Leaf, "Mutual Recognition in European Judicial Cooperation: A Step Too Far Too Soon? Case Study: The European Arrest Warrant," *European Law Journal* 10 (2004): 200–17.

37. European Commission, "European Arrest Warrant Replaces Extradition Between EU Member States," <http://ec.europa.eu/justice_home/fsj/criminal/extradition/fsj_criminal_extradition_en.htm> (accessed 10 October 2006).

38. European Commission, "European Arrest Warrant Replaces Extradition."

39. EU law bans capital punishment among EU member states and prohibits the extradition of suspects to countries where they could face the death penalty.

40. Nora Bensahel, "The Counterterror Coalitions: Cooperation with Europe, NATO, and the European Union," report prepared for the U.S. Air Force, Project Air Force, RAND, 2003, <http://www.rand.org/publications/MR/MR1746/MR1746.pdf> (accessed 6 September 2006).

41. United States Congress, *Europe and Counterterrorism: Strengthening Police*, 15.

42. Berlin, for example, insists that even basic legal assistance provided by German authorities to the United States not lead to the pursuit of a capital case or contribute to the application of the death penalty. In the past, German judicial officials refused to respond to U.S. requests for evidence in the case against Zacarias Moussaoui, who faced a possible death sentence in the United States for his alleged involvement in planning the September 11 attacks. United States Congress, *Europe and Counterterrorism: Strengthening Police*, 16.

43. John D. Occhipinti, *The Politics of EU Police Cooperation* (Boulder, CO: Lynne Rienner, 2003), 149, 165–66.

44. "'Scoreboard'" on Post-Madrid Counter-Terrorism Plans," *Statewatch*, <http://www.statewatch.org/news/2004/mar/swscoreboard.pdf>, 23 March 2004.

45. Council of the European Union. *Council Decision of 19 December 2002 on the Implementation of Specific Measures for Police and Judicial Cooperation to Combat Terrorism in Accordance with Article 4 of Common Position 2001/931/CFSP*, EN 2003/48/JHA 0068, Brussels, 22 January 2003, art.2a–2e.

46. Council of the European Union, *Council Common Position Concerning Additional Restrictive Measures Against the Taliban*, 2001/154/CFSP, Brussels, 27 February 2001.

47. Council of the European Union, *Conclusions and Plan of Action of the Extraordinary European Council Meeting on 21 September 2001*.

48. Bensahel, "The Counterterror Coalitions: Cooperation with Europe, NATO, and the European Union."

49. "'Scoreboard' on Post-Madrid Counter-Terrorism Plans," *Statewatch*, 18.

50. We are grateful to an anonymous reviewer from the *Journal of Terrorism and Political Violence* for providing this information.

51. Stevenson, "How Europe and America Defend Themselves," 87.

52. Nicola Vennemann, "Country Report on the European Union," in *Terrorism as a Challenge for National and International Law: Security Versus Liberty?*,

ed. Christian Walter, Frank Schorkopf, Silja Vöneky, and Volker Röben (New York: Springer-Verlag, 2004), 217–66.

53. In 2003 Europol had a staff of about 350, including fifty liaison officers from national police, customs, immigration, and intelligence agencies. Europol has also seen its budget double to €52 million since it became operational in 1998, but in comparison to the FBI's almost 30,000 employees and $3 billion annual budget, Europol remains miniscule. Stevenson, "How Europe and America Defend Themselves," 87.

54. United States Congress, *Europe and Counterterrorism: Strengthening Police*, 10.

55. Jitendra Joshi, "After Madrid, EU's Nascent Anti-Terror Strategy Under Focus," Agence France-Presse, 15 March 2004.

56. France, for example, has a centralized system, whereas Germany works on a more fragmented federal level. France has robust laws for detaining terrorist suspects and judges specifically trained to deal with the cases, but others do not.

57. European Commission, *Communication from the Commission to the Council and the European Parliament of 16 June 2004: Towards Enhancing Access to Information by Law Enforcement Agencies*, COM(2004) 429 Final, Brussels, 16 June 2004, <http://europa.eu/scadplus/leg/en/lvb/l14151.htm> (accessed 1 August 2006).

58. Council of the European Union, "Provisional Findings of the Two 'Peer Evaluation' Mechanisms Affecting the Union Fight Against Terrorism," *Statewatch*, <http://www.statewatch.org/news/2004/jun/eu-plan-terr-eval.pdf> (accessed 26 May 2004).

59. Judy Dempsey, "Europe at Loggerheads Over How to Co-Ordinate on Terrorism," *Financial Times* (London), 18 March 2004. At the Council level two working groups are fully devoted to the fight against terrorism. The representatives of member states' ministries of interior or law enforcement agencies have been meeting under the auspices of the Terrorist Working Group (TWG). TWG gathers three times per presidency and deals with internal threat assessments, practical law enforcement cooperation, and coordination among EU bodies in the Justice and Home Affairs pillar. The representatives of member states' Ministries of Foreign Affairs (and in some member states of external security services) meet as the Working Party on Terrorism (External Aspects) (better known as COTER). They discuss issues relating to external matters, threat assessments and policy recommendations as regards third countries and regions, implementations of UN conventions and coordination of work (particularly in the UN and in the Common Foreign and Security Policy (CFSP) pillar in general). For the last two years, TWG and COTER have held, once per presidency, a joint meeting to integrate the internal and external dimension of the EU's counter-terrorism policy. They have also functioned as "senior groups," alongside the meetings of the EU Police Chiefs Operational Task Force (PCOTF) and the Counter-Terrorism Group (CTG). PCOTF was set up to share best practices in counter-

terrorism and as such it has also been holding regular meetings with the heads of EU member states' Counter Terrorist Units to exchange information and experiences. The CTG coordinates the activities of nonpolice intelligence agencies and produces assessment reports on the threat posed by radical Sunni Islam. For more information, see Council of the European Union, "Declaration on Combating Terrorism Is Adopted in Brussels," 25 March 2004, <http://www.eu2004.ie/templates/news.asp?sNavlocator=66&list_id=462> (accessed 6 September 2006).

60. Bensahel, "The Counterterror Coalitions: Cooperation with Europe, NATO, and the European Union," 40.

61. Bensahel, "The Counterterror Coalitions: Cooperation with Europe, NATO, and the European Union," 40.

62. European Commission, "European Commission Action Paper in Response to the Terrorist Attacks on Madrid," memo/04/66, Brussels, 18 March 2004, 8.

63. Bensahel, "The Counterterror Coalitions: Cooperation with Europe, NATO, and the European Union," 40.

64. The first pillar is the European Community, where decisions are most often taken by qualified majority voting and involve all of the EU institutions. The second pillar is the Common Foreign and Security Policy (CFSP) and the third pillar is the area of Justice and Home Affairs. In both the CFSP and the JHA, each member state has the right of veto.

65. Council of the European Union, "Provisional Findings of the Two 'Peer Evaluation' Mechanisms Affecting the Union Fight Against Terrorism," 19.

66. Council of the European Union, "Provisional Findings of the Two 'Peer Evaluation' Mechanisms Affecting the Union Fight Against Terrorism," 19.

67. Bensahel, "The Counterterror Coalitions: Cooperation with Europe, NATO, and the European Union," 40.

68. Jürgen Storbeck, director, Europol, quoted in United States Congress, *Europe and Counterterrorism: Strengthening Police*, 9; originally quoted in Judy Dempsey, "Europol's Bid for Success," *Financial Times*, 27 February 2002.

69. European Union Network of Independent Experts in Fundamental Rights, "The Balance Between Freedom and Security in the Response by the European Union and Its Member States to the Terrorist Threats," thematic commentary prepared for the European Commission, Unit A5, "Citizenship, Charter of Fundamental Rights, Racism, Zenophobia, Daphne Program," DG Justice and Home Affairs, 31 March 2003, Statewatch, <http://www.statewatch.org/news/2003/apr/CFR-CDF.ThemComment1.pdf> (accessed 6 September 2006).

70. European Union Network of Independent Experts in Fundamental Rights, "The Balance Between Freedom and Security in the Response by the European Union and Its Member States to the Terrorist Threats," 20–37.

71. Council of the European Union, Justice and Home Affairs, *Conclusions Adopted by the Council (Justice and Home Affairs), Brussels, 20 September 2001*, SN 3926/6/01, Brussels, 20 September 2001.

72. Council of the European Union. *Council Decision of 28 February 2002 Setting up Eurojust with a View to Reinforcing the Fight Against Serious Crime,* EN 2002/187/JHA 0001, Brussels, 28 February 2002.

73. Vennemann, "Country Report on the European Union," 49.

74. European Commission, "Eurojust Coordinating Cross-Border Prosecutions at EU Level," <http://europa.eu.int/comm/justice_home/fsj/criminal/eurojust/fsj_criminal_eurojust_en.htm> (accessed 1 September 2006).

75. Bensahel, "The Counterterror Coalitions: Cooperation with Europe, NATO, and the European Union," 41.

76. In cases of assistance in cross-border judicial cooperation, Eurojust is working alongside another recently established unit—the European Judicial Network (EJN), which became operational in 1998. While EJN is essentially a decentralized information sharing network connecting EU lawyers and judges working on criminal cases, Eurojust is a centralized unit. European Commission, "Eurojust Coordinating Cross-Border Prosecutions at EU Level."

77. European Commission, "Eurojust Coordinating Cross-Border Prosecutions at EU Level."

78. Bensahel, "The Counterterror Coalitions: Cooperation with Europe, NATO, and the European Union," 41.

79. Dubois, "The Attacks of 11 September: EU-US Cooperation Against Terrorism in the Field of Justice and Home Affairs," 328.

80. Den Boer and Monar, "Keynote Article: 11 September and the Challenge of Global Terrorism to the EU as a Security Actor," 23.

81. Vennemann, "Country Report on the European Union," 50.

82. European Commission, "Eurojust Coordinating Cross-Border Prosecutions at EU Level."

83. European Commission, "The Fight Against Terrorism: The Commission Proposes Measures on the Exchange of Information and on the 'European Criminal Record,'" 30 March 2004, <http://europa.eu.int/rapid/start/cgi/guesten.ksh?p_action.gettxt=gt&doc=IP/04/425|0|RAPID&lg=EN&display=> (accessed 6 September 2006).

84. European Commission, "Eurojust Coordinating Cross-Border Prosecutions at EU Level."

85. Dempsey, "Europe at Loggerheads Over How to Co-Ordinate on Terrorism."

86. European Commission, "European Commission Action Paper in Response to the Terrorist Attacks on Madrid," 8.

87. Jasinski, "The European Union and Terrorism," 54.

88. We are grateful to an anonymous reviewer from the *Journal of Terrorism and Political Violence* for formulating this explanation.

89. Council of the European Union, *Proposal for a Council Framework Decision on Combating Terrorism, Outcome of Proceedings of the Council of 7 December 2001*, EN 14845/1/01 REV 1, Brussels, 7 December 2001.

90. Council of the European Union, *Council Framework Decision of 13 June 2002 on Combating Terrorism.*

91. Steve Peers, "EU Responses to Terrorism," *International and Comparative Law Qaurterly* 52 (2003): 227, 228.

92. United States Congress, *Europe and Counterterrorism: Strengthening Police*, 8.

93. Vennemann, "Country Report on the European Union," 19.

94. European Union Network of Independent Experts in Fundamental Rights, "The Balance Between Freedom and Security in the Response by the European Union and Its Member States to the Terrorist Threats," 11.

95. Peers, "EU Responses to Terrorism," 243 (original emphasis).

96. Britain, France, Germany, Italy, Portugal, and Spain. Jasinski, "The European Union and Terrorism," 43.

97. Dubois, "The Attacks of 11 September: EU-US Cooperation Against Terrorism in the Field of Justice and Home Affairs," 326.

98. European Commission, "European Commission Action Paper in Response to the Terrorist Attacks on Madrid."

99. Jörg Friedrichs, quoted in Sophie Arie, "Europe, US Clash over Terror War," *Christian Science Monitor*, 29 September 2005.

100. Ian Cuthbertson, quoted in Arie, "Europe, US Clash over Terror War."

101. Cuthbertson, quoted in Arie, "Europe, US Clash Over Terror War."

102. Council of the European Union, *Council Common Position of 27 December 2001 on the Application of Specific Measures to Combat Terrorism*, EN 2001/931/CFSP 0093, Brussels, 27 December 2001.

103. Council of the European Union, *Council Regulation of 27 December 2001 on Specific Restrictive Measures Directed Against Certain Persons and Entities with a View to Combating Terrorism*, EN (EC) No. 2580/2001, Brussels, 27 December 2001.

104. Vennemann, "Country Report on the European Union," 38.

105. Dubois, "The Attacks of 11 September: EU-US Cooperation Against Terrorism in the Field of Justice and Home Affairs," 323.

106. Council of the European Union, *Council Common Position 2004/500/CFSP of 17 May 2004 Updating Common Position 2001/931/CFSP on the Application of Specific Measures to Combat Terrorism and Repealing Common Position 2004/309/CFSP*, EN 2004/500/CFSP, Brussels, 17 May 2004, 4.

107. Council of The European Union, *Council Common Position 2001/931/CFSP of 27 December 2001 on the Application of Specific Measures to Combat Terrorism*, Brussels, 27 December 2001, L344/94.

108. European Union, *Supplementary Report by the European Union to the Committee Established Under Paragraph 6 of Security Council Resolution 1373 (2001)*.

109. European Union Network of Independent Experts in Fundamental Rights, "The Balance Between Freedom and Security in the Response by the European Union and Its Member States to the Terrorist Threats," 41.

110. As of April 2004, the list established on the basis of the Regulation (EC) No. 2580/2001 contained the names of twenty-six individuals and twenty-five entities. Council of the European Union, *Council Decision of 2 April 2004 Implementing Article 2(3) of Regulation (EC) No. 2580/2001 on Specific Restrictive Measures Directed Against Certain Persons and Entities with a View to Combating Terrorism and Repealing Decision 2003/902/EC*, EN 2004/306/EC, Brussels, 2 April 2004.

111. Bank of England, "Consolidated List of Financial Sanctions Targets in the UK," Bank of England, 2 April 2004, <http://www.bankofengland.co.uk/sanctions/terrorism.htm> (accessed 2 April 2004).

112. Vennemann, "Country Report on the European Union," 26.

113. Vennemann, "Country Report on the European Union," 26.

114. Council of the European Union, *Council Common Position Concerning Restrictive Measures against the Taliban*, EN 16/11/1999, Brussels, 16 November 1999; Council of the European Union, *Council Framework Decision of 13 June 2002 on Combating Terrorism*; Council of the European Union, *Council Common Position Concerning Restrictive Measures Against Osama Bin Laden, Members of the al-Qaeda Organization and the Taliban and Other Individuals, Groups, Undertakings and Entities Associated with Them*, EN 29/05/2002 21, Brussels, 29 November 2002.

115. Vennemann, "Country Report on the European Union," 29.

116. Edward Alden, "Europe Freezes Terrorist Assets Worth $35 Million," *Financial Times* (London), 8 April 2002, <http://specials.ft.com/attackonterrorism/FT39YWK5SZC.html> (accessed 8 April 2002).

117. Robert Wielaard, "EU Proposes Terrorist Database Following Madrid Bombings, Criticizes Foot-Dragging Since Sept. 11," Associated Press, 18 March 2004.

118. United States Department of the Treasury, "Treasury Announces Joint Action with Saudi Arabia Against Four Branches of Al-Haramain in the Fight Against Terrorist Financing," press release JS-1108, 22 January 2004, <http://www.treasury.gov/press/releases/js1108.htm> (accessed 6 September 2006).

119. Jimmy Gurulé, former U.S. Under Secretary of Treasury, "Locking Down Terrorist Finance," lecture, University of Notre Dame, 5 April 2004.

120. The EU–U.S. comparison may be somewhat misleading because the EU and U.S. definitions of *financial assets* differ substantially. Nevertheless, the difference between the amounts frozen by respective EU and U.S. authorities is so substantial that the comparison is plausible. For details about the U.S. financial sanctions model, see Richard R. Newcomb, "Targeted Financial Sanctions: The U.S. Model," in *Smart Sanctions: Targeting Economic Statecraft*, ed. David Cortright and George A. Lopez (Boulder, CO: Rowman & Littlefield, 2002), 41–64.

121. Laurence Thieux, "European Security and Global Terrorism: The Strategic Aftermath of the Madrid Bombings," *Perspectives: The Central European Review of International Affairs* 22 (Summer 2004): 62.

122. European Commission, "European Commission Action Paper in Response to the Terrorist Attacks on Madrid."

123. Throughout the preaccession process these countries were interchangeably referred to as candidate, applicant, associated, or partner countries. Since the primary discussion within this chapter is on the preaccession process, we maintain the term *former candidate country* throughout the chapter. Bulgaria, Romania, and Turkey are still officially called *candidate countries* since the European Council has determined that they are not yet ready to enter the EU. Bulgaria and Romania are currently anticipating membership in 2007, while Turkey has not yet been given a "prospective" date for accession.

124. This is not a "formula" or checklist that the EU consciously uses. We inductively identified this process using steps that the European internal evaluations repeatedly emphasized as decisive for the success of the accession process.

125. *Acquis* implementation requires not only the adoption of appropriate legislation but also the ensuring of an adequate level of administrative capacity.

126. For 1997 and 1998, 7 percent, or €71.5 million, of the Phare budget went toward the Justice and Home Affairs chapter of the *acquis*. European Commission, PLS RAMBØLL Management, and Eureval–C3E, "PHARE Ex Post Evaluation of Country Support Implemented from 1997–1998 to 2000–2001: Consolidated Background Report," 3 April 2003, <http://europa.eu.int/comm/enlargement/phare_evaluation_pdf/consolidated_background_report_english.pdf> (accessed 3 April 2003).

127. Europe created the first accession funding program, the Phare Program, in 1989 (Council Regulation 3906/89) to assist the democratic transitions of Poland and Hungary after the cold war. In 1993 it was reoriented to support all former candidate countries in their accession process. From 1989 to 1999 the Phare framework existed as the sole instrument to support institution building and *acquis*-related investment to prepare candidate countries for membership. In 1999 the Council created two other programs for accession: Special Accession Programme for Agriculture and Rural Development (SAPARD), which contributes to improve the competitiveness of the agricultural sector with respect to the *acquis*, and Instrument for Structural Policies for Pre-Accession (ISPA), which assists with strategic, large-scale infrastructure projects in the transportation and environmental sectors (in a fifty-fifty proportion). Phare projects did not support

Cyprus and Malta, which had their own dedicated financial instruments. See Council of the European Communities, *Council Regulation (EEC) No. 3906/89 of 18 December 1989 on Economic Aid to the Republic of Hungary and the Polish People's Republic,* (EEC) No. 3906/89, Brussels, 18 December 1989; see also Council of the European Union, *Special Accession Program for Agriculture and Rural Development* (SAPARD), Council Regulation 1268/1999, Brussels, 21 June 1999; see also European Commission, *Instrument for Structural Policies for Pre-accession* (ISPA), Council Regulation 1267/99, Brussels, 21 June 1999.

128. Twinning in Europe has had a long and successful history, with the first modern twinning arrangement forming between Orléans (France) and Dundee (UK) in 1946. Since 1989 Europe has officially funded these efforts, benefiting over 11,000 towns with EU grants aimed largely at increasing the sense of European identity and sharing lessons throughout the region. In 2003 the EU funded almost 1,400 town twinning partnerships worth €12 million, and 80,000 people in Europe participated in twinning activities cofinanced by the EC. A twinning program is drastically different from a traditional town twinning program's technical advice in that two (or three) partners create a close partnership to complete a complex project in a specific field, which must yield "guaranteed results." European Commission, "Belonging to the European Union," *The Magazine: Education and Culture in Europe* 20 (2003), <http://europa.eu.int/comm/dgs/education_culture/mag/20/en.pdf> (accessed 6 September 2006).

129. EU twinning projects involve the secondment of EU experts, known as preaccession advisers (PAA), to the candidate countries. They are made available for a period of at least one year to work on a project in the corresponding ministry in a candidate country. Preaccession advisers are supported by a senior project leader in their home administration, who is responsible for ensuring the overall thrust of the project implementation and coordinating all other inputs from the member state. To achieve the objective of the twinning project, it is necessary to combine different means, including short-term expertise, training, services (such as translation and interpreting), and specialized help (such as specialized computer software), in addition to the preaccession adviser.

130. In the "legislative and administrative impacts" category, projects with twinning (N = 50) had an overall effectiveness rating of 0.72 (on a scale of 0 to 1, with 1 being full achievement of intended impacts); without twinning (N = 62), 0.69. For the socioeconomic category, projects with twinning (N = 27) had an overall effectiveness rating of 0.63; without twinning (N = 45), 0.56. Based on an external review conducted by PLS Rambøll Management. European Commission, PLS RAMBØLL Management, and Eureval–C3E, "PHARE Ex Post Evaluation of Country Support Implemented from 1997–1998 to 2000–2001," 129–35.

131. European Commission, PLS RAMBØLL Management, and Eureval–C3E, "PHARE Ex Post Evaluation of Country Support Implemented from 1997–1998 to 2000–2001," 135.

132. European Commission, PLS RAMBØLL Management, and Eureval–C3E, "PHARE Ex Post Evaluation of Country Support Implemented from 1997–1998 to 2000–2001," 135.

133. European Commission, Permanent Representation of Sweden to the EU, and Permanent Representation of Austria to the EU, "The Enlargement Process and the Three Pre-Accession Instruments: Phare, ISPA, SAPARD," Proceedings of the Conference on Enlargement, Brussels, 5 March 2001, 8.

134. For the status of all treaties except those listed below, see United Nations, "Conventions on Terrorism: Current Status of Multilateral Treaties on Terrorism Deposited with the Secretary-General," *United Nations Treaty Collection* <http://untreaty.un.org/English/terrorism.asp> (accessed 22 April 2004); for the yes or no status of all maritime treaties, including SUA, see International Maritime Organization, "Status of Conventions by Country," <http://www.imo.org/Conventions/mainframe.asp?topic_id=248> (accessed 22 January 2007); for dated status of Maritime SUA and Protocol, see International Maritime Organization, "Summary of Conventions," <http://www.imo.org/Conventions/mainframe.asp?topic_id=247> (accessed 22 January 2007); for information about current (additional) Nuclear Protocols, see International Atomic Energy Agency, "Safeguards and Verification," <http://www.iaea.org/OurWork/SV/Safeguards/sg_protocol.html> (accessed 22 April 2004).

135. European Commission, "European Commission Action Paper in Response to the Terrorist Attacks on Madrid."

136. European Commission, "European Commission Action Paper in Response to the Terrorist Attacks on Madrid."

137. BBC Monitoring International Reports, "Austrian Chancellor Urges EU Cooperation in Antiterror Measures," trans. Wiener Zeitung, Vienna, BCC, 18 March 2004.

138. European Commission, "European Commission Action Paper in Response to the Terrorist Attacks on Madrid."

139. Jitendra Joshi, "EU Holds Emergency Terror Talks After Madrid Blasts," Agence France-Presse, 19 March 2004.

140. Joshi, "EU Holds Emergency Terror Talks After Madrid Blasts."

141. Council of the European Union, "European Council to Focus on Fight Against Terrorism," press release 81, Brussels, 15 March 2004, <http://europa.eu.int/rapid/start/cgi/guesten.ksh?p_action.gettxt=gt&doc=PRES/04/81|0|RAPID&lg=EN&display=> (accessed 15 March 2004).

142. Council of the European Union, "Declaration on Combating Terrorism Is Adopted in Brussels."

143. Rory Watson, "Brussels Backs Creation of Anti-Terror Czar," *Times* (London), 19 March 2004.

144. Thieux, "European Security and Global Terrorism," 60.

145. European Commission, "The Hague Programme: Ten Priorities for the Next Five Years," Brussels, 1 August 2006, <http://ec.europa.eu/justice_home/news/information_dossiers/the_hague_priorities/index_en.htm> (accessed 5 September 2006).

146. European Union, "The Hague Programme: Ten Priorities for the Next Five Years."

147. European Commission, "The Hague Programme: Ten Priorities for the Next Five Years."

148. Council of the European Union, "Declaration on Combating Terrorism Is Adopted in Brussels."

149. Vennemann, "Country Report on the European Union," 53.

150. Dubois, "The Attacks of 11 September," 330.

151. Dubois, "The Attacks of 11 September," 327.

152. Agence France-Presse, "EU Lawmakers Shoot Down US Deal on Airline Passenger Data," 18 March 2004.

153. Vennemann, "Country Report on the European Union," 53.

154. Franco Frattini, vice president and European commissioner responsible for Justice, Freedom and Security, "Internal and External Dimension of Fighting Terrorism," speech at the Fourth Congress on European Defense, Berlin, 28 November 2005, European Union, <http://europa.eu/rapid/pressReleasesAction.do?reference=SPEECH/05/735&format=HTML&aged=0&language=EN&guiLanguage=en> (accessed 1 August 2006).

8

Strategies and Policy Challenges for Winning the Fight Against Terrorism

David Cortright and George A. Lopez

An effective strategy against global terrorism requires both protective efforts to defend against the immediate threat posed by Al-Qaida and associated groups and preventive measures that alter the risk factors that give rise to terrorism. Most of the current U.S. and international efforts are protective in nature. They focus on military, police, and intelligence operations to disrupt terrorist organizations, prevent attacks, destroy training camps, and kill or capture militant leaders. Targeted UN sanctions are supplementing these efforts by isolating designated leaders of Al-Qaida and the Taliban and deterring states from supporting terrorist networks. The UN counter-terrorism program is attempting to build worldwide cooperation among nations and regional organizations to freeze terrorist finances, tighten border controls, and strengthen multinational law enforcement. The UN Non-Proliferation Committee and other bilateral and international programs are urging states to do more to keep deadly weapons and related materials out of the hands of nonstate terrorist groups. These programs have value in applying pressure on militant organizations and building international cooperation against terrorism, but on their own they are unlikely to reduce substantially the global terrorist threat. The longer-term goal of defeating terrorism depends on developing and implementing strategies that address the underlying causes of political extremism and that alter the social and political conditions that sustain Al-Qaida and similarly inspired groups.

At the United States Institute of Peace, Paul Stares and Monica Yacoubian have developed an innovative framework for strategizing against terrorism. They propose an epidemiological approach that treats militancy as if it were a virus or mutating disease.[1] The first challenge is to contain the contagion, the second is to protect those who are threatened by it, and the third is to remedy the conditions that foster its spread. Protective measures include controlling the movement of individuals in countries of concern, blocking the transmission of extremist ideology, and mobilizing moderate voices to promote nonviolent forms of political expression. Preventive measures include resolving political disputes that motivate armed violence, addressing conditions that give rise to militancy, and reducing social marginalization within Muslim countries and European diaspora communities. The cure will take many years, Stares and Yacoubian emphasize.[2]

At the Madrid International Summit on Democracy, Terrorism, and Security in March 2005, UN Secretary-General Kofi Annan outlined a general strategy against terrorism that combined prevention with protection. The Secretary-General's approach included "five Ds": dissuading disaffected groups from choosing terrorism, denying terrorists the means to carry out their attacks, deterring states from supporting terrorists, developing state capacity to prevent terrorism, and defending human rights in the struggle against terrorism. The Secretary-General's High-Level Panel on Threats, Challenges and Change likewise urged "a global strategy of fighting terrorism that addresses root causes and strengthens responsible states and the rule of law and fundamental human rights."[3] In April 2006 the Secretary-General reiterated the call to "reinforce the inexcusability and unacceptability of terrorism, while working to address the conditions that terrorists exploit."[4] He urged greater efforts to promote democracy and representative government, end military occupations, reduce poverty and unemployment, and halt state collapse. In September 2006 the White House released its *National Strategy for Combating Terrorism*, which declared that the fight against terrorism is not only a battle of arms but a "battle of ideas." The document called for "the creation of a global environment inhospitable to violent extremists."[5] It urged the advancement of freedom and human dignity and greater efforts to resolve disputes peacefully and promote the rule of law.

This chapter addresses these and other strategic dimensions of the struggle against terrorism. We examine what analyst Shibley Telhami has termed the "demand side" of terrorism, exploring ways to cut off the flow of recruits, financial support, and political sympathy for extremist groups. We look at the current global terrorist threat and identify the factors that have led to the emergence and growth of Al-Qaida and associated groups. We address the political and military grievances that militant groups exploit and the social and economic conditions from which they draw sustenance. We review the political economy of terrorism and consider the important links between terrorism and human rights. We conclude with strategic options for preventing terrorism and the challenges these strategies pose for U.S. foreign policy.

Know Thy Enemy

By declaring a "war on terror" and lumping together the many different types of terrorism into one undifferentiated category, the Bush administration has confounded the task of strategic analysis. The administration's approach obfuscates the distinct environments and political contexts in which terrorist groups operate, thereby glossing over fundamental differences between Al-Qaida and the dozens of localized groups like Hamas that operate independently. The former have a global agenda directed against the United States and its client regimes, while the latter have specific agendas rooted in particular grievances.[6] There are common points of Islamist ideology and anti-Americanism among many extremist groups, but their political agendas often differ. The challenge for strategic analysis is distinguishing between groups whose resort to terror is based on historic and possibly negotiable political demands and those with a globalist agenda that is less amenable to compromise.

Although much attention has focused on state sponsorship of terrorism, the Al-Qaida network operates beyond state control. Osama bin Laden and his followers initially received support in the 1990s from the National Islamic Front–dominated regime in Sudan and later from the Taliban in Afghanistan, but the structure of the network was always stateless and has become more so since the overthrow of the Taliban in November 2001. In its early phase Al-Qaida operated under a centralized structure controlled by bin Laden, but it has since become much more reticular. Al-Qaida is a highly decentralized network with widely dispersed cells in sixty or more countries. The separate cells follow a common jihadist ideology and strategy but operate largely on their own. They are increasingly self-financed with their own recruitment and training programs. The network is transnational and employs the tools of globalization—the Internet, international travel, and open borders—to communicate and conduct terrorist operations among disparate cells throughout the world. Marc Sageman, a former CIA officer in Afghanistan, described Al-Qaida as "a loose-knit, violent Islamic revivalist social movement held together by a common idea: the global Islamist jihad."[7]

In recent years the jihadist terror threat has become increasingly diffuse. So-called self-starter groups and "home-grown" terrorist cells with little or no connection to Al-Qaida have emerged in Europe and on other continents. The bombings of March 2004 in Madrid and July 2005 in London were the work of locally based extremists, although some of the London bombers had links to Al-Qaida operatives in Pakistan.[8] The bombers in Madrid were inspired by and sought to emulate Osama bin Laden, but they had no operational connection to the Al-Qaida network.[9] The emergence of these "self-radicalized" and less professionalized terrorist cells has compounded the challenge of identifying and countering the jihadist threat. On the one hand, self-starter groups are less competent than disciplined Al-Qaida cadres who have received training. The bombers in Madrid and London were far less capable than the hijackers of September 11 (9/11). On the other hand, the growth in the number of these terrorist militants and the unpredictability of when and where they will emerge has increased the likelihood of attack.

Increased military and law enforcement pressures against Al-Qaida since September 2001 have significantly disrupted the network. Military operations in Afghanistan and elsewhere destroyed all known training camps and eliminated much of Al-Qaida's top leadership.[10] The International Institute for Strategic Studies (IISS) estimated that half of Al-Qaida's thirty senior leaders and perhaps 2,000 rank-and-file members were killed or captured in the months after 9/11.[11] Cooperative multinational law enforcement and intelligence-sharing efforts have progressed markedly[12]—although concerns have been raised regarding questionable apprehension, detention, and interrogation methods employed by U.S. forces. Progress has been achieved in freezing terrorist-related financial assets. According to the Security Council's Analytic Support and Sanctions Monitoring Team, approximately $91 million, mainly in the form of bank accounts, was frozen by thirty-five countries under the Al-Qaida/Taliban sanctions regime as of July 2006— although most of the assets were seized in the months immediately after 9/11. Since mid-2002 the amount of frozen assets associated with Al-Qaida and the Taliban has hardly changed.[13] The staff of the 9/11 Commission reported that although Al-Qaida's funding has decreased, "it remains relatively easy for Al-Qaida to find the relatively small sums required to fund terrorist operations."[14] The costs of operations by self-starter groups are especially low (only $10,000 in the case of the Madrid bombing of March 2004), with the money raised primarily through narcotics trafficking.[15] Setbacks to the Al-Qaida network and the partial decapitation of its leadership have led to an even more decentralized, franchised mode of operation. Bin Laden's seclusion has forced operational commanders and cell leaders to become more autonomous. Al-Qaida has become "more a loose collection of regional networks with a greatly weakened centralized organization," according to the 9/11 Commission staff.[16] The IISS observed that U.S.-led military attacks in Afghanistan and elsewhere "impelled an already decentralized and evasive transnational terrorist network to become more 'virtual' and protean and therefore more difficult to identify and neutralize."[17]

Despite the worldwide pressure applied against Al-Qaida, the terrorist network has regained strength in recent years. Analysts such as political scientist John Mueller have suggested that the danger of further Al-Qaida attacks within the United States has been exaggerated,[18] but most observers believe that the global terrorist threat remains grave and is growing. Terrorism expert Bruce Hoffman testified before the House Armed Services Committee in February 2007 that Al-Qaida is "on the march" and is planning and inspiring militant attacks around the world.[19] Daniel Benjamin and Steven Simon are unequivocal in declaring that the "long-term danger of terrorism is growing."[20] While military and law enforcement pressures in recent years clearly have damaged Al-Qaida's infrastructure, the network has a large reserve of trained militants, and the flow of recruits has reportedly increased since the invasion of Iraq. Tens of thousands of men were trained by Al-Qaida during the 1980s and 1990s.[21] According to the 9/11 Commission report, as many as 20,000 militants passed through bin Laden–sponsored training camps in Afghanistan from 1996 through September 2001.[22] Since March 2003 thousands of additional recruits have come forward in response to the U.S. war and occupation in Iraq. The "Trends in Global Terrorism" National Intelligence Estimate partially released by the White House in September 2006 acknowledged that Al-Qaida "is exploiting the situation in Iraq to attract new recruits and donors."[23] As the 9/11 Commission staff concluded, Al-Qaida remains a formidable and dangerous enemy that is "actively striving to attack the United States and inflict mass casualties."[24] The growth of amorphous self-starter groups compounds this danger. The 2004 IISS *Strategic Survey* concluded, "Risks to Westerners and Western assets in Arab countries have increased since the Iraq war."[25]

U.S. government figures show that the number of major terrorist attacks in the world has increased significantly. In April 2005 controversy emerged in Washington, D.C., when the State Department failed to release its annual *Patterns of Global Terrorism* report. The department claimed that it was no longer satisfied with the methodology of the report, which has become a standard reference among policymakers and researchers worldwide. According to congressional staff who reviewed the report's findings, the number of "significant" terrorist attacks rose in 2004 to 655, three times greater than the 220 attacks reported the previous year. The number of attacks increased nine fold in Iraq, from twenty-two to 198. Even excluding Iraq from the overall figures, the number of significant terrorist attacks in the world doubled in 2004.[26] Worldwide deaths from terrorist attacks also doubled, according to an analysis of the RAND Corporation's database of terrorist incidents.[27] In April 2006 the State Department released a new document, *Country Reports on Terrorism, 2005*, intended to supplant the previous *Patterns of Global Terrorism* annual report. Because the data in the new report does not correlate with that from the previous reports, it is impossible to make exact comparisons. The new report stated there were 11,000 terrorist attacks in 2005, resulting in more than 14,600 fatalities. Nearly 70 percent of the attacks occurred outside Iraq.[28] According to an analysis by the office of Representative. Henry Waxman (D-CA), based on statistics from the Memorial Institute for the Prevention of Terrorism, established after the Oklahoma City bombings, there were 4,924 terror incidents in 2005, up from 2,646 in 2004 and 1,898 in 2003.[29] Because of the different methodologies and definitions utilized in the various reports, it is not possible to compare the data, but all assessments show a rise in global terrorist incidents.

The "New" Terrorism

The nature of the international terrorist threat has changed significantly in recent years. The number of international terrorist attacks actually declined in the period before September 11. Annual terrorist attacks peaked at 666 in 1987 and declined to 348 in 2001. In the Middle East terrorist attacks declined every year during the 1990s, as the Oslo peace process was underway, reaching their lowest totals at the time of the Camp David conference in July 2000.[30] While the number of terrorist incidents was declining, however, the number of casualties per incident was increasing. With the rise of Al-Qaida and the jihadist movement, a new form of mass casualty or "catastrophic" terrorism emerged. The number of people killed or wounded in terrorist violence increased sharply.[31] Casualty rates began to rise in the 1990s with high-profile incidents like the Khobar Towers attack in Saudi Arabia in 1996 and the bombings of U.S. embassies in Nairobi and Dar-es-Salaam in 1998. This trend peaked with the September 11 attacks and has continued with attacks in Bali in 2003, the Madrid bombing of March 2004, the school massacre at Beslan in September 2004, the London transit bombings in July 2005, and ongoing attacks in Iraq and beyond. The wave of attacks that began with September 11 has become the most sustained and lethal terrorist campaign in modern history.[32] The rise of suicide bombing, especially in Palestine and Iraq, has added a chilling and horrifying dimension to the terrorist threat. This new terrorism marks a break with the pattern of previous terrorist movements, which employed calibrated violence to achieve incremental change and a negotiated solution. Many of the new terrorists have millennial ambitions that are not subject to negotiation. They seek to achieve global impacts by maximizing violence.[33] Some analysts refer to this phenomenon as "superterrorism." As

Ekaterina Stepanova observes, "Unlimited goals imply, or even require
... unlimited means: weapons of mass destruction."[34] Al-Qaida has
attempted to obtain chemical, biological, radiological, and nuclear
weapons in an effort to acquire ultimate destructive capability.

Another important trend is the rise of religiously motivated terrorism.
According to the RAND–St. Andrews University Chronology of International Terrorist Incidents, the number of terrorist groups classified as
"religious" rose from two (out of sixty-four) in 1980 to twenty-five (out
of fifty-eight) by 1995.[35] Religiously based terrorist groups are characterized by a belief in a Manichaean struggle of good versus evil, which
justifies the most heinous acts against those considered infidels. Terrorists inspired by fanatical religious beliefs are less constrained by moral
or legal norms and are more likely to be willing to sacrifice themselves
for millennial purposes. Such groups are able to gain popular support
through their manipulation and appropriation of broadly accepted
religious symbols and language. As Reza Aslan observed, militants
distort the meaning of *jihad* "to give religious sanction to what are in
actuality social and political agendas."[36] They use religion rather than
ideology to justify their actions. These groups are not religious in any
sense of the term, but they cloak themselves in the respectability and
inspirational power of religion to win social support for their political
agenda.

Political Roots

"Terrorism is . . . essentially a political act," concluded the UN Policy
Working Group on Terrorism in 2002. "To overcome the problem of terrorism it is necessary to understand its political nature as well as its basic
criminality and psychology."[37] For many Americans, deeply scarred by
the horrors of September 11, acknowledging the political grievances of
Al-Qaida and related networks may seem offensive. Explaining why the
terrorists attacked can sound like appeasement or a justification for their
crimes. The point is not to excuse such acts, however, but to understand
why they occurred and to use this knowledge to prevent such attacks in
the future. "It is difficult to envision how one can address the terrorism
phenomenon," writes Telhami, "without addressing the central issues

that create the fertile grounds for breeding terrorism and that are exploited by organizers."[38]

The pious invocations in bin Laden's pronouncements and the religious motivations of many Al-Qaida militants have led some observers to believe that terrorism is rooted in Islam and that religion somehow causes terrorism. The agenda of Al-Qaida is not only about Islam, however. It is deeply political as well. Bin Laden and his fellow jihadists have distorted Qur'anic teachings and taken advantage of growing anti-Western sentiment in the Arab world to advance specific political purposes. The combustible mix of religion and politics thus creates a powerful motivational force. The result is a two-level challenge: a hard core of extremist militants fired by religious fanaticism and a broad base of support for the Islamist ideology in Muslim societies.[39]

The Al-Qaida political agenda is rooted in an extreme reaction to Western domination and local despotism. Bin Laden and his followers seek to free Islamic societies from occupation and exploitation and to replace the corrupt and authoritarian governments that now rule in many Muslim countries with revolutionary regimes based on Islamic fundamentalism. Their ultimate goal is to erase national boundaries and recreate the caliphate, a single Muslim theocratic superstate.[40] The immediate objectives are to overthrow U.S. client regimes in the region, end the occupation of Iraq and the Palestinian territories, and remove U.S. troops from the Islamic world.[41] These are concerns that are widely shared in the Arab and Muslim world, where many people harbor a deep sense of humiliation and resentment over oppressive conditions that they attribute primarily to the policies of the West. This has sparked a growing movement of resistance based on Islamic militance. "The most pervasive psychology in the Arab world today is collective rage and feelings of helplessness," writes Telhami.[42] This psychology of rage derives primarily from the Israeli-Palestinian conflict, but it is increasingly fueled as well by the U.S. occupation of Iraq. The Iraq war has united much of the world, writes Francis Fukuyama, "in a frenzy of anti-Americanism."[43] The Bush administration's description of Iraq as the central battleground in the war on terror has tainted efforts to curb Islamic extremism and reinforced bin Laden's assertion that the U.S. is waging war against Islam.[44]

The emergence of radical Islam is rooted in broad political, economic, and social transformations that have swept Arab and Muslim countries in recent decades. Rapid urbanization, unequal and often failed economic development, and frustrated political reform efforts have disrupted traditional cultures and societies. The failure of Arab nationalism has compounded the effects of these transitions.[45] The new national regimes that emerged in the twentieth century failed to meet rising public expectations, which were whetted by oil wealth. As autocratic governments closed off paths of peaceful protest, the mosque became one of the few places where people could gather freely to voice their grievances. Political opposition came to be expressed increasingly in religious terms. Some responded to the cultural uncertainties and social disruptions of modernization by embracing fundamentalism. A powerful Islamic revivalist movement emerged, aided by the spread of Saudi-financed salafist missionary activity. This development deepened feelings of religious identification and solidarity among Muslims.[46] Some sought to assert a distinctive Islamic identity against growing Western influence—a development that was not necessarily violent but that the extremists were able to exploit to their advantage. As Aslan notes, reactions to Western colonialism and anti-imperialist sentiment fueled the rise of Islamic radicalism.[47] Al-Qaida appropriated the Islamist and anti-Western themes of the revival movement to forge a militant ideology of revolt. As economic conditions worsened, Palestinian grievances festered, and U.S. military encroachments increased, the extremists gained ground. Their call for holy war against the United States, Israel, and corrupt Arab governments attracted growing support throughout the region.

The Deadly Logic of Suicide Terrorism

No form of terrorism is more lethal or more horrifying in its psychological impact than suicide bombing. It is difficult to deter those who are prepared to die to carry out their mission. The suicide bomber is able to strike with terrifying accuracy to murder the largest number of people and thus sow the greatest amount of emotional and social disorder. Prior to 1968 the phenomenon of suicide terrorism was practically unknown.

In recent years the danger has increased dramatically. There were three times more suicide bombings in the four years after September 11 than in the previous thirty years.[48] In his detailed study of the subject, *Dying to Win*, political scientist Robert Pape points out that nearly half of all worldwide fatalities from terrorist violence from 1980 through 2003 have resulted from suicide attacks, although these have constituted only 3 percent of the total.[49] These numbers do not include the September 11 attacks or the skyrocketing number of bombings in Iraq. More than 400 suicide attacks occurred in Iraq in the first two years of the U.S. occupation, and the number of attacks has continued to rise since.[50]

Empirical evidence shows that suicide terrorism is motivated by a desire to end military occupation. Nearly all the political scientists and sociologists who have studied the phenomenon agree, writes reviewer Christian Caryl, that "the organizations using suicide attacks have been fighting to evict an occupying power from a national homeland."[51] More than 90 percent of the 315 suicide terrorist attacks in Pape's database were motivated by a desire to remove foreign forces from territory that militants claimed as their homeland. These attacks occurred as part of organized campaigns to compel adversaries to "withdraw military forces from territory that the terrorists consider to be their homeland."[52] UN Secretary-General Kofi Annan's April 2006 report noted that "suicide terrorism campaigns often occur in the context of foreign occupation or perceived foreign occupation."[53] Whether in Sri Lanka, Kashmir, Chechnya, Palestine, or Iraq, suicide bombings have had a common purpose and political agenda: to achieve political self-determination and drive out what are seen as foreign occupation forces. This helps to explain the grim pattern of relentless suicide attack in Iraq and has ominous implications for the U.S. itself. "The presence of nearly 150,000 American combat troops in Iraq," writes Pape, "can only give suicide terrorism a boost, and the longer this campaign continues the greater the risk of new attacks in the United States."[54]

Countering Hegemony

The fight against foreign domination and occupation has been and remains a fundamental political goal of Al-Qaida. Bin Laden's network emerged during the resistance to the Soviet invasion of Afghanistan. The militants who would later create Al-Qaida ironically received an important boost from the large-scale U.S. military and financial support that flowed through Pakistan to the anti-Soviet mujahedeen in Afghanistan in the 1980s. The United States cultivated Islamic groups to fight against communism. The Saudi government and other Arab states were encouraged to mobilize religiously motivated adherents of Islam to fight against the "infidel" communists. This policy "obviously had unintended horrific consequences," observes Telhami.[55]

Fresh from the mujahedeen victory in Afghanistan, bin Laden approached the Saudi monarchy in 1990 to seek support for a jihad to retake Kuwait from the secularist regime of Saddam Hussein. When the Saudis rebuffed bin Laden and invited U.S. forces into the kingdom, bin Laden denounced the arrangement and began to mobilize against the U.S. and the Riyadh government. The jihadists were especially outraged by the stationing of U.S. forces in the Arabian peninsula. Bin Laden issued the first of his calls for attacks against the United States in 1992.[56] In 1996 he issued another self-styled fatwa, "Declaration of Holy War on the Americans Occupying the Country of the Two Holy Places," calling on Muslims worldwide to join in a campaign to remove U.S. military bases. As bin Laden told Robert Fisk of *The Independent* in 1996, "When the American troops entered Saudi Arabia . . . there was a strong protest from the ulema [religious authorities] and from students of the sharia law all over the country."[57] The United States acted to redress this grievance in 2003 in conjunction with the assault against Saddam Hussein. Emboldened by the prospect of establishing long-term military bases in Iraq, American officials shut down Prince Sultan Air Base and announced the hasty withdrawal of most U.S. forces from Saudi Arabia. This attempt to undercut bin Laden's agenda and placate Saudi resentments was too little too late, however. It was more than offset by the intense wave of popular revulsion and hostility that greeted the U.S. war and occupation in Iraq.

For decades the United States has been steadily increasing its military presence in the Arab world and has been attempting to exert political and economic domination over the oil-rich Persian Gulf and central Asian region. In the 1970s Washington picked up the mantle of imperial influence in the region after London withdrew its last forces from "east of Suez." The growing U.S. involvement was also a reaction to the oil crisis of the early 1970s and an expression of increased commitment to Israel and its post-1967 occupation of Palestinian territories. The U.S. military buildup in the region accelerated after the 1991 Gulf War and especially after 2001. In the aftermath of the September 11 attacks, the U.S. established military bases or outposts in several additional countries, all of them Islamic—not counting the many U.S. bases in Iraq. This insertion of U.S. military force into Arab and Muslim countries is unprecedented. The extensive U.S. military presence in the region has aroused intense feelings of resentment and sparked growing anti-American animosity. The U.S. military presence in Muslim countries fosters political radicalization and creates the very conditions that lead to terrorist attacks. A Defense Department Science Board report investigating the suicide bombing of Khobar Towers in Saudi Arabia in 1996 concluded, "Historical data show a strong correlation between U.S. involvement in international situations and an increase in terrorist attacks against the United States."[58] Pape likewise observed that "the presence of tens of thousands of American combat forces on the Arabian peninsula after 1990 enabled Al-Qaida to recruit suicide terrorists" and increased the risk of attacks against U.S. interests.[59]

It is not just the growing U.S. military penetration of the region that prompts enmity but also Washington's tendency to ally with and support repressive regimes. U.S. support for Israel's occupation policies has generated widespread revulsion toward American policy throughout the region. "No issue resonates with more people or does more to shape attitudes toward the United States," reports Telhami, "than the Arab-Israeli dispute."[60] Many of the governments in the region that host U.S. troops and bases and receive American support suppress political freedoms and fail to meet the social needs of their citizens. These are governments that deny democracy, violate human rights, and smother dissent. By supporting regimes that are engaged in such repressive practices, the U.S. is helping to perpetuate conditions that make terrorism more likely. The combination of increased U.S. military involvement in the region and continued U.S. support for occupation and undemocratic rule creates a volatile mixture of hostility and discontent that fuels resistance.

Some terrorism experts argue that the very extent and unrivaled primacy of American power generates countervailing pressures. "The reaction to preponderant power," argues Audrey Kurth Cronin, "is the most general explanation for international terrorism."[61] Modern terrorism, she writes, is a form of "anti-hegemonic . . . opposition to the international system led by the United States."[62] It is perceived in many Arab and Muslim countries as a struggle between the haves and have-nots. A contributing factor to this anti-American sentiment is a perception of double standards. There is a widespread belief in Islamic societies and indeed in much of the world that the United States misuses its vast military, economic, and political power to enforce an unjust system that benefits a few at the expense of the many.[63] Globalization is resented as a system of U.S. corporate and economic exploitation and a form of cultural homogenization that threatens traditional society and values. There is also concern about the U.S. political practice of exceptionalism. The United States imposes demands on the rest of the world that it refuses to accept for itself. It insists that Iran and other countries abandon their nuclear ambitions yet clings to nuclear weapons for itself. It attempts to cloak its actions in a mantle of UN respectability yet often turns its back on UN authority. It went to war ostensibly to enforce Iraqi compliance with Security Council resolutions but has blocked efforts to require Israeli implementation of such resolutions. Washington rejects the International Criminal Court and claims immunity from liability for its actions abroad. Such practices are seen around the world as an expression of imperial arrogance. They contribute to feelings of powerlessness and humiliation. They generate resentment and a greater willingness to tolerate or support anti-American extremists.

The Political Economy of Terrorism

The task of understanding the root causes of terrorism is difficult and fraught with uncertainty. Research in the subject is limited, and there is little consensus on what should be examined. We know that terrorism is a political act and that terrorist militants have political agendas, but we are less certain about the social and economic conditions that give rise to these groups. Little is known about the political and social dynamics within local communities that allow terrorist organizers to mobilize support. As Cronin notes, terrorist groups "cannot exist without the availability of broader sources of active or passive sympathy, resources, and support" within the societies where they operate.[64] Understanding these "avenues of sustenance" is the "proverbial center of gravity" for responding to the terrorist threat.[65] Separating Al-Qaida from its support base requires an understanding of the factors that sustain public sympathy and support.

Much attention has rightly focused on the financing of terror. Efforts to freeze and cut off financial support for terrorist activities have been a centerpiece of the UN counter-terrorism program. These efforts have had some success in reducing the funds available to Al-Qaida. The methods employed are essentially the same as those used in the fight against money laundering and narcotics trafficking. The financing of terror differs fundamentally from financial crime, however. Terrorists are motivated by political concerns, not economic greed. They may resort to crime or commodity predation to finance their activities, but their mission is primarily political, not economic. The financing of terror also involves much smaller amounts of money than financial crime. The September 11 attacks costs less than $500,000, whereas the drug barons of Colombia annually launder hundreds of millions of dollars.[66] Terrorist networks rely on informal hawala money-transfer systems and couriers to transfer funds. According to the staff report of the 9/11 Commission, "There is little evidence that bin Laden and his core Al-Qaida members used banks" to finance the attacks against the United States.[67] As a result of international financial pressures, Al-Qaida and the Taliban have had to resort to localized criminal activities.[68] Militant groups have also relied on charitable organizations to raise funds, combining militant political activities with social welfare programs. These factors make the task of defunding terror extremely difficult. As Mónica Serrano observed, "No war against terrorists will be won by seizing their assets."[69] Efforts to track and interdict terrorist financing remain important and they can be useful in criminal prosecutions, but they are unlikely to be successful in denying terrorists the financial means of carrying out attacks.

The political economy of terror is best understood in the traditional context of guerilla war. Terrorists, like guerilla fighters, depend on public support to survive. As Mao Tse Tung famously observed, the guerilla revolutionary is like a fish swimming in the sea. The militant depends on the supporting community to provide political sympathy, financial support, and a continuing supply of recruits. Successful terrorist movements operate in a similar manner. Whether it is the IRA in Northern Ireland, Hezbollah in southern Lebanon, or insurgents in Iraq, militants draw support from the surrounding community and receive sufficient material assistance and volunteer support to sustain armed resistance against opponents with far superior military capacity and technology. At the heart of this dynamic of social support is an informal economy of exchange. Insurgent or terrorist leaders offer their supporters an intangible good (dignity, liberation, true Islam) in exchange for political, economic, and material assistance. In many Muslim countries this exchange has important social dimensions. Jihadist groups operate charitable agencies that offer health care, education, and welfare services that local governments are unable or unwilling to provide. In the myriad places where states have failed to meet the basic needs of a growing population, religious groups operating under the banner of Islam have filled the gap and created a network of social support services. The radical movement thus creates a social and cultural infrastructure to reinforce its political support base.[70] The exchange between militants and local populations is rooted in service and sacrifice, not personal enrichment. It aims for the realization of urgent social needs and transcendent goals. The militant leader is willing to suffer and even sacrifice his or her life in the struggle for liberation. In return, members of the community offer political cover and financial and social support. This "deep financial logic" of terrorism, as Serrano describes it, resembles philanthropy more than profiteering. It is a process of giving rather than taking. The manipulation of religion, with its belief in the nobility of sacrifice, adds powerful spiritual and emotional grounding to the exchange. Martyrdom becomes the ultimate sacrifice and reward.

The Poverty Connection

Many analysts and political leaders assume that there is a direct connection between poverty and terrorism. At the G-8 Summit in

Gleneagles, Scotland, in July 2005, British prime minister Tony Blair traced the roots of terrorism to extremism and "acute and appalling forms of poverty."[71] The Bush administration has justified its international antipoverty efforts in part as a means of preventing terrorism. "We fight against poverty because hope is an answer to terror," said President Bush at the international conference on poverty reduction in Monterey Mexico in 2002. The administration's September 2002 *National Security Strategy* included a chapter highlighting the importance of economic development efforts and trade liberalization as part of the fight against terrorism. The State Department Millennium Challenge program, part of a UN effort to halve global poverty by 2015, is also justified as part of the broader campaign against terrorism.

While there is evidence of a link between armed conflict and inadequate economic development, there is no direct connection between terrorism and poverty. "Terrorism is not the inevitable by-product of poverty," observes the *National Strategy for Combating Terrorism.*[72] The relationship between socioeconomic conditions and the rise of terrorism is complex and indirect. There are distinct and important differences between the people who sympathize with terrorist movements and the hard-core militants who lead such movements and carry out terrorist strikes. International experts at the Madrid Summit in March 2005 concluded that "the leaders of militant movements are better educated and of higher status than most of the population from which they come."[73] They are not the poorest members of their society.

The September 11 hijackers were not impoverished. They were relatively well educated and lived in reasonably comfortable circumstances. Osama bin Laden came from a wealthy Saudi family. Empirical studies confirm that the militants who carry out terrorist strikes tend to come from more advantaged socioeconomic backgrounds and have higher educational levels than the people they claim to represent. An analysis of Hezbollah militants conducted by Alan B. Krueger and Jitka Malesckova found no evidence of a direct link between poverty and terrorism. The socioeconomic and educational status of Hezbollah fighters was higher than that of the average Palestinian. They were less likely to be poor than the Palestinian population as a whole and had higher educational levels than the general population.[74] Their investigation found "little support for the view that those who live in poverty or have a low level of education are disproportionately drawn to participate in terrorist activities."[75] Studies of terrorist groups in different historical and geographic settings have reached similar conclusions.

These findings about the social origins of terrorist leaders have intriguing parallels with studies of the social origins of revolutionaries. Historians have noted that many of the most prominent revolutionary leaders of the twentieth century, who claimed to fight on behalf of the economically oppressed, came from privileged socioeconomic conditions. Lenin, Trotsky, Mao Tse Tung, Ho Chi Minh, Castro, Che Guevera: all had relatively privileged backgrounds and were more educated than those whom they sought to liberate. These leaders of political rebellion responded to general conditions of underdevelopment and oppression rather than to the personal experience of poverty and illiteracy. They saw themselves as vanguards, speaking for and seeking to liberate the oppressed masses. They used their privileged social and educational backgrounds and the skills they acquired as a result to become leaders for social justice.[76] The motivations of terrorists may be similar. Although jihadists rarely come from the poorest sectors of society, their sense of grievance is often nourished by the impoverishment and oppression of their fellow Muslims.[77] Telhami observes, "The more educated segments of the public are generally less accepting of an inferior position in politics and society and are also more aware of their capacity to effect change."[78]

It is not individual poverty per se but a general lack of economic development that seems to be most strongly associated with armed conflict. Studies by Paul Collier and his colleagues at the World Bank found that civil conflict is most likely to occur in poor and underdeveloped countries, where large numbers of young men lack economic prospects.[79] Collier and his team showed that civil conflict is heavily concentrated in the poorest countries. They concluded that "the root cause of conflict is the failure of economic development."[80] Empirical analyses by scholars at the University of Maryland's Center for International Development and Conflict Management similarly concluded that "outbreaks of major collective political violence are strongly associated with various measures of poverty, underdevelopment, and maldistribution of resources."[81]

Weak regimes and poor governance were also identified as major factors related to political violence.

Specific analyses of terrorism closely parallel these findings about political violence, according to Monty G. Marshall.[82] Krueger and Malesckova report a statistical correlation between the overall level of poverty in a society and the number of terrorists emanating from that country. The poorest countries tend to spawn the greatest number of terrorists.[83] A lack of economic prospects for substantial numbers of young men creates opportunities for militants to recruit followers. As Thomas Friedman observed, "Poverty creates humiliation and stifled aspirations and forces many people to leave their traditional farms to join the alienated urban poor in the cities—all conditions that spawn terrorists there."[84] Terrorism expert Jessica Stern likewise concluded that "while there is no single root cause of terrorism, my interviews with terrorists over the past five years suggest that alienation, perceived humiliation, and lack of opportunity make young men susceptible to extremism."[85]

Poverty and lack of opportunity are likely to be most disruptive when people experience a decline in social and economic status or feel relatively disadvantaged compared to what they possessed previously or hope to gain in the future. It is not poverty per se but the experience of relative deprivation that seems to be associated with violent conflict. When rising expectations and growing social needs clash with limited or even declining opportunity, frustration and anger can result.[86] The international experts at the Madrid Summit noted that terrorism is "most likely to emerge in societies characterized by rapid modernization" where economic change "creates conditions that are conducive to instability."[87] Discontent tends to be highest when people experience a discrepancy between what they have and what they feel entitled to or if a period of improving conditions is interrupted or reversed.[88] The countries of the Middle East and Arab world have experienced abrupt and dramatic social transformations in recent decades. Urbanization, rapid population growth, and massive oil revenues (largely squandered and unequally distributed) have disrupted previous social patterns and created political and economic tensions. The resulting social and economic malaise has contributed to corruption and economic stagnation. These conditions have combined with high birth rates and declining levels of infant mortality to produce "a large, steadily increasing population of young men without any reasonable expectation of suitable or steady employment—a sure prescription for social turbulence."[89] Because of inadequate public education, many of these young men are trained in religious schools, where they acquire more ideology than productive skills and are easily influenced by Islamist radicals.

Failed Governance

Closely related to the problems of flawed development and unmet expectations is the phenomenon of weak states with poor governance. Such regimes are unable to control their borders, provide for the needs of their citizens, or guarantee the rule of law. This creates an environment in which terrorists have greater opportunity to operate and recruit supporters. The Bush administration's *National Security Strategy* noted that "America is now threatened less by conquering states than we are by failing ones."[90] In the wake of the September 11 attacks, the problem of inadequate governance has become a priority concern of international security policy.[91] The prevention of terrorism means overcoming the anarchic conditions and stark economic and social hardships that characterize failed-state environments. Inadequate governance affects the security equation in several ways. Countries like Afghanistan or Somalia become safe havens for terrorists and favored locations for training camps and bases. An inability to control borders or monitor the flow of goods and people increases the likelihood of illegal trafficking by terrorists, smugglers, and other criminal elements. A lack of security and economic development in failed states may result in humanitarian emergencies, increased refugee flows, and greater risk of disease and malnutrition. This can create a downward spiral of misery and chaos, exacerbating the conditions that give rise to terrorism.

The debacle in Iraq has produced an acute problem of failed governance and increased terrorism. The United States was able to topple the Baathist regime easily, but it has been unable to establish a new system of stable governance.[92] The ensuing violence and chaos have led to widespread terrorist recruitment within the country and the infiltration of terrorist militants from without. The ironic result, wrote Stepanova, was to turn a so-called rogue state that had suppressed Islamic terrorism into a failed state where jihadist violence ran rampant.[93] Iraqi insurgents have resorted to terrorism as their primary method of armed resistance in an attempt to offset the overwhelming military and technological advantage of the U.S. The result has been a sharp increase in terrorist attacks and widespread loss of life within Iraq and growing radicalization and terrorist recruitment in other countries. The horrendous increase in sectarian violence has compounded the anarchy and chaos in Iraq and further undermined the prospects for coherent governance. A July 2005 report from London's prestigious Chatham House concluded that the Iraq campaign "gave a boost to the Al-Qaida network's propaganda, recruitment and fundraising, caused a major split in the coalition, provided an ideal targeting and training area for Al-Qaida–linked terrorists, and deflected resources and assistance" away from the ongoing mission in Afghanistan.[94] Robert L. Hutchings, chair of the National Intelligence Council of the CIA, reported to Congress that Iraq has become "a magnet for international terrorist activity."[95]

The problems arising from failed states and inadequate governance cannot be addressed solely through military means, as the tragedy of Iraq illustrates. Security is an essential requirement in establishing the rule of law, and adequate police and military forces are necessities in every state, but the primary challenges are political and economic, not military. Creating the conditions for stable governance is a slow, laborious process that requires sustained commitment from a wide array of internal and external actors working together to ensure security and establish mechanisms of political and economic development. It requires providing hope and opportunity for the affected population and overcoming the conditions of anarchy and chaos that serve as breeding grounds for terrorism.

The Human Rights Connection

Many of the Arab and Muslim societies from which Al-Qaida draws support lack basic political freedom and civil liberties. The countries of the Middle East region have the world's lowest "freedom score" of political and civil rights, according to the ratings of the UN Development

Programme.[96] Governments in the region often deny people the opportunity to participate in political decision making. Citizens lack legitimate channels for political dissent. In many of these countries, violations of civil and political rights combine with the suppression of demands for ethnic, religious, or cultural autonomy to fuel acute political frustration. When governments respond to protest by isolating and further repressing the reformers, a vicious cycle of deepening frustration and political polarization drives people toward militancy. When the United States provides military and political support for such regimes, this feeds the anti-American character of the protest and reinforces the Al-Qaida agenda.

Empirical research has found a strong correlation between the denial of political freedom and the rise of terrorism. Measures of political repression are a statistically significant indicator of the likelihood of terrorist recruitment. They show that terrorists are most likely to come from countries that lack basic civil liberties.[97] By correlating the number of terrorists emanating from various countries with a wide range of variables, Krueger and Malesckova found the strongest association between terrorism and an index measuring the lack of political freedom. They write that "the only variable that was consistently associated with the number of terrorists was the Freedom House index of political rights and civil liberties. Countries with more freedom were less likely to be the birthplace of international terrorists."[98] Support for this finding comes from a recent study of terrorism in Latin America by Andreas Feldman and Maftu Peraelae. The authors analyzed nongovernmental terrorism in several states in the region and concluded that "the incidence of nongovernmental terrorism shows a consistently negative and significant association with the human rights of the state. The deterioration of the state's record is accompanied by an increase in non-governmental terrorist incidents one year later."[99]

Many other observers have found similar connections between the rise of terrorist movements and the denial of human rights and democratic expression. Terrorism thrives, UN Secretary-General Annan concluded, "where human rights are violated and where political and civil rights are curtailed."[100] A National Academy of Sciences study in 2002 noted that "terrorism and its supporting audiences appear to be fostered by policies of extreme political repression and discouraged by policies of incorporating both dissident and moderate groups into civil society and the political process."[101] The 2002 UN Policy Working Group observed that "a lack of hope for justice provides breeding grounds for terrorism."[102] The White House *National Strategy* likewise observed that "terrorists are recruited from populations with no voice in their own government" and who have "no legitimate way to promote change in their own country."[103] People without an opportunity to voice their opinions and organize politically often turn to violence as the only way of expressing their grievances. As Krueger observed in the *New York Times*, "The freedom to assemble and protest peacefully without interference from the government goes a long way to providing an alternative to terrorism."[104] Many of those who become political militants are motivated not by a hatred of freedom but by an extreme yearning for it. They view themselves as acting on behalf of Arab and Muslim communities that aspire to achieve freedom.

The challenge of protecting human rights while fighting against terrorism has stirred controversy. Some analysts perceive a tension between the two, while others see a necessary connection and emphasize the importance of strengthening human rights to prevent terrorism. Concerns have been raised about the human rights implications of counterterrorism measures. Many worry that efforts to broaden government surveillance, increase law enforcement powers, tighten border controls, and regulate finances will encroach on individual and social rights and threaten civil liberties. The UN High-Level Panel expressed concern that "approaches to terror focusing wholly on military, police and intelligence measures risk undermining efforts to promote good governance and human rights."[105] In his speech at the Madrid Summit Secretary-General Kofi Annan noted that human rights experts "are unanimous in finding that many measures which States are currently adopting to counter terrorism infringe on human rights and fundamental freedoms."[106] Controversy has emerged over cases in which individuals in various countries have been detained or subjected to financial restrictions without due process. In some countries officials have used the fight against terrorism as a justification for suppressing democracy and human rights and cracking down on domestic political opponents. Russian president Vladimir Putin responded to the tragic school massacre in Beslan in September

2004 by proposing sweeping restrictions on Russian democracy, ending the popular election of regional governors and eliminating local electoral districts in the lower house of the Duma. In the United States critics have charged that the Patriot Act, adopted in the wake of September 11, threatens civil liberties by authorizing the detention of immigrants without due process, expanding government authority to conduct searches and wire taps, and reducing judicial oversight of intrusive information-gathering activities.[107] Concerns also have been expressed that detention, interrogation, and prosecution procedures adopted by the Bush administration violate international legal standards.

UN declarations and resolutions have been unequivocal in urging strict adherence to human rights standards in the global fight against terrorism. As Secretary-General Kofi Annan stated in September 2003,

> There is no trade off to be made between human rights and terrorism. Upholding human rights is not at odds with battling terrorism: on the contrary, the moral vision of human rights—the deep respect for the dignity of each person—is among our most powerful weapons against it. To compromise on the protection of human rights would hand terrorists a victory they could not achieve on their own. The promotion and protection of human rights . . . should therefore be at the center of anti-terrorism strategies.[108]

At its ministerial meeting in January 2003 the Security Council adopted Resolution 1456, urging greater international compliance with UN counter-terrorism mandates but also reminding states of their duty to comply with international legal obligations, "in particular international human rights, refugee and humanitarian law."[109]

A strong case can be made that protecting human rights and strengthening democracy are essential to the fight against terrorism. Guaranteeing the freedom to voice dissenting views without government interference can help to prevent the resort to political extremism and terrorism.[110] To win the fight against terrorism, the White House *National Strategy* argued, requires the advancement of freedom and human dignity, a commitment "to uphold basic human rights, including freedom of religion, conscience, speech, assembly, and press."[111] Support for human rights principles is also essential for sustaining political support for the fight against terrorism in democratic societies. Nothing will erode the support for antiterrorism measures more quickly than the perception among ordinary law-abiding citizens that such programs are eroding basic freedoms. A broadly based strategy respectful of human rights is also necessary to win the support of people in regions from which terrorists originate. An overreliance on repressive measures could alienate many of the social groups whose cooperation is most urgently needed in the collective struggle against terrorism. As Secretary-General Annan observed, governments "that resort to excessive use of force and indiscriminate repression when countering terrorism risk strengthening the base for terrorists among the general population."[112] Coercive instruments are necessary at times to protect against specific threats, but the global counter-terrorism fight must be waged within a legal framework that is respectful of civil liberties and human rights.[113]

Assessing Strategies

The struggle against the global terrorist threat posed by Al-Qaida and associated groups is a multidimensional, long-term effort that demands a wide array of strategies and increasing levels of international cooperation. The campaign requires a two-level approach: (1) coordinated international efforts to protect against terrorist attacks and drive Al-Qaida and associated networks out of business and (2) a series of preventive measures and international policies that ameliorate the grievances and conditions that give rise to terrorism. Table 8.1 depicts this two-level approach and outlines some of the policies associated with each.

Because the Al-Qaida terrorist threat is global in nature, the strategies employed against it must be transnational as well. Every nation shares a common interest in eliminating the scourge of global terrorism and in working together to eliminate the threat posed by Al-Qaida and associated groups. A terror threat that is spread across dozens of countries can be countered only through a broadly collaborative effort involving many nations. The most effective tools in this fight are not unilateral but cooperative. International law, multilateral institutions, and collaborative action: these are the essential ingredients in a winning strategy against global terrorism.

Table 8.1
Counter-Terrorism Policy Options

Protective

Military, police, and intelligence operations against Al-Qaida
Enforcement of UN Security Council counter-terrorism resolutions
Homeland security

Preventive

Addressing political grievances:
• Supporting an Israeli-Palestinian settlement
• Ending military occupation in Iraq
• Lowering the U.S. military profile in Arab and Muslim countries
Improving governance in regions of instability:
• Assisting with nation building efforts in failed states
• Providing consistent support for democracy and human rights
Expanding economic and social opportunity:
• Supporting sustainable economic development
• Supporting poverty reduction initiatives

An effective strategy requires differentiating among target groups. Two broad categories can be distinguished: (1) hard-core militants of Al-Qaida and related groups and (2) active sympathizers, supporters, and potential recruits. Benjamin and Simon offer the image of "two concentric circles, one very small, one very large."[114] In the inner circle are those who actually commit terrorist acts or actively support them. The outer circle consists of the much larger universe of people who under the right circumstances might be persuaded to join the core group. The challenge of strategy is to employ methods that diminish the inner circle without motivating those on the outside to join the inner core. The methods employed vary with the target audience. Against bin Laden and the Al-Qaida cadre, protective measures are the priority. The emphasis is on military and police operations, defensive measures, and the enforcement of UN counter-terrorism mandates. For sympathizers and potential recruits in the outer circle, however, different approaches are needed. Military measures may be counterproductive and could drive third parties toward militancy. The goal instead is to isolate hard-core elements and separate them from their potential support base. This requires a

Table 8.2
Counter-Terrorism Policy Options and Targets

	Targets	
Policies	Hard-Core Al-Qaida Militants	Potential Recruits, Sympathizers, and Supporters
Military, police, and intelligence operations	X	
Counter-terrorism enforcement	X	
Homeland security	X	
Supporting Israeli-Palestinian settlement	X	X
Ending military occupation of Iraq	X	X
Lowering U.S. military profile	X	X
Improved governance and nation building in failed states		X
Supporting democracy and human rights		X
Supporting sustainable development		X

political approach that addresses deeply felt grievances, promotes democratic governance, and supports sustainable economic development. The creative application and interplay of these various approaches, directed strategically toward the right targets, can erode the operational capacity of existing terrorist groups and cut them off from vital sources of political, social, and economic support. Table 8.2 depicts this dual approach.

The underlying strategic objectives are to separate hard-core militants from their support base and to render the use of terrorist methods illegitimate. President Bush emphasized this approach during an August 2004 television interview. When asked if the United States could win the war on terror, the president replied, "I don't think you can win it. But I think you can create conditions so that those who use terror as a tool are less acceptable in parts of the world."[115] This means addressing the "demand side" of terrorism to ensure that the vacuum created by the destruction of a particular terrorist cell is not quickly filled by other aspirants.[116] It means cutting the cord of terrorist formation by halting the flow of recruits and money and undermining political support.

Political Priorities

If terrorism is primarily a political phenomenon, the strategies for preventing it must focus on political issues as well. Isolating hard-core militants and reducing the legitimacy of terrorist methods requires a strategy of conflict transformation: recognizing the injustices that terrorist groups exploit and engaging with affected parties to resolve grievances through political rather than military means. Addressing the grievances that drive radicalization is an essential means of preventing the creation of new terrorist cells. "Prolonged unresolved conflicts . . . often create conditions conducive to exploitation by terrorists," Secretary-General Annan observed, and "must not be allowed to fester."[117] Demonstrating that political means are available to meet a community's deeply felt needs can convince those who support militancy to resolve their grievances through political bargaining rather than armed violence. Where contending groups are involved in dialogue and political power sharing arrangements, they are less likely to resort to violence. These efforts are not always successful, but they have the potential to reduce violence and transform disputes into more manageable forms.

As a loosely confederated network of militant groups, Al-Qaida is potentially susceptible to political defection. This is a vulnerability that should be exploited. The Institute for International Security Studies recommended a strategy of "filling political vacuums with diplomatic activity."[118] Reaching political accommodation with local groups whose agendas are amenable to negotiation can help to splinter the global terrorist movement and isolate hard-core factions. Depriving Al-Qaida of potential allies would weaken the network and reduce the pool of potential recruits for its global operations. Wherever there are active Al-Qaida groups contesting local issues—in the Philippines, Indonesia, Uzbekistan, and beyond—successful dispute resolution could lower political tensions in the affected country and loosen links with Al-Qaida. By convincing militants to forgo violence in favor of political participation, conflict transformation strategies offer means of shrinking support for extremism and reducing the pool of terrorist recruits and allies.

This is not to suggest a policy of negotiating with bin Laden and the hard-core militants. There can be no bargaining with those who perpetrate mass slaughter and barbarism. The idea of bargaining with Al-Qaida over global Islamic rule and the overthrow of Arab governments is absurd. Bin Laden's millennial goals are beyond the realm of conventional politics and quite literally nonnegotiable. Bin Laden and his lieutenants would no doubt continue their murderous ways regardless of efforts to redress Arab grievances. The leadership cadre of Al-Qaida can be countered only through effective coercive pressure and law enforcement. The goal of a political strategy is not to engage with bin Laden but with those who support his cause to drive a wedge between hardcore militants and potential sympathizers. Addressing legitimate grievances and resolving political differences is not meant to appease hard-core militants but to lower political tensions and reduce the appeal of extremist methods among sympathizers.

The most salient political issue in the Arab and Muslim world has been and continues to be the Israeli-Palestinian dispute. No other issue creates such a pervasive sense of humiliation among people in the region. Al-Qaida has not been involved in the Palestinian struggle, but it has taken advantage of the resulting bitterness and despair among people throughout the region to win support for its jihadist agenda. The oppression of the Palestinians is an open wound in the Arab body politic. Healing this wound through a just settlement leading to the creation of a viable Palestinian state alongside a secure Israel would create a healthier political climate in the region and remove one of the principal sources of support for extremism.

Resolving the crisis in Iraq would be another giant step toward reducing support for militancy. The longer U.S. troops remain and the current chaos continues, the deeper will be the anger and resentment toward U.S. policies and those who support them. Al-Qaida has taken advantage of this animosity and the worldwide opposition to U.S. occupation to step up recruitment and forge operational links with Iraqi resistance groups. The cause of the Iraqi insurgency is increasingly seen in the region as a just struggle against foreign occupation and is attracting growing sympathy and political support, despite the brutal methods of many insurgents. This benefits Al-Qaida and undermines efforts to reduce support for militancy. There are no easy answers in Iraq, but it is widely agreed in the region that the crisis requires a political rather than military solution and that U.S. and other foreign troops must be removed so that Iraqis can decide their own future. Resolving this crisis is an urgent priority for the security of the region and the broader international campaign against Al-Qaida.

The political strategy against terrorism means offering a better bargain to those who now sympathize with or support the terrorist jihad. At the heart of this better offer is the promise and reality of democracy—real political participation in the decisions that affect people's lives. "Democracy is the antithesis of terrorist tyranny," the White House *National Strategy* declared.[119] A policy of supporting democracy and human rights is based on the conviction that over time the freely expressed will of the people is the best guarantee of freedom, order, and security. Citizens who have opportunities to dissent and petition for redress of grievances are less likely to resort to violence to make themselves heard. Representative governments help to build more open and productive economies and generate greater opportunity. They foster a free press that educates and informs citizens and holds government leaders accountable. Promoting these conditions would help to create improved governance and make societies less prone to political extremism. Providing consistent support for democracy and human rights is an essential long-term strategy for reducing the likelihood of violence and terrorism.

Closely related to the challenge of enhancing political participation is the need to expand economic and social opportunity. Because political extremism and violence grow out of joblessness and a lack of opportunity, a process of sustained, equitable economic development is essential to reducing the breeding grounds for terrorism. The United States and other wealthy countries can use their economic resources to support development and the expansion of economic and social opportunity in Arab and Muslim countries. This could help to ameliorate some of the conditions that lead to armed conflict and support for political extremism. Development aid, debt relief, and other forms of economic assistance can create jobs and increase living standards and thereby reduce the likelihood of armed conflict. Expanded trade and investment can boost economic development and reduce poverty, provided they are not tied to structural adjustment and financial liberalization policies that reduce employment and increase vulnerability to external financial shocks. Economic aid and trade incentives can be used as inducements to reward countries that make progress toward improved governance.[120] Countries that take steps toward greater democracy, respect for human rights, and more equitable economic and social development should be supported with every available incentive. Democracy, human rights, and economic opportunity are the antidotes to terrorism, and they should be promoted actively as core strategies for preventing the rise of political extremism.

The struggle against terrorism is ultimately a political battle. It is not a military campaign, wrote Fukuyama, but a "contest for the hearts and minds of ordinary Muslims around the world."[121] The 9/11 Commission argued that the goal of U.S. strategy must be "prevailing over the ideology that contributes to Islamic terrorism." This should be easy for a democratic country founded on principles of freedom. Winning the fight against terrorism means living up to American ideals of justice, equality, and the rule of law. It means demilitarizing the so-called war on terror and focusing instead on the use of diplomatic, law enforcement, and economic policy instruments. It means working cooperatively in the world rather than unilaterally, acting with humility rather than arrogance. In this way the United States can speak and act with moral authority in dissuading others from supporting terrorism. It can offer hope and a positive vision for the future to overcome the ideology of hatred.

Notes

1. Paul Stares and Monica Yacoubian, "Terrorism as a Virus," *Washington Post*, 23 August 2005.

2. United States Institute of Peace, "Rethinking the War on Terror," briefing, United States Institute of Peace, Washington, DC, September 2005.

3. United Nations General Assembly, *A More Secure World: Our Shared Responsibility, Report of the Secretary-General's High-Level Panel on Threats, Challenges and Change*, A/59/565, New York, 29 November 2004, 46.

4. United Nations General Assembly, *Uniting Against Terrorism: Recommendations for a Global Counter-terrorism Strategy*, A/60/825, New York, 27 April 2006, par. 7.

5. White House, *National Strategy for Combating Terrorism*, (Washington, DC: GPO, September 2006), 7.

6. Scott Atran, "America's Mission Impossible: Strategy on the Altar of Ideology," unpublished manuscript, 15 February 2004, 4.

7. Marc Sageman, "Killing the Hydra: Only Attacks on Its Ideas Can Defeat a Network Like Al-Qaida," *Los Angeles Times*, 6 June 2004.

8. Mark Mazzetti and David Rohde, "Terror officials See Qaeda Chiefs Regaining Power," *New York Times*, 19 February 2007.

9. Daniel Benjamin and Steven Simon, *The Next Attack: The Failure of the War on Terror and a Strategy for Getting It Right* (New York: Times Books, 2005), 6.

10. United States Congress, *Al-Qaida After the Iraq Conflict,* report for Congress prepared by Audrey Kurth Cronin, 108th Cong., 1st sess., 23 May 2003, Committee Print Order Code RS 21529, 4, <http://fpc.state.gov/documents/organization/21191.pdf> (accessed 2 February 2004); see also Bruce Hoffman, "The Leadership Secrets of Osama bin Laden: The Terrorist as CEO," *Atlantic Monthly* 291, no. 3 (April 2003): 26.

11. International Institute for Strategic Studies, "Perspectives," *Strategic Survey 2003/4* 104, no. 1, ed. Jonathan Stevenson (May 2004): 6.

12. International Institute for Strategic Studies, "Perspectives," *Strategic Survey 2004/5* 105, no. 1, ed. Jonathan Stevenson (May 2005): 10.

13. United Nations Security Council, *Fifth Report of the Analytic Support and Sanctions Monitoring Team Appointed Pursuant to Resolutions 1526 (2004) and 1617 (2005) Concerning Al-Qaida and the Taliban and Associated Individuals and Entities,* S/2006/750, New York, 20 September 2006, paras. 59 and 61.

14. National Commission on Terrorist Attacks upon the United States, *Overview of the Enemy,* staff statement no. 15, presented at the twelfth public hearing of the National Commission on Terrorist Attacks upon the United States, 108th Cong., 2d sess., 16 June 2004, 11, <http://www.9-11commission.gov/staff_statements/staff_statement_15.pdf> (accessed 1 September 2004).

15. United Nations Security Council, *First Report of the Analytical Support and Sanctions Monitoring Team Appointed Pursuant to Resolution 1526 (2004) Concerning Al-Qaida and the Taliban and Associated Individuals and Entities,* S/2004/679, New York, 25 August 2004, par. 45.

16. National Commission on Terrorist Attacks upon the United States, *Overview of the Enemy.*

17. International Institute for Strategic Studies, *The Military Balance 2003–2004,* ed. Christopher Langton (London: Oxford University Press, 2003), 354.

18. John Mueller, "Is There Still a Terrorist Threat?," *Foreign Affairs* 85, no. 5 (September–October 2006), 8.

19. Bruce Hoffman, "Challenges for the U.S. Special Operations Command Posed by the Global Terrorist Threat: Al Qaeda on the Run or on the March?," written testimony submitted to the House Armed Services Subcommittee on Terrorism, Unconventional Threats and Capabilities, 101st Cong., 2d sess.,

Washington, DC, 14 February 2007. Available online at the House Armed Services Committee, <http://www.house.gov/hasc/hearing_information.shtml> (accessed 22 February 2007).

20. Benjamin and Simon, *The Next Attack*, 127.

21. United States Congress, *Al-Qaida After the Iraq Conflict*; see also Eric Leser, "The Iraq Quagmire: The Endless War Against Terrorism," *Le Monde*, 14 November 2003.

22. National Commission on Terrorist Attacks upon the United States, *The 9/11 Commission Report, Final Report of the National Commission on Terrorist Attacks upon The United States* (New York: Norton, 2004), 67.

23. "Excerpt from the National Intelligence Estimate," *Washington Post*, 27 September 2006.

24. National Commission on Terrorist Attacks upon the United States, *Overview of the Enemy*, 11.

25. International Institute for Strategic Studies, "Perspectives," *Strategic Survey 2003/4*, 8.

26. Susan Glasser, "U.S. Figures Show Sharp Global Rise in Terrorism," *Washington Post*, 27 April 2005.

27. Charles J. Hanley, "AP Survey: Experts See New Kind of War," Associated Press, 9 July 2005.

28. United States Department of State, *Country Reports on Terrorism 2005* (Washington, DC: GPO, 7 April 2006), Statistical Annex.

29. See the database of the Memorial Institute for the Prevention of Terrorism (MIPT), Knowledge Base, which incorporates the RAND Terrorism Chronology 1968–1997, RAND-MIPT Terrorism Incident Database 1998–present, the Terrorism Indictment Database at the University of Arkansas, and DFI International's research on terrorist organizations, Incident Reports by Date, <http://www.tkb.org/Home.jsp> (accessed 28 December 2005). As investigations of terrorist activities continue and as the concept of what constitutes a terrorist act is fine-tuned, this number has been adjusted upward since December 2005.

30. Shibley Telhami, *The Stakes: America in the Middle East: The Consequences of Power and the Choice for Peace*, updated ed. (Boulder, CO: Westview Press, 2004), 108.

31. Audrey Kurth Cronin, "Transnational Terrorism and Security," in *Grave New World: Security Challenges in the Twenty-first Century*, ed. Michael E. Brown (Washington, DC: Georgetown University Press, 2003), 291.

32. Daniel Benjamin, Thomas E. McNamara, and Steven Simon, "The Neglected Instrument: Multilateral Cooperation," paper presented at the conference on Prosecuting Terrorism: The Global Challenge, Florence, Italy, 3–5 June 2004, 2.

33. Benjamin, McNamara, and Simon, "The Neglected Instrument," 2.

34. Ekaterina Stepanova, "War and Peace Building," *Washington Quarterly* 27, no. 4 (Autumn 2004): 128–29.

35. Bruce Hoffman, *Inside Terrorism* (New York: Columbia University Press, 1998), 90–91.

36. Reza Aslan, *No God but God: The Origins, Evolution, and Future of Islam* (New York: Random House, 2006), 81.

37. United Nations General Assembly and Security Council, *Report of the Policy Working Group on the United Nations and Terrorism*, A/57/273 and S/2002/875 (identical documents), New York, 6 August 2002, par. 13.

38. Telhami, *The Stakes*, 14.

39. Cronin, "Transnational Terrorism," 282, 285.

40. Benjamin, McNamara, and Simon, "The Neglected Instrument," 2.

41. Rob de Wijk, "The Limits of Military Power," *Washington Quarterly* 25, no. 1 (Winter 2002): 86.

42. Telhami, *The Stakes*, 33.

43. Francis Fukuyama, "After Neo-Conservatism," *New York Times Magazine*, 19 February 2006, 62.

44. Benjamin, McNamara, and Simon, "The Neglected Instrument," 2.

45. National Commission on Terrorist Attacks, *The 9/11 Commission Report*, 52.

46. Benjamin and Simon, *The Next Attack*, 51–52.

47. Aslan, *No God but God*, 86.

48. See the MIPT Knowledge Base, <http://www.tkb.org/home.jsp> (accessed 31 August 2006), data cited in Benjamin and Simon, *The Next Attack*, 73.

49. United States Congress, *Terrorists and Suicide Attacks*, report for Congress prepared by Audrey Kurth Cronin, 108th Cong., 1st sess., 28 August 2003, Committee Print Order Code RL32058, 9, *Federation of American Scientists*, <http://www.fas.org/irp/crs/RL32058.pdf> (accessed 1 September 2006), cited in Robert Pape, *Dying to Win: The Strategic Logic of Suicide Terrorism* (New York: Random House, 2005), 4, and also cited in Christian Caryl, "Why They Do It," *New York Review of Books* 52, no. 14 (22 September 2005).

50. Benjamin and Simon, *The Next Attack*, 39.

51. Caryl, "Why They Do It."

52. Robert Pape, "Blowing Up an Assumption," *New York Times*, 18 May 2005.

53. United Nations General Assembly, *Uniting Against Terrorism*, par. 28.

54. Pape, "Blowing Up an Assumption."

55. Telhami, *The Stakes*, 28.

56. National Commission on Terrorist Attacks, *The 9/11 Commission Report*, 48.

57. Robert Fisk, "In His Last Recorded Interview, Usama bin Ladin Tells Robert Fisk Why He So Despises America," 6 December 1996, <http://www.robert-fisk.com/fisk_interview3.htm> (accessed 15 November 2004).

58. United States Department of Defense, Office of the Under Secretary of Defense for Acquisition and Technology, Defense Science Board, "Organizing a DOD Response: A Major DOD Mission," in *The Defense Science Board 1997 Summer Study Task Force on DOD Responses to Transnational Threats*, vol. 1, final report, October 1997, 15, <http://www.acq.osd.mil/dsb/reports/trans.pdf> (accessed 1 September 2006), quoted in Scott Atran, "The Strategic Threat from Suicide Terror" (AEI-Brookings Joint Center for Regulatory Studies, related publication 03–33, December 2003), 14.

59. Pape, "Blowing Up an Assumption."

60. Telhami, *The Stakes*, 59.

61. Cronin, "Transnational Terrorism," 279.

62. Cronin, "Transnational Terrorism," 279.

63. Rama Mani, "The Root Causes of Terrorism and Conflict Prevention," in *Terrorism and the UN: Before and After September 11*, ed. Jane Boulden and Thomas G. Weiss (Bloomington: Indiana University Press, 2004), 230–31.

64. Cronin, "Transnational Terrorism," 297.

65. Cronin, "Transnational Terrorism," 297.

66. International Institute for Strategic Studies, "Perspectives," *Strategic Survey 2003/4*, 8.

67. National Commission on Terrorist Attacks upon the United States, *Overview of the Enemy*.

68. United Nations Security Council, *Third Report of the Analytical Support and Sanctions Monitoring Team Appointed Pursuant to Resolution 1526 (2004) Concerning Al-Qaida and the Taliban and Associated Individuals and Entities*, S/2005/572, New York, 9 September 2005, par. 67.

69. Mónica Serrano, "The Political Economy of Terrorism," in *Terrorism and the UN: Before and After September 11*, ed. Jane Boulden and Thomas G. Weiss (Bloomington: Indiana University Press, 2004), 202.

70. de Wijk, "The Limits of Military Power," 86.

71. "Blair: Poverty, Extremism Cause Terrorism," *USA Today*, 9 July 2005, <http://www.usatoday.com/news/world/2005-07-09-tony-roots_x.htm> (accessed 18 July 2005).

72. White House, *National Strategy for Combating Terrorism*, September 2006, 9.

73. Ted Robert Gurr, "Economic Factors," in *Addressing the Causes of Terrorism: The Club de Madrid Series on Democracy and Terrorism*, proceedings of the International Summit on Democracy, Terrorism and Security, Club de Madrid, Madrid, Spain, 8–11 March 2005, vol. 1, 19.

74. Alan B. Krueger and Jitka Malesckova, "Education, Poverty and Terrorism: Is There a Causal Connection?," *Journal of Economic Perspectives* 17, no. 4 (Fall 2003): 131–32.

75. Krueger and Malesckova, "Education, Poverty and Terrorism," 135.

76. Lewis Kriesberg, *Constructive Conflicts: From Escalation to Resolution*, 2d ed. (Lanham, MD: Rowman and Littlefield, 2003), 70.

77. Benjamin and Simon, *The Next Attack*, 86.

78. Telhami, *The Stakes*, 29.

79. Paul Collier et al., *Breaking the Conflict Trap: Civil War and Development Policy* (Washington, DC: World Bank, 2003).

80. Collier et al., *Breaking the Conflict Trap*, 53.

81. Monty G. Marshall, "Global Terrorism: An Overview and Analysis," in *Peace and Conflict 2005: A Global Survey of Armed Conflicts, Self-Determination Movements, and Democracy*, ed. Monty G. Marshall and Ted Robert Gurr (College Park, MD: University of Maryland Center for International Development and Conflict Management, 2005), 68, <http://www.cidcm.umd.edu/paper.asp?id=15> (accessed 18 July 2005).

82. Marshall, "Global Terrorism," 68.

83. Krueger and Malesckova, "Education, Poverty and Terrorism," 138.

84. Thomas Friedman, "Connect the Dots," *New York Times*, 25 September 2003.

85. Jessica Stern, "How America Created a Terrorist Haven," *New York Times*, 20 August 2003.

86. See the classic study by Ted Robert Gurr, *Why Men Rebel* (Princeton, NJ: Princeton University Press, 1970).

87. Gurr, "Economic Factors," 19.

88. Lewis Kriesberg, *Constructive Conflicts: From Escalation to Resolution*, 2d ed. (Lanham, MD: Rowman and Littlefield, 2003), 68.

89. National Commission on Terrorist Attacks, *The 9/11 Commission Report*, 53–54.

90. George W. Bush, speech at West Point, New York, 1 June 2002, cited in White House, "Overview of America's International Strategy," in *The National Security Strategy of the United States of America*, September 2002, 1, <http://www.whitehouse.gov/nsc/nss.pdf> (accessed 1 September 2006).

91. John J. Gershman et al., *A Secure America in a Secure World*, special report, Task Force on Terrorism (Washington, DC: Foreign Policy in Focus, 2004), 34.

92. See Larry Diamond, "What Went Wrong in Iraq," *Foreign Affairs* 83, no. 5 (September–October 2004): 34–56, for a firsthand account of the incompetence of the U.S.-led occupation.

93. Stepanova, "War and Peace Building," 130.

94. Chatham House, "Security, Terrorism and the UK," ISP/NSC Briefing Paper 05/01, Royal Institute of International Affairs, London, July 2005, 3, <http://www.chathamhouse.org.uk/pdf/research/niis/BPsecurity.pdf> (accessed 1 September 2006).

95. Dana Priest, "Iraq New Terror Breeding Ground; War Created Haven, CIA Advisers Report," *Washington Post*, 14 January 2005.

96. Telhami, *The Stakes*, 92–93.

97. Krueger and Malesckova, "Education, Poverty and Terrorism," 142.

98. Alan B. Krueger and Jitka Malesckova, "Seeking the Roots of Terrorism," *Chronicle of Higher Education* 49, no. 39 (6 June 2003): b10.

99. Andreas Feldman and Maftu Peraelae, "Reassessing the Causes of Nongovernmental Terrorism in Latin America," *American Politics and Society* 42, no. 2 (Summer 2004): 120.

100. United Nations General Assembly, *Uniting Against Terrorism*, par. 32.

101. Gershman, *A Secure America*, 34.

102. United Nations General Assembly and Security Council, *Report of the Policy Working Group on the United Nations and Terrorism*, par. 16.

103. White House, *National Strategy for Combating Terrorism*, September 2006, 9.

104. Alan Krueger, "Economic Scene," *New York Times*, 29 May 2002.

105. United Nations General Assembly, *A More Secure World*, par. 147.

106. Kofi Annan, "A Global Strategy for Fighting Terrorism," keynote address, closing plenary of the International Summit on Democracy, Terrorism and Security, Club de Madrid, Madrid, 10 March 2005, <http://english.safe-democracy .org/keynotes/a-global-strategy-for-fighting-terrorism.html> (accessed 18 July 2005).

107. Gershman, *A Secure America*, 10–11.

108. Kofi Annan, "Conference Report," keynote address, Conference on Fighting Terrorism for Humanity, International Peace Academy, New York, 22 September 2003, 10.

109. United Nations Security Council, *Resolution 1456 (2003)*, S/RES/1456, New York, 20 January 2003, par. 6.

110. Krueger, "Economic Scene."

111. White House, *National Strategy for Combating Terrorism*, 9.

112. United Nations General Assembly, *Uniting Against Terrorism*, par. 33.

113. United Nations General Assembly, *A More Secure World*, paras. 147–48.

114. Benjamin and Simon, *The Next Attack*, 126.

115. Elisabeth Bumiller, "Bush Cites Doubt America Can Win War on Terror," *New York Times*, 31 August 2004.

116. Telhami, *The Stakes*, 177.

117. United Nations General Assembly, *Uniting Against Terrorism*, par. 28.

118. International Institute for Strategic Studies, *The Military Balance 2003–2004*, 357.

119. White House, *National Strategy for Combating Terrorism*, September 2006, 9.

120. Cronin, "Transnational Terrorism," 299.

121. Fukuyama, "After Neo-Conservatism," 62.

Bibliography

Abbott, Kenneth W., et al. "The Concept of Legalization." *International Organization* 54, no. 3 (2000): 401–19.

Ackerman, Gary, and Laura Snyder. "Would They If They Could?" *Bulletin of the Atomic Scientists* 58, no. 3 (May–June 2002): 40–47.

Agence France-Presse. "EU Lawmakers Shoot Down US Deal on Airline Passenger Data." 18 March 2004.

———. "Sahel States Call for UN Inquiry into Sanctions on Libya." 17 August 1997.

———. "South Africa Calls for Lifting of Sanctions on Libya." 22 October 1997.

———. "U.S. Intelligence Concludes Theft of Russian Nuclear Material 'Has Occurred.' " 23 February 2005.

Agureyev, Aleksey. "Two Lithuanians Sentenced in Missile Plot in USA." ITAR-TASS, 20 August 1998.

Akgül, Deniz A. "The European Union Response to September 11: Relations with the US and the Failure to Maintain a CFSP." *Review of International Affairs* 1, no. 4 (Summer 2002): 1–24.

Albright, David. "Al Qaeda's Nuclear Program: Through the Window of Seized Documents." Nautilus Institute Policy Forum 47, 6 November 2002. <http://www.nautilus.org/archives/fora/Special-Policy-Forum/47_Albright.html> (accessed March 18, 2005).

Albright, Madeleine. *Madame Secretary: A Memoir.* New York: Hyperion, 2003.

Alden, Edward. "Europe Freezes Terrorist Assets Worth $35 Million." *Financial Times* (London), 8 April 2002. <http://specials.ft.com/attackonterrorism/FT39YWK5SZC.html> (accessed 8 April 2002).

Alegre, Susie, and Marisa Leaf. "Mutual Recognition in European Judicial Cooperation: A Step Too Far Too Soon? Case Study: The European Arrest Warrant." *European Law Journal* 10 (2004): 200, 200–17.

Alexander, Yonah, ed. *International Terrorism: National, Regional and Global Perspectives.* New York: Praeger, 1976.

al-Fadl, Jamal. Testimony cited in *United States of America v. Usama Bin Laden et al.* S(7) 98 Cr. 1023, (S.D.N.Y. 2001). <http://cns.miis.edu/pubs/reports/binladen.htm> (accessed 18 March 2005).

Allison, Graham. Nuclear Terrorism: *The Ultimate Preventable Catastrophe.* New York: Times Books, 2004.

Anderson, Malcolm. "Counterterrorism as an Objective of European Police Cooperation." In *European Democracies Against Terrorism: Governmental Policies and Intergovernmental Cooperation*, edited by Fernando Reinares, 227–43. Burlington, VT: Ashgate, 2000.

"Angered by US Sanctions, EU Threatens to Go to WTO." *New York Times*, 22 August 1996.

Annan, Kofi. "Conference Report." Keynote address, Conference on Fighting Terrorism for Humanity, International Peace Academy, New York, 22 September 2003.

———. "A Global Strategy for Fighting Terrorism." Keynote address, closing plenary of the International Summit on Democracy, Terrorism, and Security, Club de Madrid, Madrid, 10 March 2005. <http://english.safe-democracy.org/keynotes/a-global-strategy-for-fighting-terrorism.html> (accessed 18 July 2005).

———. *Mandating and Delivering: Analysis and Recommendations to Facilitate the Review of Mandates.* Report of the Secretary General of the United Nations General Assembly. A/60/733. New York, 30 March 2006.

———. "Menace of Terrorism Requires Global Response, Says Secretary-General, Stressing Importance of Increased United Nations Role." United Nations Press Release, SG/SM/8583; SC/7639, New York, 20 January 2003.

———. Statement at the 4688th meeting of the United Nations Security Council [High-Level Meeting of the Security Council: Combating Terrorism], S/PV.4688, New York, 20 January 2003.

———. "Statesmanship, Confidence-Rebuilding Required for UN Capable of Coping with Today's Crises." Address to United Nations Association of the United Kingdom, Central Hall, Westminster, United Kingdom, 31 January 2006.

———. *Uniting Against Terrorism: Recommendations for a Global Counter-Terrorism Strategy.* Report of the Secretary-General to the United Nations General Assembly. A/60/825. New York, 27 April 2006. <http://www.un.org/unitingagainstterrorism/sg-terrorism-2may06.pdf> (accessed 24 September 2006).

Apple, R. E., Jr. "U.S. Now Casting Doubt on Allies' Libyan Policy." *New York Times*, 24 April 1986.

Applegarth, Claire. "G-8 Global Partnership Selects Ukraine for Nonproliferation Funds." *Arms Control Today* 34, no. 10 (December 2004): 41.

Arbatov, Alexei. "Deep Cuts and De-alerting: A Russian Perspective." In *The Nuclear Turning Point: A Blueprint for Deep Cuts and De-Alerting of Nuclear*

Weapons, edited by Harold Feiveson, 305–24. Washington, DC: Brookings Institution, 1999.

Arie, Sophie. "Europe, US Clash over Terror War." *Christian Science Monitor,* 29 September 2005.

Arkin, William M. "Early Warning: A New Trident II Is an Illusion of Defense." *Washington Post,* 22 May 2006. <http://blog.washingtonpost.com/earlywarning/2006/05/a_new_trident_ii_is_an_illusio.html> (accessed 8 August 2006).

Aslan, Reza. *No God but God: The Origins, Evolution, and Future of Islam.* New York: Randon House, 2006.

Associated Press. "Abu Nidal Tied to Turkish Attack." *New York Times,* 7 November 1986.

———. "Qaddafi Says He Sponsored and Now Forsakes Terrorists." *New York Times,* 26 October 1989.

———. "U.N. General Assembly Adopts Counter-terrorism Strategy." *International Herald Tribune,* 9 September 2006. <http://www.iht.com/articles/ap/2006/09/08/news/UN_GEN_UN_Counter_Terrorism.php> (accessed 28 September 2006).

———. "U.S. Criticizes Turkish Leader for Libya Trip and Trade Deal." *New York Times,* 8 October 1996.

———. "U.S.: Terror Funding Stymied." *CBS News,* 11 January 2005. <http://www.cbsnews.com/stories/2005/01/11/terror/main666168.shtml> (accessed 24 September 2006).

Atran, Scott. "America's Mission Impossible: Strategy on the Altar of Ideology." Unpublished manuscript, 15 February 2004.

———. "The Strategic Threat from Suicide Terror." AEI-Brookings Joint Center for Regulatory Studies, related publication 03–33, December 2003.

Baker, Howard, and Lloyd Cutler. *A Report Card on the Department of Energy's Nonproliferation Programs with Russia.* Draft paper of the Secretary of Energy Advisory Board, United States Department of Energy, 10 January 2000 (released 10 January 2001). <http://www.seab.energy.gov/publications/rpt.pdf> (accessed 24 August 2006).

Baker, Peter. "Pakistani Scientist Who Met with Bin Laden Failed Polygraphs, Renewing Suspicions." *Washington Post,* 3 March 2002.

Bank of England. "Consolidated List of Financial Sanctions Targets in the UK." Bank of England, 2 April 2004. <http://www.bankofengland.co.uk/sanctions/terrorism.htm> (accessed 2 April 2004).

Basile, Mark. "Going to the Source: Why Al Qaeda's Financial Network Is Likely to Withstand the Current War on Terrorist Financing." *Studies in Conflict and Terrorism* 27, no. 3 (May–June 2004): 169–85.

Bayefsky, Anne. "U.N.derwhelming Response: The U.N.'s Approach to Terrorism." *National Review Online,* 24 September 2004. <http://www.nationalreview.com/comment/bayefsky200409240915.asp> (accessed 8 September 2006).

BBC Monitoring International Reports. "Austrian Chancellor Urges EU Cooperation in Antiterror Measures." Translated by *Wiener Zeitung* (Vienna). BBC, 18 March 2004.

Benjamin, Daniel, Thomas E. McNamara, and Steven Simon. "The Neglected Instrument: Multilateral Cooperation." Paper presented at the Prosecuting Terrorism: The Global Challenge conference, Florence, Italy, 3–5 June 2004.

Benjamin, Daniel, and Steven Simon. *The Next Attack: The Failure of the War on Terror and a Strategy for Getting It Right.* New York: Times Books, 2005.

Bensahel, Nora. "The Counterterror Coalitions: Cooperation with Europe, NATO, and the European Union." Report prepared for the U.S. Air Force, Project Air Force, RAND, 2003. <http://www.rand.org/publications/MR/MR1746/MR1746.pdf> (accessed 6 September 2006).

Biersteker, Thomas, and Sue E. Eckert. "Strengthening Targeted Sanctions Through Fair and Clear Procedures." Report, Watson Institute for International Studies, Brown University, Providence, March 2006.

Bin Laden, Osama. "The Nuclear Bomb of Islam." Statement in *International Islamic Front for Fighting the Jews and the Crusaders,* 29 May 1998. Cited in *United States of America v. Usama Bin Laden et al.,* S (9) 98 Cr. 1023 (LBS)(S.D.N.Y. 1998), 7 March 2001. <http://cns.miis.edu/pubs/reports/pdfs/binladen/indict.pdf> (accessed 17 March 2005).

Black, Ian. "Lockerbie Families Cheered by Hague Court Ruling; Venue Choice for Trial of Libyans Is Setback for Britain and US." *The Guardian* (London), 28 February 1998.

———. "UN Fury at Sanctions Defiance." *The Guardian* (London), 23 September 1997.

Blair, Tony. "Moment of Reconciliation." Foreign policy speech delivered at Georgetown University, Washington, DC, 26 May 2006. Government of the United Kingdom. <http://www.number-10.gov.uk/output/Page9549.asp> (accessed 29 September 2006).

"Blair: Poverty, Extremisim Cause Terrorism." *USA Today,* 9 July 2005.

Bokhari, Farhan et al. "Pakistan's 'Rogue Nuclear Scientist': What Did Khan's Government Know about his Deals?" *Financial Times* (London), 6 April 2004.

Bolton, John. "Bolton Outlines Bush Administration's Nonproliferation Efforts." US Info, United States Department of State, 19 October 2004. <http://usinfo.state.gov/eap/Archive/2004/Oct/20-535618.html> (accessed 30 August 2006).

Bonner, Raymond, and Craig S. Smith. "Pakistani Said to Have Given Libya Uranium." *New York Times,* 21 February 2004.

Boulden, Jane, and Thomas G. Weiss, eds. *Terrorism and the UN: Before and After September 11.* Bloomington: Indiana University Press, 2004.

Buchan, David. "Libya Claims Victory in Lockerbie Ruling." *Financial Times* (London), 28 February 1998.

Bumiller, Elisabeth. "Bush Cites Doubt America Can Win War on Terror." *New York Times*, 31 August 2004.

Bunn, Matthew. "Preventing a Nuclear 9/11." *Issues in Science and Technology* (Winter 2005): 55–62.

Bunn, Matthew, John P. Holdren, and Anthony Wier. *Securing Nuclear Weapons and Materials: Seven Steps for Immediate Action*. Report, Project on Managing the Atom and Nuclear Threat Initiative, Belfer Center for Science and International Affairs, John F. Kennedy School of Government, Harvard University, Cambridge, MA, 20 May 2002. <http://bcsia.ksg.harvard.edu/publication .cfm?ctype=book&item_id=90> (accessed 17 March 2005).

Burgess, John, et al. "Allies Cool to U.S. Call for Sanctions on Libya; Bonn Rejects Plea, Saying Tactics Futile." *Washington Post*, 9 January 1986.

Burns, Robert. "Defense Secretary Says Potentially Deadly Link Between Terrorist Networks and 'Terrorist States' Must Be Stopped." Associated Press, 31 January 2002.

Burrows, William, and Robert Windrem. *Critical Mass: The Dangerous Race for Superweapons in a Fragmenting World*. New York: Simon and Schuster, 1994.

Bush, President George H. W. "The U.S. and Asia: Building Democracy and Freedom." Excerpts from remarks before the Asia Society, New York, 12 November 1991. U.S. Department of State dispatch, vol. 2, no. 46, 18 November 1991. University of Illinois at Chicago Federal Depository Library. <http:// dosfan.lib.uic.edu/ERC/briefing/dispatch/1991/html/Dispatchv2no46.html> (accessed 9 September 2006).

Bush, President George W. *The National Security Strategy of the United States of America*. Washington, DC: GPO, 2006. <http://www.whitehouse.gov/nsc/ nss/2006/nss2006.pdf#search=%22The%20National%20Security%20Strategy %20of%20the%20United%20States%20of%20America%202006%22> (accessed 23 August 2006).

———. Speech at West Point, New York, 1 June 2002. Cited in "Overview of America's International Strategy." In *The National Security Strategy of the United States of America*. Washington, DC: GPO, September 2002. <http://www.whitehouse.gov/nsc/nss.pdf> (accessed 1 September 2006).

Cameron, Iain. "Protecting Legal Rights: On the (In)security of Targeted Sanctions." In *International Sanctions: Between Words and Wars in the Global System*, edited by Peter Wallensteen and Carina Staibano, chap. 14. London: Frank Cass, 2005.

Cannon, Lou. "U.S. Makes New Bid for Sanctions." *Washington Post*, 16 January 1986.

Cannon, Lou, and Bob Woodward. "Reagan's Use of Force Marks Turning Point; More Terror and Retaliation Seen." *Washington Post*, 16 April 1986.

Cardona, Meliton. "The European Response to Terrorism." *Terrorism and Political Violence* 4, no. 4 (Winter 1992): 245–54.

Carrell. Severin, and Jenny Booth. "Lockerbie Trial Move Welcomed by Libya's Allies." *New York Times*, 26 August 1998.

Carson, J. Mark, et al. "Can Terrorists Build Nuclear Weapons?" Paper prepared for International Task Force on the Prevention of Nuclear Terrorism, Nuclear Control Institute, Washington, DC, 1987. <http://www.nci.org/k-m/makeab .htm> (accessed 18 March 2005).

Caryl, Christian. "Why They Do It." *New York Review of Books* 52, no. 14 (22 September 2005).

Center for Nonproliferation Studies, trans. "The Russian Federation and Nonproliferation of Weapons of Mass Destruction and Delivery Systems: Threats, Assessments, Problems and Solutions." A Russian government paper translated by Monterey Institute for International Affairs, Center for Nonproliferation Studies, Monterey, CA, June 2006. <http://cns.miis.edu/pubs/other/rusfed.htm> (accessed 8 August 2006).

Center for Social and Economic Studies. *Discouraging Terrorism: Some Implications of 9/11 (2002)*. Available at National Academies Press. <http://darwin .nap.edu/books/0309085306/html/1.html> (accessed 8 September 2006).

Chatham House. "Security, Terrorism, and the UK." ISP/NSC Briefing Paper 05/01. Royal Institute of International Affairs, London, July 2005. <http://www.chathamhouse.org.uk/pdf/research/niis/BPsecurity.pdf> (accessed 1 September 2006).

Chesterman, Simon. "Shared Secrets: Intelligence and Collective Security." Paper #10, Lowy Institute for International Policy, Sydney, Australia, 2006.

Chyba, Christopher F. "Toward Biological Security." In *Terrorism and Counterterrorism: Understanding the New Security Environment—Readings and Interpretations*, revised and updated by Russell D. Howard and Reid Sawyer, chap. 5.2. Guilford, CT: McGraw-Hill/Dushkin, 2003. Previously published in *Foreign Affairs* 81, no. 3 (May–June 2002): 122–36.

Clarke, Richard A. et al. *Defeating the Jihadists: A Blueprint for Action*. Washington, DC: Century Foundation Press, 2004.

Collier, Paul et al. *Breaking the Conflict Trap: Civil War and Development Policy*. Washington, DC: World Bank, 2003.

Commission of the European Communities. *Commission Staff Working Paper, EC External Assistance Facilitating the Implementation of UN Security Council Resolution 1373: An Overview*. SEC(2002) 231. Brussels, 25 February 2002.

———. *Proposal for a Council Framework Decision on Combating Terrorism*. 2001/0217 (CNS). Brussels, 19 September 2001.

Commission on the Intelligence Capabilities of the United States Regarding Weapons of Mass Destruction. *Report to the President of the United States*. Washington, DC: GPO, 2005. <http://www.wmd.gov/report/index.html> (accessed 24 August 2006).

Cooper, Christopher. "Shunned in Sweden: How the Drive to Block Funds for Terrorism Entangled Mr. Aden." *Wall Street Journal*, 6 May 2002.

Cooper, Helene. "Libya Hands Over Pan Am 103 Suspects, as U.N. but not U.S. Suspends Sanctions." *Wall Street Journal,* 6 April 1999.

Cortright, David, and George A. Lopez. *Sanctions and the Search for Security: Challenges to UN Action.* Boulder, CO: Lynne Rienner, 2002.

———. *The Sanctions Decade: Assessing UN Strategies in the 1990s.* Boulder, CO: Lynne Rienner, 2000.

Cortright, David, George A. Lopez, Alistair Millar, and Linda Gerber. *An Action Agenda for Enhancing the United Nations Program on Counter-Terrorism.* Goshen, IN: Fourth Freedom Forum, 2004. <http://www.fourthfreedom.org/pdf/Action_Agenda.pdf> (accessed 26 July 2005).

Council of the European Communities. *Council Regulation (EEC) No. 3906/89 of 18 December 1989 on Economic Aid to the Republic of Hungary and the Polish People's Republic.* (EEC) No. 3906/89. Brussels, 18 December 1989.

Council of the European Union. *Conclusions and Plan of Action of the Extraordinary European Council Meeting on 21 September 2001.* Brussels, 21 September 2001. <http://europa.eu.int/comm/external_relations/110901/actplan01.pdf> (accessed 6 September 2006).

———. *Council Common Position Concerning Additional Restrictive Measures Against the Taliban.* 2001/154/CFSP. Brussels, 27 February 2001.

———. *Council Common Position Concerning Additional Restrictive Measures Against the Taliban.* EN 27/02/2001. Brussels, 29 November 2001.

———. *Council Common Position Concerning Restrictive Measures Against Osama Bin Laden, Members of the al-Qaeda Organization and the Taliban and Other Individuals, Groups, Undertakings and Entities Associated with Them.* EN 29/05/2002 21. Brussels, 29 November 2002.

———. *Council Common Position Concerning Restrictive Measures Against the Taliban.* EN 16/11/1999. Brussels, 16 November 1999.

———. *Council Common Position of 27 December 2001 on the Application of Specific Measures to Combat Terrorism.* EN 2001/931/CFSP 0093. Brussels, 27 December 2001.

———. *Council Common Position 2004/500/CFSP of 17 May 2004 Updating Common Position 2001/931/CFSP on the Application of Specific Measures to Combat Terrorism and Repealing Common Position 2004/309/CFSP.* EN 2004/500/CFSP. Brussels, 17 May 2004.

———. *Council Common Position 2001/931/CFSP of 27 December 2001 on the Application of Specific Measures to Combat Terrorism.* Brussels, 27 December 2001.

———. *Council Decision of 3 December 1998 Instructing Europol to Deal with Crimes Committed or Likely to Be Committed in the Course of Terrorist Activities Against Life, Limb, Personal Freedom or Property.* EN 30/01/1999 0022 (1999). Brussels, 3 December 1998.

————. *Council Decision of 28 February 2002 Setting up Eurojust with a View to Reinforcing the Fight Against Serious Crime.* EN 2002/187/JHA 0001. Brussels, 28 February 2002.

————. *Council Decision of 19 December 2002 on the Implementation of Specific Measures for Police and Judicial Cooperation to Combat Terrorism in Accordance with Article 4 of Common Position 2001/931/CFSP.* EN 2003/48/JHA 0068. Brussels, 22 January 2003.

————. *Council Decision of 2 April 2004 Implementing Article 2(3) of Regulation (EC) No. 2580/2001 on Specific Restrictive Measures Directed Against Certain Persons and Entities with a View to Combating Terrorism and Repealing Decision 2003/902/EC.* EN 2004/306/EC. Brussels, 2 April 2004.

————. *Council Framework Decision of 13 June 2002 on Combating Terrorism.* EN 2002/475/JHA 0003. Brussels, 13 June 2002. <http://europa.eu.int/eur-lex/pri/en/oj/dat/2002/l_164/l_16420020622en00030007.pdf#search=%22Framework%20Decision%20on%20Combating%20Terrorism%22> (accessed 6 September 2006).

————. *Council Framework Decision of 13 June 2002 on the European Arrest Warrant and the Surrender Procedures Between Member States: Statements Made by Certain Member States on the Adoption of the Framework Decision.* EN 2002/584/JHA 0001. Brussels, 26 June 2002.

————. *Council Regulation of 27 December 2001 on Specific Restrictive Measures Directed Against Certain Persons and Entities with a View to Combating Terrorism.* EN (EC) No. 2580/2001. Brussels, 27 December 2001.

————. "Declaration on Combating Terrorism Is Adopted in Brussels." Press release, 25 March 2004. <http://www.eu2004.ie/templates/news.asp?sNavlocator=66&list_id=462> (accessed 6 September 2006).

————. "European Council to Focus on Fight Against Terrorism." Press release 81, 15 March 2004. <http://europa.eu.int/rapid/start/cgi/guesten.ksh?p_action.gettxt=gt&doc=PRES/04/81|0|RAPID&lg=EN&display=> (accessed 15 March 2004).

————. *Proposal for a Council Framework Decision on Combating Terrorism, Outcome of Proceedings of the Council of 7 December 2001.* EN 14845/1/01 REV 1. Brussels, 7 December 2001.

————. *Proposal for a Framework Decision on the European Arrest Warrant and the Surrender Procedures Between the Member States, Outcome of Proceedings of the Council.* EN 14867/1/01 REV1. Brussels, 12 December 2001.

————. "Provisional Findings of the Two 'Peer Evaluation' Mechanisms Affecting the Union Fight Against Terrorism." *Statewatch.* <http://www.statewatch.org/news/2004/jun/eu-plan-terr-eval.pdf> (accessed 26 May 2004).

————. *Special Accession Program for Agriculture and Rural Development* (SAPARD). Council Regulation 1268/1999. Brussels, 21 June 1999.

————. *Treaty on European Union.* Maastricht, 7 February 1992. <http://www.eurotreaties.com/maastrichteu.pdf>.

Council of the European Union, Justice and Home Affairs. *Conclusions Adopted by the Council (Justice and Home Affairs), Brussels, 20 September 2001.* SN 3926/6/01. Brussels, 20 September 2001.

Council on Foreign Relations. *Update on the Global Campaign Against Terrorist Financing: Second Report of an Independent Task Force on Terrorist Financing.* New York: Council on Foreign Relations, 2004.

"Counter-Proliferation in Asia: No Place to Hide, Maybe." *Economist*, 30 October–5 November 2004.

Counter-Terrorism Executive Directorate. "Framework for the Collection, Analysis, Development and Dissemination of Best Practices Relative to United Nations Security Council Resolutions 1373 (2001) and 1624 (2005)." Unpublished, n.d.

Crenshaw, Martha. "The Logic of Terrorism: Terrorist Behavior as a Product of Strategic Choice." In *Origins of Terrorism: Psychologies, Ideologies, Theologies, States of Mind*, edited by Walter Reich, 7–24. Washington, DC: Woodrow Wilson Center Press, 1998.

———. "The Psychology of Terrorism: An Agenda for the Twenty-first Century." *Political Psychology* 21, no. 2 (2001): 405–20.

Cronin, Audrey Kurth. "Behind the Curve: Globalization and International Terrorism." *International Security* 27, no. 3 (Winter 2002–2003): 30–58.

———. "Rethinking Sovereignty: American Strategy in the Age of Terrorism." *Survival* 44, no. 2 (2002): 119–39.

———. "Transnational Terrorism and Security." In *Grave New World: Security Challenges in the Twenty-first Century*, edited by Michael E. Brown, 279–304. Washington, DC: Georgetown University Press, 2003.

de Margerie, Emanuel. "Why France Said No." *New York Times*, 20 May 1986.

Dempsey, Judy. "Europe at Loggerheads Over How to Co-Ordinate on Terrorism." *Financial Times* (London), 18 March 2004.

———. "Europol's Bid for Success." *Financial Times*, 27 February 2002.

den Boer, Monica, and Jörg Monar. "Keynote Article: 11 September and the Challenge of Global Terrorism to the EU as a Security Actor." In *The European Union: Annual Review of the EU 2001/2002*, edited by Geoffrey Edwards and Georg Wiessala, 11–28. Oxford, UK: Blackwell, 2002.

de Wijk, Rob. "The Limits of Military Power." *Washington Quarterly* 25, no. 1 (Winter 2002): 75–92.

DeYoung, Karen. "British Dubious About Sanctions: View That Moves Are Counterproductive Is Restated in London." *Washington Post*, 8 January 1986.

Diamond, Larry. "What Went Wrong in Iraq." *Foreign Affairs* 83, no. 5 (September–October 2004): 34–56.

Dionne, E. J., Jr. "France Weighing Troops for Chad." *New York Times*, 12 July 1983.

"Doctor Describes 'Terror' Among Qaddafi Family." *New York Times,* 16 April 1986.

Drozdiak, William, and George Lardner Jr. "French Seek Four Libyans in Jet Bombing; One Suspect Also Linked to 1988 Pan Am Blast." *Washington Post,* 31 October 1991.

Dubois, Dorine. "The Attacks of 11 September: EU-US Cooperation Against Terrorism in the Field of Justice and Home Affairs." *European Foreign Affairs Review* 7 (2002): 317–35.

Dunne, Nancy, and Robert Corzine. "Politics Sets Tone for Trade Barriers." *Financial Times* (London), 25 July 1996.

Dunnigan, James. "Patterns of Islamic Terror." Strategy Page, 28 October 2004. <http://www.strategypage.com/dls/articles/2004102822.asp> (accessed 20 July 2005).

Eastern and Southern Africa Anti–Money Laundering Group. "Welcome." <http://www.esaamlg.org> (accessed 8 September 2006).

ElBaradei, Mohamed. "Nuclear Non-Proliferation: Global Security in a Rapidly Changing World." Statement, Carnegie International Non-Proliferation Conference, Washington, DC, 21 June 2004. International Atomic Energy Agency. <http://www.iaea.org/NewsCenter/Statements/2004/ebsp2004n004.html> (accessed 21 March 2005).

———. "Nuclear Security: Measures to Protect Against Nuclear Terrorism." Report by the director general to the International Atomic Energy Agency, Board of Governors General Conference, GOV/2004/50-GC(48)/6, Washington, DC, 11 August 2004. <http://www.globalsecurity.org/security/library/report/2004/gc48-6.pdf> (accessed 21 March 2005).

El-Kikhia, Mansour O. *Libya's Qaddafi: The Politics of Contradiction.* Jacksonville, FL: University of Florida Press, 1998.

Erlanger, Steven. "U.S. to Ask Wider Libya Ban If Trial Is Refused." *New York Times,* 25 August 1998.

"EU Charges House Iran Sanctions Legislation Violates WTO." *Inside U.S. Trade,* 9 February 1996.

European Commission. "Belonging to the European Union." *The Magazine: Education and Culture in Europe* 20 (2003). <http://europa.eu.int/comm/dgs/education_culture/mag/20/en.pdf> (accessed 6 September 2006).

———. *Communication from the Commission to the Council and the European Parliament of 16 June 2004: Towards Enhancing Access to Information by Law Enforcement Agencies.* COM(2004) 429 Final. Brussels, 16 June 2004. <http://europa.eu/scadplus/leg/en/lvb/l14151.htm> (accessed 1 August 2006).

———. "Eurojust Coordinating Cross-Border Prosecutions at EU Level." February 2005. <http://europa.eu.int/comm/justice_home/fsj/criminal/eurojust/fsj_criminal_eurojust_en.htm> (accessed 1 September 2006).

————. "European Arrest Warrant Replaces Extradition between EU Member States." <http://ec.europa.eu/justice_home/fsj/criminal/extradition/fsj_criminal _extradition_en.htm> (accessed 10 October 2006).

————. "European Commission Action Paper in Response to the Terrorist Attacks on Madrid." Memo/04/66. Brussels, 18 March 2004.

————. "Extradition and Surrender Procedures Across the EU." Brussels, updated May 2005. <http://europa.eu.int/comm/justice_home/fsj/criminal/ extradition/fsj_criminal_extradition_en.htm> (accessed 6 September 2006).

————. "The Fight Against Terrorism: The Commission Proposes Measures on the Exchange of Information and on the 'European Criminal Record.'" 30 March 2004. <http://europa.eu.int/rapid/start/cgi/guesten.ksh?p_action.gettxt =gt&doc=IP/04/425|0|RAPID&lg=EN&display=> (accessed 6 September 2006).

————. "The Hague Programme: Ten Priorities for the Next Five Years." Brussels, 1 August 2006. <http://ec.europa.eu/justice_home/news/information _dossiers/the_hague_priorities/index_en.htm> (accessed 5 September 2006).

————. *Instrument for Structural Policies for Pre-accession* (ISPA). Council Regulation 1267/99. Brussels, 21 June 1999.

————. "On Time, on Target: Training to Combat Organized Crime in Hungary." *Phare National Programmes Highlights* 4 (February 2000): 40.

————. *Proposal for a Council Framework Decision on Combating Terrorism.* 2001/0217 (CNS). Brussels, 19 September 2001.

European Commission, Permanent Representation of Sweden to the EU, and Permanent Representation of Austria to the EU. "The Enlargement Process and the Three Pre-Accession Instruments: Phare, ISPA, SAPARD." Proceedings of the Conference on Enlargement, 5 March 2001.

European Commission, PLS RAMBØLL Management, and Eureval–C3E. "PHARE Ex Post Evaluation of Country Support Implemented from 1997–1998 to 2000–2001: Consolidated Background Report," 3 April 2003. <http://europa .eu.int/comm/enlargement/phare_evaluation_pdf/consolidated_background _report_english.pdf> (accessed 3 April 2003).

European Union. *Declaration on Combating Terrorism. Council of the European Union Documents*, Brussels, 25 March 2004. <http://www.eu2004.ie/ templates/document_file.asp?id=10707> (accessed 8 September 2006).

————. *Supplementary Report by the European Union to the Committee Established Under Paragraph 6 of Security Council Resolution 1373 (2001).* Technical report no. S/2002/928. New York: UN, 2002.

European Union. Network of Independent Experts in Fundamental Rights. "The Balance Between Freedom and Security in the Response by the European Union and Its Member States to the Terrorist Threats." Thematic commentary prepared for the European Commission, Unit A5. "Citizenship, Charter of Fundamental Rights, Racism, Zenophobia, Daphne Program." DG Justice and Home Affairs, 31 March 2003. Statewatch, <http://www.statewatch.org/news/2003/apr/ CFR-CDF.ThemComment1.pdf> (accessed 6 September, 2006).

"Excerpt from the National Intelligence Estimate." *Washington Post*, 27 September 2006.

Feldman, Andreas, and Maftu Peraelae. "Reassessing the Causes of Nongovernmental Terrorism in Latin America." *American Politics and Society* 42, no. 2 (Summer 2004): 101–32.

Ferguson, Charles D. *Preventing Catastrophic Nuclear Terrorism*, Council on Foreign Relations Special Report No. 11. New York: Council on Foreign Relations Press, March 2006.

Ferguson, Charles D., Evan S. Medeiros, and Phillip C. Saunders. "Chinese Tactical Nuclear Weapons." In *Tactical Nuclear Weapons: Emerging Threats in an Evolving Security Environment*, edited by Brian Alexander and Alistair Millar, 110–26. Washington, DC: Brassey's, 2003.

Ferguson, Charles D., and William C. Potter et al. *The Four Faces of Nuclear Terrorism*. Monterey, CA: Monterey Institute of International Affairs, 2005.

Fidler, Stephen, and Mark Suzman. "Gadaffi Warily Backs Trial Plan." *Financial Times* (London), 28 August 1998.

Financial Action Task Force. *Annual Report 1996–1997*. Paris: Organisation for Economic Cooperation and Development, June 1997. <http://www .fatf-gafi.org>.

————. *Annual Report 2003–2004*. Paris: OECD, 2 July 2004.

————. *Annual Report 2003*. Paris: OECD, 20 June 2003.

————. *Annual Report 2004–2005*. Paris: OECD, 2005.

————. *Annual and Overall Review of Non-Cooperative Countries or Territories, 2005–2006*. Paris: OECD, 23 June 2006.

————. *Annual Review of Non-Cooperative Countries and Territories, 27 February 2004*. Paris: OECD, 27 February 2004.

————. *Annual Review of Non-Cooperative Countries or Territories 2003–2004*. Paris: OECD, 2 July 2004.

————. *Annual Review of Non-Cooperative Countries or Territories 2002–2003*. Paris: OECD, 10 June 2003.

————. "Developments in Non-Cooperative Countries and Territories." Press release, OECD, 7 September 2001.

————. "Combating the Abuse of Alternative Remittance Systems: International Best Practices." In *FATF Annual Report 2002–2003*, annex B. Paris: OECD, June 2003.

————. *FATF Decides to Impose Countermeasures Against Nauru*. Paris: OECD, 2001. <http://www.fatf-gafi.org>.

————. "FATF Intensifies Anti-Terrorist Financing Campaign." Press release, OECD, Paris, 3 October 2003. <http://www.fatf-gafi.org/dataoecd/43/32/33690944.pdf> (accessed 10 September 2006).

———. "Russia, Dominica, Niue, and Marshall Islands Removed from FATF's List of Non-Cooperative Countries and Territories." Press release, OECD, 11 October 2002. <http://www.fatf-gafi.org/dataoecd/45/31/33693981.pdf> (accessed 18 September 2006).

———. "FATF Tackles Terrorism Financing, Delists Guatemala." Press release, OECD, Paris, 2 July 2004. <http://www.fatf-gafi.org/dataoecd/29/36/33616642.pdf> (accessed 10 September 2006).

———. "FATF Withdraws Counter-Measures with Respect to Ukraine and Decides on Date for Counter-Measures to Philippines." Press release, OECD, 14 February 2003.

———. *Forty Recommendations of the FATF on Money Laundering (MF)*. Paris: OECD, 1990.

———. *Methodology for Assessing Compliance with Anti-Money Laundering Standards and Combating Terrorist Financing Standards*. Paris: OECD, 11 October 2002.

———. *Methodology for Assessing Compliance with the FATF Forty Recommendations and the FATF Nine Special Recommendations*. Paris: OECD, 27 February 2004.

———. *Money Laundering and Terrorist Financing Typologies 2004–2005*. Paris: OECD, 10 June 2005.

———. *Report on Non-Cooperative Countries or Territories*. Paris: OECD, 14 February 2000.

———. *Review to Identify Non-Cooperative Countries or Territories: Increasing the Worldwide Effectiveness of Anti–Money Laundering Measures 2001*. Paris: OECD, 22 June 2001.

———. *Review to Identify Non-Cooperative Countries or Territories: Increasing the World-Wide Effectiveness of Anti–Money Laundering Measures*. Paris: OECD, 21 June 2002.

———. *Special Recommendations on Terrorist Financing*. Paris: OECD, October 2001; revised 22 October 2004. <http://www.fatf-gafi.org/dataoecd/8/17/34849466.pdf> (accessed 1 September 2006).

Fingar, Thomas. "Current and Projected National Security Threats to the United States." Statement Before the Senate Select Committee on Intelligence, 109th Cong., 1st sess., Washington, DC, 16 February 2005.

Fishman, Charles. "For Missing Pilots' Relatives, 'the News Is Nothing Good.'" *Washington Post*, 16 April 1986.

Fisk, Robert. "In His Last Recorded Interview, Usama bin Laden Tells Robert Fisk Why He So Despises America," 6 December 1996. <http://www.robert-fisk.com/fisk_interview3.htm> (accessed 15 November 2004).

Flores, David A. "Export Controls and the U.S. Effort to Combat International Terrorism." *Law and Policy in International Business* 13 (1981): 521–90.

Frattini, Franco. "Internal and External Dimension of Fighting Terrorism." Speech at the Fourth Congress on European Defense. Berlin, 28 November 2005. European Union <http://europa.eu/rapid/pressReleaseAction.do?reference =SPEECH/05/735&format=HTML&aged=0&language=EN&guiLanguage=en> (accessed 1 August 2006).

Friedman, Thomas. "Connect the Dots." *New York Times*, 25 September 2003.

Fukuyama, Francis. "After Neo-Conservatism." *New York Times Magazine*, 19 February 2006.

Gabbitas, Andrea. "Non-Strategic Nuclear Weapons: Problems of Definition." In *Controlling Non-Strategic Nuclear Weapons: Obstacles and Opportunities*, edited by Jeffrey Larsen and Kurt Klingenberger, 23–38. Colorado Springs, CO: United States Air Force Academy and Institute for National Security Studies, 2001.

"Gaddafi Defies UN Sanctions with Trip to Nigeria." *The Independent* (London), 10 May 1997.

Gershman, John. *A Secure America in a Secure World*. Special Report of the Task Force on Terrorism. Washington, DC: Foreign Policy in Focus, September 2004. <http://www.fpif.org/papers/04terror/index_body.html> (accessed 18 September).

Getler, Michael. "U.S. Navy Fighters Shot Down Two Libyan Jets." *Washington Post*, 20 August 1981.

Glasser, Susan. "U.S. Figures Show Sharp Global Rise in Terrorism." *Washington Post*, 27 April 2005.

Global Security. "Operation Attain Document." *Global Security. org*, <http://www.globalsecurity.org/military/ops/attain_document.htm> (accessed 14 July 2005).

———. "Weapons of Mass Destruction (WMD): A. Q. Khan." <http://www.globalsecurity.org/wmd/world/pakistan/khan.htm> (accessed 18 March 2005).

Goshko, John M. "Libya Sanctions Debated at U.N.: Gadhafi's Backers Call Them Vindictive; Victims' Families Demand They Go On." *Washington Post*, 21 March 1998.

———. "OPEC Turns Down Libya's Request for Retaliation; Oil Companies Bow to Reagan's Wishes; Oil Firms Bow to President on Pullout." *Washington Post*, 12 December 1981.

Gowers, Andrew. "Crisis in the Gulf; Abu Nidal May Launch Attacks on U.S. Targets." *Financial Times* (London), 11 August 1990.

Gration, Jonathan S. "United States Assistance to Chad: Qadhafi-Bashing?" Paper written for National Security Policy Process, National War College, Fort McNair, Washington, DC, 18 December 1992. National Defense University Special Collections. <http://www.ndu.edu/library/n3/93-E-031.pdf> (accessed 14 July 2005).

Gray, Jerry. "Foreigners Investing in Libya or in Iran Face U.S. Sanctions," *New York Times*, late edition, 23 July 1996.

Greenberg, Karen. "From the Editor: European Counterterrorism and Its Implications for the U.S. War on Terror." *New York University Review of Law and Security* (Summer 2005): 2–3.

Greenberg, Maurice, William F. Wechsler, and Lee S. Wolosky. *Terrorist Financing: Independent Task Force Report*. Washington, DC: Brookings Institution, 2002.

Group of Eight. "G8 Statement on Strengthening the UN's Counter-Terrorism Program." St. Petersburg, Russia, 16 July 2006. <http://en.g8russia.ru/docs/18.html> (accessed 24 September 2006).

Gunaratna, Rohan, ed. *The Changing Face of Terrorism*. London: Easter Universities Press, 2004.

Gurr, Ted Robert. "Economic Factors." In *Addressing the Causes of Terrorism: The Club de Madrid Series on Democracy and Terrorism*. Proceedings of the International Summit on Democracy, Terrorism and Security, Club de Madrid, Madrid, Spain, 8–11 March 2005, vol. 1.

———. *Why Men Rebel*. Princeton, NJ: Princeton University Press, 1970.

Gurulé, Jimmy. "The Global Effort to Stop Terrorist Financing." *U.S. Foreign Policy Agenda* 8, no. 1 (2003): 21–24. <http://www.ciaonet.org.lib-proxy.nd.edu/olj/fpa/fpa_aug03_gurule.pdf> (accessed 20 September 2006).

———. "Locking Down Terrorist Finance." Lecture, University of Notre Dame, 5 April 2004.

Gwertzman, Bernard. "U.S. Expels Libyans and Closes Mission, Charging Terrorism." *New York Times*, 7 May 1981.

———. "Why Reagan Shuns Attack." *New York Times*, 8 January 1986.

Handler, Joshua. "The September 1991 PNIs and the Elimination, Storing, and Security Aspects of TNWs." Presentation at the Time to Control Tactical Nuclear Weapons seminar hosted by the United Nations Institute for Disarmament Research et al., New York, 24 September 2001. <http://www.princeton.edu/~globsec/publications/pdf/untalk.pdf> (accessed 18 March 2005).

Hanley, Charles J. "AP Survey: Experts See New Kind of War." Associated Press, 9 July 2005.

Hayden, Patrick et al., eds. *America's War on Terror*. London: Ashgate Press, 2003.

Hershey, Robert D., Jr. "U.S. Effort on Libya Oil Said to Gain." *New York Times*, 1 July 1986.

Hoagland, Jim. "Mitterand: U.S., France Are United on Essentials; French Leader, Reagan to Meet Wednesday." *Washington Post*, 29 June 1986.

Hoffman, Bruce. "Challenges for the U.S. Special Operations Command Posed by the Global Terrorist Threat: Al Qaeda on the Run or on the March?" Written testimony submitted to the House Armed Services Subcommittee on Terrorism, Unconventional Threats and Capabilities, 110th Cong., 1st sess., Washington, DC, 14 February 2007. House Armed Services Committee. <http://www.house.gov/hasc/hearing_information.shtml> (accessed 22 February 2007).

———. *Inside Terrorism.* Revised and expanded edition. New York: Columbia University Press, 2006.

———. "The Leadership Secrets of Osama bin Laden: The Terrorist as CEO." *Atlantic Monthly* 291, no. 3 (April 2003): 26.

Hoffman, David. "President Orders Freeze on Libyans' U.S. Assets: 'Hundreds of Millions' Affected, Official Says." *Washington Post*, 9 January 1986.

Hoge, Warren. "New Libyan Cooperation Leads to Renewed Ties with Britain." *New York Times*, 8 July 1999.

House, Karen Elliott. "U.S. Will End Libya Oil Buying, Technology Sales." *Wall Street Journal*, 11 March 1982.

Hoyt, Timothy D. "The Buddha Frowns? Tactical Nuclear Weapons in South Asia." In *Tactical Nuclear Weapons: Emerging Threats in an Evolving Security Environment*, edited by Brian Alexander and Alistair Millar, 95–109. Washington, DC: Brassey's, 2003.

Huband, Mark. "Lockerbie Bomb Suspects Will Face Trial, Says Libya Gadaffi in Pledge to Mandela on Hand-Over." *Financial Times* (London), 20 March 1999.

Hufbauer, Gary Clyde, Jeffrey J. Schott, and Kimberly Ann Elliott. *Economic Sanctions Reconsidered: History and Current Policy.* 2d ed. Washington, DC: Institute for International Economics, 1990.

Human Rights Watch. "Open Letter to the United Nations Counter-Terrorism Committee." 25 January 2005. <http://hrw.org/english/docs/2005/01/25/uzbeki10074_txt.htm> (accessed 8 September 2006).

Interfax. "Moscow Rally Calls to Prevent US Control Over Russian Nuclear Facilities." 20 February 2005.

International Atomic Energy Agency. "Budget and Finance." IAEA. <http://www.iaea.org/About/budget.html> (accessed 24 September 2006).

———. "Calculating the New Global Nuclear Terrorism Threat." Press release, 1 November 2001. <http://www.iaea.org/NewsCenter/PressReleases/2001/nt_pressrelease.shtml> (accessed 21 March 2005).

———. "IAEA Staff." IAEA. <http://www.iaea.org/About/staff.html> (accessed 24 September 2006).

———. "List of Confirmed Incidents Involving HEU or Pu." International Atomic Energy Agency. <http://www.iaea.org/NewsCenter/Features/RadSources/table1.html> (accessed 18 March 2005).

———. "Safeguards and Verification." IAEA. <http://www.iaea.org/OurWork/SV/Safeguards/sg-protocol.html> (accessed 22 April 2004).

Ibrahim, Youssef M. "Arab Militants Release Three After Qaddafi Intervenes." *New York Times*, 11 April 1990.

———. "Libya Denies Link to Airline Blasts." *New York Times*, 28 June 1991.

———. "Planned U.S. Sanctions Anger Europeans." *New York Times*, 25 July 1996.

International Institute for Strategic Studies. *The Military Balance 2003–2004*. Edited by Christopher Langton. London: Oxford University Press, 2003.

———. "Perspectives." Edited by Jonathan Stevenson. *Strategic Survey 2003/4* 104, no. 1. (May 2004): 6.

———. "Perspectives." Edited by Jonathan Stevenson. *Strategic Survey 2004/5* 105, no. 1 (May 2005): 10.

International Maritime Organization. "Status of Conventions by Country." IMO. <http://www.imo.org/Conventions/mainframe.asp?topic_id=248> (accessed 22 January 2007).

———. "Summary of Conventions." IMO. <http://www.imo.org/Conventions/mainframe.asp?topic_id=247> (accessed 22 January 2007).

"Iran and Israel: Chain Reaction." Editorial, *Christian Science Monitor*, 9 July 2004.

"Italy's ENI Has Deal with Libya." *Wall Street Journal*, 5 November 1996.

Ivanov, H. E. Igor S. *Statement to the Non-Proliferation Treaty 2000 Review Conference*, New York, April 25, 2000. Federation of American Scientists. <http://www.fas.org/nuke/control/npt/news/00_04_25.htm> (accessed 18 March 2005).

Jackson, Brian A., et al. *Aptitude for Destruction*. Vol. 1, *Organizational Learning in Terrorist Groups and Its Implications for Combating Terrorism*. Monograph prepared for the National Institute of Justice. Santa Monica, CA: RAND Corporation Monograph, 2005.

Jacoby, Vice Admiral Lowell E. "Current and Projected National Security Threats to the United States." Statement, Senate Select Committee on Intelligence, 109th Cong., 1st sess., Washington, DC, 16 February 2005.

Jasinski, Filip. "The European Union and Terrorism." *Polish Quarterly of International Affairs* 11, no. 2 (2002): 35–55.

Jentleson, Bruce W., and Christopher A. Whytock. "Who 'Won' Libya? The Force-Diplomacy Debate and Its Implications for Theory and Policy." *International Security* 30, no. 3 (Winter 2005–2006): 47–86.

Johnson, Haynes. "The Believe It or Not Show: On Libya, a New Standard of Incredibility." *Washington Post*, 8 December 1981.

Jönsson, Christer, and Jonas Tallberg. "Compliance and Post-Agreement Bargaining." *European Journal of International Relations* 4, no. 4 (1998): 371–408.

Joshi, Jitendra. "After Madrid, EU's Nascent Anti-Terror Strategy Under Focus." Agence France-Presse, 15 March 2004.

————. "EU Holds Emergency Terror Talks After Madrid Blasts." Agence France-Presse, 19 March 2004.

"Judges Find Libyan Guilty of Murder in Pan Am Bombing, Co-Defendant Acquitted in '88 Crash." *New York Times*, 1 February 2001.

Kaplan, Eben. "The Rise of Al-Qaedism." Background paper, Council on Foreign Relations, New York, 30 June 2006. <http://www.cfr.org/publication/11033/rise_of_alqaedism.html> (accessed 8 September 2006).

————. "Tracking Down Terrorist Financing." Background paper, Council on Foreign Relations, New York, 4 April 2006. <http://www.cfr.org/publication/10356/tracking_down_terrorist_financing.html> (accessed 10 October 2006).

Katz, Lee Michael. "Gadhafi Demands Negotiations Before Turning in Suspects." *USA Today*, 28 August 1998.

Keeble, Richard. "The Secret War Against Libya." N.d. *Medialens*. <http://www.medialens.org/articles/the_articles/articles_2002/rk_secret_war.html> (accessed 13 July 2005).

Kifner, John. "Hijacking in Karachi; Clues to Attackers Point in Confusing Directions." *New York Times*, 7 September 1986.

Kriesberg, Lewis. *Constructive Conflicts: From Escalation to Resolution.* 2d ed. Lanham, MD: Rowman and Littlefield, 2003.

Krueger, Alan. "Economic Scene." *New York Times*, 29 May 2002.

————. "Economic Scene." *New York Times*, 29 May 2003.

Krueger, Alan B., and Jitka Malesckova. "Education, Poverty and Terrorism: Is There a Causal Connection?" *Journal of Economic Perspectives* 17, no. 4 (Fall 2003): 119–44.

————. "Seeking the Roots of Terrorism." *Chronicle of Higher Education* 49, no. 39 (6 June 2003): B10.

Landler, Mark. "German 9/11 Retrial Gets Exculpatory Evidence from U.S." *New York Times,* 12 August 2004.

Lane, Charles et al. "In Baghdad, a Welcome Mat for Terrorists." *Newsweek*, 3 September 1990.

Lang, Cosmo Gordon, Archbishop of Canterbury. "Archbishop's Appeal: Individual Will and Action," *London Times,* 28 December 1937.

Lee, Rensselaer. "Nuclear Smuggling from the Former Soviet Union: Threats and Responses." *Global Beat*, 27 April 2001. <http://www.bu.edu/globalbeat/nuclear/FPRI042701.html> (accessed 25 August 2006).

Leser, Eric. "The Iraq Quagmire: The Endless War Against Terrorism." *Le Monde*, 14 November 2003.

Leverett, Flynt. "Why Libya Gave Up the Bomb." *New York Times,* 25 January 2004.

Lewis, Jeffrey. "Nuclear Numerology Chinese Style." Letter to the editor. *Arms Control Today* 35, no. 2 (March 2005).

Lippman, Thomas W. "Trade Ban Irks Libyans; Tripoli Prefers Boeings, but U.S. Won't Sell Them." *Washington Post*, 11 August 1978.

————. "U.S., Britain Announce Plan for Pan Am Trial; Libya Challenged to Deliver Bomb Suspects." *Washington Post*, 25 August 1998.

"Lockerbie Impasse in Libya." *The Independent* (London), 30 October 1997.

Locy, Toni. "Families Suing Libya over Pan Am Blast." *Washington Post*, 7 May 1996.

Lodge, Juliet. "Terrorism and the European Community: Towards 1992." *Terrorism and Political Violence* 1, no. 1 (January 1989): 28–47.

Luck, Edward C. "Tackling Terrorism." In *The United Nations Security Council: From the Cold War to the Twenty-first Century*, edited by David M. Malone, 85–100. Boulder, CO: Lynne Rienner, 2004.

————. "The Uninvited Challenge: Terrorism Targets the United Nations." In *Multilateralism Under Challenge: Power, International Order and Structural Change*, edited by Edward Newman, Ramesh Thakur, and John Tirman, 336–55. Tokyo: United Nations University and the Social Science Research Council, 2005. Available online from Center on International Organization, School of International and Public Affairs, Columbia University. <http://www.sipa.columbia.edu/cio/cio/projects/LuckSSRCUNU.pdf> (accessed 7 December 2005).

Lynch, Colum. "French Imperil Libyan Deal on Flight 103." *Washington Post*, 19 August 2003.

————. "U.N. Votes to Outlaw Nuclear Terrorism, No New Restrictions Put on Atomic Arms." *Washington Post*, 14 April 2005.

Mani, Rama. "The Root Causes of Terrorism and Conflict Prevention." In *Terrorism and the UN: Before and After September 11*, edited by Jane Boulden and Thomas G. Weiss, 219–42. Bloomington: Indiana University Press, 2004.

Marshall, Monty G. "Global Terrorism: An Overview and Analysis." In *Peace and Conflict 2005: A Global Survey of Armed Conflicts, Self-Determination Movements, and Democracy*, edited by Monty G. Marshall and Ted Robert Gurr, 62–73. College Park, MD: University of Maryland Center for International Development and Conflict Management, 2005. <http://www.cidcm.umd.edu/paper.asp?id=15> (accessed 18 July 2005).

Mazzetti, Mark. "Spy Agencies Say Iraq War Worsens Terror Threat." *New York Times*, 24 September 2006.

Mazzetti, Mark, and David Rohde. "Terror Officials See Qaeda Chiefs Regaining Power." *New York Times*, 19 February 2007.

McBride, Janet. "Libya Wins a Round in Pan Am 103 Case." *Washington Post*, 28 February 1998.

McIntyre, Jamie. "Zubaydah: Al Qaeda Had 'Dirty Bomb' Know-How." *CNN*, 22 April 2002. <http://archives.cnn.com/2002/US/04/22/Subaydah.dirty.bomb> (accessed 17 March 2005).

McNamara, Robert S. "Apocalypse Soon," *Foreign Policy* 148 (May–June 2005). <http://www.foreignpolicy.com/story/cms.php?story_id=2829> (accessed 24 August 2006).

Middle East and North Africa Financial Action Task Force (MENAFATF) against Money Laundering and Terrorist Financing. "Inaugural Ministerial Meeting of the Middle East and North Africa Financial Action Task Force (MENAFATF) against Money Laundering and Terrorist Financing." Press release, MENAFATF, Kingdom of Bahrain, 30 November 2004. <http://www.menafatf.org/ArticleDetail.asp?rid=548> (accessed 18 September 2006).

Milhollin, Gary. "Can Terrorists Get the Bomb?" *Commentary* 113, no. 2 (February 2002): 45–49.

Millar, Alistair, and Morten Bremer Maerli. "Nuclear Non-Proliferation and UNSC Resolution 1540." In *Policy Briefs on the Implementation of the Treaty on the Non-Proliferation of Nuclear Weapons*. Oslo: Norwegian Institute of International Affairs, 2005. <http://www.nupi.no/IPS/filestore/PolicyBriefsApril2005.pdf> (accessed 26 July 2005).

Miller, Judith. "In Rare Talks with Libyans, U.S. Airs View on Sanctions." *New York Times*, 12 June 1999.

Mir, Hamid. "Osama Claims He Has Nukes: If US Uses N-Arms, It Will Get Same Response." *Dawn*, 9 November 2001. <http://www.dawn.com/2001/11/10/top1.htm> (accessed 17 March 2005).

Mitchell, Ronald B. "Sources of Transparency: Information Systems in International Regimes." *International Studies Quarterly* 42, no. 1 (March 1998): 109–30.

Monblatt, Steven. "Developing Regional Cooperation." Statement of the Executive Secretary, Inter-American Committee Against Terrorism, Organization of American States, at the UN Counter-Terrorism Committee special meeting, Almaty, Kazakhstan, 26–27 January 2005.

Mossberg, Walter S. "U.S. Firms Urged to Bring Home Americans Who Have Jobs in Libya." *Wall Street Journal*, 11 December 1981.

Mueller, John. "Is There Still a Terrorist Threat?" *Foreign Affairs* 85, no. 5 (September–October 2006): 2–8.

Müller, Harold, and Annette Schaper. "Part II: Definitions, Types, Missions, Risks and Options for Control: A European Perspective." In *Tactical Nuclear Weapons: Options for Control*, edited by William Potter et al., 19–78. Geneva: United Nations, 2001.

Murphy Sean D., ed. "Contemporary Practice of the United States Relating to International Law: Multilateral Listing of States as Money-Laundering Havens." *American Journal of International Law* 94, no. 4 (October 2000): 695–96.

Myers, Joseph. "International Standards and Cooperation in the Fight against Money Laundering." *Economic Perspectives* 6, no. 2 (May 2001). Electronic journal, U.S. Department of State. <http://usinfo.state.gov/journals/ites/0501/ijee/treasury.htm> (accessed 20 September 2006).

Naftali, Timothy. *Blind Spot: The Secret History of American Counterterrorism.* Cambridge, MA: Basic/Perseus Books, 2005.

Nathan, Adam, and David Leppard. "Al-Qaeda's Men Held Secret Meetings to Build 'Dirty Bomb'." *Sunday Times* (London), 14 October 2001.

National Intelligence Council. *Annual Report to Congress on the Safety and Security of Russian Nuclear Facilities and Military Forces.* 108th Cong., 2d sess. Washington, DC, December 2004. <http://www.cia.gov/nic/special_russiannuke04.html> (accessed 18 March 2005).

———. *Title Classified.* ICA 2001-07HC. 22 October 2001.

National Memorial Institute for the Prevention of Terrorism Knowledge Base database (incorporates RAND Terrorism Chronology 1968–1997, RAND-MIPT Terrorism Incident Database 1998–present, the Terrorism Indictment Database of the University of Arkansas, and DFI International's research on terrorist organizations). <http://www.tkb.org/Home.jsp> (accessed 31 August 2006).

Newcomb, Richard R. "Targeted Financial Sanctions: The U.S. Model." In *Smart Sanctions: Targeting Economic Statecraft,* edited by David Cortright and George A. Lopez, 41–64. Boulder, CO: Rowman & Littlefield, 2002.

"Exposing the Libyan Link." *New York Times,* 21 June 1981.

"Trade Briefs: Sanctions on Libya Seen Behind Repatriation Plan." *New York Times,* 20 October 1995.

Norris, Robert S., William M. Arkin, Hans M. Kristensen, and Joshua Handler. "British Nuclear Forces, 2001." NRDC: Nuclear Notebook. *Bulletin of the Atomic Scientists* 57, no. 6 (November–December 2001): 78–79.

———. "French Nuclear Forces, 2001." NRDC: Nuclear Notebook. *Bulletin of the Atomic Scientists* 57, no. 4 (July–August 2001): 70–71. <http://www.thebulletin.org/article_nn.php?art_ofn=ja01norris>.

———. "Israeli Nuclear Forces, 2002." NRDC Nuclear Notebook. *Bulletin of the Atomic Scientists* 58, no. 5 (September–October 2002): 73–75. <http://www.thebulletin.org/article_nn.php?art_ofn=so02norris> (accessed 25 August 2006).

Norris, Robert S., and Hans M. Kristensen. "India's Nuclear Forces, 2005." NRDC: Nuclear Notebook. *Bulletin of the Atomic Scientists* 61, no. 5 (September–October 2005): 73–75. <http://www.thebulletin.org/article_nn.php?art_ofn=so05norris>.

———. "Russian Nuclear Forces, 2006." NRDC: Nuclear Notebook. *Bulletin of the Atomic Scientists* 62, no. 2 (March–April 2006): 64–67. <http://www.thebulletin.org/article_nn.php?art_ofn=ma06norris> (accessed 25 August 2006).

———. "U.S. Nuclear Weapons in Europe: 1954–2004." NRDC: Nuclear Notebook. *Bulletin of the Atomic Scientists* 60, no. 6 (November–December 2004): 76–77. <http://www.thebulletin.org/article_nn.php?art_ofn=nd04norris>.

———. "U.S. Nuclear Forces, 2005," *Bulletin of the Atomic Scientists* 61, no. 1 (January–February 2005): 73–75. <http://www.thebulletin.org/article_nn.php?art_ofn=jf05norris> (accessed 25 August 2006).

Norris, Robert S., Hans M. Kristensen, and Joshua Handler. "Pakistan's Nuclear Forces, 2001." *Bulletin of the Atomic Scientists* 58, no. 1 (January–February 2002): 70–71. <http://www.thebulletin.org/article_nn.php?art_ofn=jf02norris>.

Nunn, Sam. "The Race Between Cooperation and Catastrophe: Reducing the Global Nuclear Threat." Speech delivered at the National Press Club, Washington, DC, 9 March 2005. <http://www.ntinitiative.org/c_press/speech_nunnpressclub_030905.pdf> (accessed 17 March 2005).

Oberdorfer, Don. "Reagan Appeals to Allies Not to Thwart Sanctions." *Washington Post*, 10 January 1986.

Occhipinti, John D. *The Politics of EU Police Cooperation*. Boulder, CO: Lynne Rienner, 2003.

"Officials: Nuclear Strategy a Deterrent." 10 March 2002. *CBS News*. <http://www.cbsnews.com/stories/2002/03/13/national/main503608.shtml> (accessed 17 March 2005).

Organisation for Economic Co-operation and Development. *The Challenge of Capacity Development: Working Towards Good Practice*. DCD/DAC/GOVNET(2005)5/REV/1, DAC Network on Governance [GOVNET], Paris, 1 February 2006. <http://www.oecd.org> (accessed 12 September 2006).

———. *A Development Co-operation Lens on Terrorism Prevention: Key Entry Points for Action*. Paris: OECD Publications, 2003. <http://www.oecd.org> (accessed 12 September 2006).

———. *Helping Prevent Violent Conflict* (Paris: OECD Publications, 2001), 37. Available at <http://www.oecd.org> (accessed 12 September 2006).

Organisation of the Islamic Conference. *Convention on Combating International Terrorism*. Annex to Resolution no. 59/26P, completed at the Organisation of the Islamic Conference Convention on Combating International Terrorism, Ouagadougou, 1 July 1999. <http://www.oic-un.org/26icfm/c.html> (accessed 24 September 2006).

Organization of African Unity. *Convention on the Prevention and Combating of Terrorism*. Algiers, 14 July 1999.

Oudraat, Chantal de Jonge. "Combating Terrorism." *Washington Quarterly* 26, no. 4 (Autumn 2003): 163–76.

———. "The Role of the UN Security Council." In *Terrorism and the UN: Before and After September 11*, edited by Jane Boulden and Thomas G. Weiss, 151–72. Bloomington: Indiana University Press, 2004.

Pape, Robert. "Blowing Up an Assumption." *New York Times*, 18 May 2005.

————. *Dying to Win: The Strategic Logic of Suicide Terrorism*. New York: Random House, 2005.

Parrish, Scott, and William Potter. "Central Asian States Establish Nuclear-Weapons-Free-Zone Despite U.S. Opposition." Research story, Monterey Institute for International Studies, Center for Nonproliferation Studies, Monterey, CA, 8 September 2006.

Parker, Andrew, and Stephen Fidler. "Proposal for Libyans' Trial Unveiled." *Financial Times* (London), 25 August 1998.

Peers, Steve. "EU Responses to Terrorism." *International and Comparative Law Quarterly* 52 (2003): 227–28.

Perry, William J. Keynote Address at the Conference on Post–Cold War U.S. Nuclear Strategy: A Search for Technical and Policy Common Ground. Committee on International Security and Arms Control, National Academy of Sciences, Washington, DC, 11 August 2004. <http://www7.nationalacademies.org/cisac/Perry_Presentation.pdf>

Pike, John. "Nuclear Weapon Effects." In *Special Weapons Primer, Federation of American Scientists.* <http://www.fas.org/nuke/intro/nuke/effects.htm> (accessed 17 March 2005).

Pincus, Walter. "Pentagon Revises Nuclear Strike Plan Strategy; Includes Preemptive Use Against Banned Weapons." *Washington Post*, 11 September 2005.

Potter, William, and Nikolai Sokov. *Tactical Nuclear Weapons: The Nature of the Problem.* Monterey, CA: Monterey Institute of International Studies, 4 January 2001. Center for Nonproliferation Studies. <http://cns.miis.edu/pubs/reports/tnw_nat.htm> (accessed 18 March 2005).

Powell, Colin L. "U.S. Forces: Challenges Ahead." *Foreign Affairs* 71, no. 5 (Winter 1992–1993): 32–45.

Preparatory Committee of Austria, Sweden, and Ukraine. "Reductions of Non-Strategic Nuclear Weapons." Working paper prepared for Conference of the Parties to the Treaty on the Non-Proliferation of Nuclear Weapons, Third Session, New York, NPT/CONF.2005/PC.III/WP.13, 29 April 2004. Reaching Critical Will, <http://www.reachingcriticalwill.org/legal/npt/prepcom04/WPX.pdf> (accessed 7 July 2005).

Priest, Dana. "Iraq New Terror Breeding Ground; War Created Haven, CIA Advisers Report." *Washington Post*, 14 January 2005.

Priest, Dana, and Josh White. "War Helps Recruit Terrorists, Hill Told; Intelligence Officials Talk of Growing Insurgency." *Washington Post*, February 17, 2005.

Rauf, Tariq. *Towards NPT 2005: An Action Plan for the '13-Steps' Towards Nuclear Disarmament Agreed at NPT 2000.* Monterey, CA: Monterey Institute for International Studies, 2001. Center for Nonproliferation Studies. <http://www.cns.miis.edu/pubs/reports/pdfs/npt2005.pdf> (accessed 18 March 2005).

Reagan, Ronald. "Transcript of Address by Reagan on Libya." *New York Times*, 15 April 1986.

"Reagan's Response: U.S. Aircraft Attack Libyan Targets in Bid to Preempt Terrorism; Military Airport, Barracks Are Hit; President Vows Further Action If Needed." *Wall Street Journal*, 15 April 1986.

Record, Jeffrey. "Bounding the Global War on Terrorism." Monograph, Strategic Studies Institute of the U.S. Army War College, Carlisle, Pennsylvania, December 2003. <http://www.carlisle.army/mil/ssi> (accessed 4 January 2005).

Reuter, Peter, and Edwin M. Truman. *Chasing Dirty Money: The Fight Against Money Laundering*. Washington, DC: Institute for International Economics, 2004.

Reuters. "Chad Says Rebels Hold a Third of the Country." *New York Times*, 26 June 1983.

―――. "OAU Breaks Libya Sanctions." *The Guardian* (London), 10 June 1998.

―――. "Qaddafi Flies to Niger, in Defiance of U.N. Ban." *New York Times*, 9 May 1997.

―――. "UN Sanctions Prompt Gadaffi to Send Home One Million Africans." *Financial Times* (London), 19 October 1995.

―――. "Vatican Establishes Full Ties with Libya." *New York Times*, 11 March 1997.

Richter, Paul. "Tactical Devices Still Present Major Threat." *Los Angeles Times*, 25 May 2002.

Ricks, Thomas. *Fiasco: The American Military Adventure in Iraq*. New York: Penguin Press, 2006.

Riding, Alan. "Four Libyans Charged by France in Air Bombing." *New York Times*, 31 October 1991.

Rogers, Paul. *A War on Terror: Afghanistan and After*. London: Pluto Press, 2004.

Rosand, Eric. "Current Developments: Security Council Resolution 1373, the Counter-Terrorism Committee, and the Fight Against Terrorism." *American Journal of International Law* 97, no. 2 (April 2003): 335, 341.

―――"Current Developments: The Security Council's Efforts to Monitor the Implementation of Al Qaeda/Taliban Sanctions," *American Journal of International Law* 98 (2004): 745–63.

―――. "The Security Council as 'Global Legislator': Ultra Vires or Ultra Innovative." *Fordham International Law Journal* 28 (May 2005): 542, 542–90.

―――. "Security Council Resolution 1373 and the Counter-Terrorism Committee: The Cornerstone of the United Nations Contribution to the Fight Against Terrorism." In *Legal Instruments in the Fight Against International Terrorism: A Transatlantic Dialogue*, edited by Cyrille Fijnaut, Jan Wouters, and Frederik Naert, 603–32. Boston: Brill Academic, 2004.

————. "The UN Security Council's Counter-Terrorism Efforts." Presentation at the American Society of International Law Regional Centennial Meeting, San Francisco, 7 April 2005.

Rosenthal, Andrew. "U.S. Accuses Libya as Two Are Charged in Pan Am Bombing." *New York Times*, 15 November 1991.

Rostow, Nicholas. "Before and After: The Changed UN Response to Terrorism Since September 11th." *Cornell International Law Journal 95*, no. 3 (Winter 2002): 475, 482.

————. "Statement on the Work of the 1267 Committee, in the Security Council." USUN Press Release no. 136 (05), 20 July 2005. <http://www.un.int/usa/05_136.htm> (accessed 8 December 2005).

Rupérez, Javier. "A Response to the Recommendations for Improving the United Nations Counter-Terrorism Committee's Assessment and Assistance Coordination Function." Remarks, International Peace Academy Policy Forum on the Counter-Terrorism Committee/Counter-Terrorism Committee Directorate, New York, 22 November 2005.

Rubin, Barnett R. *Still Ours to Lose: Afghanistan on the Brink*. Prepared testimony for the House Committee on International Relations, 109th Cong., 2d. sess., 20 September 2006, and the Senate Committee on Foreign Relations, 21 September 2006.

"Sanctions on Libya Seen Behind Repatriation Plan." Journal of Commerce, Trade Briefs. *New York Times*, 20 October 1995.

Sageman, Marc. "Killing the Hydra: Only Attacks on Its Ideas Can Defeat a Network Like Al Qaeda." *Los Angeles Times*, 6 June 2004.

————. *Understanding Terror Networks*. Philadelphia: University of Pennsylvania Press, 2004.

————. "Sahel States Call for UN Inquiry into Sanctions on Libya." Agence France-Presse, 17 August 1997.

————. "South Africa Calls for Lifting of Sanctions on Libya." Agence France-Presse, 22 October 1997.

Sanger, David E. "In Face of Report, Iran Acknowledges Buying Nuclear Components." *New York Times*, 23 February 2004.

Scheuer, Michael. "Bin Laden Expert Steps Forward: Ex-CIA Agent Assesses Terror War in *60 Minutes* Interview." By Steve Kroft. *60 Minutes*, CBS, 14 November 2004. <http://www.cbsnews.com/stories/2004/11/12/60minutes/main655407.shtml> (accessed 24 August 2006).

Schmidt, Susan, and Walter Pincus. "Al Muhajir Alleged to Be Scouting Terror Sites; U.S. Says Al Qaeda Had Instructed Suspect." *Washington Post*, 12 June 2002.

Schmitt, Eric, and Thom Shanker. "New Name for 'War on Terror' Reflects Wider U.S. Campaign." *New York Times*, 26 July 2005.

Schmoll, Vincent. "Liechtenstein Dialogue on the Future of Financial Markets." Summary of remarks for focus group 2. <http: //www.dialogue.Li/0/Downloads/2005_referenten_summary_schmoll.pdf> (accessed 10 October 2006).

Schneider, Howard. "U.N. Chief, Gadhafi Meet on Suspects; Annan Praises Libyan's Commitment to Resolving 1998 Lockerbie Bombing Case." *Washington Post*, 6 December 1998.

Schott, Jeffrey J. *Trade Sanctions and U.S. Foreign Policy*. Washington, DC: Carnegie Endowment for International Peace, 14 September 1982.

Schumacher, Edward. "Libya a Week After Raid: Qaddafi Seems Firmly in Control." *New York Times*, 24 April 1986.

————. "Wide Damage Seen: Daughter of Qaddafi Is Said to Have Died." *New York Times*, 16 April 1986.

Sciolino, Elaine. "Abu Nidal Backing Is Said to Be Wide." *New York Times*, 19 January 1986.

"'Scoreboard' on Post-Madrid Counter-Terrorism Plans." Statewatch <http://www.statewatch.org/news/2004/mar/swscoreboard.pdf> (accessed 23 March 2004).

"Senate Approves Amended Iran Sanctions Bill That also Targets Libya." *Inside U.S. Trade*, 22 December 1995.

Serrano, Mónica. "The Political Economy of Terrorism." In *Terrorism and the UN: Before and After September 11*, edited by Jane Boulden and Thomas G. Weiss, 198–218. Bloomington: Indiana University Press, 2004.

Shelton, Dinah. "Introduction: Law, Non-Law and the Problem of 'Soft Law'." In *Commitment and Compliance: The Role of Non-Binding Norms in the International Legal Systems*, edited by Dinah Shelton, 1–20. Oxford: Oxford University Press, 2000.

Shenon, Philip. "A Decision Is Due Today from Libya." *New York Times*, 26 August 1998.

Shipler, David K. et al. "Trail of Mideast Terror: Seeking a Link to Libya." *New York Times*, 5 January 1986.

Shultz, George P. *Turmoil and Triumph: My Years as Secretary of State*. Woodbridge, CT: Charles Scribner's Sons, 1993.

Silke, Andrew. "An Introduction to Terrorism Research." In *Research on Terrorism: Trends, Achievements and Failures*, edited by Andrew Silke. London: Frank Cass, 2004.

Simmons, Beth. "International Efforts Against Money Laundering." In *Commitment and Compliance: The Role of Non-Binding Norms in the International Legal Systems*, edited by Dinah Shelton, 244–62. Oxford: Oxford University Press, 2000.

Slevin, Peter. "Libya Accepts Blame in Lockerbie Bombing, Letter on Flight 103 Is Bid to Ease Sanctions." *Washington Post*, 17 August 2003.

Smith, Craig S. "Libya and France Reach Agreement on Victim Compensation." *New York Times*, 12 September 2003.

Sokov, Nikolai. "CNS Analysis of the Russian Government's White Paper on WMD Nonproliferation." Monterey Institute for International Affairs, Center for Nonproliferation Studies, Monterey, CA, 25 July 2006. <http://cns.miis.edu/pubs/week/060726.htm> (accessed 8 August 2006).

———. "South Africa Calls for Lifting of Sanctions on Libya." Agence France-Presse, 22 October 1997.

Stares, Paul, and Monica Yacoubian. "Terrorism as a Virus." *Washington Post*, 23 August 2005.

Stepanova, Ekaterina. "War and Peace Building." *Washington Quarterly* 27, no. 4 (Autumn 2004): 128–29.

Stern, Jessica. "How America Created a Terrorist Haven." *New York Times*, 20 August 2003.

———. *Terror in the Name of God: Why Religious Militants Kill*. New York: Harper Collins, 2003.

Stevenson, Jonathan. "How Europe and America Defend Themselves." *Foreign Affairs* 82, no. 2 (March–April 2003): 75–90.

Stiles, Kendall W. "The Power of Procedure and the Procedures of the Powerful: Anti-Terror Law in the United Nations." *Journal of Peace Research* 43, no. 1 (January 2006): 37–54.

Talmon, Stefan. "The Security Council as World Legislature." *American Journal of International Law* 99 (January 2005): 175, 175–93.

"Tarnoff Presses House on Changes to Iran, Libya Sanctions Bill." *Inside U.S. Trade*, 10 May 1996, 16.

Taubman, Philip. "Libya Using U.S. Trucks to Haul Soviet Tanks." *New York Times*, 21 January 1982.

Telhami, Shibley. *The Stakes: America in the Middle East: The Consequences of Power and the Choice for Peace*. Updated ed. Boulder, CO: Westview Press, 2004.

"Text of State Department Report in Libya Under Qaddafi." *New York Times*, 9 January 1986.

Thieux, Laurence. "European Security and Global Terrorism: The Strategic Aftermath of the Madrid Bombings." *Perspectives: The Central European Review of International Affairs* 22 (Summer 2004): 59–74.

Townsend, Adam. "Can the EU Achieve an Area of Freedom, Security and Justice?" Opinion, Center for European Reform, October 2003. <http://www.cer.org.uk/pdf/opinion_at_jhaoct.pdf> (accessed 6 September 2006).

"Transcript of President Reagan's News Conference on Foreign and Domestic Issues." *New York Times*, 8 January 1986.

Tsoukala, Anastassia. "Democracy Against Security: The Debates About Coun-terterrorism in the European Parliament, September 2001–June 2003." *Alternatives: Global, Local, Political* 29, no. 4 (August–October 2004): 417–39.

United Nations. *Convention for the Suppression of Unlawful Acts Against the Safety of Civil Aviation.* Signed at Montreal on 23 January 1971. UN Treaty Collection. <http://untreaty.un.org/English/Terrorism.asp>.

———. "Conventions on Terrorism: Current Status of Multilateral Treaties on Terrorism Deposited with the Secretary-General." United Nations Treaty Collection <http://www.untreaty.un.org/English/terrorism.asp> (accessed 22 April 2004).

———. *Convention on Offences and Certain Other Acts Committed on Board Aircraft.* Tokyo, 14 September 1963. UN Treaty Collection. <http://untreaty .un.org/English/Terrorism.asp>.

———. *International Convention Against the Taking of Hostages.* Adopted on 17 December 1979. New York, 18 December 1979. <http://untreaty.un.org/ English/Terrorism.asp>.

———. *International Convention for the Suppression of Acts of Nuclear Terrorism.* New York, 14 September 2005.

———. *International Convention for the Suppression of Terrorist Bombings.* UN Treaty Collection. <http://untreaty.un.org/English/Terrorism.asp> (accessed 7 September 2006).

———. *International Convention for the Suppression of the Financing of Terrorism* (1999). UN Treaty Collection. <http://untreaty.un.org/English/ Terrorism.asp> (accessed 7 September 2006).

———. *International Convention for the Suppression of Unlawful Seizure of Aircraft.* Signed at The Hague on 16 December 1970. UN Treaty Collection. <http://untreaty.un.org/English/Terrorism.asp>.

———. *Second Report of the Monitoring Group Established Pursuant to Security Council Resolution 1363 (2001).* S/2003/1070. New York, 2 December 2003.

———. "Secretary-General Offers Global Strategy for Fighting Terrorism, in Address to Madrid Summit." SG/SM/9757. Madrid, 10 March 2005.

United Nations Counter-Terrorism Committee. "Facilitating the Provision of Technical Assistance." <http://www.un.org/Docs/sc/committees/1373/tat.html> (accessed 8 September 2006).

United Nations Counter-Terrorism Executive Directorate. "Framework for the Collection, Analysis, Development and Dissemination of Best Practices Relative to United Nations Security Council Resolutions 1373 (2001) and 1624 (2005)." Undated and unpublished report.

United Nations Economic and Social Council. *Promotion and Protection of Human Rights: Report of the Special Rapporteur on the promotion and protection of human rights and fundamental freedoms while countering terrorism, Martin Scheinin.* E/CN.4/2006/98. New York, 28 December 2005.

United Nations General Assembly. *Convention on the Prevention of Punishment of Crimes Against Internationally Protected Persons, Including Diplomatic Agents.* Resolution 3166 (XXVIII). New York, 14 December 1973.

———. *Declaration on Measures to Eliminate International Terrorism,* New York, 9 December 1994.

———. *Estimates in Respect of Special Political Missions, Good Offices and Other Political Initiatives Authorized by the General Assembly and/or the Security Council.* A/59/534/Add.1. New York, 23 November 2004.

———. "General Assembly Adopts Global Counter-Terrorism Strategy." Press release, unnumbered resolution, and plan of action. New York, 8 September 2006.

———. *In Larger Freedom: Towards Development, Security, and Human Rights for All.* A/59/2005, New York, 21 March 2005.

———. "Legal Committee Ends Discussion of Counter-Terrorism Measures; To Receive Group Report on Comprehensive Convention." Press release GA/L/3277. New York, 10 October 2005.

———. "Legal Committee, Reviewing Issues on Completion of Overall Anti-Terrorism Treaty, Notes Outstanding Differences." Press release GA/L/3275, New York, 10 June 2005.

———. *Measures to Eliminate International Terrorism.* A/RES/49/60. New York, 17 February 1995. <http://daccessdds.un.org/doc/UNDOC/GEN/N95/768/19/PDF/N9576819.pdf?OpenElement> (accessed 22 September 2006).

———. *A More Secure World: Our Shared Responsibility, Report of the Secretary-General's High-Level Panel on Threats, Challenges and Change.* A/59/565. New York, 29 November 2004.

———. *Reduction of Non-Strategic Nuclear Weapons.* A/RES/57/58. New York, 22 November 2002.

———. *Special Subjects and Questions Relating to the Programme Budget for the Biennium 2004–2005.* A/RES/59/29. New York, 31 August 2005.

———. *2005 World Summit Outcome.* A/RES/60/1. New York, 24 October 2005.

———. *Uniting Against Terrorism: Recommendations for a Global Counter-Terrorism Strategy.* A/60/825. New York, 27 April 2006.

United Nations General Assembly and Security Council. *Report of the Policy Working Group on the United Nations and Terrorism.* A/57/273, S/2002/875. New York, 6 August 2002.

United Nations Office of the High Commissioner for Human Rights. *Protection of Human Rights and Fundamental Freedoms While Countering Terrorism.* Human Rights Resolution 2005/80. <http://ap.ohchr.org/documents/E/CHR/resolutions/E-CN_4-RES-2005–80.doc> (accessed 8 September 2006).

———. "Terrorism." Office of the United Nations High Commissioner for Human Rights. <http://www.ohchr.org/english/issues/terrorism/index.htm> (accessed 8 September 2006).

United Nations Office on Drugs and Crime. "GPML Technical Assistance." UNODC.   <http://www.unodc.org/unodc/en/money_laundering_technical _assistance.html> (accessed 8 September 2006).

————. "Conventions Against Terrorism." UNODC. <http://www.unodc.org/ unodc/terrorism_conventions.html> (accessed 19 September 2006).

United Nations Office on Drugs and Crime, Terrorism Prevention Branch. *Delivering Counter-Terrorism Assistance.* Brochure, New York, April 2005. <http://www.unodc.org/pdf/crime/terrorism/Brochure_GPT_April2005.pdf> (accessed 8 September 2006).

United Nations Security Council. Analytical Support and Sanctions Monitoring Team. *First Report of the Analytical Support and Sanctions Monitoring Team Appointed Pursuant to Resolution 1526 (2004) Concerning Al-Qaida and the Taliban and Associated Individuals and Entities.* S/2004/679. New York, 25 August 2004.

————. *Third Report of the Analytical Support and Sanctions Monitoring Team Appointed Pursuant to Resolution 1526 (2004) Concerning Al-Qaida and the Taliban and Associated Individuals and Entities.* S/2005/572. New York, 9 September 2005.

————. *Fourth Report of the Analytical Support and Sanctions Monitoring Team Appointed Pursuant to Security Council Resolutions 1526 (2004) and 1617 (2005) Concerning Al-Qaida and the Taliban and Associated Individuals and Entities.* S/2006/154. New York, 10 March 2006.

————. *Fifth Report of the Analytic Support and Sanctions Monitoring Team Appointed Pursuant to Resolutions 1526 (2004) and 1617 (2005) Concerning A1-Qaida and the Taliban and Associated Individuals and Entities.* S/2006/750. New York, 20 September 2006.

————. *5229th Meeting.* S/PV.5229 (Resumption 1). New York, 20 July 2005. <http://daccessdds.un.org/doc/UNDOC/PRO/N05/431/30/PDF/N0543130.pdf? OpenElement> (accessed 24 September 2006).

————. *Programme of Work of the Security Council Committee Established Pursuant to Resolution 1540 (2004).* New York, 2006.

————. *Proposal for the Revitalisation of the Counter-Terrorism Committee.* S/2004/124. New York, 19 February 2004.

————. *Report of the Counter-Terrorism Committee to the Security Council for Its consideration as part of Its comprehensive review of the Counter-Terrorism Committee Executive Directorate.* S/2005/800. New York, 16 December 2005, par. 14.

————. *Reports by Chairs of Eight Subsidiary Bodies to the Security Council,* 5332nd Meeting (PM). SC/8591. New York, 19 December 2005. <http://www.un.org/News/Press/docs/2005/sc8591.doc.htm> (accessed 30 August 2006).

————. *Resolution 242 (1967).* S/RES/242. New York, 22 November 1967.

————. *Resolution 338 (1973)*. S/RES/338. New York, 22 October 1973.

————. *Resolution 487 (1981)*. S/RES/487. New York, 19 June 1981.

————. *Resolution 687 (1991)*. S/RES/687. New York, 3 April 1991.

————. *Resolution 731 (1992)*. S/RES/731. New York, 21 January 1992.

————. *Resolution 748 (1992)*. S/RES/748. New York, 31 March 1992.

————. *Resolution 883 (1993)*. S/RES/883. New York, 11 November 1993.

————. *Resolution 1054 (1996)*. S/RES/1054. New York, 26 April 1996.

————. *Resolution 1192 (1998)*. S/RES/1192. New York, 27 August 1998.

————. *Resolution 1267 (1999)*. S/RES/687. New York, 15 October 1999.

————. *Resolution 1373 (2001)*. S/RES/1373. New York, 28 September 2001.

————. *Resolution 1377 (2001)*. S/RES/1377. New York, 12 November 2001.

————. *Resolution 1390 (2002)*. S/RES/1390. New York, 28 January 2002.

————. *Resolution 1456 (2003)*. S/RES/1456. New York, 20 January 2003.

————. *Resolution 1526 (2004)*. S/RES/1535. New York, 30 January 2004.

————. *Resolution 1535 (2004)*. S/RES/1535. New York, 26 March 2004.

————. *Resolution 1540 (2004)*. S/RES/1540. New York, 28 April, 2004.

————. *Resolution 1566 (2004)*. S/RES/1566. New York, 1 October, 2004.

————. *Resolution 1617 (2005)*. [Peace and security—terrorist acts]. S/RES/1617. New York, 29 July 2005.

————. *Resolution 1624 (2005)*. S/RES/1624. New York, 14 September 2005.

————. *Resolution 1673 (2006)*. S/RES/1673. New York, 27 April 2006.

————. "Security Council Briefed by Chairmen of Three Anti-Terrorism Committees; Status of Reporting, Technical Assistance, Among Issues Addressed." Press release SC/8536. New York, 26 October 2005. <http://www.un.org/News/Press/docs/2005/sc8536.doc.htm> (accessed 24 September 2006).

————. "Security Council Extends for Two Years Mandate of Committee Monitoring Implementation of Resolution 1540 (2004) on Mass Destruction Weapons." Press release, SC8708. New York, 27 April 2006. <http://www.un.org/News/Press/docs/2006/sc8708.doc.htm> (accessed 24 September 2006).

————. "Security Council Reviews Work of Committees on Nuclear Non-Proliferation, Counter-Terrorism, Al-Qaida and Taliban." Press release, DC/8730. New York, 30 May 2006. <http://www.un.org/News/Press/docs/2006/sc8730.doc.htm> (accessed on 30 July 2006).

————. *Statement by the President of the Security Council*. S/PRST/2005/16. New York, 25 April 2005.

————. *Statement by the President of the Security Council*. S/PRST/2005/34. New York, 20 July 2005.

———. *Summaries Provided by Participants in the Counter-Terrorism Committee/Commonwealth of Independent States Special Meeting, 26 to 28 January 2005.* S/2005/87. New York, 14 February 2005.

———. "The 1267 (Al-Qaeda/Taliban) Committee and the 1540 (WMD) Sanctions Committee." Security Council Report, Update Report no. 5, 16 January 2006.

———. *Work Programme of the Counter-Terrorism Committee.* S/2005/663. New York, 21 October 2005.

United Nations Security Council Committee Established Pursuant to Resolution 1267 (1999) Concerning Al-Qaida and the Taliban and Associated Individuals and Entities. *The New Consolidated List of Individuals and Entities Belonging to or Associated with the Taliban and Al-Qaida Organisation as Established and Maintained by the 1267 Committee.* Updated 24 August 2006. <http://www.un.org/Docs/sc/committees/1267/1267ListEng.htm> (accessed 6 September 2006).

United States Congress. *Al Qaeda After the Iraq Conflict.* Report for Congress prepared by Audrey Kurth Cronin, 108th Cong., 1st sess., 23 May 2003, Committee Print Order Code RS 21529. <http://fpc.state.gov/documents/organization/21191.pdf> (accessed 2 February 2004).

———. *Europe and Counterterrorism: Strengthening Police and Judicial Cooperation.* Report for Congress prepared by Kristin Archick, 108th Cong., 2d sess., updated 23 August 2004, Committee Print Order Code RL31509.

———. *The Iran-Libya Sanctions Act (ILSA).* Report for Congress prepared by Kenneth Katzman, 109th Cong., 2d sess., updated 26 April 2006, Committee Print Order Code RS 20871. <http://fpc.state.gov/documents/organization/66441.pdf#search=%22%22edward%20Kennedy%22%20ILSA%22> (accessed 10 June 2006).

———. *Terrorists and Suicide Attacks.* Report for Congress prepared by Audrey Kurth Cronin, 108th Cong., 1st sess., 28 August 2003. <http://www.fas.org/irp/crs/RL32058.pdf> (accessed 1 September 2006).

———. *Trade Expansion Act of 1962.* Public Law 87–794, 87th Cong., 2d sess. 11 October 1962. 76 Stat. 872, sec. 232 as amended by (19 U.S.C. 1862) amendment 4907, sec. 1e, 10 March 1982.

United States Department of Defense. *Proliferation: Threat and Response.* 3d ed. Washington, DC: GPO, 10 January 2001.

United States Department of Defense, Office of the Under Secretary of Defense for Acquisition and Technology, Defense Science Board. "Organizing a DOD Response: A Major DOD Mission." In *The Defense Science Board 1997 Summer Study Task Force on DOD Responses to Transnational Threats,* vol. 1, final report. Washington, DC: October 1997. <http://www.acq.osd.mil/dsb/reports/trans.pdf> (accessed 1 September 2006).

United States Department of State. *Communiqué on Libya.* 10 June 1998.

———. *Country Reports on Terrorism 2005.* Washington, DC: GPO, 2006.

———. "Overview of State-Sponsored Terrorism." *Patterns of Global Terrorism–1996*. Washington, DC: GPO, 30 April 1996. Federation of American Scientists, <http://www.fas.org/irp/threat/terror_96/overview.html> (accessed 12 November 2005).

———. *Patterns of Global Terrorism–1985*. Washington, DC: GPO, 1986.

———. *Patterns of Global Terrorism–1986*. Washington, DC: GPO, 1987.

———. *Patterns of Global Terrorism–1989*. Washington, DC: GPO, 1990.

———. *Patterns of Global Terrorism–1990*. Washington, DC: GPO, 1991.

———. *Patterns of Global Terrorism–1991*. Washington, DC: GPO, 1992.

United States Department of State, Bureau for International Narcotics and Law Enforcement Affairs. *International Narcotics Control Strategy Report 2003*. Vol. 2, *Money Laundering and Financial Crimes*. Washington, DC: Bureau for International Narcotics and Law Enforcement Affairs, 1 March 2004.

United States Department of State, Bureau of Nonproliferation. "Proliferation Security Initiative Frequently Asked Questions (FAQ)" Fact Sheet. 11 January 2005. <http://www.state.gov/t/np/rls/fs/32725.htm> (accessed 21 March 2005).

United States Department of the Treasury. "Treasury Announces Joint Action with Saudi Arabia Against Four Branches of Al-Haramain in the Fight Against Terrorist Financing." Press release JS-1108. 22 January 2004. <http://www.treasury.gov/press/releases/js1108.htm> (accessed 6 September 2006).

United States Department of Treasury, Office of Public Affairs. "U.S. Designates Individual Tied to Attacks on European Tourists." Press release, JS-1043. 5 December 2003. <http://treas.gov/press/releases/js1043.htm> (accessed 24 September 2006).

United States General Accounting Office. *Libyan Trade Sanctions*. GAO/NSIAD-87-132BR. Washington, DC: GPO, May 1987.

———. *Nuclear Nonproliferation: U.S. Efforts to Help Other Countries Combat Nuclear Smuggling Need Strengthened Coordination and Planning*. GAO-02-426. Washington, DC: GAO, 2002.

———. *Terrorist Financing: U.S. Agencies Should Systematically Assess Terrorists' Use of Alternative Financing Mechanisms*. GAO-04-163, no. 24. Report to Congressional requesters, 108th Cong., 1st sess., Washington, DC, November 2003.

United States Institute of Peace. *American Interests and UN Reform: Report of the Task Force on the United Nations*. Report, 109th Cong., 1st sess. U.S. Institute of Peace, Washington, DC, 2005.

———. "Rethinking the War on Terror." Briefing, United States Institute of Peace, Washington, DC, September 2005.

———. "U.S. Intelligence Concludes Theft of Russian Nuclear Material 'Has Occurred.'" Agence France-Presse, 23 February 2005.

United States Mission to the United Nations. "Written Statement of the U.S. Delegation for Inclusion in the Record of the Briefing by the Chairs of the 1267 Al-Qaida/Taliban Sanctions Committee, the 1373 Counter Terrorism Committee, and the 1540 Committee on Non-Proliferation of Weapons of Mass Destruction, in the Security Council, April 25, 2005." USUN Press Release #80(05). New York, 25 April 2005. <http://www.un.int/usa/05_080.htm> (accessed 8 September 2006).

United States National Commission on Terrorist Attacks upon the United States. *Monograph on Terrorist Financing.* Staff report to the commission prepared by John Roth, Douglas Greenburg, and Serena Wille, 108th Cong., 2d sess., 2004, Committee Print.

———. *The 9/11 Commission Report, Final Report of the National Commission on Terrorist Attacks upon the United States.* New York: Norton, 2004.

———. *Overview of the Enemy,* Staff Statement No. 15. Presented at the twelfth public hearing of the National Commission on Terrorist Attacks upon the United States, 108th Cong., 2d sess., 16 June 2004. <http://www.9-11commission.gov/staff_statements/staff_statement_15.pdf> (accessed 1 September 2004).

Vandewalle, Dirk, *A History of Modern Libya.* New York: Cambridge University Press, 2006.

Vandewalle, Dirk, ed. *Qadhafi's Libya, 1969–1994.* London: Macmillan, 1995.

Vennemann, Nicola. "Country Report on the European Union." In *Terrorism as a Challenge for National and International Law: Security Versus Liberty?,* edited by Christian Walter, Frank Schorkopf, Silja Vöneky, and Volker Röben, 217–66. New York: Springer-Verlag, 2004. <http://edoc.mphil.de/conference-on-terrorism/index.cfm> (accessed 1 March 2004).

von Hippel, Karin. "Democracy by Force: A Renewed Commitment to Nation Building." In *The Battle for Hearts and Minds: Using Soft Power to Undermine Terrorist Networks,* edited by Alexander T. J. Lennon, 108–29. Cambridge, MA: MIT Press, 2003.

———. "Improving the International Response to the Transnational Terrorist Threat." In *Terrorism and the UN: Before and After September 11,* edited by Jane Boulden and Thomas G. Weiss, 102–19. Bloomington: Indiana University Press, 2004.

Wadhams, Nick. "UN General Assembly Adopts New Counterterrorism Strategy." *San Diego Union-Tribune,* 8 September 2006. <http://www.signonsandiego.com/news/nation/terror/20060908-1635-un-counter-terrorism.html> (accessed 9 September 2006).

Walcott, John. "Fast End to Mutual Hostility Unlikely as U.S. Reopens Dialogue with Syria." Washington Insight, *Wall Street Journal,* 6 July 1987.

Walker, William. "Weapons of Mass Destruction and International Order." Adelphi Paper 370, International Institute for Strategic Studies, London, November 2004.

Walt, Stephen M. *Taming American Power: The Global Response to U.S. Primacy*. New York: W. W. Norton, 2006.

Walt, Stephen M., and John J. Mearsheimer. "An Unnecessary War." *Foreign Policy* 134 (January–February 2003): 50–59.

Ward, Curtis A. "Purposes and Scope: Technical Assistance Activities in the Counter-Terrorism Committee." Unpublished paper, 2004.

Watson, Rory. "Brussels Backs Creation of Anti-Terror Czar." *Times* (London), 19 March 2004.

Weapons of Mass Destruction Commission. "Reviving Disarmament," in *Weapons of Terror: Freeing the World of Nuclear, Biological and Chemical Arms*. Stockholm: Weapons of Mass Destruction Commission, 2006. <http://www.wmdcommission.org/files/Weapons_of_Terror.pdf> (accessed 23 August 2006).

Weinberger, Caspar W. *Fighting for Peace: Seven Critical Years in the Pentagon*. New York: Warner Books, 1990.

———. "The Uses of Military Power." Speech given at the National Press Club, Washington, DC, 28 November 1984. Airforce Magazine online <http://www.afa.org/magazine/Jan2004/0104keeperfull.asp> (accessed 24 September 2006).

Weintraub, Bernard. "Terrorists Train at Fifteen Libyan Sites, U.S. Officials say." *New York Times*, 6 January 1986.

———. "Response to Terrorism: How President Decided." *New York Times*, 12 January 1986.

Weiss, Edith Brown, and Harold K. Jacobson, eds. *Engaging Countries: Strengthening Compliance with International Environmental Accords*. Cambridge, MA: MIT Press, 2000.

Weldon, Rep. Curt. "Opening Statement of the Chairman, Military Research and Development Subcommittee, at the Hearing on Nuclear Terrorism and Countermeasures." Remarks before the House Committee on National Security, Military Research and Development Subcommittee, 105th Cong., 1st sess., 1 October 1997, Terrorism Research Center. <http://www.terrorism.org/modules.php?op=modload&name=News&file=article&sid=5695> (accessed 20 May 2005).

White House. *The National Security Strategy of the United States of America*. Washington, DC: GPO, September 2002.

———. *National Strategy for Combating Terrorism*. Washington, DC: GPO, September 2006.

———. "Overview of America's International Strategy." In *The National Security Strategy of the United States of America*, 1–2. Washington, DC: GPO, September 2006.

White House. *Progress Report on the Global War on Terrorism*. Washington, DC: GPO, September 2003. <http://www.whitehouse.gov/homeland/progress/progress_report_0903.pdf> (accessed 2 February 2004).

Whitlock, Craig. "Germany Arrests Two Al-Qaeda Suspects; Men Accused of Planning Attacks in Iraq." *Washington Post,* 24 January 2005.

Whitney, Craig R. "Europe Gives Cold Shoulder to Clinton on Cuba Law." *New York Times,* 18 July 1996.

———. "France: Libya Pays for Bombing Plane." *New York Times,* 17 July 1999.

———. "World Court Claims Jurisdiction in Pan Am Flight 103 Case." *New York Times,* 28 February 1998.

Wielaard, Robert. "EU Proposes Terrorist Database Following Madrid Bombings, Criticizes Foot-Dragging Since Sept. 11." Associated Press, 18 March 2004.

Wikipedia. s.v. "Pan Am Flight 103." <http://en.wikipedia.org/wiki/Pan_Am_flight_103> (accessed 20 July 2004).

———. s.v. "Pan Am Flight 73." <http://en.wikipedia.org/wiki/Pan_Am _Flight_73> (accessed 20 July 2005).

Wilkinson, Paul. *Terrorism and the Liberal State.* London: Macmillan, 1986.

———. *Terrorism Versus Democracy: The Liberal State Response.* London: Frank Cass, 2003.

Wilson, George C. "Qaddafi Was a Target of U.S. Raid; 'Hoped We'd Get Him,' Official Says;' At Least One Jet Aimed at Compound." *Washington Post,* 18 April 1986.

Wilson, George C., and David Hoffman. "U.S. Ends Naval Exercises off Libya." *Washington Post,* 28 March 1986.

Wilton, Dave. *Etymologies and Word Origins,* s.v. "weapons of mass destruction." <http://www.wordorigins.org/wordorw.htm> (accessed 15 June 2005).

Woodward, Bob. *Veil: The Secret Wars of the CIA, 1981–1987.* New York: Simon and Schuster, 1987.

Woodward, Bob, and Barbara Feinman. "CIA Anti-Qaddafi Plan Backed: Reagan Authorized Covert Operation to Undermine Libyan Regime." *Washington Post,* 3 November 1985.

"Working Paper on Reductions of Non-Strategic Nuclear Weapons." Working paper submitted by the representatives of Austria, Sweden, and Ukraine to the Third [2004] Preparatory Committee for the 2005 Review Conference of the NPT. NPT/CONF. 2005/PC.III/WP.13. New York, 29 April 2004.

Yost, David. "Russia and Arms Control for Non Strategic Forces," in *Controlling Non-Strategic Nuclear Weapons: Obstacles and Opportunities,* edited by Jeffrey Larsen and Kurt Klingenberger, 133–37. Colorado Springs, CO: United States Air Force Academy and Institute for National Security Studies, 2001.

Yusufzai, Rahimullah. "Wrath of God: Osama bin Laden Lashes Out Against the West" (interview). *Time Asia,* 11 January 1999. <http://www.time.com/time/asia/asia/magazine/1999/990111/osama1.html> (accessed 24 August 2006).

Zagari, M. P. M. "Combating Terrorism: Report to the Committee of Legal Affairs and Citizens' Rights of the European Parliament." *Terrorism and Political Violence* 4, no. 4 (Winter 1992): 288–300.

About the Authors

Stephanie Ahern currently serves as professor of social science at the United States Military Academy. Her research interests focus primarily on military interventions and organizational learning. She also has an interest in the European Union.

Oldrich Bures is on the faculty of political science and European studies at Palacky University, the Czech Republic. His research focuses on conflict resolution and international security, emphasizing United Nations peacekeeping operations, private military companies, and EU counterterrorism policy. His recent work is published in various periodicals, including the *Journal of Terrorism, Violence and Insurgency*, and *International Peacekeeping*.

David Cortright is president of the Fourth Freedom Forum in Goshen, Indiana, and a research fellow at the Joan B. Kroc Institute for International Peace Studies at the University of Notre Dame. He has served as consultant or adviser to various governments and agencies of the United Nations, the Carnegie Commission on Preventing Deadly Conflict, and the International Peace Academy. He has written widely on counterterrorism, nuclear disarmament, nonviolent social change, and the use of incentives and sanctions as tools of international peacemaking.

Linda Gerber-Stellingwerf is research director of the Fourth Freedom Forum. She received her master of library science degree from the School of Library and Information Science at Indiana University, Bloomington. She participates in the joint Fourth Freedom Forum/Kroc Institute Sanctions and Security Project and has helped write and edit various reports and books produced by the Fourth Freedom Forum. She is a member of the American Library Association.

Lee H. Hamilton is director of the Woodrow Wilson International Center for Scholars in Washington and the Center on Congress at Indiana University. He served for thirty-four years as a U.S. representative from Indiana's 9th district, during which time he was chairman and ranking member of the House Committee on Foreign Affairs. Recently, he was vice-chairman of the 9/11 Commission and co-chairman of the Iraq Study Group.

Jason Ipe is a research associate at the Center on Global Counter-Terrorism Cooperation in Washington, D.C. He has provided research and written contributions to numerous book chapters and reports on issues of counter-terrorism, money laundering, terrorist financing, and nonproliferation. He received his B.A. in international relations from Connecticut College in New London, Connecticut, and his master of arts degree in international security policy from the Elliott School of International Affairs at The George Washington University in Washington, D.C.

Kathryn L. Gardner is completing a Ph.D. in the department of political science at the University of Notre Dame. She is interested in compliance issues generally as well as the theoretical application of compliance theories, counter-terrorism, and Islamic movements. Her research on the Financial Action Task Force has been published in *Global Governance.*

George A. Lopez is the Reverend Theodore M. Hesburgh, CSC Professor of Peace Studies at the Joan B. Kroc Institute for International Peace Studies at the University of Notre Dame. His coauthored book with David Cortright, *The Sanctions Decade: Assessing UN Strategies in the 1990s,* was named a Choice Outstanding Book in 2000. His work on political violence has been published in *International Studies Quarterly,* the *Bulletin of the Atomic Scientists, Human Rights Quarterly,* and other journals.

Thomas E. McNamara, a career diplomat, is a senior official in the Office of the Director of National Intelligence and an adjunct professor at The George Washington University. After September 11, 2001, he served as the secretary of state's senior adviser for terrorism and homeland security. His career has included service as assistant secretary of state, special negotiator for Panama, ambassador-at-large for counter terrorism, special assistant to the president, ambassador to Colombia, National Security Council director, and other senior positions. He has extensive experience in political-military affairs, counter-terrorism, and counter narcotics, and also in Latin American, Middle Eastern, African, European, and Russian affairs. His lectures and writings on security issues are extensive. He has appeared on *The NewsHour*, NPR, other major networks, Univision, and on talk radio programs.

Alistair Millar is vice president and director of the Washington, D.C., office of the Fourth Freedom Forum and director of the Center on Global Counter-Terrorism Cooperation. He has written several articles and reports on sanctions, incentives, and nuclear nonproliferation. He edited *Tactical Nuclear Weapons: Emergent Threats in an Evolving Security Environment* (2003). Millar also teaches at the Elliott School of International Affairs at The George Washington University in Washington, D.C., and he is a Ph.D. candidate at the University of Bradford in the UK.

Eric Rosand is currently a senior fellow at the Center on Global Counter-Terrorism Cooperation. Previously he served in the U.S. Department of State for nearly nine years. Most recently, he was chief of the Multilateral Affairs Unit in the Department of State's Office of the Counterterrorism Coordinator, where he was responsible for developing and coordinating the U.S. government's counter-terrorism policies at the UN and other multilateral institutions.

From 2002 to 2005 he was the deputy legal counselor at the U.S. Mission to the UN, where he served as the mission's counter-terrorism expert and representative to the Security Council's Counter-Terrorism Committee and General Assembly's Ad Hoc Committee on Terrorism.

He has been intimately involved in nearly all of the major counter-terrorism developments at the UN since September 11, 2001. Prior to that he served as a lawyer at the Department of State, where he worked on rule-of-law issues in Bosnia and Holocaust-era compensation and restitution issues. He is the author of numerous articles and book chapters on the appropriate role for the UN in the counter-terrorism campaign. He is coauthor with Alistair Millar of *Allied Against Terrorism: What's Needed to Strengthen Worldwide Commitment* (2006).

Index

Abu Nidal Organization (ANO),
88–90, 93–95, 100
Ackerman, Gary, 149n19
Action Plan of the European Council,
191
Action Plan for Freedom, Justice, and
Security, 219–220
Ad Hoc Committee on Terrorism
(United Nations), 53
Afghanistan, 1, 21n23, 125, 239
Al-Qaida and, 129
Bush administration and, 3
failed governance and, 257
ideology and, 6
Soviet invasion of, 248
UN sanctions and, 9
U.S. military and, 241
Afghan war, 5, 84
African National Congress (ANC),
109
African Union (AU), 53
Ahern, Stephanie, 17–18, 187–236
Air-Sol Moyenne Porté (ASMPs),
136t5.4nf
Albania, 26
Albright, Madeleine, 110
Allison, Graham, 130
Al-Meghrahi, Abdel Basset, 111
Al-Qaida, vii–ix, 237
Afghanistan and, 129
anti-Americanism and, 245
asset seizures and, 210–211
bargaining with, 264–265

bombings and, 51
Bush administration and, 3
countering hegemony and,
247–250
failed governance and, 257
human rights and, 258
jihadist ideology and, 5–6, 240,
243–244
leader deaths of, 240
Madrid bombings and, 187
military pressures on, 240–241
money laundering and, 160,
170–171
political grievances of, 244–246
reducing allies of, 264
sanctions and, 41–42, 45–46,
57–58, 61–62, 67, 241
social dynamics of, 250–252
strengthening of, 1
structure of, 2, 239–240
trained reserve of, 241–242
understanding, 239–243
weapons of mass destruction
(WMD) and, 15–16, 124–131,
146, 244
winning strategies for, 261–266
Al-Qaida/Taliban Sanctions
Committee (United Nations), 43,
45–46, 57–58, 61–62
Al-Qaida/Taliban Sanctions
Monitoring Team (United Nations),
3, 13, 36
Amman, 1

Analysis work files (AWFs) (European Union), 196
Analytic Support and Sanctions Monitoring Team (United Nations), 42–43, 57, 241
Annan, Kofi, 10–11, 18, 36, 111, 238
    on civil liberties, 37, 258–261
    priority alignment and, 264
    suicide bombers and, 247
    on United Nations Counter-Terrorism Committee (CTC), 23–24
Anti–money laundering (AML). *See* Money laundering
Aouzou Strip, 87
Archick, Kristin, 196
Asia-Pacific Economic Cooperation (APEC), 40
Asia/Pacific Group on Money Laundering (APG), 182n38
Aslan, Reza, 244
Asset seizures, 58, 78n20, 233n120, 240–241
    Al-Qaida and, 210–211
    Common Position and, 208–210
    European Union and, 208–212
    Financial Action Task Force (FATF) and, 158–161
    Taliban and, 210
    United States and, 211
Association of Southeast Asian Nations (ASEAN), 40
Australia, 143
Austria, 88–89, 94, 217

Baathists, 256
Baker, Howard, 130–131
Bali, 160, 243
Bank of England, 210
Basel Committee on Banking Supervision (BCBS), 32
Basque Fatherland and Liberty (ETA), 208
Belgium, 143, 217
Benjamin, Daniel, 4, 36, 241, 262

Beslan massacre, 13, 58, 243, 259–260
Binalshibh, Ramzi, 7
bin Laden, Osama, vii, 57, 220, 239, 241
    anti-Americanism and, 245
    bargaining with, 264–265
    countering hegemony and, 247–250
    fatwa and, 126t5.1, 248
    political grievances of, 244–246
    Saudi rebuff and, 248
    training camps of, 242
    wealth of, 253
    weapons of mass destruction (WMD) and, 125–128
Black September, 96
Blair, Tony, 74, 253
Blix, Hans, 123
Blunkett, David, 217, 219
Bolton, John, 142, 154n54
Bombings, 1, 124
    Al-Qaida and, 51
    Amman and, 1
    Bali and, 160
    financial costs of, 160, 241, 251
    Germany and, 89–90, 93, 124
    Hague Programme and, 219–220
    international law and, 53–54
    Libya and, 89–90
    Lockerbie families and, 110–111
    London and, 1, 160, 240, 243
    Madrid and, 160, 187, 199, 202–203, 206–207, 211, 216–220, 240, 243
    Pan Am flight 73 and, 93–95
    Pan Am flight 103 and, 9, 51, 95, 98–102, 107–112
    Sharm el-Sheikh and, 1
    suicide logic and, 246–247
    U.S. barracks and, 96–97
    U.S. embassies and, 51, 160, 243
    USS Cole and, 160
    UTA flight 772 and, 9, 51, 99–101, 111–112
Boogerd-Quaak, Johanna, 222
Brazil, 152n38

Brussels, 188, 198, 216
Bures, Oldrich, 17–18, 187–236
Burkina Faso, 108
Bush, George H. W., 14
 Libya and, 83, 98, 100–102,
 113–114
 Presidential Nuclear Initiatives
 (PNIs) and, 134, 138
Bush, George W., 2, 74, 263
 European arrest warrant (EAW) and,
 196
 global war on terror and, 4
 Libya and, 114
 military emphasis of, 4–5
 multilateral coalition and, 3–4
 National Security Strategy and, 253,
 256
 *National Strategy for Combating
 Terrorism* and, 6
 poverty and, 253
 United Nations and, 8–9
 "war on terror" metaphor and, 4

Camp David, 84–85, 243
Canada, 92
Candidate countries (CCs), 188
Caribbean Community (CARICOM),
 80n26
Caribbean Financial Action Task
 Force (CFATF), 40
Carly, Christian, 247
Carter, Jimmy, 84–86
Casey, William, 87, 115n15
Castro, Fidel, 254
Center for Nonproliferation Studies,
 139
Central Asian Nuclear Weapons Free
 Zone, 140
Centre for Defence Studies, 5
Chad, 86–88, 99, 108
Charities, 180
Chatham House, 257
Chechnya, 131, 247
Che Guevara, 254
Chesterman, Simon, 64
China, 56, 103, 124

Chirac, Jacques, 107
Civil liberties, 6, 37
 defining terrorism and, 204–208
 failed governance and, 256–257
 Geneva Conventions and, 205–206
 Patriot Act and, 260
 poverty and, 252–256
 Putin and, 260
 terrorist societies and, 257–261
 United Nations and, 11
Clinton, Bill, 107, 114, 138
Cohen, William, 148n8
Collier, Paul, 254
Colombia, 209
Common Foreign and Security Policy
 (CFSP) (European Union), 228n59,
 229n64
Common Position, 208–210
Commonwealth of Independent States
 (CIS), 40
Commonwealth Secretariat, 39
"Communication on the Fight
 Against Terrorism" (European
 Commission), 202
Communism, viii
Confrontation Arabs, 85
Consolidated List of Financial
 Sanctions Targets in the UK, 210
Consolidation issues, 66–71
Convention on Simplified Extradition
 Procedures Between Member States
 of the European Union, 190
Convention on the Physical
 Protection of Nuclear Materials,
 144
Convention Relating to Extradition
 Between Member States of the
 European Union, 190
Cook, Robin, 110
Cooperative Threat Reduction (CTR),
 133
Cortright, David, viii
 strategic counter-terrorism and, 1–22
 United Nations Counter-Terrorism
 Committee (CTC) and, 23–50
 winning policies and, 237–274

Costa Rica, 14, 64, 70
Council of Europe, 188
Select Committee of Experts on the
Evaluation of Anti–Money
Laundering Measures
(MONEYVAL) and, 182n38
Council on Foreign Relations, 14, 74
Counter-Terrorism Action Group
(CTAG), 39
Counter-terrorism financing (CTF).
See Financial Action Task Force
(FATF)
Counter-terrorism policy options,
262t8.1, 263t8.2
Counter-terrorism strategies, vii–x
assessment of, 261–263
bilateral confrontation and, 85–98
coalitions and, 4
countering hegemony and, 247–250
current debate over, 3–6
European Union and, 196–200,
208–212 (see also European
Union)
FATF and, 157–179 (see also
Financial Action Task Force
(FATF))
"go it alone" approach and, 6–7
increased extremism and, 1
institutional approaches and, 6–9
international law and, 51–76
knowing enemy and, 239–243
law enforcement and, 1–2, 7 (see
also Law enforcement)
Libyan case study and, 83–114
military and, 4–5 (see also Military)
multilateral approach and, 2–9, 19,
98–114
new terrorism and, 243–244
regional approaches and, 6–9
tools and, viii-ix
unilateral approach and, 102–105
United Nations and, 1, 3, 9–11, 23
(see also United Nations)
"war on terror" metaphor and, 4
weapons of mass destruction
(WMD) and, 123–147

Counter Terrorism Task Force
(CTTF) (Asia-Pacific Economic
Co-operation), 197
Country Reports on Terrorism (U.S.
State Department), 242
Crenshaw, Martha, 6
Cronin, Audrey Kurth, 250
Cuba, 106
Customer due diligence (CDD), 161
Cuthbertson, Ian, 207
Cutler, Lloyd, 130–131
Cyberterrorism, 149n18
Cyprus, 212
Czech Republic, 143, 212

Dar-es-Salaam, 243
"Declaration of Holy War on the
Americans Occupying the Country
of the Two Holy Places" (fatwa),
248
Declaration on Combating Terrorism
(European Council), 40
Declaration on Measures to Eliminate
International Terrorism (United
Nations), 53
Defense Intelligence Agency, 125
Democracy, 266
den Boer, Monica, 191
Denmark, 143
Development aid, 37–39
Djibouti, 103
Dublin Agreement, 188–189
Dubois, Dorine, 192, 206, 208
Dying to Win (Pape), 247

Eastern and Southern Africa Anti–
Money Laundering Group
(ESAAMLG), 182n38
Egypt, 53, 99, 105, 109
Abu Nidal Organization and, 89
Libya and, 85
Sadat and, 85
weapons of mass destruction
(WMD) and, 141, 152n38
Eight Special Recommendations on
Terrorist Financing (FATF), 163

ElBaradei, Mohamed, 142, 144–145
ELF, 107
el-Motassadeq, Mounir, 7–8
Estonia, 212
Eurasian Group on Combating
Money Laundering and Financing
of Terrorism (EAG), 182n38
Europe Agreements, 213–214, 216
European arrest warrant (EAW),
17–18, 192–196
European Commission
"Action Paper in Response to
Terrorist Attacks on Madrid," 203,
206–207, 211
European Judicial Network (EJN)
and, 230n76
Libya and, 102–105
Regulation No. 2580/2001 and, 208
European Convention on the
Suppression of Terrorism (ECST),
188–190
European Council, 40
Action Plan of the, 191, 219–220
European arrest warrant (EAW) and,
192–196
Europol and, 196–200
Madrid bombings and, 218
European Court of Justice (ECJ), 202
European Judicial Cooperation Unit
(Eurojust), 187–188, 200–203
European Police (Europol), 187–188,
190, 196–200
European Political Cooperation
(EPC), 188
Single European Act (SEA) and,
227n1
European Union (EU), 2–3, 12, 17
Abu Nidal Organization and, 88–89
acquis communautaire approach
and, 213–216, 233n125
Action Plan of the European
Council and, 191, 219–220
air base use of, 8
Anti-fraud Office and, 201
asset seizures and, 208–212,
233n120

candidate countries and, 188
Common Position and, 208–210
Convention on Simplified
Extradition Procedures Between
Member States of the European
Union and, 190
Convention Relating to Extradition
Between Member States of the
European Union and, 190
Counter-Terrorism Group (CTG)
and, 228n59
Counter Terrorism Task Force
(CTTF) and, 197
defining terrorism and, 187–189,
204–208
Dublin Agreement and, 188–189
enlarging cooperation in, 212–216
Eurojust and, 187–188, 200–203
Europol and, 187–188, 190,
196–200
Europol Drugs Unit (EDU) and,
190
former candidate countries (FCCs)
and, 212–216, 233n123
Framework Decision and, 193–197,
204–207, 221
Hague Programme and, 219–220
institutional approach of, 7–9
Iran and Libya Sanctions Act (ILSA)
and, 106–112
Justice and Home Affairs (JHA),
187–192, 196–201, 213–216,
221–222
Libya and, 90–93
London bombings and, 160, 240,
243
Maastricht treaty and, 189–191,
210
Madrid bombings and, 160, 187,
199, 202–203, 206–207, 211,
216–220, 240, 243
Network of Independent Experts in
Fundamental Rights (CFR-CDF)
and, 200, 206, 209
Phare Programme, 215, 233nn126,
127

European Union (EU) (cont.)
Plan of Action and, 17, 187, 192,
200, 218
Police Chiefs Operational Task
Force (PCOTF) and, 228–229n59
Police Working Group on Terrorism
(PWGT) and, 200
post-9/11 counter-terrorism policy,
192, 216–223
preaccession advisers and, 234n129
pre-9/11 counter-terrorism policy,
188–191
Revised Plan of Action and,
218–220
Situation Centre and, 198
Special Accession Programme for
Agriculture and Rural Development
(SAPARD) and, 233n127
terrorist identification and, 208–212
Terrorist Working Group (TWG)
and, 228n59
Treaty of Amsterdam and, 191
Treaty on European Union (TEU)
and, 189, 202 (see also Maastricht
treaty)
TREVI Group and, 189
twinning and, 213–214, 234nn128,
129
United Nations and, 8–9
Euskadi Ta Askatasuna (Basque
Fatherland and Liberty, ETA),
208
Extraordinary European Council,
196–197, 200, 221, 225n23
Exxon, 86

FATF-style regional bodies (FSRBs),
168–170
Fatwa, 248
Federation of American Scientists,
148n11
Feldman, Andreas, 258
Fhimah, Al-Amin Khalifa, 111
Financial Action Task Force (FATF),
3, 12, 16–17
assessment of, 175–178

asset seizures and, 158–161
charities and, 180
compliance and, 166–168, 175–176,
184n58, 185n60
Council on Foreign Relations and,
178–179
creation of, 157–158
*Eight Special Recommendations on
Terrorist Financing* and, 163
*Forty Recommendations on Money
Laundering* and, 161–170,
175–176
G-7 countries and, 157
as global solution, 178–179
hawala system and, 180
International Best Practices papers
and, 165, 178
"Know Your Customer" approach
and, 163, 177
membership status in, 181n22
model of, 161–170, 175–178
money laundering and terrorist
financing (ML/TF) and, 157–166
mutual review and, 166–168
*Nine Special Recommendations on
Terrorist Financing* and, 162–169,
173, 175–176, 178
Noncooperative Countries and
Territories (NCCTs) Initiative and,
167, 170–171, 172t6.2, 183n51
peer review and, 167–168,
171–175
political commitments to, 158
regional bodies of, 168–170
self-reporting and, 166–168
typology exercises and, 165–166
United Nations Counter-Terrorism
Committee (CTC) and, 31–32, 39
Financial intelligence units (FIUs),
163
Financial Times, 211
Fingar, Thomas, 128, 149n20
Fisk, Robert, 248
Foreign Policy, 4
Former candidate countries (FCCs),
212–216, 233n123

Forty Recommendations on Money Laundering (FATF), 161, 173, 175–176
compliance issues and, 166–170
peer review mechanism and, 167–168
regional FATFs and, 168–170
standards process and, 162–166
France, 87, 91–92, 96, 217
Iran and Libya Sanctions Act (ILSA) and, 107–108
Libya and, 9, 51, 99–110
UTA flight 772 and, 9, 51, 99–101, 110–112
Freedom House, 258
Friedman, Thomas, 255
Fukuyama, Francis, 245, 267

G-7 countries, 16, 92, 157
G-8 countries, 35
Counter-Terrorism Action Group (CTAG) and, 39
United Nations Counter-Terrorism Committee (CTC) and, 39
weapons of mass destruction (WMD) and, 143–147
G-8 Summit, 7, 252–253
Gardner, Kathryn L., 16–17, 157–186
Geneva Conventions, 205
Gerber-Stellingwerf, Linda, 12, 23–50
Germany, 199, 217, 227n42
Guernica bombings and, 124
West Berlin disco bombing, 89–93
Gorbachev, Mikhail, 134, 138
Greenberg, Karen, 7
Greenstock, Jeremy, 26
Grupo de Acción Financiera de Sudamerica (GAFISUD), 182n38
Guantanamo, 8
Guerillas, 251–252
Gulf of Sidra, 86, 89
Gulf War, 141, 249
Gurulé, Jimmy, 178

Habre, Hissen, 87
Hadley, Steven J., 4
Hague, The, 9, 95, 109–111, 219–220
Hamas, 239
Hamilton, Lee H., vii–x
Hawala system, 180
Hegemony, 247–250
Helms-Burton Act, 106–107
Hezbollah, 252–254
Highly enriched uranium (HEU), 132t5.3
Hit squads, 86, 88, 90
Ho Chi Minh, 254
Hoffman, Bruce, 5–6, 241
Hostages, 58, 96
Abu Nidal Organization (ANO) and, 100
defining terrorism and, 204–208
Iran and, 52, 84–85
Hungary, 212, 214
Hussein, Saddam, 15, 113, 248
Hutchings, Robert L., 257

Ideology, vii–viii
Afghan war and, 84
bombings and, 53–54
jihadists and, 5–6, 126t5.1, 240, 243–244
Libya and, 84–85, 113
pan-Islamic, 84
weapons of mass destruction (WMD) and, 131
Incentives-based diplomacy, 12
Independent, The, 248
India, 28
Indonesia, 264
In Larger Freedom: Towards Development, Security, and Human Rights for All (UN Report), 11
Institute for International Law and Justice, 64
Institutional approaches, 6–9
Instrument for Structural Policies for Pre-Accession (European Council), 233n127

Inter-American Committee Against
Terrorism (CICTE), 40
Intergovernmental Action Group
Against Money Laundering
(GIABA), 182n38
International Atomic Energy Agency
(IAEA), 71, 73, 75, 129, 139,
141–142, 145, 153n42
International Best Practices (Financial
Action Task Force), 165, 178
International Civil Aviation
Organization (ICAO), 32, 39, 52,
73
*International Convention for the
Suppression of Acts of Nuclear
Terrorism* (United Nations), 53,
146
*International Convention for the
Suppression of the Financing of
Terrorism* (United Nations), 29
*International Convention for the
Suppression of Terrorist Bombings*
(United Nations), 29
International Court of Justice,
109–110
International Emergency Economic
Powers Act (IEEPA), 89–90
International Institute for Strategic
Studies (IISS), 240, 242
International law, 76
Al-Qaida/Taliban Sanctions
Committee and, 57–58
asset seizures and, 58, 78n20 (*see
also* Asset seizures)
Beslan hostages and, 58
bombings and, 53–54
consolidation options and, 66–71
Counter-Terrorism Committee and,
55
*Declaration on Measures to
Eliminate International Terrorism*
(United Nations) and, 53
duplication issues and, 61–62,
79n26
European arrest warrant (EAW) and,
17–18, 192–196
future institutional options and,
73–75
General Assembly and, 51–54
Global Programme Against Money
Laundering (GPML) and, 60–61,
68–69
legal framework for, 52–59
Libya and, 106–110
nonproliferation and, 56–57
Office on Drugs and Crime,
59–61
pro-Western orientation and,
53
Resolution 1566 and, 58–59
sanctions and, 106–110 (*see also*
Sanctions)
9/11 and, 51, 55, 57
short-term solutions and, 71–73
streamlining efforts and, 62–65
UNODC/TPB and, 59–61
weapons of mass destruction
(WMD) and, 123–147
International Maritime Organization
(IMO), 32, 39
International Monetary Fund (IMF),
32, 35, 169, 171, 175, 179n5
International Organization for
Migration, 39
Interpol, 32
Ipe, Jason, 15–16, 123–155
IRA, 252
Iran, 65
Contra scandal and, 95
Iran and Libya Sanctions Act
(ILSA), 106–112
Iran Sanctions Act (ISA), 107
U.S. hostages in, 52, 84–85
weapons of mass destruction
(WMD) and, 129, 141–142
Iraq, ix, 1, 243, 245, 252
failed governance in, 256–257
ideology and, 6
invasion of, 4
pedagogic value of, 15
resolving crisis in, 265–266
suicide bombers and, 247

war as military blunder, 4–5
weapons of mass destruction
(WMD) and, 142
Ireland, 144, 152n38, 218, 252
Islam. *See* Muslims
Israel
Abu Nidal Organization and, 89
Middle East stability and, 249
Palestinians and, 96, 265
Sadat and, 85
weapons of mass destruction
(WMD) and, 141
Italy, 108, 193, 226n27
Milan hostages and, 207–208
Rome airport attacks and, 88–89,
92, 94
Ivanov, Igor, 151n35

Jacoby, Lowell E., 125
Japan, 92, 133
Jasinski, Filip, 194
Jentleson, Bruce W., 15
JFK Airport, 93, 107
Jihadists, 2
ideology of, 5–6, 126t5.1, 240,
243–244
U.S. military and, 248
Jordan, 26, 53

Kashmir, 247
Kazakhstan, 41, 140
Kennedy, Edward, 106, 108
Kenya, 26, 51
Khan, A. Q., 131, 133, 144
Khobar Towers, 243, 249
King's College, 5
"Know Your Customer" approach,
163, 177
Krueger, Alan B., 253–255, 258–259
Kurdistan Worker's Party, 208
Kuwait, 25, 248
Kyrgyzstan, 140

Lang, Gordon, 124
Lantos, Tom, 15
Latvia, 212

Law enforcement, 1–2, 7
Al-Qaida leaders and, 240
assessment of, 261–263
asset seizures and, 208–212 (*see also*
Asset seizures)
defining terrorism and, 204–208
Dublin Agreement and, 188–189
Eurojust and, 200–203
European arrest warrant (EAW) and,
192–196
Europol and, 196–200
international law strengthening and,
51–76
Maastricht treaty and, 189–191
money laundering and, 157–161
(*see also* Financial Action Task
Force [FATF])
Police Working Group on Terrorism
(PWGT) and, 200
terrorist identification and, 208–212
United Nations Counter-Terrorism
Committee (CTC) and, 32, 37
weapons of mass destruction
(WMD) and, 123–147
Lebanon, 65, 96–97, 252
Legal issues, 7, 12, 28–29
Action Plan of the European
Council and, 191
asset seizures and, 58, 78n20,
208–212
Common Position and, 208–210
Convention Relating to Extradition
Between Member States of the
European Union and, 190
Convention on Simplified
Extradition Procedures Between
Member States of the European
Union and, 190
defining terrorism and, 204–208
European arrest warrant and,
17–18, 192–196
freedom of navigation maneuvers
and, 86
Global Programme Against Money
Laundering (GPML) and, 60–61,
68–69

Legal issues (cont.)
    Guantanamo and, 8
    torture and, 8
    Treaty of Amsterdam and, 191
    TREVI Group and, 189
    United Nations Counter-Terrorism
        Committee (CTC) and, 23, 31
Lenin, Vladimir Ilych, 254
Leverett, Flynt, 15
Liberia, 142
Libya, ix, 14–15
    Abu Nidal Organization and,
        88–90, 93–95, 100
    Aouzou Strip and, 87
    April 1986 strikes and, 90–92
    bilateral confrontation and, 85–98
    Bush (George H. W.) and, 83,
        100–102, 113–114
    Bush (George W.) and, 114
    Carter administration and, 84–86
    Chad and, 86–88
    Clinton administration and, 114
    Egypt and, 85
    Europe and, 90–93
    four-year standoff against,
        105–106
    France and, 9, 51, 99–110
    Gulf of Sidra and, 86, 89
    Helms-Burton Act and, 106–107
    hit squads and, 86, 88, 90
    International Emergency Economic
        Powers Act (IEEPA) and, 89–90
    Iran and Libya Sanctions Act (ILSA)
        and, 106–112
    isolation of, 104
    Karachi attack and, 94–95
    Lockerbie families and, 110–111
    multilateral approach and, 98–114
    oil firms and, 86
    Palestine Liberation Organization
        (PLO) and, 85, 96
    Pan Am flight 73 and, 93–95
    Pan Am flight 103 and, 9, 51, 95,
        98–102, 107–112
    Reagan administration and, 83,
        85–87, 96–98
    sanctions and, 9, 86, 88–92, 99,
        102–114
    unilateral approach and,
        102–105
    UN Security Council and, 103
    U.S. military and, 86, 89–92
    U.S. policy changes and, 84–85,
        100–102
    UTA flight 772 and, 9, 51, 99–101,
        110–112
    weapons of mass destruction
        (WMD) and, 83, 143
    Weinberger Doctrine and, 97–98
    West Berlin bombing and, 89–90,
        93
Lithuania, 212
London Times, 124
Lopez, George A., viii
    strategic counter-terrorism and,
        1–22
    United Nations Counter-Terrorism
        Committee (CTC) and, 23–50
    winning policies and, 237–274
Lugar, Richard, 150n29

Maastricht treaty, 189–191, 210. *See
    also* European Union
Macedonia, 26
McNamara, Thomas E., 14–15,
    83–122
Madrid Summit, 10–11, 18, 238
Malesckova, Jitka, 253–255, 258
Mali, 108
Malta, 212
Mandela, Nelson, 109–111
Mao Tse Tung, 252, 254
Marshall, Monty G., 255
Mearsheimer, John J., 4
Members of the European Parliament
    (MEPs), 222
Memorial Institute for the Prevention
    of Terrorism, 243, 269n29
Mexico, 152n38
Middle East and North Africa FATF-
    style regional body (MENAFSRB),
    40, 169–170

Middle East and North Africa
  Financial Action Task Force
  (MENAFATF), 182nn38, 40, 41
Middle East and North Africa Region
  (MENA), 40
Military, vii, 2
  Al-Qaida and, 240–241
  excessive emphasis on, 4–5
  guerillas and, 251–252
  increased Arab buildup and,
  248–249
  jihadists and, 248
  Libya and, 86, 89–92
  nuclear weapons and, ix (*see also*
    Weapons of mass destruction
    (WMD))
  Qaddafi and, 85
  solving Iraq crisis and, 265–266
  U.S. barracks bombing and, 96–97
  U.S. support in Pakistan and, 248
  Weinberger Doctrine and, 97–98
  winning strategy for, 262–263
Millar, Alistair
  international law and, 51–82
  strategic counter-terrorism and,
  12–16
  United Nations Counter-Terrorism
  Committee (CTC) and, 23–50
  weapons of mass destruction and,
  123–155
Mitchell, Ronald, 173–174
Mitterand, François, 100
Monar, Jörg, 191
Money laundering (ML), 16, 25,
  251–252. *See also* Financial Action
  Task Force (FATF)
  Al-Qaida and, 160, 170–171
  charities and, 180
  gatekeepers and, 162–163
  Global Programme Against Money
    Laundering (GPML) and, 60–61,
    68–69
  informal banking systems (hawala)
    and, 159
  precious stones and metals, 159
  profit in, 159

self-sufficient cells and, 160–161
  shell banks and, 162–163
  suspicious transaction reports
    (STRs) and, 161, 181n21
  terrorist financing and, 157–161
Morocco, 26, 103
Mueller, John, 241
Mujahedeen, 248
Multilateral Affairs Unit, 13
Musharraf, 131
Muslims, viii
  fatwa and, 248, 126t5.1
  hit squads and, 88
  politics and, 244–246, 264–267
  radicalism and, 244–246
  sharia law and, 248
Myers, Richard, 148n8

Nairobi, 243
Nasser, Gamal Abdel, 85
National Academy of Sciences,
  258–259
National Intelligence Council (U.S.),
  131
National Intelligence Estimate (U.S.),
  242
National Security Council (NSC)
  (U.S.), 4
National Security Strategy (Bush
  administration), 253, 256
*National Strategy for Combating
  Terrorism* (White House), 6, 238,
  253, 259–260, 266
National Transportation Safety Board
  (NTSB) (U.S.), 107
Natural Resources Defense Council
  (NRDC), 151n30
Netherlands, 9, 110
New Agenda Coalition (NAC),
  152n38
New terrorism, 243–244
New York Times, 4–5, 259
New York University School of Law,
  64
New Zealand, 144, 152n38
Niger, 99, 108

Nine Special Recommendations on Terrorist Financing (FATF), 162–169, 173, 175–176, 178
Non-Aligned Movement (NAM), 105
Noncooperative Countries and Territories (NCCTs) Initiative, 167, 170–171, 172t6.2
Nongovernmental organizations (NGOs), 209–210, 222
Nonproliferation, 56–57, 129, 140, 145, 237
North Africa, 141
North Atlantic Treaty Organization (NATO), 84, 90, 140
North Korea, 129, 142
Nuclear Nonproliferation Treaty (NPT), 129, 140, 145
Nuclear weapon-free zones (NWFZs), 140–141
Nuclear weapons, ix, 15–16. *See also* Weapons of mass destruction (WMD)
Nunn, Sam, 124, 138, 150n29

Office of the Coordinator for Counterterrorism (U.S. Dept. of State), 13
Offshore Group of Banking Supervisors (OGBS), 182n38
Oil, 86, 88, 106, 255
OLAF, 201
Order of Good Hope, 109
Organisation of African Unity (OAU), 53, 110
Organisation for Economic Co-operation and Development (OECD), 31, 37–39, 168
Development Co-operation Directorate (DAC) and, 37–38
Organisation of the Islamic Conference (OIC), 53, 59
Organization of American States (OAS), 28, 40
Organization for the Prohibition of Chemical Weapons (OPCW), 39, 73, 75

Organization for Security and Co-operation in Europe (OSCE), 16
Oslo peace process, 243

Pakistan, 93–94, 103, 240
international law and, 53, 56
U.S. military support and, 248
weapons of mass destruction (WMD) and, 131, 133
Palestine, 100, 243, 249, 265
Abu Nidal Organization and, 88–90, 93–94
Popular Front for the Liberation of Palestine-General Command (PFLP-GC), 98
suicide bombers and, 247
weapons of mass destruction (WMD) and, 141
Palestine Liberation Organization (PLO), 85, 96
Panama, 142
Pan Am flight 73, 93–95
Pan Am flight 103, 51, 95, 98, 99–102, 107–112
Pape, Robert, 247, 249
Patriot Act, 260
Patterns of Global Terrorism (U.S. State Department), 101, 105, 242
Pelindaba Treaty, 140
Peraelae, Maftu, 258
Perry, William, 15, 138
Persian Gulf, 141, 248
Philippines, 264
Plutonium, 129
Poland, 212
Police Working Group on Terrorism (PWGT), 200
Policy, 3
bargaining and, 264–265
bilateral, 85–98
Convention on the Physical Protection of Nuclear Materials and, 144
Cooperative Threat Reduction (CTR) and, 133

democracy and, 266
European Union and, 188–196,
216–220 (*see also* European
Union)
"go it alone" approach and, 6–7
Helms-Burton Act and, 106–107
International Convention for the
Suppression of Acts of Nuclear
Terrorism (United Nations) and,
146
Iran and Libya Sanctions Act (ILSA)
and, 106–112
Iran Sanctions Act (ISA) and,
107
legal issues and, 190–191 (*see also*
Legal issues)
Libya and, 83–114
multilateral, 98–114
Nuclear Nonproliferation Treaty
(NPT) and, 129, 145
options and, 262t8.1
peer review and, 167–168,
171–175
Pelindaba Treaty and, 140
poverty and, 252–256
Presidential Nuclear Initiatives
(PNIs) and, 134, 138
priority alignment and, 264–267
Proliferation Security Initiative (PSI)
and, 142–143
Protocol of the United Nations
Transnational Organised Crime
Convention and, 217
social opportunity expansion and,
266–267
torture and, 8
Trade Expansion Act and, 87
transparency and, 32
Treaty of Amsterdam and, 191
Treaty of Nice and, 201
Treaty of Rarotonga and, 140
Treaty of Tlatelolco and, 140
unilateral, 102–105
weapons of mass destruction
(WMD) and, 123–147
winning strategy for, 261–263

Politics
anti-Americanism and, 245
bilateral confrontation and, 85–98
countering hegemony and,
247–250
democracy and, 266
human rights and, 257–261
multilateral approach and, 98–114
poor governance and, 256–257
poverty and, 252–256
priorities for, 264–267
radicalism and, 244–246
religion and, 244–246, 264–267
sanctions enforcement and, 45–46
terrorism and, 244–246, 250–252,
264–267
unilateral approach and, 102–105
"war on terror" metaphor and, 4
Popular Front for the Liberation of
Palestine–General Command
(PFLP–GC), 98
Population growth, 255
Poverty, 252–256
Presidential Nuclear Initiatives
(PNIs), 134, 138
Proliferation Security Initiative (PSI),
142–143
Protocol of the United Nations
Transnational Organised Crime
Convention, 217
Putin, Vladimir, 139, 259–260

Qaddafi, Mohamar. *See also* Libya
Abu Nidal Organization and,
88–90, 93–94
Chad and, 87–88
Europe and, 102
ideology of, 85, 113
Karachi attack and, 94–95
Mandela and, 109–111
Palestine Liberation Organization
(PLO) and, 85
Pan Am flight 73 and, 93–95
Reagan administration and, 83,
85–87, 96–98
Sadat and, 85

RAND Corporation, 5–6, 199, 242, 244
Reagan, Ronald, 92
hit squads and, 86, 88, 90
International Emergency
Economic Powers Act (IEEPA) and, 89–90
Iran hostage crisis and, 84
Libya and, 83, 85–87, 96–98
Pan Am flight 103 and, 96
SALT II Treaty and, 84, 130–131
Regional approaches, 6–9
Rejectionist Arabs, 85
Religion, 53–54, 104
anti-Americanism and, 245
fatwa and, 126t5.1, 248
politics and, 244–246, 264–267
radicalism and, 244–246
sharia law and, 248
terrorism and, 244
Vatican and, 108
Republic of Korea, 144
Revolutionary Armed Forces of
Colombia, 208
Rosand, Eric, 13–14, 51–82
Rumsfeld, Donald, 123
Rupérez, Javier, 32
Russia, 103
Beslan massacre and, 13, 58, 243, 259–260
Chechen separatists and, 131
Cooperative Threat Reduction
(CTR) and, 133
Gorbachev and, 134, 138
Presidential Nuclear Initiatives
(PNIs) and, 134, 138
Putin and, 139, 259–260
Soviet Union and, 10, 16, 84
tactical nuclear weapons (TNWs)
and, 133–140
United Nations Counter-Terrorism
Committee (CTC) and, 33
weapons of mass destruction
(WMD) and, 129–140, 143, 151n35
Yeltsin and, 134, 138

Sadat, Anwar, 85
Sageman, Marc, 5, 240
Sanctions, 12, 67
Afghanistan and, 9
Al Qaida/Taliban and, 41–42, 45–46, 57–58, 61–62, 67, 241
Analytic Support and Sanctions
Monitoring Team (United Nations)
and, 42–43, 57, 241
asset seizures and, 58, 78n20, 158–161, 208–212
Consolidated List of Financial
Sanctions Targets in the UK and, 210
duplication issues and, 61–62
enforcement issues and, 45–46
Global Programme Against Money
Laundering (GPML) (United
Nations) and, 60–61, 68–69
Helms-Burton Act and, 106–107
International Emergency Economic
Powers Act (IEEPA) and, 89–90
Iran and Libya Sanctions Act (ILSA)
and, 106–112
Iran Sanctions Act (ISA) and, 107
Libya and, 9, 86, 88–92, 99, 102–114
multilateralization of, 102–105
Resolution 1267 and, 57–58
Sudan and, 9
targeted, 104
United Nations Counter-Terrorism
Committee (CTC) and, 24, 33, 41–46
Saudi Arabia, 243, 248–249
Scotland
Iran and Libya Sanctions Act (ILSA)
and, 106–112
Lockerbie attack and, 51, 95, 98–102, 107–112
Self-radicalization, 240
Self-starter groups, 240, 242
9/11, vii, 1–2, 4, 9–10, 243, 247
el-Motassadeq and, 7–8
European Union and, 188–192, 216–223

Financial Action Task Force (FATF)
and, 16–17
financial costs of, 251
hijackers' wealth and, 253
international law and, 51, 55, 57,
60
Patriot Act and, 260
terrorist financing and, 158–163,
251
United Nations Counter-Terrorism
Committee (CTC) and, 23
UNODC/TPB and, 60
U.S. military buildup and, 249
weapons of mass destruction
(WMD) and, 125
9/11 Commission, 160, 241, 242,
267
Serrano, Mónica, 159, 251
Sharia law, 248
Sharm el-Sheikh, 1
Simon, Steven, 4, 36, 241, 262
Slovak Republic, 212
Slovenia, 212
Snyder, Laura, 149n19
Sokov, Nikolai, 139–140
South Africa, 28, 152n38
Southeast Asia Nuclear Weapons Free
Zone, 140
Soviet Union, 10, 16, 84
Spain, 124
Madrid bombings and, 160, 187,
199, 202–203, 206–207, 211,
216–220, 240, 243
Madrid Summit and, 238, 253
weapons of mass destruction
(WMD) and, 217
Sri Lanka, 247
Stares, Paul, 237–238
Stepanova, Ekaterina, 244, 256–257
Stern, Jessica, 5, 255
Stevenson, Jonathan, 197–198
Stiles, Kendall W., 52–53
Storbeck, Jürgen, 200
Strategic Arms Limitation Talks II
(SALT II) Treaty, 84, 130–131
Strategic Survey (IISS), 242

Sudan, 9, 30, 99
Suicide bombers, 1, 243, 246–247
Superterrorism, 18, 243–244
Suspicious transaction reports (STRs),
161, 181n21
Sweden, 152n38
Switzerland, 14, 64, 70, 209
Syria, 100, 118n43
Abu Nidal Organization (ANO)
and, 88, 93, 95
international law and, 53, 65
weapons of mass destruction
(WMD) and, 142

Tactical nuclear weapons (TNWs).
See Weapons of mass destruction
(WMD)
Tajikistan, 140
Taliban, vii, 237
asset seizures and, 210
Bush administration and, 3
overthrow of, 239
sanctions and, 41–42, 45–46,
57–58, 61–62, 67, 241
understanding, 239
weapons of mass destruction
(WMD) and, 125
Tampere European Council, 191, 201
Tanzania, 51
Task Force of EU Police Chiefs, 217
Technology, 36, 86, 149n18, 240
Telhami, Shibley, 18, 238–239,
244–245
Terrorism
anti-Americanism and, 245
bargaining with, 264–265
Common Position and, 208
cyberterrorism and, 149n18
defining, viii, 44–45, 187–189,
204–208
democracy and, 266
Global Programme Against Money
Laundering (GPML) (United
Nations) and, 60–61, 68–69
global war on, 1 (*see also* Counter-
terrorism strategies)

Terrorism (cont.)
  growing danger of, 241–244
  guerillas and, 251–252
  hit squads and, 86, 88, 90
  home-grown cells and, 240
  human rights and, 257–261
  ideology and, vii–viii, 5–6 (*see also*
    Ideology; Religion)
  international law and, 51–76
  Libya and, 83–114
  literature on, 3
  money laundering and, 157–161,
    251–252 (*see also* Money
    laundering)
  motivations for, 6
  new terrorism and, 1, 243–244
  political roots of, 244–246,
    250–252, 264–267
  poor governance and, 256–257
  poverty and, 252–256
  priority alignment and, 264–267
  public support of, 251–252
  recruitment for, 5–6
  self-radicalized cells and, 240
  self-starter groups and, 240, 242
  self-sufficient cells and, 160–161
  social dynamics of, 250–252
  suicide logic of, 246–247
  superterrorism and, 18, 243–244
  weapons of mass destruction
    (WMD) and, 123–147 (*see also*
    Weapons of mass destruction
    (WMD))
Terrorist Working Group (TWG),
  228n59
Thailand, 26
Thatcher, Margaret, 91
Theater nuclear forces (TNF), 84
Torture, 8
Total, 107
Trade Expansion Act, 87
Transparency, 32
Treaty of Amsterdam, 191
Treaty of Nice, 201
Treaty of Rarotonga, 140
Treaty of Tlatelolco, 140

Treaty on European Union (TEU),
  189, 202 (*see also* Maastricht
  treaty)
"Trends in Global Terrorism"
  (National Intelligence Estimate),
  242
TREVI (Terrorism, Radicalism,
  Extremism, and Political Violence)
  Group, 189
Trotsky, Leon, 254
Tsoukala, Anastassia, 191
Tunisia, 99
Turkey, 89, 108
Turkmenistan, 140
Twinning, 213–214, 234nn128,
  129

Ulema, 248
United Against Terrorism (UN
  Report), 64
United Arab Emirates, 25
United Kingdom, 92
  Consolidated List of Financial
    Sanctions Targets in the UK and,
    210
  Europol and, 199
  Libya and, 90, 102–110
  London bombings and, 160, 240,
    243
  Madrid bombings and, 217
  technical assistance fund and, 36
  United Nations Counter-Terrorism
    Committee (CTC) and, 27–28, 33
United Nations, 1
  Annan and, 10–11, 18, 23–24,
    36–37, 111, 238, 247, 258–261,
    264
  asset seizures and, 208–212
  Chapter VII of Charter of, 23, 51,
    67, 104
  Common Position and, 208–210
  consolidation efforts and, 66–71
  Counter-Proliferation Committee
    and, 3, 16
  Counter-Terrorism Implementation
    Task Force and, 11

counter-terrorism strategies and, 2–3
duplicated efforts in, 13–14
Economic and Social Council
(ECOSOC) and, 68
General Assembly and, 27–28,
52–54, 73–75
*International Convention for the
Suppression of Acts of Nuclear
Terrorism* and, 53, 146
international law strengthening and,
51–76
Libyan sanctions and, 9, 103
Madrid Summit and, 10–11, 18
Non-Proliferation Committee and,
237
Protocol of the United Nations
Transnational Organised Crime
Convention and, 217
relevance of, 2–3
Resolution 242 and, 154n50
Resolution 338 and, 154n50
Resolution 487 and, 142
Resolution 687 and, 141
Resolution 731 and, 103–104
Resolution 748 and, 9, 103–104
Resolution 883 and, 103–105
Resolution 1054 and, 9
Resolution 1192 and, 121n92
Resolution 1267 and, 9, 13, 41,
57–58, 210
Resolution 1373 and, 27–29, 144,
146, 208–216 (*see also* United
Nations Counter-Terrorism
Committee [CTC]), 29
Resolution 1377 and, 33–34
Resolution 1390 and, 41–42
Resolution 1456 and, 260
Resolution 1526 and, 67, 160
Resolution 1535 and, 9, 13, 26–27
Resolution 1540 and, 3, 10, 13, 16,
24, 27, 42–43, 56–57, 142–147
Resolution 1566 and, 10, 13, 24,
28, 43, 58–59, 69
Resolution 1617 and, 13, 67
Resolution 1624 and, 80n27
Resolution 1673 and, 56–57

role of, 2–3, 9–11
Secretary-General's High-Level Panel
on Threats, Challenges and
Change, 10–11, 33, 44–45, 58,
238
U.S./European differences over, 8–9
United Nations Counter-Terrorism
Committee (CTC)
Analytic Support and Sanctions
Monitoring Team and, 42–43
Annan on, 23–24
civil liberties and, 37
as committee of the whole, 23–24
compliance criteria and, 32–33
consolidation options and, 66–71
coordination and, 41–44
Counter-Terrorism Executive
Directorate (CTED) and, 3, 9–10,
13, 24, 32, 36, 42
defining terrorism and, 44–45
developing countries and, 28, 37–39
duplication issues and, 61–62
enforcement issues and, 45–46
evaluation criteria and, 32–33
expanded staff of, 26–27
Financial Action Task Force (FATF)
and, 31–32, 39
financial mechanisms and, 31
as forum, 27
future options for, 74
G-8 countries and, 35, 39
Greenstock and, 42
implementation challenges and,
30–33
increased membership of, 29
information sharing and, 29, 34
international cooperation and,
24–26, 39–41, 55
International Monetary Fund (IMF)
and, 32, 35
investigations and, 24
law enforcement and, 32, 37
measuring progress of, 29–30
member state obligations and, 23
mixed record of, 24–28
money laundering and, 25

United Nations Counter-Terrorism
  Committee (CTC) (cont.)
Organization of American States
  (OAS) and, 40
overlap issues and, 41–44
performance standards and,
  31–32
primary function of, 24
Resolution 1373 and, 8–9, 12–13,
  19, 23, 27–40, 55, 61–62, 67, 72
Resolution 1377 and, 33–34
Resolution 1535 and, 26–27
Resolution 1540 and, 27, 42–43,
  62–63, 67–68
Resolution 1566 and, 28
revitalization of, 26–27
sanctions and, 24, 33, 41–46
Security Council and, 26–27, 30,
  33, 54–55, 103
short-term solutions and, 72–73
site visits and, 25–26
state reports and, 25–26, 29
streamlining efforts and, 63
as switchboard, 24–25
technical assistance and, 33–39
transparency and, 32
UN Charter and, 23, 28
uneven leadership in, 26–27
United Kingdom and, 27–28
United States and, 8, 27–28, 33
UNODC/TPB and, 35, 39
United Nations Development
  Programme (UNDP), 36, 60, 75,
  257–258
United Nations Economic and Social
  Council (ECOSOC), 68
United Nations Global Programme
  Against Money Laundering
  (GPML), 60–61, 68–69
United Nations High Commission for
  Refugees, 75
United Nations Office on Drugs and
  Crime/Terrorism Prevention Branch
  (UNODC/TPB), 13–14, 27
consolidation issues and, 68–70
future options for, 74

Global Programme Against Money
  Laundering (GPML) and, 60–61,
  68–69
international law and, 59–61
9/11 and, 60
short-term solution limitation and,
  71
United Nations Counter-Terrorism
  Committee (CTC) and, 35, 39
United Nations Policy Working
  Group on Terrorism, 244, 259
United States, vii–x
Al-Qaida leaders and, 240
anti-Americanism and, 245
asset seizures and, 211
Bush (George H. W.) and, 83,
  100–102, 113–114
Bush (George W.) and, 3–4 (*see also*
  Bush, George W.)
Carter administration and, 84–86
Clinton administration and, 107,
  114, 138
Cooperative Threat Reduction
  (CTR) and, 133
defining terrorism and, 207
detention issues of, 8
embassy attacks and, 51, 160,
  243
European arrest warrant (EAW) and,
  196
fatwa against, 126t5.1, 248
"go it alone" approach of, 6–7
Guantanamo and, 8
hegemony and, 248–250
Helms-Burton Act and, 106–107
increased Arab involvement of,
  248–249
Iran-Contra scandal and, 95
Iran hostage crisis and, 52, 84–85
Iran and Libya Sanctions Act (ILSA)
  and, 106–112
Iran Sanctions Act (ISA) and, 107
Israeli support by, 249
law-enforcement approaches and,
  1–2
Libya and, 83–114

multilateral approach and, 98–114
National Intelligence Council and, 131
National Intelligence Estimate and, 5
Pakistan and, 248
Patriot Act and, 260
political priorities for, 264–267
Presidential Nuclear Initiatives (PNIs) and, 134, 138
Proliferation Security Initiative (PSI) and, 142–143
Reagan administration and, 83–92, 96–98, 130–131
SALT II Treaty and, 84, 130–131 (*see also* Weapons of mass destruction [WMD])
secretive approach of, 8
9/11 Commission and, 160, 241–242, 267
technical assistance and, 36
torture and, 8
unilateral approach and, 102–105
United Nations Counter-Terrorism Committee (CTC) and, 27–28, 33
United States Institute of Peace, 237–238
Uniting Against Terrorism: Recommendations for a Global Counter-Terrorism Strategy (UN Report), 11, 18
University of Maryland's Center for International Development and Conflict Management, 254
Uranium, 16, 87, 129
Urbanization, 255
U.S. Central Intelligence Agency (CIA), 5, 87, 115n15, 207, 217, 240, 257
U.S. Defense Department, 249
U.S. Department of the Treasury, 211
"Uses of Military Power, The" (Weinberger), 97
U.S. Federal Bureau of Investigation (FBI), 199

U.S. General Accounting Office (GAO), 115n18, 179n5, 180nn10, 12, 16
U.S. House Armed Services Committee, 241
U.S. National Intelligence Estimate, 5
USS *Cole*, 160
U.S. Senate Select Committee on Intelligence, 128
U.S. Sixth Fleet, 86, 89–90
U.S. State Department, 13, 101, 105, 242, 253
UTA flight 772, 9, 51, 99–101, 111–112
Uzbekistan, 140, 264

Vatican, 108
Voice of America, viii
von Hippel, Karen, 5

Walt, Stephen M., 4
Waxman, Henry, 242–243
Weapons of mass destruction (WMD), 9, 62, 67–69, 244
Al-Qaida and, 15–16, 124–131, 146, 244
biological, 244
black market and, 131, 133
Center for Nonproliferation Studies and, 139
Chechen separatists and, 131
chemical, 125, 144, 244
Convention on the Physical Protection of Nuclear Materials and, 144
Cooperative Threat Reduction (CTR) and, 133
cyberterrorism and, 149n18
defining, 123–124
Egypt and, 141
fissile material for, 125, 128–130, 132t5.3, 143, 153n42
G-8 countries and, 143–147
global approaches and, 142–146
Gulf War and, 141

Weapons of mass destruction
(WMD) (cont.)
International Atomic Energy Agency
(IAEA) and, 73, 129, 139,
141–142, 145, 153n42
International Convention for the
Suppression of Acts of Nuclear
Terrorism and, 146
Iran and, 141–142
Iraq and, 142
Islamic ideology and, 126t5.1, 131
Israel and, 141
Khan and, 131, 133
Libya and, 83, 143
Madrid bombings and, 217
NATO and, 140
nonproliferation committee and,
56–57
North Korea and, 129, 142
nuclear effects and, 124
Nuclear Nonproliferation Treaty
(NPT) and, 129, 140, 145
nuclear smuggling and, 132t5.3
nuclear weapon-free zones (NWFZs
and), 140–141
Pakistan and, 131, 133
Palestine and, 141
Pelindaba Treaty and, 140
portable, 133
Presidential Nuclear Initiatives
(PNIs) and, 134, 138
Proliferation Security Initiative (PSI)
and, 142–143
radiological, 244
regional approaches and, 140–142
Resolution 687 and, 141
Resolution 1540 and, 144–147
Russia and, 129–140, 143, 151n35
SALT II Treaty and, 84, 130–131
9/11 and, 125
Syria and, 142
tactical nuclear weapons (TNWs)
and, 125, 133–140, 151n35,
152n37
Taliban and, 125

terrorist networks and, 123,
125–128
Treaty of Rarotonga and, 140
Treaty of Tlatelolco and, 140
vulnerable locations and, 130–133
Weapons of Mass Destruction
Commission (WMD Commission),
123
Weinberger, Caspar, 97–98
Weiss, Edith Brown, 162
Weldon, Curt, 138–139
Whitehead, John, 90
White House, 5–6, 238, 253,
259–260, 266
Whytock, Christopher A., 15
Working Party on Terrorism
(External Aspects) (COTER)
(European Union), 228n59
World Bank, 36
Financial Action Task Force (FATF)
and, 169, 171, 175, 179n5
poverty and, 254
World Customs Organization
(WCO), 32, 39
World Policy Institute, 207
World Summit, 58, 69
World Trade Organization (WTO),
107
World War II, 4

Yacoubian, Monica, 237–238
Yeltsin, Boris, 134, 138